The ActionScript 3.0 Quick Reference Guide

For Developers and Designers Using Flash CS4 Professional

*David Stiller, Rich Shupe, Jen deHaan, and
Darren Richardson*

O'REILLY®

Beijing · Cambridge · Farnham · Köln · Sebastopol · Taipei · Tokyo

The ActionScript 3.0 Quick Reference Guide: For Developers and Designers Using Flash CS4 Professional
by David Stiller, Rich Shupe, Jen deHaan, and Darren Richardson

Published by O'Reilly Media, Inc., 1005 Gravenstein Highway North, Sebastopol, CA 95472.

O'Reilly books may be purchased for educational, business, or sales promotional use. Online editions are also available for most titles (*http://safari.oreilly.com*). For more information, contact our corporate/institutional sales department: (800) 998-9938 or *corporate@oreilly.com*.

Editor: Robyn Thomas
Production Editor: Michele Filshie
Copyeditor: Sohaila Abdulali
Technical Editors: Matthew Woodruff, Anselm Bradford, and Eric Kramer
Proofreader: Nancy Bell

Indexer: Ellen Troutman Zaig
Cover Designer: Karen Montgomery
Interior Designer: David Futato
Illustrators: Robert Romano and Jessamyn Read

Printing History:
    October 2008:   First Edition.

RepKover.
 This book uses RepKover, a durable and flexible lay-flat binding.

ISBN: 978-0-596-51735-9

[M]

1223315717

Adobe Developer Library

Adobe Developer Library, a copublishing partnership between O'Reilly Media Inc. and Adobe Systems, Inc., is the authoritative resource for developers using Adobe technologies. These comprehensive resources offer learning solutions to help developers create cutting-edge interactive web applications that can reach virtually anyone on any platform.

With top-quality books and innovative online resources covering the latest tools for rich-Internet application development, the *Adobe Developer Library* delivers expert training, straight from the source. Topics include ActionScript, Adobe Flex®, Adobe Flash®, and Adobe Acrobat® software.

Get the latest news about books, online resources, and more at *adobedeveloper-library.com*.

*To Scott Joplin, for doing his
thing like nobody's business, then
sharing it.*

-- David Stiller

*To Jodi, Sally, and Claire for
putting up with so much.*

-- Rich Shupe

Table of Contents

Part II. ActionScript and the Flash CS4 Authoring Tool

Part III. How Do I?

Foreword

The battle, as it stood, had clearly defined lines. The artists liked ActionScript 1.0 and the programmers, let's just say they weren't happy (if they used Flash at all!).

Then ActionScript 2.0 appeared and many artists started getting nervous until they realized that they could basically ignore it. Programmers were a bit more happy until they realized that the changes were mostly superficial. But in many cases, it was enough to bring new programmers to Flash—which made the artists even more nervous.

Fast forward to just a couple of years ago and ActionScript 3.0 rears its head. The programmers embrace it like a brother, like the saviour of the Flash platform. The artists, for the most part, ran and hid. As they dashed away from terms like "classes" and "interfaces" they bemoaned the loss of what, for many of them, was their first programming language.

This was real programming, they said. ActionScript 3.0 had wandered into the land populated by frightening giants like Java and C++. It wasn't fun anymore, it was just scary.

Enter this book and its talented authors.

For the developers reading this, I have a confession to make that will probably ring true with you as well. At first, ActionScript 3.0 intimidated the heck out of me. Everything that I knew how to do was different. It felt like the ground had been ripped out from under me. It was all sort of familiar, but so many little things were different, I often felt like it would have been easier for me if I hadn't ever learned ActionScript 1.0 and 2.0. It took me quite a long time to get a good sense of the language and to get back to that level of comfort I had with earlier versions.

The good news for you, dear coder, is that if you haven't yet made that transition and gained that level of comfort, your road is going to be a lot easier thanks to this book. Honestly, I'm a bit jealous.

For the artists reading this, the authors of this book are here to explain that no, it's not hard, it's just different. Different in a way that is more powerful, that lets your ideas go further. You have been doing "real" programming all along and this is just the next logical step.

ActionScript 3.0 is a giant of a programming language. There is a lot to learn, and conquering will take time and patience. But at the end of day (and the end of this book) you will find that by learning ActionScript 3.0 not only are you a better Flash developer, but also a better developer period. You'll have under your belt a good understanding of many core object-oriented concepts and can take them to any other language you want to tackle—whether that be Python, Java, C++, or just about anything else.

No matter what your background, the pages that follow will provide you with some excellent knowledge, insight, and even a little bit of wisdom in the realm of Flash and ActionScript. I'm lucky enough to personally know some of the authors of this book so I can honestly tell you that you're about to learn from some of the best developers and teachers I know.

Happy learning!

—Branden Hall
CTO, Automatic Studios Ltd.
September 2008

Preface

ActionScript 3.0 introduced Flash developers to a new realm. In this improved territory, ActionScript has emerged from the gym with a new physique. The language is more powerful, more efficient, and—thanks to a new internal consistency—easier to learn for those new to the Flash Platform. As the saying goes, change is a good thing. On the other hand, too much of anything can be, well, nerve-wracking. For many, ActionScript's change equates to a chronic attack of growing pains. Others, used to the paradigms and occasional quirks of ActionScript 2.0, find the new ActionScript 3.0 practically unrecognizable.

In any case, the ongoing support for ActionScript 1.0 and 2.0, in both the Flash authoring environment and Flash Player, means that learning ActionScript 3.0 is, for the immediate future, still an option. For now, you can choose when to learn the new version of the language (and to what degree), applying your newly earned knowledge on a project-by-project basis, if you want. Sometimes, it'll be easier to decide when to use ActionScript 3.0 than to decide whether you should migrate existing code or start from scratch. For example, if you want significant performance gains, or to use a new feature specific to Action-Script 3.0, using the new language may be a foregone conclusion. How to arrive at completed ActionScript 3.0 code, however, is another question, and that's where this book is useful.

This book aims to show you where Flash CS4 Professional and ActionScript 3.0 differ from prior releases of Flash and ActionScript, respectively. You can use this text as a guide, helping you decide if new application features warrant an upgrade, and assisting with the steeper learning curve imposed by the more robust new language. Perhaps most importantly, this book will increase your familiarity with ActionScript 3.0 structure and syntax, letting you adjust (or abandon) ActionScript 2.0 coding practices more easily.

What Sets This Book Apart

Simple: Essentially, we've created two books in one. Or put another way, there are two sections to the book, each using its own learning methodology.

Part I and Part II are written in classic tech-book formatting and prose. General concepts are introduced and followed with expository prose and simple, demonstrative tutorials as necessary.

Part III and Part IV (especially Part III) are pure reference sections, designed for you to quickly look up and learn from "How Do I...?" scenarios.

Think of the book as a seminar. The first half is presentation; the latter half is Q&A.

What's in This Book

When ActionScript 3.0 hit the streets, the reaction from the Flash crowd was enormous, and not without a tremor of intimidation. Certain questions have emerged—on the forums, in classrooms, user groups, and at conferences— more often than others. This book answers the questions we most often encounter, questions that seem to pose the biggest stumbling blocks for longtime users. The book's in a hybrid format to serve two needs. The first half of the book is something like a fireside chat, providing fairly broad coverage of Flash CS4 Professional, and select overviews of ActionScript 3.0. The second half presents many focused examples of ActionScript 3.0 syntax in small, digestible chunks. Both halves are chock-full of hands-on demonstrations. Ideally, you can hop between the two, and gear up or down to the pace that best suits your needs at the time. Navigate the Table of Contents and/or Index to find quick answers to specific questions about ActionScript 3.0 and its application.

Part I: Introduction to ActionScript 3.0

Part I of the text introduces a variety of tools to write ActionScript 3.0, while relying on Flash CS4 Professional as its primary authoring environment. It then discusses some of the attributes that make ActionScript 3.0 stand head and shoulders above its predecessors. Topics include power and performance, the benefits of strong data typing (including robust compile time warnings and error messages) and how the new language architecture can improve your workflow.

Chapter 1, *Introducing ActionScript 3.0*

Chapter 2, *Discovering What You Need to Work with ActionScript 3.0*

Part II: ActionScript and the Flash CS4 Authoring Tool

Part II walks you through the Flash CS4 authoring tool with keen attention to ActionScript-related interface elements, and helps you decide when to use the timeline, and when to use classes, for coding. It also discusses the creation of assets at runtime, how to convert timeline animation into ActionScript (for manipulation and reuse), how to use, skin, and style user interface components, and how to troubleshoot your code when things go awry.

Part III: How Do I?

Part III switches to cookbook-style—a concise look at a problem, solution, and discussion for each of several issues. This format lets you hone in on syntax and methodology in easily digestible recipes. It starts off by highlighting the Graphics class, formerly the Drawing API, which the second half of the book uses extensively for highly portable, code-only examples. It then discusses the most significant changes introduced by ActionScript 3.0: the new display architecture and event model. Next, you'll discover new ways of using text for display and interactivity. Finally, you'll concentrate on input/output processes, including sending and loading XML and variables, as well as loading images, external SWFs, sound, and video.

Part IV: Migration

Part IV distills everything covered in Part I through Part III, and applies those skills to the issue of migration—updating existing projects written in Action-Script 2.0 to use ActionScript 3.0 code. This concept's first application is the migration of a simple particle system. The exercise highlights as many migration issues as possible in a short example, and helps you ask an important question related to your own projects: should you migrate or rewrite? The final chapter of the book serves as a cross-reference, and a code-comparison guide. Specific migration issues are demonstrated in quick syntax examples, comparing ActionScript 2.0 and 3.0 uses. Where applicable, references to more complete discussions elsewhere in the book are included, and select new material in the same comparative format is also added.

Chapter 18, *A Sample Migration*

Chapter 19, *Where Did It Go?*

What's Not in This Book

Due to the size and focus constraints of this book, many aspects of ActionScript usage are necessarily excluded. First and foremost, this book focuses specifically on Flash CS4 Professional, although most of the examples work just fine in Flash CS3. The Flash Platform has grown considerably, so if you prefer other ActionScript coding environments, including Flex Builder, FDT, or FlashDevelop (or even text editors, such as Notepad or TextMate, in conjunction with the Flex SDK command-line compiler), you may want to skim through several of the examples to see if you think they'll be helpful. In general, you can easily adapt most of the book's examples for ActionScript 3.0 projects written in other tools, and you are introduced to a handful of those tools in Chapter 2. However, very little additional material, such as Flex Builder MXML documents or project files, is supplied. This book is a migration reference for Flash professionals, so you'll see mostly FLA and AS files.

Secondly, this book is aimed at relatively experienced ActionScript 2.0 coders who are making the move to ActionScript 3.0. It neither provides language essentials nor serves as a comprehensive reference. As such, if you're not already comfortable with ActionScript, and want to focus a bit more on fundamentals, you should seek out *Learning ActionScript 3.0: A Beginner's Guide* by Rich Shupe and Zevan Rosser (O'Reilly, 978-0-596-52787-7). Conversely, if you're looking for more of an in-depth reference book, you may prefer *Essential ActionScript 3.0* by Colin Moock (O'Reilly, 978-0-596-52694-8).

Finally, while it hits many of the high points, this volume doesn't cover all areas of ActionScript 3.0 interest, and may not satisfy advanced users' needs. If you want to immerse yourself in the more elaborate capabilities of the language, you can either acquire the aforementioned *Essential ActionScript 3.0* for broad coverage, or look into additional specialized books such as *ActionScript 3.0 Design Patterns: Object Oriented Programming Techniques* by William Sanders and Chandima Cumaranatunge (O'Reilly, 978-0-596-52846-1) for OOP and design patterns expertise.

Conventions Used in This Book

This book uses the following typographical conventions:

Menu options
> Menu options are shown using the → character, such as File→Open.

Italic
> Indicates new terms, URLs, email addresses, file names, and file extensions.

`Constant width`
> Used for program listings, as well as within paragraphs to refer to program elements such as variable or function names, databases, data types, environment variables, statements, and keywords.

`Constant width bold`
> Shows commands or other text that the user should type literally.

`Constant width italic`
> Shows text that should be replaced with user-supplied values or by values determined by context.

> This is a note. It contains useful information about the topic at hand, often highlighting important concepts or best practices.

> This is a warning. It helps you solve and avoid annoying problems. Ignore at your own peril.

This Book's Example Files

You can download the example files for this book at:

> *http://www.oreilly.com/catalog/9780596517359*

Note that, although alternative development platforms are discussed briefly, the examples in this book are presented in the context of classes or timeline frame scripts intended for use with the Flash authoring tool. Self-contained examples are typically intended for inclusion in FLA files or as Flash document classes, but you can adapt them for use in other environments (such as Flex Builder) without support for those tools.

Using Code Examples

This book is here to help you get your job done. In general, you may use the code in this book in your programs and documentation. You don't need to contact us for permission unless you're reproducing a significant portion of the code. For example, writing a program that uses several chunks of code from this book doesn't require permission. Selling or distributing a CD-ROM of examples from O'Reilly books does require permission. Answering a question by citing this book and quoting example code doesn't require permission. Incorporating a significant amount of example code from this book into your product's documentation does require permission.

We appreciate, but don't require, attribution. An attribution usually includes the title, author, publisher, and ISBN. For example: "*The ActionScript 3.0 Quick Reference Guide: For Developers and Designers Using Flash CS4 Professional*" by David Stiller, Rich Shupe, Jen deHaan, and Darren Richardson Copyright © 2009 David Stiller and Rich Shupe, 978-0-596-51735-9."

If you feel your use of code examples falls outside fair use or the permission given above, feel free to contact us at *permissions@oreilly.com*.

Safari® Books Online

Safari When you see a Safari® Books Online icon on the cover of your favorite technology book, that means the book is available online through the O'Reilly Network Safari Bookshelf.

Safari offers a solution that's better than e-books. It's a virtual library that lets you easily search thousands of top tech books, cut and paste code samples, download chapters, and find quick answers when you need the most accurate, current information. Try it for free at *http://safari.oreilly.com*.

How to Contact Us

Please address comments and questions concerning this book to the publisher:

O'Reilly Media, Inc
1005 Gravenstein Highway North
Sebastopol, CA 95472
800-998-9938 (in the United States or Canada)
707-829-0515 (international or local)
707-829-0104 (fax)

We have a web page for this book, where we list errata, examples, and any additional information. You can find this page at:

http://oreilly.com/catalog/ 9780596517359

Acknowledgments

From David

Thanks to Rich, Jen, Darren, and the gang at O'Reilly. We took a trip to Oz and had enough adventures to write a book about it! (Rich, you owe me a face-to-face sit-down with Pentago!) For technical assistance and encouragement, I'd like to extend gratitude to Marisa Bozza, Tink (Stephen Downs), Greg Dove, Chris Georgenes, Tom Green, Branden Hall, Keenan Keeling, San Khong, John Mayhew, Colin Moock, Robert Penner, Nivesh Rajbhandari, Robert Reinhardt, Steve Schelter, and Kenneth J. Toley. Thanks and love to my #1 woman, Dawn, who introduced me to Georges Méliès, and my #1 girl, Meridian, *für unser Abenteur mit Andersen und den Brüdern Grimm.*

From Rich

Thanks to David, Jen, and Darren for making me part of the team. Thanks to Robyn Thomas, Michele Filshie, Steve Weiss, and Dennis Fitzgerald for working with me again. You're unmatched in my professional experience. Thanks to our tech editors Matthew Woodruff, Eric Kramer, and Anselm Bradford. Thanks to Marisa Bozza, Lee Brimelow, John Dowdell, Richard Galvan, Mally Gardner, Stefan Gruenwedel, Jeff Kamarer, Vishal Khandpur, San Khong, John Mayhew, Tony Mowatt, John Nack, Chris Nuuja, Ted Patrick, Nivesh Ragbhandari, and Adobe. Special thanks to my staff at FMA and Mike Wills, and my family for endless support. Last but not least, extra special thanks go to Jodi, Sally, and Claire for everything.

ActionScript 3.0 Introduced

Part I seats you comfortably in the ActionScript 3.0 bistro, offers to take your coat, and gives you a free basket of fresh bread, hot from the oven. You'll get drinks, of course, and be presented with a menu that unveils the variety of tools you can use while exploring ActionScript 3.0. Specials include the Flash authoring tool and Flash Player 10, with a dash of Flex Builder 3. You'll also see a few third-party script editors.

The first chapters touch on a number of ActionScript concepts, explored further in Part II, Part III, and Part IV. These introductory tidbits are intended to whet your appetite. They give you an overview of the new features of Action-Script 3.0: what makes it easier to use and more powerful than its predecessor, how to benefit from its richer warnings and error messages, and how the new language can improve your workflow by helping you get organized.

Chapter 1, *Introducing ActionScript 3.0*

Chapter 2, *Discovering What You Need to Work with ActionScript 3.0*

Chapter 3, *Looking at the Changes in ActionScript 3.0*

Chapter 4, *Exploring the Benefits of Using ActionScript 3.0*

Introducing ActionScript 3.0

If you chase perfection, you often catch excellence.

—William Fowble

The term "perfect" is a powerful word. From a practical standpoint, it represents a state that arguably cannot be achieved. Hey, that's a relief already! This book doesn't expect the impossible. This isn't the print version of an office know-it-all, itching for you to slip up. You won't hear any anxious hand wringing in these pages over why you haven't yet upgraded to, much less mastered, ActionScript 3.0. (Yes, even though it was available in Flash CS3 Professional.) Instead, the following chapters will take their cue from a sage observation by William Fowble: If you chase perfection, you often catch excellence. In other words, chin up! Aim for the best and enjoy the road trip. ActionScript 3.0—the current version of the programming language for the Adobe Flash Platform—is a language that indeed catches excellence. This book is designed to explain a bit about why that is. In so doing, our hope is to help you chase perfection by introducing you to the improved organization, syntax, and workflows of the new language. Catching excellence, for all of us, is a matter of practice, and comes with time.

This book is going to introduce you to new ways of thinking about the Flash Platform. ActionScript 3.0 requires these new ways because the language is actually structured around them. That's a big part of why the new language improves on previous versions. Like its precursor, but to a greater extent, ActionScript 3.0 is based on a specification called ECMAScript, which is a standard proposed by a body of experts known as Ecma International. This group is something like the World Wide Web Consortium (W3C), whose responsibility includes HTML, XML, CSS, and other widely used markup languages. Such a standard's benefit is that ActionScript 3.0 isn't just an arbitrary language invented to meet Adobe's needs. ECMAScript is a relatively mature specification, already in its third revision. The Ecma International team includes authorities from industry powerhouses like Microsoft, the Mozilla Foundation, and Adobe. The specification is built on the collective insight and success of these diverse experts in the field. Of all the versions of ActionScript, the current version comes closest into full compliance with this specification —at this point, closer even than the other famous ECMAScript derivative, JavaScript. This makes ActionScript 3.0 a model of best practices, habits you can use in both Flash CS4 Professional and Flex Builder 3. In many cases, you may even find that these practices benefit your involvement with existing projects coded in previous versions of ActionScript. Sure, the syntactical details change, but achievement in programming is all about structure and purpose. It's the concepts and good habits that carry you.

For the nuts and bolts, the relevant ActionScript Language Reference is always a mere keystroke away (the F1 key). Even so, a new set of Help docs can be daunting, especially if you're already well-versed in ActionScript 2.0. Fortunately, the ActionScript 3.0 documentation is every bit as helpful as it used to be, even if it looks different. The layout of the Help docs is still organized around the layout of the language itself—around the classes that define the objects you will use—and its class entries still summarize the usable apparatus of each object: its characteristics, called *properties*; the things it can do, called *methods*; and the things it can react to, called *events*. In the new documentation, code samples are presented as custom classes, rather than frame scripts. This requires you test them as standalone, simple text files, according to the new *document class* concept described in Chapter 6. Fortunately, this also means you can test these classes in other programs, such as Flex Builder. This book will help you get familiar not only with the new language, but also with the documentation that explains it.

Keep in mind, ramping up to ActionScript 3.0 isn't merely about learning the latest syntax: it's about becoming a better, more efficient programmer. This isn't meant to slight ActionScript 2.0 at all, but plenty has changed since its introduction in late 2003. It's no exaggeration to say that several aspects of the language have been completely overhauled. In fact, ActionScript 3.0 requires an entirely new virtual machine, which is the module inside Flash Player that interprets compiled ActionScript. As of Flash Player 9, the runtime that displays Flash movies does so with *two* virtual machines: AVM1 for legacy SWF files based on ActionScript 1.0 and 2.0, and the new AVM2 for ActionScript 3.0. That's a first in the history of Flash Player. Thanks to the new virtual machine, ActionScript 3.0 runs faster and more efficiently by an order of magnitude. This bodes well for the overriding goal of the new language: to facilitate a wide range of interactive media and Rich Internet Applications (RIAs)—to do so simply, with better performance, and highly compatible with industry standards. As you can imagine, an upgrade of this scale means you may have to reshape some of your current habits. But take heart. Reshape doesn't necessarily mean tear down and rebuild. As ActionScript has matured, it has consistently moved in the direction it currently stands. Again, honing your skills in light of ActionScript 3.0 will help you in your current projects and also in legacy project maintenance. Migration can be intimidating, but much of that uncertainty comes from trying to find your stride. Once you take the first few steps, the momentum keeps you going.

Here's a look at some of the new features.

Examining ActionScript 3.0, the Language

Section 4 of the ECMAScript standard (*http://www.ecma-international.org/ publications/files/ECMA-ST/Ecma-262.pdf*) defines an important facet of any language that implements it. Such languages "will provide not only the objects and other facilities described in this specification but also certain environment-specific *host* objects, whose description and behaviour are beyond the scope of this specification." In other words, any ECMAScript derivative needs a set core functionality that stands on its own and will then provide additional functionality specific to the environment that interprets it. This is exactly what ActionScript 3.0 does, and its host environments include Flash Player for web browsers, intended for Flash-enabled websites such as *http://YouTube.com*; Flash Lite for devices, such as video games for your cell phone; and Adobe Integrated Runtime (AIR) for applications installed on the hard drive, such as eBay Desktop (*http://desktop.ebay.com/*).

Here is a brief summary of a number of core updates.

Runtime Exceptions

In ActionScript 2.0, many runtime errors failed without drawing attention to themselves. On the plus side—and this is a very weak plus—this meant that errors of this sort often failed "gracefully." In other words, they might not halt someone's experience with something abrupt or laden with technical jargon, such as an alert or dialog box. On the minus side, this also meant such errors might go unnoticed by the developer—until complaints started rolling in that people were experiencing slow playback or even lockups. Such errors could be hard for developers to pinpoint and repair, precisely because they were silent.

ActionScript 3.0 allows for a variety of runtime exceptions to be handled with purpose. This includes `Error` objects generated both by the runtime environment and, potentially, by the programmer. In ActionScript 3.0, the `Error` class is considerably more robust than its forerunner, and tailor-made

Error objects can be built from this class as desired, inheriting and extending its functionality to provide highly customized error messages. Exceptions can even provide source file and line number information, which greatly enhances the debugging experience, letting developers quickly track down errors.

Runtime Types

ActionScript 2.0 introduced the ability to strongly type variables, parameters, and function return values. This was, and still is, an optional way to let Flash know exactly what sort of data a particular variable, parameter, or return value could cope with. This ability was a boon to developers in terms of debugging, because it gave you a way to display error messages in cases of a *type mismatch*. For example, if you were going to perform a math operation on two numbers provided by the user, you might take those numbers from input text fields. This would actually make them strings, which meant your math operation would give you unexpected results (for example, 1 + 2 would become "12" instead of 3). By strongly typing the parameters of the function that performed this operation—in other words, by specifying intended variable types with a colon (:), then the type—you could benefit from a meaningful error message in the Output panel such as this:

```
// ActionScript 2.0
var userVar1:String = inputField1.text;
var userVar2:String = inputField2.text;

function getSum(a:Number, b:Number):Number {
    return a + b;
}

trace(getSum(userVar1, userVar2));
// Displays:
**Error** Scene=Scene 1, layer=Layer 1, frame=1:Line 8: Type mismatch.
    getSum(userVar1, userVar2);.
```

A type mismatch notice is a great reminder to use something like `parseInt()` or `parseFloat()` to convert those strings into numeric values. Useful indeed, but this was only a first step in a good direction. In ActionScript 2.0, this sort of error checking only occurred at compile time. Under many circumstances —such as evaluating data from dynamic sources like XML—the feature wasn't "smart" enough to catch every contingency. In ActionScript 3.0, it is.

Sealed Classes

Following in the same vein as runtime exceptions and runtime types, Action-Script 3.0 establishes the concept of *sealed classes* in a stricter, more formalized way than in ActionScript 2.0. A sealed class is one that can't have properties or methods assigned to it at runtime, such as String. By default, classes in ActionScript 3.0 are sealed, but this can be overruled when you write your own.

```
var str:String = "" // Or: new String();
str.customProperty = "This generates a compiler error.";
// Displays: Access of possibly undefined property customProperty
// through a reference with static type String.
```

In contrast, a class that actually can have properties and methods assigned to it at runtime is called *dynamic*. One of the most familiar dynamic classes is MovieClip, though historically speaking, many frame script developers haven't considered movie clips in terms of a class. The same could be said of buttons and text fields, because you can create such elements with Flash's drawing tools. (Of the elements just mentioned, only movie clips are dynamic.) For frame script coders, movie clips are often thought of simply as symbols or timelines, and timelines have always been able to receive new variables at runtime. True enough. What's really going on, though, is that variables defined in keyframe scripts are in reality dynamic properties of a MovieClip instance; functions are actually dynamic methods.

Declaring a variable in a keyframe of the main timeline or in a movie clip's timeline is conceptually the same as the following:

```
var mc:MovieClip = new MovieClip();
mc.customProperty = "This is perfectly acceptable.";
```

Custom classes in ActionScript 3.0 can behave this way too, if and only if they are declared with the **dynamic** attribute:

```
package {
    public dynamic class CustomClass() {
        // class code here
    }
}
```

On paper, this is also how it was in ActionScript 2.0, but in fact, even non-dynamic classes could be altered at runtime by manipulation of the Object.prototype property (inherited by all objects) or by the array access operator ([]). Advanced programmers who used such an approach in the past will find it no longer works in ActionScript 3.0 for sealed classes.

```
// ActionScript 2.0
var str:String = "";
str.customProperty = "Secret back door.";
// Displays: There is no property with the name 'customProperty'.

str["customProperty"] = "Secret back door.";
// Works just fine in ActionScript 2.0, but in 3.0 displays:
    Cannot create property customProperty on String.
```

In ActionScript 3.0, non-dynamic classes actually are what they claim to be. This makes for stricter compile-time checking and improves memory usage because class instances can now be guaranteed to require no more than a predeclared amount of system memory.

Method Closures

Of all the updates to ActionScript 3.0, it's no surprise that developers, regardless of skill level, encounter one in particular early on: *method closures*. Why? Because the introduction of method closures changes the point of view, or *scope*, of methods in ActionScript 3.0.

Scope refers to the conceptual area of a program in which code executes. The availability of code definitions, such as variables, functions, properties, and methods, depends on the scope of the code being executed. For example, if a variable is declared in a timeline frame, that variable can be referenced by any other code in that frame, as long as that code appears after the declaration. Even a function defined in that frame can reference the variable scoped to the timeline, because scopes can be nested, and the flow moves from outer scope to inner: the timeline's definitions become available to the function.

```
// A variable declared here ...
var favoriteCereal:String = "Star Crunchers!";

// can be referenced here ...
trace(favoriteCereal); // Displays: Star Crunchers!

function myFunction():void {
    // and here ...
    trace(favoriteCereal); // Displays: Star Crunchers!
}
myFunction();
```

In contrast, a variable declared inside a function can only be referenced by that function, because the scope of the function is confined to itself.

```
function myFunction():void {
    // A variable declared here ...
    var favoriteCereal:String = "Star Crunchers!";

    // can only be referenced here ...
    trace(favoriteCereal); // Displays: Star Crunchers!
}
myFunction();

// but not in the outer scope ...
trace(favoriteCereal);
// Displays:
**Error** Scene=Scene 1, layer=Layer 1, frame=1:Line 10:
    Access of undefined property favoriteCereal.
```

Up to now, this should be familiar to ActionScript 2.0 developers. How, then, have things changed? Consider the next few examples.

In ActionScript 2.0, a button click might be handled like this:

```
// ActionScript 2.0
myButton.onRelease = buttonHandler;
function buttonHandler():Void {
    trace(this); // Displays: _level0.myButton
    // other event handler code
}
```

Prior to ActionScript 3.0, the scope of the function shown belonged to the myButton instance. In this case, the button code could conveniently be abbreviated with the use of the this keyword, which self-referenced the current scope (myButton). In some cases, this made for a handy way to achieve certain goals. For example, to repeatedly loop a Sound instance in ActionScript 2.0, the following would do:

```
// ActionScript 2.0
var audio:Sound = new Sound();
audio.loadSound("externalFile.mp3", true);
audio.onSoundComplete = completeHandler;
function completeHandler():Void {
    this.start();
}
```

Again, the function is scoped to the instance. In this case, the expression this.start() amounts to invoking the Sound.start() method on the audio instance. Although convenient in this sort of situation, difficulties arose when the event handler needed to reference objects outside the scope of the function, especially in custom classes.

To a large extent, this issue could be addressed in ActionScript 2.0 with the Delegate class, which allowed you to reroute the scope as desired:

```
// ActionScript 2.0
import mx.utils.Delegate;
var audio:Sound = new Sound();
audio.loadSound("externalFile.mp3", true);
audio.onSoundComplete = Delegate.create(this, completeHandler);

function completeHandler():Void {
    audio.start();
}
```

The Delegate.create() method accepted two parameters: first, the desired scope; second, the function or method to execute in that scope. Note that because of this change, the function invokes audio.start() directly. In this case, the this keyword no longer refers to the audio instance to which the listener was attached, but rather to the timeline frame in which the listener was assigned.

In ActionScript 3.0, method closures let a function or method remember where it was defined. In short, you get the best of both worlds. In the following ActionScript 3.0, written in a keyframe, the reference to this shows that the scope belongs to the main timeline—to the frame in which the function is defined, rather than to the myButton instance. No extra baggage, like the Delegate class, is required.

```
myButton.addEventListener(MouseEvent.CLICK, buttonHandler);
function buttonHandler(evt:MouseEvent):void {
    trace(this); // Displays: [object MainTimeline]
}
```

To reference the button rather than the frame, use the Event.target property of the parameter that is passed into the function automatically by the event. In this snippet, the parameter is arbitrarily named evt:

```
myButton.addEventListener(MouseEvent.CLICK, buttonHandler);
function buttonHandler(evt:MouseEvent):void {
    trace(evt.target);      // Displays: [object SimpleButton]
    trace(evt.target.name); // Displays: myButton
}
```

ECMAScript for XML (E4X)

Flash has long supported XML, but the addition of *ECMAScript for XML* (E4X) syntax is a significant productivity boost. Like ActionScript, E4X is an Ecma International specification, which affords a powerful yet concise set of language constructs for retrieving data from XML, and manipulating it.

In ActionScript 2.0, you can certainly navigate among the nodes of a loaded XML document, but the effort becomes progressively more tedious as the XML's complexity increases. The ActionScript 2.0 XML class provides a handful of necessary navigation properties, such as firstChild, nextSibling, lastChild, and childNodes. Choosing from these, and assuming an XML document has already been loaded and parsed into an XML instance named myXML, you might select the title of the fifth track of The Beatles' *Abbey Road* album ("Octopus's Garden") like this:

```
// ActionScript 2.0
myXML.firstChild.firstChild.firstChild.childNodes[4].attributes.¬
    title;

// Contents of the loaded XML document
<?xml version="1.0" encoding="iso-8859-1"?>
<library>
    <artist name="The Beatles">
        <album name="Abbey Road">
```

```
          <track title="Come Together" />
          <track title="Something" />
          <track title="Maxwell's Silver Hammer" />
          <track title="Oh! Darling" />
          <track title="Octopus's Garden" />
          <track title="I Want You (She's So Heavy)" />
          <track title="Here Comes the Sun" />
          <track title="Because" />
          <track title="You Never Give Me Your Money" />
          <track title="Sun King" />
          <track title="Mean Mr. Mustard" />
          <track title="Polythene Pam" />
          <track title="She Came in Through the Bathroom Window" />
          <track title="Golden Slumbers" />
          <track title="Carry That Weight" />
          <track title="The End" />
          <track title="Her Majesty" />
      </album>
    </artist>
  </library>
```

In the preceding whopping expression, myXML refers to the parsed XML document; the three mentions of firstChild refer, respectively, to the <library>, <artist>, and <album> nodes; and childNodes[4] refers to the fifth <track> node (bear in mind, childNodes returns an array, and arrays start at zero). Finally, the attributes property leads to the title attribute of the selected node.

E4X lets parsed XML be referenced as if it were a native object. This lets you traverse the loaded data incredibly more intuitively. In the ActionScript 3.0 equivalent, the same track can be referenced like this:

```
// ActionScript 3.0
myXML.artist[0].album[0].track[4].@title;
```

or, thanks to the descendent accessor operator (..), even something as short as this:

```
myXML..track[4].@title;
```

Which would you rather type?

In addition, you can compare data using a familiar set of operators. For example, if the XML document at hand contains numerous recording artists, The Beatles' <artist> node could be singled out as easily as this:

```
myXML.artist.(@name == "The Beatles")
```

The E4X specification is available in Adobe PDF format at the Ecma International website: *http://www.ecma-international .org/publications/files/ECMA-ST/Ecma-357.pdf.*

Regular Expressions

The term *regular expressions* refers to a set of specialized language constructs for retrieving data from strings (that is, text content), and manipulating such data. In this regard, regular expressions (often abbreviated as *regex*) shares a number of similarities with E4X: both mechanisms are compact and efficient in their tasks. The syntax of regex tends to be initially harder to grasp than E4X—here, normal letters and punctuation are used to represent whole sets of characters, in addition to filtering rules—but the results are well worth the effort.

What can you do with regular expressions? To answer that, consider two familiar methods of the String class, indexOf() and lastIndexOf(), which have been available in ActionScript for years. These methods both accept two parameters: first, a string to look for within a container string; second, optionally, where to start looking within the container string. Each method takes its starting point from opposite ends of the container string.

```
var pangram:String = "The quick, brown fox jumps over a lazy dog.";

trace(pangram.indexOf("o"));      // Displays 13
trace(pangram.indexOf("o", 14)); // Displays 18
trace(pangram.lastIndexOf("o")); // Displays 40
```

In the first trace() statement, only one parameter is supplied, "o", and the return value is 13 because the letter "o" makes its first appearance at index 13 (starting with 0, the thirteenth character in the string pangram). In the second statement, the return value is 18 because of the optional second parameter 14, which instructs the method to begin after the index of the first "o". In the third statement, the return value is 40 because the method lastIndexOf() begins its search from the end of the string.

For simple searches, indexOf() and lastIndexOf() fit the bill, but what if the requirement is something like "find all US ZIP codes," which could be any 5-number combination, or "find all words in this paragraph that contain three or more vowels"? Suddenly, the task seems considerably more difficult, if not impossible. Believe it or not, the RegExp class in ActionScript 3.0 handles this requirement very easily. The solution requires a *pattern* of specialized characters, expressed either as an instance of the RegExp class or passed as a parameter to one of the regex-related methods of the String class (match(), replace(), or search()).

Given a variable, paragraph, set to the text content of the previous paragraph, the following code shows how to retrieve words with three or more vowels:

```
var re:RegExp = /\b(\w*[aeiou]\w*){3}\b/gi;

var result:Object = re.exec(paragraph);
```

```
while (result != null) {
    trace(result[0]);
    result = re.exec(paragraph);
}
// Displays: searches, indexOf, lastIndexOf, requirement,
// something, and other words with three or more vowels
```

A full discussion of regular expressions syntax is beyond the scope of this book, but here's a brief overview of how the previous example works. A variable, `re`, is set to an instance of the `RegExp` class by way of the RegExp delimiter operator (`/pattern/flags`). Between the two slashes of this operator, the pattern `\b(\w*[aeiou]\w*){3}\b` spells out the search requirement. After the second slash, the flags (`gi`) configure the pattern as global and case insensitive. The `RegExp.exec()` method executes the pattern on the string `paragraph` and returns an object (`result`) that contains information about the search. The search is repeated until `result` is `null`.

If the preceding example seems outlandish, imagine the same sort of power applied to the validation of user input. You can manage even potentially complex requirements without much difficulty. These include questions such as, "Is this email address correctly formed?" (Checking for the "@" character isn't enough!) "Is this a valid telephone number?" (People might enter anything from (123) 456-7890 to 123.456.46789 to 123456789.) "Has the user tried to sneak in an inappropriate word by using a nonstandard spelling?" Patterns that match these requirements not only find the strings in question, but can also manipulate them in order to, for example, format telephone numbers consistently or replace questionable words with Xs.

 For an exhaustive and highly regarded treatise on regular expressions, be sure to read *Mastering Regular Expressions*, by Jeffrey Friedl (O'Reilly). Numerous tutorials are also available online at the unrelated *http://www.regular-expressions.info/* website.

Namespaces

In advanced programming scenarios, the concept of *namespaces* brings a valuable new mechanism to ActionScript 3.0. In short, namespaces are essentially custom access specifiers—like `public`, `private`, `protected`, and `internal`—except with names you choose. Namespaces let you control the visibility of your properties and methods, even to the point of overriding package structures. They also let you qualify members under various guises. As a quick example, you might develop an AIR application that performs one behavior while an Internet connection is present, and another when no connection is present. By using namespaces, you can define multiple versions of the same method that, for instance, checks an online inventory when the user's WiFi connection is available but defaults to a cached version otherwise. Or you might define series of variables in several languages, where the value of a variable depends on the user's regional settings. These distinctions are determined by custom prefixes and the name qualifier operator (::):

```
// Three versions of the same String variable
english::newFeatures // Value of "Lots of new stuff"
german::newFeatures  // Value of "Viele neue Sachen"
french::newFeatures  // Value of "Plien de nouvelles choses"
```

Namespaces are outfitted with a Universal Resource Identifier (URI) to avoid collisions, and are also used to represent XML namespaces when working with E4X.

New Primitive Types

ActionScript 3.0 introduces two new primitive types, int and uint, bringing the full list to Boolean, int, Null, Number, String, uint, and void (note the change in capitalization from Void). These new numeric types reduce memory usage in cases when a numeric value need only be an integer. How? The familiar Number data type is an IEEE-754 double-precision floating-point number, which, thanks to its structure, always requires 64 bits of memory. Number objects range from 1.79e+308 (1.79 with over 300 zeroes after it!) down to 5e-324. That's an unimaginably large range, which isn't always necessary. Sometimes you just want to count through a for loop, and all you need is an integer.

Enter int, which is a relatively small 32-bit number (only 4 bytes), whose range is still an impressive 2,147,483,647 (over two billion) down to –2,147,483,648. That range should do for most of the for loops you'll encounter. By contrast, uint numbers (unsigned integers) range from 0 to 4,294,967,295, which is the same span as int, but entirely on the positive side of the number line. If your for loop's counter, or any other integer value, needs a higher range than offered by int, uint makes a good choice—provided the range doesn't dip below zero. Neither type ever requests more than 32 bits of system memory.

 One note of caution: because uint values are always positive, take care when trying to subtract a uint into negative territory. A uint rolls around to 4,294,967,295 if you subtract it past zero, as the following code demonstrates.

```
var n:uint = 0;
trace(n); // Displays 0

n--;
trace(n); // Displays 4294967295
```

Exploring Flash Player API Updates

In the "ActionScript 3.0, the Language" section of this chapter, you learned that the ECMAScript specification on which ActionScript is based actually expects the language to provide functionality tailored to the platform that hosts it. In the case of ActionScript, hosts include Flash Player, AIR, and Flash Lite —all various flavors of the Flash Platform. Though each host is designed to meet specific needs—websites, desktop applications, and mobile content, respectively—their overlap is considerable. ActionScript 3.0 institutes a significant restructuring of its *application programming interface* (API), summarized handily in the colossal migration table available on the Adobe LiveDocs website (*http://help.adobe.com/en_US/AS3LCR/Flash_10.0/migration.html*) and also in the Help panel in the appendices of the ActionScript 3.0 Language and Component Reference, under the heading "ActionScript 2.0 Migration". In large part, existing functionality has been restructured into packages that make better sense from an organizational standpoint. However, Flash does have a number of philosophical changes in the way it carries out its fundamental tasks. The following paragraphs list some of the more notable updates.

> As of the publication of this book, Flash Lite does not yet support ActionScript 3.0, due to the inherent processor and memory limitations of mobile devices. The features recounted here apply to Flash Player 9 (and higher) and AIR, but won't apply to Flash Lite until that runtime adds support for ActionScript 3.0.

DOM3 Event Model

Before ActionScript 3.0, you could handle events in Flash in at least five different ways, some of which were interchangeable:

- The legacy on() handler, available since Flash 2 and still in wide use, even in ActionScript 2.0 scenarios, but gone in ActionScript 3.0

- The legacy onClipEvent() handler, also widely used and unavailable in ActionScript 3.0

- The dot notation syntax that combined and replaced on() and onClipevent() (for example Button.onPress = *functionDefinition*, MovieClip.onEnterFrame, and so on)

- The addListener() method of several—but not all!—ActionScript 2.0 classes, such as TextField, Mouse, and MovieClipLoader

- The addEventListener() method used by the v2 component set (user interface, data, and media components)

This varied assortment was a result of incremental improvements to Action-Script with every new release of the authoring tool, with the older approaches retained for backward compatibility. For longtime Flash developers, each new technique was simply a small addition to the workflow, but newcomers to recent versions, such as Flash 8 or Flash CS3, were understandably confused by an API with so many seemingly arbitrary possibilities.

Are on() and onClipEvent() really so bad? From a workflow standpoint, no. From a practical standpoint, they aren't nearly as valuable as their dot notation replacement. In ActionScript 2.0, the combination of on() and onClipEvent() provide access to only slightly more than half the events available to movie clips and buttons. In addition, you can't assign, manipulate, or remove their event handlers at runtime. Their absence in ActionScript 3.0 marks the end of a long transition period from ActionScript 1.0 through 2.0.

Because ActionScript 3.0 relies on a new virtual machine, it can afford to make a clean break in the way it handles events. With one small exception (discussed in Chapter 4), event handling is now consolidated across the board into a single, consistent approach: the EventDispatcher.addEventListener() method. This mechanism is based on the W3C's Document Object Model (DOM) Level 3 Events Specification (*http://www.w3.org/TR/DOM-Level-3 -Events/*). This means that in ActionScript 3.0, event handling syntax is the same in nearly all cases, no matter if the event dispatcher is a button, an audio clip, or a loader object for XML or JPEG files. The basic structure looks like this:

```
eventDispatchingObject.addEventListener(
    EventType,
    functionToPerform
);
```

Display List API

In ActionScript 3.0, movie clips can be instantiated with the new keyword as easily as this:

```
var mc:MovieClip = new MovieClip();
```

which is more intuitive than what it took in ActionScript 2.0:

```
var mc:MovieClip = existingMovieClip.createEmptyMovieClip(¬
    instanceName, depth);
```

And it gets better. Depth management is now automatic. Notice that the expression new MovieClip() does not require a depth parameter. This change is due to a fundamental new approach to the display of visual objects in Action-Script 3.0: a concept called the *display list*, which represents the hierarchical display of all graphical objects in Flash Player. This concept is embodied in the `DisplayObjectContainer` class, the base class for all objects that can serve as visual containers, including movie clips, the new `Sprite` and `Loader` classes, and more. Thanks to inheritance, `DisplayObjectContainer` provides new methods to these classes for considerably better control over the management of object z-order. For example, while the `MovieClip` class in ActionScript 2.0 featured `getDepth()` and `swapDepths()`, the ActionScript 3.0 version offers all of these:

- `addChild()`
- `addChildAt()`
- `contains()`
- `getChildAt()`
- `getChildByName()`
- `getChildIndex()`
- `removeChild()`
- `removeChildAt()`
- `setChildIndex()`
- `swapChildren()`
- `swapChildtenAt()`

How's that for control?

These methods are also available to `Sprite`, which is effectively a movie clip without the overhead of a timeline; `Loader`, which loads external SWF files and image files (JPEG, PNG, or GIF) at runtime; and any other class in the `DisplayObjectContainer` family tree.

Under the display list system, objects can be re-parented at any time. This ability simplifies cases in which groups of objects need to be manipulated at once. Consider a jigsaw puzzle game, for example. If you want to combine partially solved areas, so that snapped-together pieces move as one unit, you can simply remove the piece from its current parent and add it as a child to the parent that represents the partially solved group. Before ActionScript 3.0, this action would have required individual sophisticated tracking of each jigsaw piece.

New Sound APIs

Flash Player 8 was the first to support 32 simultaneous sound channels, a significant increase from the original eight-sound channel limit. Although present for as long as Flash Player has supported sound, these sound channels, as such, had no clear representation in code before ActionScript 3.0. In previous versions of the language, the Sound class was self-contained, handling all of its functionality in a relatively simple manner, but at the cost of some clarity of purpose. For example, in order to control the volume and panning of one sound distinctly from another, you had to associate each sound with its own movie clip. You made this association by way of an optional "target" parameter in the Sound constructor function. Because target movie clips might or might not contain other content, their ambiguous roles had the potential to confuse.

ActionScript 3.0 clarifies programmed sound by complementing the Sound class with three companions: SoundChannel, SoundTransform, and SoundMixer. These new APIs give you more explicit control over imported and embedded sounds. The SoundMixer.computeSpectrum() method even lets you retrieve spectral data from sounds, which you can use to program responses to changes in audio pitch and volume.

Binary Data and Sockets

The new ByteArray class enables interoperability with existing custom protocols, and lets advanced developers read, write, and manipulate data on the byte level. This has led adventurous programmers to cultivate projects previously unheard of in Flash, such as Tinic Uro's PNG encoder (*http://www .kaourantin.net/2005/10/png-encoder-in-as3.html*, now updated and featured in the as3corelib library at *http://code.google.com/p/as3corelib/*) and a dynamic tone generator by André Michelle and Joa Ebert, capable of playing MIDI-like Amiga MOD files (*http://8bitboy.popforge.de/*).

Understanding Players and Support

Although this book focuses primarily on the Flash authoring tool, it's important to realize that Adobe offers two official ActionScript 3.0 compilers. One of these compilers is built into Flash CS4 itself. As you would expect, this one takes into consideration objects in the document's Library, as well as global SWF file settings, such as background color and frame rate, as configured in the Property inspector. This compiler can also compile previous versions of ActionScript. Separate from that, there's the command line compiler included with the free Flex Software Development Kit (SDK) available at *www.adobe .com/go/flex_trial/*. This second compiler is the one used by the Flex Builder *integrated development environment* (IDE), which doesn't include drawing tools, timelines, or a library. In addition to ActionScript 3.0, the Flex compiler understands MXML, the declarative markup language used for laying out Flex applications. For want of a library, the second compiler lets metadata embed assets into resultant SWF files. The Flash authoring tool supports only limited metadata, an undocumented feature at the time of writing.

These distinct compilers serve independent workflows. To facilitate the development of RIAs, the Flex SDK features an elaborate framework of user controls and data handlers that aren't available to the Flash authoring tool, even though the framework is written in ActionScript 3.0. By comparison, Flash offers a modest subset of user controls in its Components panel, including support for the playback and manipulation of Flash video files (FLV).

In the end, there's only one ActionScript 3.0, and it behaves the same when compiled under either tool. The reason for this consistency is that Flash CS4 and the Flex SDK both publish SWF files for the same Flash Player 9 or higher. It's quite possible—and often done—to create custom classes that can be used under either circumstance. The concept of the *document class* (see Chapter 6), introduced in Flash CS3, means that an entire application, composed of numerous external classes, can be compiled by Flash or the Flex command line compiler (including Flex Builder) from identical source files.

Because ActionScript 3.0 requires AVM2, as mentioned earlier in this chapter, Flash Player 9 is the minimum required runtime to display such content. Flash Player 9 runs on numerous operating systems, including several versions of Windows, Macintosh, Linux, and Solaris. Due to the varied nature of these operating systems and occasional bug fixes required by each, in addition to ongoing new features, Flash Player 9 includes a number of minor point releases, as summarized in Table 1-1. Flash CS4's default output is aimed at Flash Player 10, which may eventually see a list of minor point releases just as long. Time will tell. To determine what version of Flash Player the user has installed, reference the static `version` property of the `Capabilities` class.

Table 1-1. Flash Player 9 minor point releases

Flash Player version	Notable changes
9.0.16.0	ActionScript 3.0, including runtime exceptions and error handling, sealed classes, method closures, ECMAScript for XML (E4X), regular expressions, namespaces, new primitive types, DOM3 event model, display list APIs, new sound APIs, and binary data and sockets.
9.0.20.0	Bug fixes and optimizations related to the Intel-based Macintosh platform.
9.0.28.0	Support for Windows Vista operating system. Addition of ADDED_TO_STAGE and REMOVED_FROM_STAGE event constants to let a DisplayObject monitor and know when it can or cannot access its stage property. Security enhancements.

Flash Player version	Notable changes
9.0.31.0	Support for Linux operating systems.
9.0.45.0	Bug fixes and improvements for Adobe Flash CS3 Professional. Affects only Windows and Macintosh platforms.
9.0.47.0	Support for Solaris operating system. Security enhancements.
9.0.48.0	Linux security enhancements.
9.0.115.0	H.264 video and High Efficiency AAC (HE-AAC) audio codec support. Hardware acceleration, hardware scaling, multi-threaded video decoding, and enhanced image scaling. Flash Player cache enables common components, such as the Flex Framework, to be cached locally and then used by any SWF from any domain. Flash Media Server buffering maintains stream buffer while a stream is paused.
9.0.124.0	Media streaming security patch and minor display update for Windows Vista.

 A full listing of all Flash Player release notes, including bug fixes, can be found at *http://www.adobe.com/support/documen tation/en/flashplayer/releasenotes.html*.

Learning ActionScript 3.0 on the Heels of 2.0

Pretend for a moment you're a carpenter. For years, you were making do with a hand-crank drill, but then the Macromedia Hardware Company introduced an electric model called ActionScript 1.0 stamped with gold letters on the handle. Beautiful thing! No reason to ever use anything else. Sure, you could operate the drill only within six feet of an electrical outlet (because that was the length of the cord), but the advantages were resoundingly clear. Plus, you could always carry around an extension cable. A few years later, Macromedia announced a new and improved ActionScript 2.0 model. This drill had an optional battery back. For some, the new battery pack was a godsend, because it freed them from the previous six foot limitation. They embraced the new feature and literally found themselves running with it. Other carpenters found the battery pack a bit too advanced. They weren't sure, for example, if they were supposed to drain the batteries completely before recharging. And honestly, that was fine: the drill still had a cord, of course, so they continued within their previous comfort zone, which was still a considerable improvement over the hand-crank days. Carpenters were a happy bunch. Eventually, the Macromedia Hardware Company became Adobe. Everyone looked forward to the new drill—ActionScript 3.0—and when it came ... they found that the cord had been replaced with a docking station. Suddenly, carpenters who had opted not to use the ActionScript 2.0 battery pack felt trapped. They had no experience with batteries, but if they were going to use an ActionScript 3.0 model, they had no choice.

It goes without saying that every analogy has its flaws. Certainly, the changes in ActionScript 3.0 amount to more than the obvious benefit of a battery pack. Clearly, the new APIs are more complex than the question of how to recharge a set of batteries. In any case, ActionScript does a lot more than drill holes! Still, it can be useful to think of ActionScript 2.0 as a preparatory transitional period between, on one hand, the very roots of the language—that is, Action-Script 1.0 and even earlier—and, on the other hand, the current version. As with the carpenter story, numerous features in ActionScript 2.0, such as strict typing (:Number, :Void, etc.) and formalized custom class files, were optional. (Unlike the analogy, those particular features are still optional in ActionScript 3.0.) Voluntary though they were, such then-new conventions were an early invitation to practice a more efficient workflow. Developers who opted to experiment with *object-oriented programming* (OOP), to the point of writing their own custom classes, may feel more at home with ActionScript 3.0 than others. For those who were perfectly comfortable with the conventions of ActionScript 1.0, they might understandably feel trepidation in light of the current version, especially now that ActionScript 3.0 has dropped support for some previously optional features, such as on() and onClipEvent(). Flipping through the ActionScript 3.0 Language and Components Reference takes considerably longer than before. Everything has been arranged into a potentially overwhelming new hierarchy of packages. Most of the Help panel sample code has been written as class files, to make it applicable both for keyframe and class file programmers.

These changes are big, but not insurmountable. One of this book's driving purposes is to help you feel caught up, whether or not you pursued the optional new conventions of ActionScript 2.0—the features that, in hindsight, were a gentle ramp up to today's recommended best practices. The important thing to keep in mind is that ActionScript 3.0 is scalable in terms of complexity. If you want to plunge headlong into OOP principles such as inheritance and design patterns, ActionScript 3.0 will oblige. If you prefer to stick with traditional timeline coding, ActionScript 3.0 will oblige—with a number of provisos covered in the following chapters.

Deciding to Migrate or Write Code from Scratch

If you work with a set of in-house templates, be they FLA files, custom classes, or a combination of both, sooner or later you'll have to decide how to update them. For the sake of discussion, these files are stable ones that have made your company money for years, and they work just fine. Nonetheless, you'd like to take advantage of the speed increases—or any of the other benefits—afforded by ActionScript 3.0. Should you painstakingly tinker with existing files, tweaking as you go, or should you ditch everything and start from square one? Which approach would require less effort?

For better or worse, there is no sure-fire way to determine which endeavor is more advantageous in a given situation. While you can theoretically upgrade a FLA file's Publish Settings to ActionScript 3.0 and compile without errors or warnings, the prospect becomes progressively more unlikely as a project gains in complexity. Chances are high that one incompatibility will occur in concert with many: in other words, when it rains, it pours. That said, here are a few thoughts to consider.

If all or most of your code exists on frames in a FLA file, you may have no realistic choice but to migrate the ActionScript in place, for the obvious reason that the code is so closely tied to the file's visual design. To start from scratch could require careful transportation of symbols from one FLA file to another, possibly including intricate nested timeline effects. For simple banner ads and linear slideshows, an in-place update may not be as difficult as it sounds. Standalone calls to stop(), gotoAndPlay(), and the like, will carry over without a hitch. By all means, select File→Publish Settings→Flash→Script→ActionScript 3.0, and then hold your breath and see what happens.

Don't forget to exhale if the compile works, and frankly, prepare yourself now for numerous entries in the Compiler Errors panel. If any of the frame code involves event handlers, loads external assets, or even calls a new web page (getURL() is now navigateToURL()), you'll have to update it. The good news is, the Compiler Errors panel is one of many helpful new tools in Flash CS4 (introduced in Flash CS3). This panel not only tells you where the erroneous code is, by class file, scene, layer, keyframe, and line number, it often makes suggestions on what to change, including a list of common migration issues.

 The Compiler Errors panel and other debugging tools are covered in Chapter 11.

If most of your code exists in external class files, your project probably involves more than a smattering of ActionScript. Although this likely means you'll spend more time on code migration (because there's more of it!), the fact that your code is separate means you can test and revise each class individually. In either case, frame code or class files, this book will help you get your bearings.

CHAPTER 2

Discovering What You Need to Work with ActionScript 3.0

Working with ActionScript 3.0 is an equation composed of two parts: you need something to compile a program written in the language, and you need something to display the results of that programming. In compiler territory, you have quite a few development choices. In the most basic approach, Adobe makes the Flex Software Development Kit (SDK) available to the public free of charge (*http://www.adobe.com/go/flex_trial/*). This SDK includes the full ActionScript 3.0 *application programming interface* (API), which is the full list of core and Flash Player API classes described in the ActionScript 3.0 Language and Components Reference, published on the Adobe LiveDocs website (*http://help.adobe.com/en_US/AS3LCR/Flash_10.0/*). In addition, the SDK includes the Flex framework (component class library) and Flex command line compiler, letting programmers freely develop and deploy Flex applications using any scripting *integrated development environment* (IDE). Because the Flex framework is, itself, written in ActionScript 3.0, you don't necessarily have to learn a new language to use Flex. Without spending a dime, interested programmers can build anything from basic ActionScript 3.0 class files—which you can also write in the Script window of Flash CS4 Professional—to full-scale Flex applications that you can write with Flex Builder 3.

Displaying the results of your work requires Flash Player 9 or higher (Flash CS4 publishes to Flash Player 10 by default). That may seem like the easy half the equation, but there are actually several versions of Flash Player 9 and will likely be several versions of Flash Player 10. The following sections give a brief overview of the tools necessary to work with ActionScript 3.0. Later in the chapter, you'll learn about alternative scripting IDEs that you can use in co-operation with the Flash authoring tool.

Flash CS4 Professional/Flex Builder 3

The Flash CS4 Professional authoring tool is the latest in a running line of the production tool that originally began life as a vector animation program. When designers and developers hear the word "Flash," they probably think first of the Flash authoring tool, rather than Flex Builder, even though both applications are Adobe products that publish SWF files for the same Flash Player runtime. In a few words, Flash CS4 can be summed up as the most appropriate tool for traditional Flash designers and developers. This authoring tool features numerous panels aimed at drawing and animation—consider the Timeline, Color, Align, Transform, and Tools panels.

Flash authoring techniques often take advantage of a *timeline metaphor*, in which the goings-on of a SWF file are thought of in terms of a playhead moving along a timeline: navigation from one display state to another is the result of "going to" and "playing" desired keyframes. In contrast, Flex Builder can be summed up as the most appropriate tool for traditional programmers, especially those familiar with tools like Borland JBuilder for Java and Microsoft Visual Studio for Visual Basic or C#. In fact, Flex Builder is built on the popular open source Eclipse platform (*http://www.eclipse.org/*), and you can even buy it as an Eclipse plug-in. Flex Builder is a coder's environment and, as such, provides no drawing tools or timelines, and only the most basic of color palettes. Even though ActionScript's `MovieClip` class features methods such as `play()`, `stop()`, and `gotoAndPlay()`, a Flex Builder developer is more likely to think of movie clips—that is, timelines—in an abstract way, in terms of an *object-oriented programming* (OOP) point of view.

To program and deploy ActionScript 3.0, you need only an ActionScript 3.0 compiler. Flash CS4 provides one, which is used when a FLA file's publish settings are configured for ActionScript 3.0. The Flex SDK also provides one, which you can use with a command line interface (no graphical user interface, just typing) or Flex Builder 3, which does the command line typing for you. If Flash CS4 (or CS3) isn't used, then you don't need (indeed, you can't create) the FLA file familiar to traditional Flash developers. In either case, you may use any simple text editor at a bare minimum, such as Notepad on Windows or TextEdit on Mac, though most developers type their code into the Actions panel or a Script window of Flash CS4, an edit window in Flex Builder, or one of the external script editors discussed later in this chapter.

Flash Player 9 or Higher

Once a SWF file is compiled, it must be viewed in some version of Flash Player; specifically, Flash Player 9 or higher, if the SWF file contains ActionScript 3.0.

Generally speaking, this tends to be a straightforward enterprise. As a reader of this book, you're presumably a Flash professional, which means you build your content in the Flash authoring tool, and publish using either File→Publish or Control→Test Movie. You already have Flash Player installed, of course, so when you launch the SWF file, or view it in an HTML document, you see the content, and then decide whether or not to upload it to a web server. For simple projects, this process is often all it takes.

You might, however, find yourself in need of a particular minor point release of Flash Player 9 or 10, like those listed in Table 1-1 of Chapter 1. If you want to display your SWF file in full screen mode, for example, you need to test in Flash Player 9.0.28.0 or higher. If you want to display H.264-encoded high definition video, you need to test in Flash Player 9.0.115.0 or higher. Further, you need to ensure that people visiting your website also have the same minor point release. The Flash authoring tool gives you more than one version of Flash Player for testing during development: debug and release players.

Debug Vs. Release Players

The application folder of Flash CS4 Professional includes installation files for two distinct versions of Flash Player. These versions are located in Debug and Release subfolders of the following locations:

- Windows: *C:\Program Files\Adobe\Adobe Flash CS4\Players*
- Mac: */Applications/Adobe Flash CS4/Players/*

These installation files include:

- **Debug**:
  - *Install Flash Player 10 ActiveX.exe*: Debug installer for the ActiveX version of Flash Player used by Internet Explorer on Windows.
  - *Install Flash Player 10 Plugin.exe*: Debug installer for the plug-in version of Flash Player used by Mozilla compatible browsers.
  - *Install Flash Player 10 UB.dmg*: Debug installer for Flash Player on Mac.
- **Release:**
  - *Install Flash Player 10 ActiveX.exe*: Release installer for the ActiveX version of Flash Player used by Internet Explorer on Windows.
  - *Install Flash Player 10 Plugin.exe*: Release installer for the plug-in version of Flash Player used by Mozilla compatible browsers.
  - *Install Flash Player 10 UB.dmg*: Release installer for Mac Flash Player.

Both folders, Debug and Release, contain identically named files. Don't let that confuse you!

These installation files let you install debug versions of Flash Player for testing locally inside a browser—then to switch back to release versions any time you please. Debug versions are identical to the non-debug-enabled (release) versions, except that the debug versions contain additional code to communicate with Flash CS4. While convenient, because they avoid the delay of a download from *http://adobe.com*, these files are limited to whatever minor point release they represent. If the Adobe update utility hasn't yet updated Flash CS4 on your computer, these installation files might not let you test everything you'd like to from within the authoring tool.

The latest installation files are available at *http://www.adobe.com/support/flash player/downloads.html*. Older versions are archived at *http://www.adobe.com/go/tn_14266/* for testing purposes. To ensure that installations succeed, Adobe recommends that you uninstall existing ActiveX controls and/or plug-ins before re-installing different versions. This can become tedious, so you may want to consider downloading Flash Switcher, a third party Firefox extension to do the work for you. Flash Switcher was written by Alessandro Crugnola and is freely available on his website for Firefox 3 on Windows, Mac, and Linux:

> *http://www.sephiroth.it/weblog/archives/2008/04/flash_switcher_for_win dows_osx_and_li.php*

 Flash Switcher includes the files necessary to test many, but not all, versions of Flash Player. To make additional versions available to the extension, install the desired version by hand from *http://www.adobe.com/go/tn_14266/*, then select the extension's icon from within Firefox and select Save As, as shown in Figure 2-1.

In addition to installation files, the Release and Debug folders contain a stand-alone executable: *FlashPlayer.exe* on Windows and *Flash Player.app* on Mac. Flash CS4 uses this executable to create Projectors or view standalone content. When you select Control→Test Movie, for example, the executable inside the Release folder displays your SWF file in the authoring tool. When you select Debug→Debug Movie, the executable inside the Debug folder is used instead.

The parent folder, Players, contains a copy of this executable. This copy is the one used when you launch a local SWF file outside of the authoring tool, for example by double-clicking a SWF file from the desktop. You can control

Figure 2-1. Adding a version of the Flash Player plug-in to the Flash Switcher Firefox extension

which version is used—debug or release—by copying (not moving!) the desired executable from its respective Debug or Release folder into the Players folder.

Debug versions of Flash Player are capable of logging `trace()` statement output to a text file. For more information on this topic, see Chapter 11.

Making Sure Users Have the Necessary Version of Flash Player

Flash CS4 provides a convenient mechanism for ensuring that website visitors have the version of Flash Player they need in order to view your content. It's a simple configuration under File→Publish Settings→HTML, as seen in Figure 2-2. Select "Detect Flash Version" as shown, and specify the desired version numbers—here, 10, 0, and 2—which indicate the minimum version of Flash Player your content requires. The fourth number, seen in the series 10.0.2.0, identifies the internal build number, which may run a wide range during private Adobe beta testing but is typically 0 for public releases; in any event, the fourth number is irrelevant for ensuring compatibility in this context.

The first number isn't editable from the HTML tab of this dialog box, and, in any case, needs to be 9 or higher to support ActionScript 3.0. If you choose to

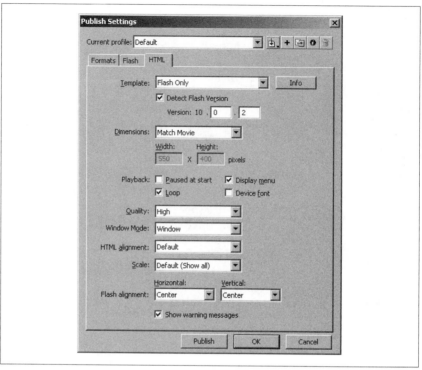

Figure 2-2. Detecting Flash Player version in HTML publish settings

publish to older versions of Flash Player, you may change the first number in the version series by selecting this dialog box's Flash tab, and then changing the Version listbox selection to a previous version of Flash Player. Anything lower than Flash Player 9 will force the Script listbox to change to ActionScript 2.0 or lower.

 Version detection requires publishing for Flash Player 4 or greater.

Employing version detection changes the way the authoring tool writes the HTML it uses to embed a published SWF file. For that reason, it's useful to understand how the HTML is written by default. At the time this book was being written (before the public release of Flash CS4), the default HTML template—that is, no Flash Player version detection—generated an HTML document with inline JavaScript (not an external *.js* file). This JavaScript embedded the SWF file dynamically, a feature that was necessary for the Internet Explorer browser between February of 2006 and April of 2008. Without such Java-

Script, Internet Explorer users had to signify their intention to interact with Active Content—that is, Flash, QuickTime, Java applets, and so on—by first clicking the Active Content in their browser.

It may be that the commercial release of Flash CS4 no longer includes Java-Script with its default HTML template, in which case the parameters in the HTML tab of the Publish Settings dialog box will only affect the HTML itself.

 As of November 2007, Microsoft announced its intention to remove the "click to activate" behavior from Internet Explorer in April 2008. Regardless, JavaScript embedding remains useful because it allows for version detection and progressive enhancement, as discussed later in this chapter. For more information, see Adobe's Active Content Development Center (*http://www.adobe.com/devnet/activecontent/*).

The configuration parameters shown in Figure 2-2 affect the HTML `<param>` tags that appear as children of the `<object>` tag used by Internet Explorer. These, in turn, correspond almost point for point with attributes of the companion `<embed>` tag used by Mozilla compatible browsers.

One of these settings—codebase, which only appears in the HTML, not the dialog box—is used only by Internet Explorer. If a user has an older version of Flash Player installed, Internet Explorer compares the version number of the installed ActiveX control against the `codebase` attribute to determine if an upgrade is merited, in which case the user is prompted as shown in Figure 2-3. If Flash Player is absent altogether, the same installation prompt occurs. For an example of the former case, consider that, as of the time this chapter was written, the default `codebase` value was 10.0.2.0. In Flash CS3, this value was 9.0.0.0, a "perfect" initial release number that has no real-life Flash Player counterpart. If you needed to use, say, the `Event.ADDED_TO_STAGE` event constant introduced in minor point release 9.0.28.0, then you could change the `codebase` value by hand after Flash CS3 generated the HTML. You can do the same with Flash CS4, if a higher minor point release is required. Just make sure, if JavaScript is included, to update any mention of `codebase` both in the JavaScript and the HTML.

In a sense, this is a rudimentary approximation of version detection, but it's essentially flawed. Why? From an aesthetic and usability standpoint, you want to avoid an interruption of the user's experience. In addition, Mozilla compatible browsers ignore `codebase` in favor of the roughly analogous `pluginspage` attribute to determine whether to present a similar prompt. The difference is that `pluginspage` makes no distinction among Flash Player

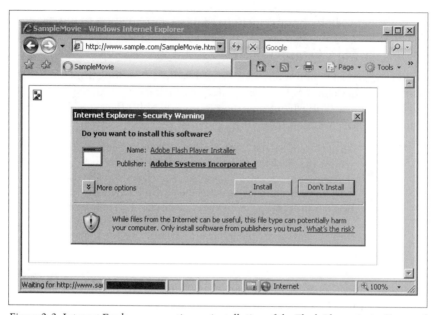

Figure 2-3. Internet Explorer prompting an installation of the Flash Player ActiveX control

versions: Mozilla browsers always install the latest version, even if you don't need the latest.

By and large, encouraging the latest version of Flash Player seems to make sense. Generally speaking, installation is a relatively trivial affair, even if it is an interruption. If your website visitor has the latest version installed, it doesn't matter if your content requires only, say, 9.0.16.0. Modern browsers make installation or upgrades practically effortless for most home users, but not every user scenario occurs at home.

In most corporate, government, and educational settings (think libraries!), individual users are rarely given administrative rights to the computers they use. These content viewers can't agree to an upgrade when prompted by the browser—in fact, the prompt may not even happen—so at best, such viewers may be faced with an upgrade proposition they can't act on and at worst, a webpage with obviously missing content. By leaving the `codebase` attribute at the lowest required value, you might steer clear of a few unnecessary interruptions for Internet Explorer users, but your best bet is version detection.

When "Detect Flash Version" is selected on in the HTML tab of the Publish Settings dialog box, the JavaScript code is slightly altered, which comes as no surprise. (Remember, if the HTML templates change in the commercial release of Flash CS4, then it won't be that the JavaScript is altered, but rather, that it is introduced into the publish process.)

The detection-specific JavaScript provides a mechanism more reliable than the codebase or pluginspage HTML tag attributes. With detection engaged, the user's installed Flash Player can be checked against major, minor, and revision values, as specified below the "Detect Flash Version" checkbox in the dialog box.

In addition, a notable change happens to the HTML. In this case, content inside the <noscript> tag no longer contains the backup <object> and <embed> tags. Instead, you're expected to provide your own alternate content. This might be an explanatory line of text, as suggested by the generated markup, but could just as easily be an image or any other valid HTML, including, if you want to risk it, an alternate SWF file published for an older version of Flash Player.

```
<noscript>
    // Provide alternate content for browsers that do not
        support scripting
    // or for those that have scripting disabled.
    Alternate HTML content should be placed here. This content
        requires the Adobe Flash Player.
    <a href="http://www.macromedia.com/go/getflash/">Get Flash</a>
</noscript>
```

This markup is mirrored in an else clause just a few lines prior:

```
} else {  // flash is too old or we can't detect the plugin
        var alternateContent = 'Alternate HTML content should ¬
            be placed here.'
        + 'This content requires the Adobe Flash Player.'
        + '<a href=http://www.macromedia.com/go/getflash/>
            Get Flash</a>';
        document.write(alternateContent);  // insert non-flash content
}
```

This code is what gets displayed if the user has JavaScript enabled, but not the minimum required version of Flash Player. Here too, the HTML written out by JavaScript can be replaced with more appropriate or targeted content of your own choosing. In this way, you can provide an experience of *progressive enhancement*, in which essential content is presented to the user in all cases, and augmented for the user who has Flash Player installed.

Using SWFObject

Be aware that the authoring tool's built-in code templates aren't your only option for embedding a SWF file with JavaScript. SWFObject, a popular third-party solution, provides an alternative approach that many consider even easier to use. The required *swfobject.js* JavaScript file, as well as additional sample files, are freely available from a Google Code project maintained by Geoff Stearns, who wrote the original script.

Download the *swfobject_2_0.zip* archive from *http://code.google.com/p/swfob ject/*. At a minimum, you need to extract the *swfobject.js* file into the folder that contains your HTML document. This JavaScript file replaces the *AC_RunActiveContent.js* file that ships with Flash CS4, so you don't need the HTML document generated by the authoring tool when you use SWFObject. Instead, create a new HTML document of your own. Use the SWFObject generator tool (an interactive form) at *http://www.swffix.org/swfobject/generator/* to create the necessary HTML and JavaScript code. Paste this code into your HTML document and upload the HTML, JavaScript and SWF files to your server.

Using Other Code Editors with Flash

With an ActionScript 3.0 compiler in hand and Flash Player 9 or 10 to display compiled content, you're ready to start producing. If your projects involve mainly timeline code, especially nested movie clip techniques, you'll likely find that the Actions panel is the most convenient place to compose ActionScript. For more complex projects, where custom classes are in order, you also—or exclusively—have to use a Script window. Script windows in Flash CS4 are not true panels, so they don't appear in the file menu like the Actions panel does, under Window→Actions. To use a Script window, simply select File→New→ActionScript file, or open an existing AS file. Although the Actions panel and Script windows share some features, only Script windows deal with the external text files necessary for custom classes.

 For a detailed overview of changes to the Actions panel and Script windows, see Chapter 5.

Of course, you have alternatives to coding in the Flash authoring tool, even if you use the authoring tool's compiler for deployment. The remainder of this chapter focuses on a simple drag-and-drop application to demonstrate work-flows in which a designer is responsible for FLA file maintenance while a developer writes ActionScript in an external script editor. The same person could very well play both designer and developer roles. In such a case, the designer/developer multitasks between the Flash authoring tool and an external script editor, which becomes a sort of "superhero Actions panel." Coding is done externally, but SWF files are generally compiled in Flash CS4.

In team environments, this scenario may or may not be suitable. In cases where virtually all content is generated by code, or where assets are loaded at runtime, designers and developers may indeed comfortably work in isolation. The only purpose of FLA files in this case might be to store artwork, audio, fonts, and the like for export as SWC files, which can be used as components in Flex Builder 3. These assets might also be dynamically loaded as SWF files, if not in their native formats. Under these circumstances, a project would almost certainly be positioned as a Flex endeavor, and deployed with the Flex SDK compiler.

In general terms, then, when ActionScript classes depend on library assets, the Flash authoring tool should perform the compiling. For this reason, the following example specifically relies on library assets to demonstrate both the benefits and considerations involved in separating code from content, especially when coding occurs outside of Flash.

Creating DragParrot, a Sample Class File

Although you can reproduce the functionality of the following class with timeline code, doing so would largely defeat the purpose of using an external code editor. This code defines a custom `DragParrot` class that, when configured as the *document class* of a specific FLA file, results in a pre-drawn parrot in a circle that you can drag only when a checkbox is selected (Figure 2-4). The Action-Script is stored in an external text file, *DragParrot.as*, saved in the same folder as its companion, *DragParrotExample.fla*. You can use the exact same code in each of the script editors discussed in the following sections.

 For more information on the new document class concept, see Chapter 6.

It's important to keep in mind that some of the assets required by `DragParrot` are stored in a separate FLA file, included with the samples that accompany this book. These assets are configured to be exported for Action-Script in the Linkage area of the Symbol Properties dialog box accessible from the Library panel. They don't appear anywhere on the FLA file's stage. Prior to ActionScript 3.0, these assets would have been assigned a linkage identifier, but the attaching mechanism has changed in the new language. Attachable assets are now assigned a *linkage class*, which defines the asset in terms of an appropriate base class, such as `MovieClip` or `Sprite`. This linkage class can be composed of custom ActionScript, but it doesn't have to be. In fact, by default, the Flash authoring tool automatically writes this class for you, in which case the class isn't saved as a separate AS file, but included virtually into the SWF

Figure 2-4. The DragParrot class in action

file. If you're coding in an external script editor and compiling in Flash CS4, you can trust that linkage classes are "magically" available at compile time.

For more information on the new linkage paradigm, see Chapter 8.

The DragParrot class, shown in the following code, begins by importing a set of external classes it needs to perform its tasks. The first of these, Parrot, obviously stands out as a custom class. This is the linkage class handled by the Flash authoring tool. As it happens, CheckBox is also a library asset (an instance of the CheckBox component) and must be present in the library. After class properties are declared, the constructor function, DragParrot(), calls on a handful of descriptively named methods.

```
package {

    import Parrot;
    import fl.controls.CheckBox;
    import flash.display.Sprite;
```

```
import flash.events.MouseEvent;

public class DragParrot extends Sprite {

    private var _ball:Sprite;
    private var _parrot:Sprite;
    private var _checkbox:CheckBox;

    public function DragParrot() {
        drawBall();
        addParrot();
        makeCheckBox();
        assignEventHandlers();
    }
```

These methods are fairly basic. The first, drawBall(), calls on a special set of functionality from the Graphics class, collectively known as the Drawing API, to draw a light blue circle into a Sprite instance, and then adds this object to the display list, so that it can be seen.

```
    private function drawBall():void {
        _ball = new Sprite();
        _ball.graphics.lineStyle();
        _ball.graphics.beginFill(0xB9D5FF);
        _ball.graphics.drawCircle(0, 0, 60);
        _ball.graphics.endFill();
        _ball.x = stage.stageWidth / 2;
        _ball.y = stage.stageHeight / 2;
        _ball.buttonMode = true;
        addChild(_ball);
    }
```

The addParrot() method attaches pre-drawn artwork from the companion FLA file's library by instantiating the linkage class Parrot. This object is added to the display list of _ball (created in the previous method), which makes the artwork a child of that object.

```
    private function addParrot():void {
        _parrot = new Parrot();
        _ball.addChild(_parrot);
        _parrot.x = _parrot.width / -2;
        _parrot.y = _parrot.height / 2 - ¬
            _ball.height / 2;
    }
```

There's a reason why the _ball, _parrot, and _checkbox variables are preceded by an underscore. By popular convention, many developers set private variables apart by using this punctuation. This was a source of potential conflict in ActionScript 2.0, because many built-in properties formerly featured underscores for unrelated reasons. Their removal in ActionScript 3.0 eliminates this confusion.

The makeCheckBox() method attaches a component from the companion FLA file's library by instantiating the linkage class CheckBox. The checkbox is positioned in the lower left corner of the stage, given a label "Allow drag", and then added to the display list.

```
private function makeCheckBox():void {
        _checkbox = new CheckBox();
        _checkbox.x = 10;
        _checkbox.y = stage.stageHeight - 30;
        _checkbox.label = "Allow drag";
        _checkbox.selected = true;
        addChild(_checkbox);
}
```

Finally, assignEventHandlers() associates _ball with two event handler methods. Thanks to an if statement, the dragParrot() handler responds only when the checkbox is turned on.

```
private function assignEventHandlers():void {
        _ball.addEventListener(MouseEvent.MOUSE_DOWN, ¬
            dragParrot);
        _ball.addEventListener(MouseEvent.MOUSE_UP, ¬
            dropParrot);
}
private function dragParrot(evt:MouseEvent):void {
    if (_checkbox.selected) {
        _ball.startDrag();
    }
}
private function dropParrot(evt:MouseEvent):void {
    _ball.stopDrag();
}
}
}
```

This class could have been written in a Script window of the Flash authoring tool or in any simple text editor. The remaining sections touch on four popular alternative ActionScript editors. Bear in mind, none of these applications exclude the use of one another. If you like, sample each one to get a feel for their nuances. You might just decide you like them all!

Coding with Flex Builder 3

As mentioned earlier in this chapter, Flex Builder 3 is Adobe's answer to traditional programmers interested in developing for the Flash Platform. To be sure, Flex Builder is hardly just a script editor. Its full benefit becomes clear when you use it to leverage the Flex framework, which includes dozens of *user interface* (UI) components and data classes not available in the Flash authoring tool (though freely available with the Flex SDK). These elements are geared toward the development of *Rich Internet Applications* (RIAs), which are Flex's specific focus. In addition to ActionScript 3.0, Flex Builder can create and edit MXML, an XML-based markup language used to declaratively lay out interface elements and, in conjunction with ActionScript 3.0, implement business logic and facilitate remote procedure calls (RPCs). Built on the Eclipse platform, Flex Builder benefits from hundreds of third-party plug-ins, which extend basic functionality across a wide range of topics. Many of these plug-ins are free (see *http://www.eclipseplugincentral.com/*) and work with both the stand alone version of Flex Builder and the version that is, itself, a plug-in for Eclipse.

 For some comprehensive guides to Flex, including Flex Builder 3, read *Learning Flex 3* (O'Reilly), by Alaric Cole; *Programming Flex 3* (O'Reilly), by Joey Lott and Chafic Kazoun; and *Flex 3 Cookbook* (O'Reilly), by Joshua Noble and Todd Anderson.

Muscle notwithstanding, Flex Builder 3 is perfectly capable of creating and editing straightforward ActionScript 3.0 classes. Although the Flash authoring tool's Actions panel and Script windows get the job done, the powerful editing capabilities of Flex Builder raise the bar considerably.

1. If you don't already have Flex Builder 3 installed, you can download a 60-day trial version from *http://www.adobe.com/products/flex/*. Once the application is installed, launch Flex Builder.

2. Select File→New→ActionScript Project from the File menu or right-click (Command-click) in the Navigator view, as shown in Figure 2-5.

3. In the New ActionScript Project dialog box, name the project **DragParrotExample**. Turn off "Use default location", as shown in Figure 2-6, and then browse to the folder on your hard drive that contains *DragParrotExample.fla*.

Click Next to continue.

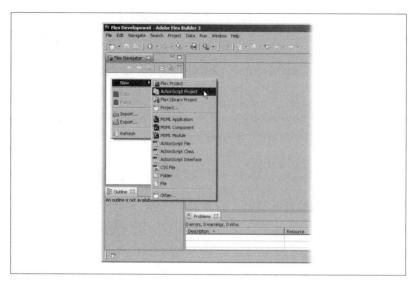

Figure 2-5. Creating a new ActionScript project in Flex Builder 3

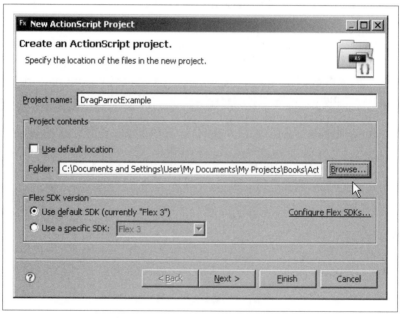

Figure 2-6. Storing the project in the same folder as a companion FLA file

4. In the Create an ActionScript Project dialog box (Figure 2-7), you have the option of including additional source folders and assets with the Source path and Library path tabs. Although they sound otherwise, these tabs

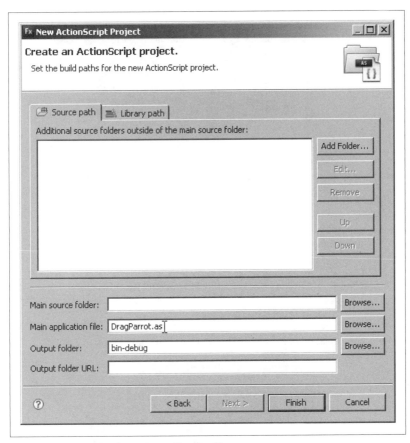

Figure 2-7. Assigning the main application file

aren't related to the Library panel in Flash. Ignore them, and change the Main application file from the default *DragParrotExample.as* (automatically named after the project) to *DragParrot.as*. By doing this, you're creating a brand new AS file, rather than reusing the class file you wrote in Flash CS4.

Click Finish to conclude.

5. At this point, you're ready to code. As Figure 2-8 shows, Flex Builder has already created a basic outline for you. A package and class have already been declared; `DragParrot` extends `Sprite`, which is already imported; and the constructor function, `DragParrot()`, is already written.

6. Add code to the existing ActionScript so that it looks like the code that follows (new code in bold).

Figure 2-8. Reviewing the basic outline of DragParrot

```
package {
    import flash.display.Sprite;

    public class DragParrot extends Sprite
    {
        private var _ball:Sprite;

        public function DragParrot()
        {
            _ball = new Sprite();
        }
        private function assignEventHandlers():void
        {

        }
    }
}
```

> Flex Builder places open curly braces ({) on a new line.
> This is a stylistic preference that has no effect on code
> execution.

This detours slightly from the code shown earlier, but it's enough to showcase a number of Flex Builder enhancements. Like the Flash authoring tool, Flex Builder features code coloring and code hinting. In addition, note that the Outline view (Figure 2-9) maintains a running catalog of *class members*, including import statements, properties, and methods.

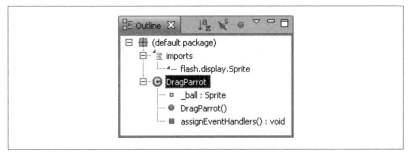

Figure 2-9. The Outline view helps you navigate code

Each kind displays its own icon to distinguish it from the others, and even the constructor function is set apart from other methods by a green dot. If you select any of the items in the Outline view, then the corresponding section of code is highlighted. Likewise, as you click various elements in the code editor, such as property and method declarations, the Outline view changes to reflect your selection.

7. Complete the `assignEventHandlers()` method so that it looks like this:

```
private function assignEventHandlers():void
{
    _ball.addEventListener(MouseEvent.MOUSE_DOWN, ¬
        dragParrot);
    _ball.addEventListener(MouseEvent.MOUSE_UP, ¬
        dropParrot);
}
```

Ensure that Project→Build Automatically is turned on. Save the file. When you do, you see a powerful troubleshooting tool as shown in Figure 2-10. Circular red X icons appear next to lines with errors. In the Problems view (bottom center), errors are conveniently summarized in a group. Clicking any of these rows highlights the relevant line of ActionScript. As you correct issues, they automatically remove themselves from the Problems view, and the red X icons disappear.

In this case, one of the errors is that the `MouseEvent` event hasn't been defined. Scroll to the existing `import` statement, and then add the following new line beneath it:

```
import flash.events.MouseEvent;
```

Save the file, and two of the four error messages go away. The remaining errors show that the event handler methods, `dragParrot()` and `dropParrot()`, haven't yet been written.

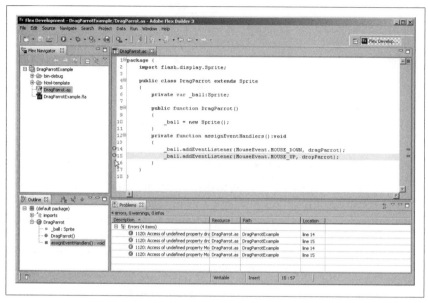

Figure 2-10. Errors are displayed and summarized as they occur

8. Revise the ActionScript so that it looks like this:

```
package {

    import flash.display.Sprite;
    import flash.events.MouseEvent;

    public class DragParrot extends Sprite {

        private var _ball:Sprite;

        public function DragParrot()
        {
            drawBall();
            assignEventHandlers();
        }
        private function drawBall():void
        {
            _ball = new Sprite();
            _ball.graphics.lineStyle();
            _ball.graphics.beginFill(0xB9D5FF);
            _ball.graphics.drawCircle(0, 0, 120);
            _ball.graphics.endFill();
            _ball.x = stage.stageWidth / 2;
            _ball.y = stage.stageHeight / 2;
            _ball.buttonMode = true;
            addChild(_ball);
        }
```

```
private function assignEventHandlers():void
{
    _ball.addEventListener(MouseEvent.MOUSE_DOWN, ¬
        dragParrot);
    _ball.addEventListener(MouseEvent.MOUSE_UP, ¬
        dropParrot);
}
private function dragParrot(evt:MouseEvent):void
{
    _ball.startDrag();
}
private function dropParrot(evt:MouseEvent):void
{
    _ball.stopDrag();
}
    }
}
```

At this point, nothing in the class file yet relies on the FLA file with which
it shares a folder. To prove it, select Run→Debug DragParrot, and then
wait a few moments while Flex Builder 3 compiles the class. Before long,
a browser opens, as shown in Figure 2-11, and a draggable circle appears.
The teal background color is a result of Flex's default preference settings.

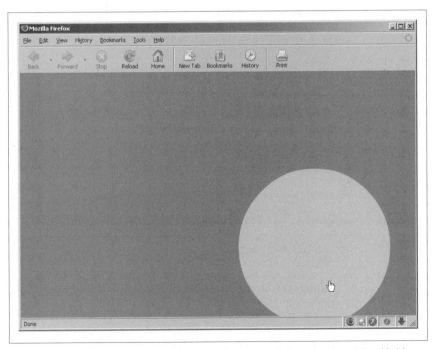

*Figure 2-11. Compiling in Flex Builder succeeds when code doesn't rely on FLA file library
assets*

Because of the default scale mode used by Flex Builder 3, the blue circle may not appear centered when the browser opens. Don't be surprised if you have to resize the browser repeatedly and look in the corners. You could address this in the Drag Parrot class, but remember, this SWF file is ultimately going to be compiled in Flash CS4.

9. Close the browser, and return to Flex Builder 3. Locate the `drawBall()` method by selecting it in the Outline view. Hover over the term `_ball` in the final line, `addChild(_ball);`. When you do, a tooltip appears (Figure 2-12) that tells you the data type of `_ball`, which is `Sprite`, and that this `Sprite` instance belongs to the `DragParrot` class.

Hold down the Ctrl (Command) key, and then move the mouse over various lines of code. The Ctrl (Command) key adds a temporary underline to properties and methods. With the key still pressed, click `_ball` once again. The ActionScript editor jumps to the definition of this term near the top of the class. These hover and click techniques assist considerably in code navigation.

```
        assignEventHandlers();
    }
    private function drawBall():void
    {
        _ball = new Sprite();
        _ball.graphics.lineStyle();
        _ball.graphics.beginFill(0xB9D5FF);
        _ball.graphics.drawCircle(0, 0, 120);
        _ball.graphics.endFill();
        _ball.x = stage.stageWidth / 2;
        _ball.y = stage.stageHeight / 2;
        _ball.buttonMode = true;
        addChild(_ball);
    }                    Sprite _ball - DragParrot
    private function assignEventHandlers():void
    {
```

Figure 2-12. Tooltips display data types

10. Time to wrap things up. Update the ActionScript one last time to look like the code that follows.

```
package {

    import Parrot;
    import fl.controls.CheckBox;
    import flash.display.Sprite;
```

```
import flash.events.MouseEvent;

public class DragParrot extends Sprite {

    private var _ball:Sprite;
    private var _parrot:Sprite;
    private var _checkbox:CheckBox;

    public function DragParrot()
    {
        drawBall();
        addParrot();
        makeCheckBox();
        assignEventHandlers();
    }
    private function drawBall():void
    {
        _ball = new Sprite();
        _ball.graphics.lineStyle();
        _ball.graphics.beginFill(0xB9D5FF);
        _ball.graphics.drawCircle(0, 0, 120);
        _ball.graphics.endFill();
        _ball.x = stage.stageWidth / 2;
        _ball.y = stage.stageHeight / 2;
        _ball.buttonMode = true;
        addChild(_ball);
    }
    private function addParrot():void
    {
        _parrot = new Parrot();
        _ball.addChild(_parrot);
        _parrot.x = _parrot.width / -2;
        _parrot.y = _parrot.height / 2 -
            _ball.height / 2;
    }
    private function makeCheckBox():void
    {
        _checkbox = new CheckBox();
        _checkbox.x = 10;
        _checkbox.y = stage.stageHeight - 30;
        _checkbox.label = "Allow drag";
        _checkbox.selected = true;
        addChild(_checkbox);
    }
    private function assignEventHandlers():void
    {
        _ball.addEventListener(MouseEvent.MOUSE_DOWN, ¬
            dragParrot);
        _ball.addEventListener(MouseEvent.MOUSE_UP, ¬
            dropParrot);
    }
    private function dragParrot(evt:MouseEvent):void
    {
        if (_checkbox.selected) {
```

```
        _ball.startDrag();
    }
}
private function dropParrot(evt:MouseEvent):void
{
    _ball.stopDrag();
}
  }
}
```

 Error notices occur because of the references to Parrot and CheckBox, which the Flex SDK compiler can't locate. For a detailed look at collaboration between Flash CS4 Professional and Flex Builder 3, read about the Flex Component Kit for Flash CS3 extension on the Adobe Exchange website *http://www.adobe.com/cfusion/ex change/index.cfm?event=extensionDetail&extid= 1273018*.

Open *DragParrotExample.fla* in Flash CS4. Ensure that the Property inspector indicates DragParrot as the document class, and then select Control→Test Movie to compile the FLA file (and class) in the Flash compiler.

Coding with SE|PY

SE|PY is a free ActionScript editor for Windows and Mac written in Python by Alessandro Crugnola. It was originally developed for ActionScript 2.0, yet continues to be very popular and works quite well with ActionScript 3.0 and even JavaScript. Information on SE|PY and downloads are available at *www .sephiroth.it/python/sepy.php*. Helpful tips are occasionally posted at *http:// www.sepy.it/*. If you like what you see, consider making a PayPal donation.

Compared with Flex Builder 3, SE|PY (Figure 2-13) is a svelte application, and purposefully so. It offers a quick-loading interface with a Swiss Army knife assortment of practical minitools. When working with ActionScript 3.0, you'll use SE|PY to write your ActionScript, and then switch over to Flash to compile. Here are a handful of the goodies that await you.

A number of tabs run down SE|PY interface's left edge. The tab selected in Figure 2-14, Members, is similar to the functionality of Flex Builder's Outline view. Class members are indicated by icons and, when double-clicked, highlight the corresponding section of code. In this implementation, members are displayed alphabetically, regardless of their order in the ActionScript, which eases navigation. The input field at the top filters members as you type (Figure 2-14), so you can easily locate methods in complex class files. Notice that the letters "dr" have highlighted methods whose names start with those char-

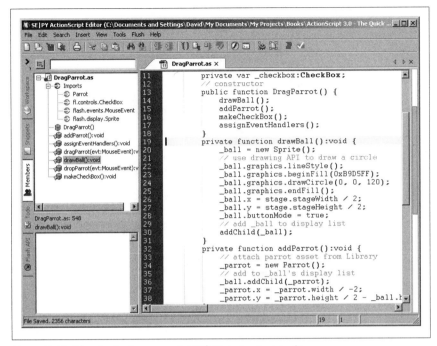

Figure 2-13. The slender but powerful SE|PY ActionScript editor

acters. Adding "a" ("dra") omits `dropParrot()` from the list, and so on. To clear filtering, delete the contents of the input field.

The Snippets tab gives you a handy way to reduce the tedium of typing common blocks of code, fittingly known as snippets. The green cogwheel icon (Figure 2-15) lets you categorize snippets by folder on your hard drive. You might create folders for ActionScript 3.0, 2.0, JavaScript, and XML.

The next few steps walk you through the creation of a SE|PY snippet.

1. Download and install SE|PY, and then launch the application. Select the Snippets tab, and then click the green cogwheel icon to locate or create a folder for snippets.

2. Once a folder is created, right-click (Command-click) on the folder's name, and then select "Create new snippet".

3. In the New Snippet dialog box, enter the name **for..in trace**, which you'll supply with a bit of templated code in a moment. Click OK to continue. This action opens a new document tab.

4. In the new document tab, type the following ActionScript (and save):

```
trace("for..in obj trace");
for (var prop:String in obj) {
```

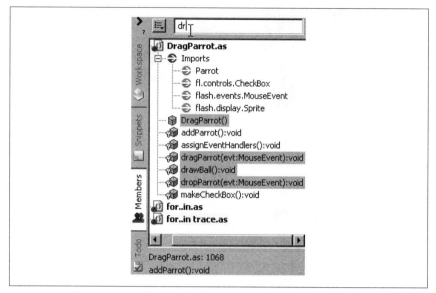

Figure 2-14. The Members tab supports filtering

Figure 2-15. Snippets make it easier to type common blocks of code

```
        trace(prop + ": " + obj[prop]);
}
```

5. Select File→New to open a new document. Double-click your newly created snippet in the Snippets tab to see it appear in the new document. So far, this is only slightly better than pasting from the Clipboard. Here's where it gets interesting.

6. Right-click (Command-click) the snippet, and then select Edit. Update the existing code to look like this:

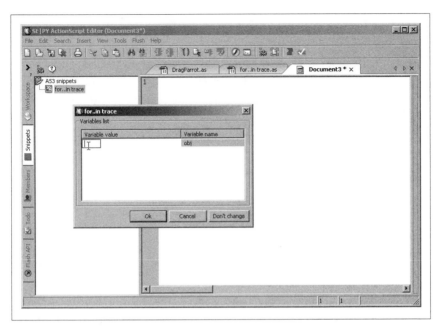

Figure 2-16. Using a more sophisticated snippet

```
trace("for..in @@obj@@ trace");
for (var prop:String in @@obj@@) {
    trace(prop + ": " + @@obj@@[prop]);
}
```

The addition of the @@ characters establishes obj as a kind of snippet-specific variable. Save and switch to the new document. Double-click the snippet again. This time, a dialog box opens, as shown in Figure 2-16.

This dialog box shows the obj variable on the right, and lets you provide a custom value on the left. Enter the term **this**, click OK, and see the custom snippet appear in the new document:

```
trace("for..in this trace");
for (var prop:String in this) {
    trace(prop + ": " + this[prop]);
}
```

You may add numerous variables to each snippet in this manner, which gives you shortcuts to tailor-made blocks of code. If you wish, you can even provide default (but changeable) values for these variables by using the following syntax inside the snippet:

```
trace("for..in @@obj=[defaultValueHere]@@ trace");
for (var prop:String in @@obj@@) {
    trace(prop + ": " + @@obj@@[prop]);
}
```

You have nearly a dozen additional tabs and tools, including:

- **Todo:** Keeps track of commented reminders (for example, `// TODO optimize this loop!`). Reminders are displayed in a clickable tree view, like the Members tab, sorted by line number and script file.
- **Variables:** Displays declared variables in a clickable table, similar to the Members tab.
- **Unicode chars:** Displays Unicode and ANSI character codes for basic and extended character sets.
- **Clipboard:** Displays text content of the current Clipboard contents.
- **XML Reader:** Displays XML files in a collapsible tree view. Supports XPath expressions for quick navigation.
- **Class Explorer:** Displays packages and classes like the Members tab, even if those classes aren't open as documents. Double-clicking a member opens the relevant class file, and highlights the corresponding section of code.
- **Stickies:** Maintains virtual "paper" sticky notes, configurable by color.
- **SharedObject Reader:** Displays the content of SharedObject files, the Flash equivalent of a browser cookie. (This item and the remaining ones are found in the file menu under Tools.)
- **Regular Expression Toolkit:** Provides an interface for testing regular expressions patterns.
- **Compare Files:** Compares text files, which is great for locating changes among multiple revisions, and compares file directories.

Coding with FlashDevelop

FlashDevelop is a compelling open source script editor for Windows designed for ActionScript 3.0 and 2.0 development. Built on the Microsoft .NET Framework, this application functions comfortably as a standalone IDE or in conjunction the Flash authoring tool. FlashDevelop is produced by Mika Palmu, Philippe Elsass, Nick Farina, and contributors. Information and downloads are available at *http://www.flashdevelop.org/* or *http://osflash.org/flashdevelop/*.

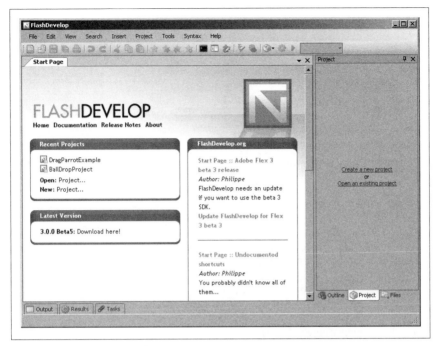

Figure 2-17. The FlashDevelop Start Page

1. Once FlashDevelop is installed, launch the application and note the Start Page (Figure 2-17), which is similar to the Welcome Screen in Flash CS4. The first time you run FlashDevelop, you may have to let it know where your Flex SDK compiler is, if you plan to optionally compile ActionScript 3.0 SWF files without Flash.

2. Select Tools→Program Settings. This action opens the Settings dialog box. Select AS3Context, locate the Flex SDK Location selection (Figure 2-18), and then, on your hard drive, browse to the SDK. If you have Flex Builder 3 installed, you'll find the SDK located within the application folder for Flex Builder (for example, *C:\Program Files\Adobe\Flex Builder 3\sdks \3.0.0*); otherwise, download and install the free Flex SDK, and then navigate to that folder.

   Click Close to continue.

3. Close the Start Page, and then select Project→New Project. This action opens the New Project dialog box. Scroll to the ActionScript 3 section, and then select Empty Project. Name this project **DragParrotExample**, and then set its location to a folder that contains *DragParrotExample.fla*, as shown in Figure 2-19. Click OK.

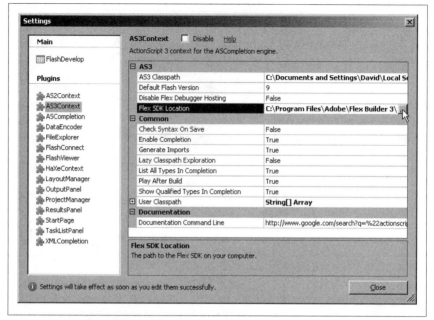

Figure 2-18. Configuring the Flex SDK location

4. FlashDevelop creates a new document for you named *Untitled1.as*. Select File→Save to save this file into the project folder as *DragParrot.as*. In the Project tab (Figure 2-20), right-click *DragParrot.as*, and then select Always Compile. Doing so configures this class as the project's main file.

5. At this point, you're ready to start coding. Type the following ActionScript into the *DragParrot.as* document (note, this is everything in the class that doesn't rely on library assets in the FLA file):

```
package {

    import flash.display.Sprite;
    import flash.events.MouseEvent;

    public class DragParrot extends Sprite {

        private var _ball:Sprite;

        public function DragParrot(){
            drawBall();
            assignEventHandlers();
        }
        private function drawBall():void {
            _ball = new Sprite();
            _ball.graphics.lineStyle();
            _ball.graphics.beginFill(0xB9D5FF);
            _ball.graphics.drawCircle(0, 0, 120);
```

```
            _ball.graphics.endFill();
            _ball.x = stage.stageWidth / 2;
            _ball.y = stage.stageHeight / 2;
            _ball.buttonMode = true;
            addChild(_ball);
        }
        private function assignEventHandlers():void {
            _ball.addEventListener(MouseEvent.MOUSE_DOWN, ¬
                dragParrot);
            _ball.addEventListener(MouseEvent.MOUSE_UP, ¬
                dropParrot);
        }
        private function dragParrot(evt:MouseEvent):void {
            _ball.startDrag();
        }
        private function dropParrot(evt:MouseEvent):void {
            _ball.stopDrag();
        }
    }
}
```

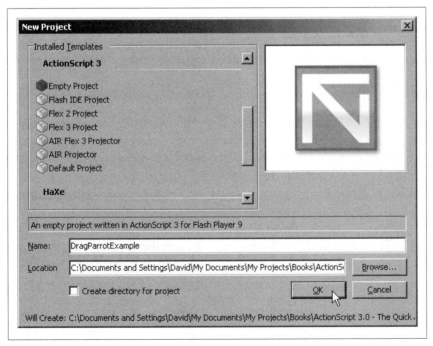

Figure 2-19. Creating an ActionScript 3.0 project

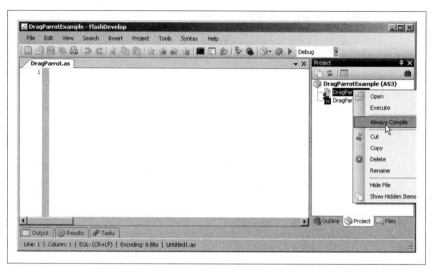

Figure 2-20. Choosing the project's main class file

6. Select Project→Properties, which opens a dialog box that configures the settings for the DragParrotExample project. This project requires the name of an output file—this is the SWF file that the Flex SDK compiler will generate—so type **DragParrotExample.swf** in the Output File field, as shown in Figure 2-21. Experiment with the Dimensions, Background Color, and Framerate settings, if you like. The Test Movie area lets you specify how the SWF file should be opened. Choose Popup for now, and then click OK to close the dialog box.

7. Select Project→Test Movie to compile the SWF file. For now, the compile succeeds, because **DragParrot** doesn't rely on the FLA file's library assets. As soon as you update your code to include the **Parrot** and **CheckBox** classes —along with the ActionScript that references them—you' have to compile in the Flash authoring tool, because the Flex SDK compiler can't locate the necessary assets. As with Flex Builder 3, you have workarounds for dealing with this situation in FlashDevelop. Forums on the FlashDevelop website offer a handful of tutorials on the subject.

   Double-click *DragParrotExample.fla* in the Project tab to launch Flash CS4. Return to Project→Properties, and then select the checkbox next to "No output, only run pre/post build commands" (Figure 2-22).

   Click OK to exit the dialog box.

8. Select Project→Test Movie, and note that FlashDevelop automatically brings the Flash authoring tool to the forefront. In this way, FLA file library

---

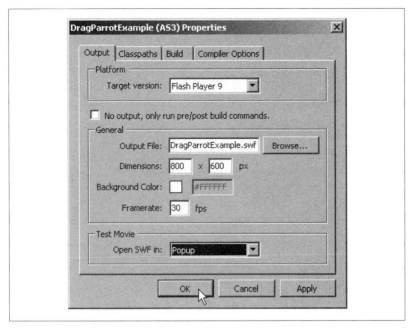

Figure 2-21. Configuring SWF file settings

assets are properly located by `DragParrot`, so that when your class is revised to reference them, the compile succeeds.

FlashDevelop supports a remarkable number of the tools featured in the other script editors discussed in this chapter. Naturally, individual nuances differ from application to application, but FlashDevelop includes its own version of the following:

- Outline tab similar to the Outline view in Flex Builder 3
- Code folding and code bookmarks
- Syntax checking and error warnings, by way of the Flex SDK
- Tasks interface for commented TODO reminders
- Introspective tooltips that display class member details
- Snippets
- SharedObject reader
- File comparison interface
- Built-in web browser

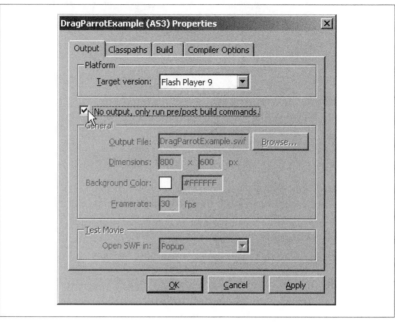

Figure 2-22. Selecting the No output checkbox switches FlashDevelop to the Flash authoring tool compiler

Coding with PrimalScript

PrimalScript, by SAPIEN Technologies, is a powerhouse script editor for Windows. This application is conversant in ActionScript 2.0 and also 3.0—provided you help it out, which is discussed in the following steps. PrimalScript gives you much of the expected code coloring, autoformatting, and code completion seen in the Flash authoring tool and Flex Builder. If you want to explore other languages, you're in luck, because PrimalScript supports over 40 more, including HTML, CSS, JavaScript, Java, C#, PHP, Python, Ruby, Perl, Tcl, and the list goes on. Application information and downloads are available at *http://www.primalscript.com/*, with three editions to choose from: Standard, Professional, and Enterprise. Fully functioning 45-day trials are available for all editions.

Longtime users of PrimalScript may notice that the application manages just fine in ActionScript 2.0 but offers minimal support in ActionScript 3.0 out the box. To work around this limitation, you have to give the application access to a set of specially formatted class definitions for ActionScript 3.0 called *intrinsic classes*. Fortunately, FlashDevelop (discussed in the previous section) includes an unofficial set of intrinsics, which you can re-use with PrimalScript:

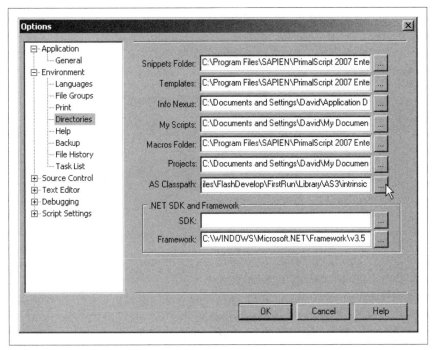

Figure 2-23. Providing ActionScript 3.0 intrinsic classes to PrimalScript

1. Download and install PrimalScript, and then launch the application. Select Tools→Options.

2. In the Options dialog box, select Environment→Directories. Use the ellipsis (...) button next to the AS Classpath field to browse for the intrinsic classes, as shown in Figure 2-23. Select the *C:\Program Files\FlashDevelop \FirstRun\Library\AS3\intrinsic* path from your FlashDevelop installation.

3. Restart PrimalScript.

4. To verify that ActionScript 3.0 code hinting is now supported, select File→New File→Script Files→ActionScript Class. Create a `Sprite` instance —or some other ActionScript 3.0 class instance—such as this:

   ```
   var s:Sprite = new Sprite();
   ```

Add a new line to your code and repeat the variable name (here, s), then type dot (.) to bring up the PrimalSense menu, as shown in Figure 2-24.

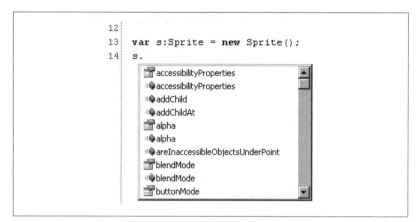

Figure 2-24. Adding intrinsic classes provides ActionScript 3.0 code completion

Like the other scripting IDEs mentioned in this chapter, PrimalScript features numerous additional amenities, all of which can boost your workflow *productivity:*

- Code folding and code bookmarks
- Advanced snippets
- Clipboard viewer
- Code browser, similar to Outline view in Flex Builder 3
- Integration with source control software
- File comparison interface
- Visual query builder and XML editor
- Built-in web browser and FTP client
- Configurable tools browser to launch related applications, such as Dreamweaver

CHAPTER 3

Looking at the Changes in ActionScript 3.0

The documentation for Flash CS4 Professional includes a tremendously useful table titled "ActionScript 2.0 Migration." An introductory caption humbly states, "The following table describes the differences between ActionScript 2.0 and 3.0," which leads to a catalog so lengthy, it would fill over 50 pages if reproduced in this book. To locate this document, look in the appendixes of the ActionScript 3.0 Language and Components Reference or search the term "migration" in the Help panel. This document is also available on the Adobe online Help Resource Center:

http://help.adobe.com/en_US/AS3LCR/Flash_10.0/migration.html

This chapter will help you find your bearings from a migration standpoint, and navigate among these changes.

Major Changes and Obsolete Code

As programming languages evolve, existing workflows may change, new features are usually added, and older features are sometimes removed. This is as true for ActionScript as it is for Java, C#, Python, PHP, and countless others. In the company of programmers at large, you're not alone. The changes in ActionScript 3.0 may seem startlingly plentiful, but historically speaking, Flash has been through this sort of remodeling before. Developers encountered a similar paradigm shift when Macromedia Flash 5 introduced the language that, for clarity, was later renamed ActionScript 1.0. The original naming scheme didn't include version numbering, and was therefore referred to simply as "ActionScript." This was true even in Flash 4, which featured a fundamentally different syntax in which objects were referenced by a relatively uncommon mechanism called *slash notation*. The dot notation syntax of ActionScript 1.0, in which nested objects are distinguished from one another by a dot (.), was a major step toward making the language more accessible to developers from other platforms. ActionScript 2.0 established a formalized structure for custom classes and, in many ways, introduced a transitional period, in which many of the current recommended best practices found a whispered beginning. ActionScript 3.0 expands and refines this formal class structure, while continuing to extend a welcoming hand to traditional timeline programmers. The pithy description by Adobe's Kevin Lynch is apt: think of ActionScript 3.0 as evolutionary, not revolutionary.

So yes, there are changes in the language. The good news is that they're designed to increase performance in Flash Player 9, 10, and future runtimes. Even better, the changes are designed to help you stay more organized.

Major Changes in the API, Classes, and Language

One of the first things Flash developers often notice in ActionScript 3.0 is the absence of underscores. Familiar MovieClip properties like _x, _y, _width, and _height are now referenced simply as x, y, width, and height. This is a bit of a jolt at first, but easy enough to remember with a mindset for change and authoring tool assistance like code completion. It was only the original property set, anyway, that featured the underscore prefixes. More recent ActionScript 1.0 and 2.0 properties, such as blendMode and cacheAsBitmap (introduced in Flash Player 8), had already dropped the underscores, so developers generally welcome the consistency offered by ActionScript 3.0. Values that used to range in integers from 0 to 100, such as MovieClip._alpha and Sound.setVolume(), now range in decimal values from 0 to 1. Even tweaks like these are straightforward enough, and arguably more cosmetic than anything else. The profound change comes in the very nature in which ActionScript 3.0 is organized. This understructure has shifted significantly, and insists on greater attention to detail.

ActionScript has historically been a very forgiving language. In some ways, you can draw a comparison between older versions of ActionScript and older versions of HTML. In the early days of web development, HTML was deceptively unfussy. Styling was handled with straightforward <font> tags, which all too often became a redundant jumble. Closing </p> tags were optional, nested tags could be closed out of sequence from how they were opened, and dozens of other lenient practices led—or had the tendency to lead—to overtime headaches. Popular websites like The Web Standards Project (*http://www.webstan dards.org/*) and CSS Zen Garden (*http://www.csszengarden.com/*) have since sparked a surge of interest in a practice called *semantic markup*, in which great care is taken to cleanly separate styling and formatting from content. This separation usually relies on XHTML specifications, which are considerably stricter than HTML, and coupled with Cascading Style Sheets (CSS). Ironic as it may seem, adherence to a stricter standard has gradually made things easier for web developers. It's a bit like the idea that picking up after yourself throughout the day saves you from facing an overwhelming mess at the end of the week. ActionScript 3.0 is more disciplined than its predecessors in a similarly helpful way.

ActionScript 3.0 is stricter

As an example of ActionScript 3.0's strictness, consider one of programming's most basic building blocks: variables. Since its introduction in ActionScript 1.0, the var keyword has been optional (but always recommended!) for time-line code. The following lines work just fine in a FLA file configured for ActionScript 1.0 or 2.0 and placed in a frame script:

```
lumps = 2;
trace("I'll have " + lumps + " lumps, please.");
// Displays: I'll have 2 lumps, please.
```

Ideally, this variable should be declared with the var keyword:

```
var lumps = 2;
```

but before ActionScript 3.0, the compiler can (and does) declare lumps automatically. While convenient on one level, this relaxed approach can lead to unexpected behavior. How? The var keyword does more than merely announce new arrivals; it defines variables in terms of a specific *scope*, which, in a few words, determines a variable's "point of view," its availability to other objects. Take a look at this revision (changes in bold):

```
function sample() {
    lumps = 2;
    trace(lumps); // Displays: 2
}
sample();

trace("I'll have " + lumps + " lumps, please.");
// Displays: I'll have 2 lumps, please.
```

Here, the lumps variable is declared and traced inside a custom sample() function, which is immediately called after the function is defined. This is followed by a second trace() statement *outside* the function that also references lumps. Because of the omission of the var keyword, both traces are successful, even if the developer's intention is to keep this variable corralled to its function. Add a second function, and all three scopes can still see the variable:

```
function sample() {
    lumps = 2;
    trace(lumps); // Displays: 2
```

```
}
sample();

trace("I'll have " + lumps + " lumps, please.");
// Displays: I'll have 2 lumps, please.

function test() {
    trace(lumps); // Displays: 2
}
test();
```

This sort of spillover can be detrimental in cases where typical naming conventions overlap among numerous functions. For example, if a temporary string, str, is used to manipulate data in one function, havoc could ensue in another if the same variable name is used elsewhere. Think of how often n, i, or x are used to represent numeric values!

You're much better off purposefully declaring a variable in its intended scope. If spillover happens to be the *desired* effect, it's still possible … it just depends on where the variable's scope occurs. Note the output differences in these revisions. In the first example, the variable is only available to one function; in the second, the variable is available to two functions and the timeline. First, when lumps is scoped to the sample() function:

```
function sample() {
    var lumps = 2;
    trace(lumps); // Displays: 2
}
sample();

trace("I'll have " + lumps + " lumps, please.");
// Displays: I'll have undefined lumps, please.

function test() {
    trace(lumps); // Displays: undefined
}
test();
```

Second, when it's scoped to the main timeline:

```
var lumps = 2;

function sample() {
    trace(lumps); // Displays: 2
}
sample();

trace("I'll have " + lumps + " lumps, please.");
// Displays: I'll have 2 lumps, please.

function test() {
    trace(lumps); // Displays: 2
```

```
    }
    test();
```

To underscore the notion of ActionScript 2.0 as a transitional language, consider that undeclared variables aren't allowed in classes, even if they do sneak by in timeline code. When compiled, this no-frills ActionScript 2.0 class generates a compiler error, "There is no property with the name 'lumps'.":

```
class Sample {
    public function Sample() {
        lumps = 2;
        trace("I'll have " + lumps + " lumps, please.");
    }
}
```

You can address this error by preceding the lumps variable with the var keyword, which scopes it to the class's constructor function, Sample(), or by declaring the variable as a class property, which scopes it to the whole class, available to any method:

```
class Sample {
    private var lumps:Number;
    public function Sample() {
        lumps = 2;
        trace("I'll have " + lumps + " lumps, please.");
        demo();
    }
    private function demo():Void {
        trace(lumps); // Also available here
    }
}
```

 Class constructor functions must not define a return data type, which explains the omission of :Void after Sample(), but the presence of :Void after demo().

In ActionScript 3.0, FLA files, as a whole, are associated with something called a *document class*, which defines the main timeline's functionality. While you may optionally write your own document class, you certainly don't have to. By default, the compiler automatically generates one for you. This default document class is called MainTimeline and extends the MovieClip class. On the surface, nothing has changed. The main timeline is still a movie clip, as it always has been, but under the hood, a new structure is in place. The main timeline is now defined by a class, which means that even timeline variables must be formally declared, just as they were in ActionScript 2.0 classes.

The main timeline can also extend the `Sprite` class, if you like. For more information on document classes, see Chapter 7.

In an ActionScript 3.0 FLA file, the following, now-familiar keyframe script generates the compiler error "1120: Access of undefined property lumps" because of the missing var keyword:

```
lumps = 2;
trace("I'll have " + lumps + " lumps, please.");
```

Adding var corrects the situation:

```
var lumps = 2;
trace("I'll have " + lumps + " lumps, please.");
```

Holding to a stricter standard encourages you to give more thought to the code you write. Variables are just the beginning.

ActionScript 3.0 encourages programming with purpose

In ActionScript 2.0, all classes and functions in the Flash Player API were global. These classes were aimed specifically at functionality provided by the Flash Player runtime, over and above the core functionality outlined in the ECMAScript specification. In this free-for-all, if you wanted to refer to the MovieClip class in your code, you could do so without using an import directive, even inside a custom class. An obvious benefit is that you could save a bit of typing:

```
import MovieClip; // This line is not needed,
                  // because the MovieClip class
                  // is already understood
var mc:MovieClip = this.createEmptyMovieClip("myClip", 0);
```

The import directive lets the compiler know which class definition to use for interpreting the code you've written. Even in ActionScript 2.0, import was necessary for classes in packages like flash.filters, flash.geom, and flash.external, and was often necessary for custom classes.

In ActionScript 3.0, only core classes are considered global, in the sense that they belong to the top level of the overhauled *packages* hierarchy. Packages are an organizational means of arranging classes into groups, usually based on similar functionality. The lion's share of ActionScript 3.0 classes is now arranged into such packages. The remainder, global functions and core classes, is listed under the All Packages→Top Level classes topic in the ActionScript 3.0 Language and Components Reference.

As with ActionScript 2.0, top-level classes don't require the import directive—either in timeline code or custom classes—but in contrast to how it used to be, MovieClip is now categorized under flash.display.MovieClip, and must be imported when used in external class files:

```
package {
    public class SampleClass {
        import flash.display.MovieClip;
        public function SampleClass() {
            var mc:MovieClip = new MovieClip();
            // Additional code here ...
        }
    }
}
```

In frame scripts, classes in the flash package join top-level classes in not requiring an import compiler directive. This line, for example, works just fine on its own in an ActionScript 3.0 frame script:

```
var mc:MovieClip = new MovieClip();
```

The concepts of packages and importing are discussed in greater detail in the section "Major Syntax and Structure Changes" on page 77 in this chapter. The subject is worth touching on at this point, however, because it helps prepare you for the massive organizational shift you'll find in the documentation's ActionScript 2.0 Migration table. This new structure's benefit may not be self evident, but it does reinforce a developer's motivation to program with purpose.

Here's an example of how the new packages arrangement can lead to better focus. Before ActionScript 3.0, you had numerous ways to load external assets into a SWF file. The loadMovie() function was among the first and is still in surprisingly wide use in ActionScript 2.0, as indicated by Adobe support forum questions. In the beginning, this function was capable only of loading external SWF files, but this changed as successive versions of Flash Player added support for other dynamically loadable file types, including JPEG, GIF, and PNG. Note that a hint of potential confusion has already raised its head for newcomers: this function, loadMovie(), expressly alludes to a "movie." This is a term commonly used to describe SWF files, but doesn't suggest support for images, even though loadMovie() easily loads image files in recent versions of Flash Player. ActionScript 3.0 helps clear up such pitfalls in semantics.

Consider the following code exercises from the standpoint of an evolutionary journey—a journey that, comparatively speaking, begins in somewhat ambiguous terms and develops into ActionScript that more clearly states its purpose.

1. In a new ActionScript 2.0 FLA file, select frame 1 in the Timeline, and then open the Actions panel. Type the following minimal ActionScript:

```
loadMovie("sample.png", container);
```

Create a new movie clip symbol and position it on the stage. Using the Property inspector, give the new symbol the instance name *container*. Put a PNG file named *sample.png* into the same folder as the FLA file, and then select Control→Test Movie to see the image appear on the stage at runtime. On its own, this code is all you need to load an image prior to ActionScript 3.0, but it doesn't provide any data on load progress or completion. If you want to display load progress or reposition the image when loading completes, then you have to set up a loop of some sort to continuously compare the number of loaded bytes against the total number of bytes the image contains.

2. Using the Actions panel, enter these additional lines of code:

```
var timer:Number = setInterval(checkProgress, 50);
function checkProgress():Void {
    container._visible = false;
    var loaded:Number  = container.getBytesLoaded();
    var total:Number   = container.getBytesTotal();
    var percent:Number = Math.round(loaded/total * 100);
    trace(percent);
    if (percent == 100 && container._width > 0) {
        clearInterval(timer);
        container._x = Stage.width / 2  - ¬
            container._width / 2;
        container._y = Stage.height / 2 - ¬
            container._height / 2;
        container._visible = true;
    }
}
```

Here, setInterval() repeatedly executes a custom checkProgress() function every 50 milliseconds. This function turns off the visibility of *container*, so that it doesn't seem to jump when later repositioned, and then declares and sets the values of three variables. The first two, loaded and total, are taken directly from the getBytesLoaded() and getBytesTotal() methods of the MovieClip class, as invoked on *container*. The third, percent, pits the previous values against each other to derive a percentage, which could potentially be routed to a text field. Here, the value is traced to the Output panel.

Finally, an if statement checks if percent is equal to 100. As a safety backup, it also checks to see if *container* has a width greater than 0. The second condition is present because of a timing issue. In this particular solution, percent might actually reach 100 before the image is displayed, even if only by a few milliseconds. That could be enough to throw off the repositioning code, because until the image shows up, *container* has a default width of 0. When both of these conditions are met, `clearInterval()` exits the `setInterval()` loop, centers *container* to the stage, and then turns its visibility on.

Go ahead and test this revision. In the menu bar of the resultant SWF file, select View→Simulate Download to imitate the loading at a slower pace. The Output panel displays a mounting percentage, which leads to the centered image at 100 percent.

So far, you've seen one approach out of many possible solutions. While it makes reasonable sense when explained, the `loadMovie()`–`setInterval()` combination isn't as graceful as something that relies on event handlers. Introduced with ActionScript 2.0, the `MovieClipLoader` class transforms this loading process into something more like a conversation. After an instance of the `MovieClipLoader` class is created, it is "spoken to" by way of the `loadClip()` method and then "listened to" by way of the `onLoadProgress` and `onLoadInit` event handlers.

3. Delete the existing code in your FLA file and replace it altogether with the following new ActionScript 2.0:

```
var mcl:MovieClipLoader = new MovieClipLoader();
mcl.loadClip("sample.png", container);

var listener:Object = new Object();
listener.onLoadProgress = progressHandler;
listener.onLoadInit = loadInitHandler;
mcl.addListener(listener);

function progressHandler(mc:MovieClip, loaded:Number, ¬
    total:Number):Void {
    var percent:Number = Math.round(loaded/total * 100);
    trace(percent);
}
function loadInitHandler(mc:MovieClip):Void {
    mc._x = Stage.width / 2  - mc._width / 2;
    mc._y = Stage.height / 2 - mc._height / 2;
}
```

The percentage calculation and repositioning portions are identical in principle to the previous version. The difference comes in the way these portions are now carried out. In this case, the instruction to load is given to an instance of the `MovieClipLoader` class (`mcl`), which manages the necessary looping internally. This action removes a bit of clutter because it sidesteps the need for something like `setInterval()`. Now that the timing issue has been remedied, you no longer need to temporarily hide the *container* symbol and reveal it later.

To manage the events, an arbitrarily named variable, `listener`, is declared and set to an instance of the `Object` class. This simple object acts on behalf of `mcl`, pairing up functions with the `onLoadInit` and `onLoadProgress` events of the `MovieClipLoader` class. These functions receive parameters automatically, which `progressHandler()` uses to determine percentage and repositioning values.

 As mentioned in Chapter 1, earlier versions of the language had at least five ways to handle events. In ActionScript 3.0, these five have been consolidated into a single streamlined approach (with a few minor exceptions). For more information, see the "DOM3 Event Model" on page 15 of Chapter 1; the "ActionScript Can No Longer Be Attached to Objects" on page 117 of Chapter 6; and the practical examples in Part IV of this book.

4. Select Control→Test Movie to verify that the SWF file behaves the same as before, including the View→Simulate Download exercise.

This revision arranges the endeavor into coherent, simplified steps, where separate functions perform the sub-goals of percentage reporting and repositioning. Bear in mind, the previous all-in-one function, `checkProgress()`, is perfectly valid. From a nuts-and-bolts technical standpoint, neither approach is superior, but if support forum questions are any reflection of common workday scenarios, many developers take a copy-and-paste approach to learning. They do what it takes to get the job done and, under hectic schedules, acquire knowledge as time allows. When solutions come in single blocks of code, the underlying principles can be harder to digest.

ActionScript 3.0 tightens up the benefits initiated by the `MovieClipLoader` class, reinforcing the theme of programming with purpose. For starters, the loading mechanism is now defined by the `Loader` class, which drops the seemingly "movie"-specific bias of previous functions and classes. At this point, neither the **listener** object nor the *container* movie clip is needed.

5. So it's time to change gears. In a new ActionScript 3.0 FLA file, type the following code into a frame script in frame 1:

```
var myLoader:Loader = new Loader();
myLoader.load(new URLRequest("sample.png"));
addChild(myLoader);

myLoader.contentLoaderInfo.addEventListener(
    ProgressEvent.PROGRESS,
    progressHandler
);
```

```
myLoader.contentLoaderInfo.addEventListener(
    Event.COMPLETE,
    completeHandler
);

function progressHandler(evt:ProgressEvent):void {
    var loaded:int  = evt.bytesLoaded;
    var total:int   = evt.bytesTotal;
    var percent:int = Math.round(loaded / total * 100);
    trace(percent);
}
function completeHandler(evt:Event):void {
    myLoader.x = stage.stageWidth / 2  - ¬
        myLoader.width / 2;
    myLoader.y = stage.stageHeight / 2 - ¬
        myLoader.height / 2;
}
```

Once again, the percentage calculation and repositioning portions are nearly the same. In this updated version, a variable myLoader is declared and set to an instance of the Loader class, which is capable of loading SWF files and image files (JPEGs, GIFs, and PNGs). Note that in this case, the file path to *sample.png* isn't merely a string, as before. In this case, it's an instance of the URLRequest class. In addition, the event handlers are associated not with myLoader itself, but with a contentLoaderInfo property of that object.

These objects are certainly new, presumably useful, and possibly overwhelming. But what exactly *are* they? Clutter? Not a bit of it! Flash has always been a creative toolbox. ActionScript 3.0 has tidied up the toolbox and put labels next to each tool. You'll learn more about this rigorously organized new arrangement in the very next section.

6. Select Control→Test Movie to see that the SWF file behaves the same as before. In the file menu of the SWF file, select View→Simulate Download to test the percentage output.

ActionScript 3.0 is more organized, which makes it more efficient

On the face of it, the URLRequest class, seen in the previous example, acts as nothing more than a container for storing file locations. It seems to be a five-dollar way of saying "*sample.png*," much like "salutations" is a five-dollar way of saying "hello." So what's the point? Is URLRequest really necessary? What was wrong with the simple string approach of earlier functions and classes? To answer these questions, think again of the overhauled ActionScript 3.0 packages structure.

Before ActionScript 3.0, the MovieClip class supported a loadMovie() method, which was practically equal in purpose to the standalone loadMovie() function.

Wait a minute! Were there formerly two versions of `loadMovie()`? There were. This sort of redundancy was frequent in older ActionScript. There were also two versions of `gotoAndPlay()`—both function and method—and many others, besides. This duplication was introduced in Flash 5, when the `MovieClip` class began taking ownership of movie-clip–related functionality. Longstanding functions became `MovieClip` methods overnight, yet the function versions remained for backward compatibility.

The trouble is, this duplication sometimes went too far. The `loadMovie()` method, especially, is a case in point. Because the `MovieClip` class defines movie clip objects, these objects should certainly be able to do the things a movie clip symbol can do: display animated timelines, move around the stage, change dimensions, and so on—but the act of loading is a categorically distinct *discipline*.

It makes good sense to coordinate the traits and functionality of loading into an object that specializes in the field, so to speak. In ActionScript 3.0, precisely this sort of thoughtful arrangement has occurred. As a subject matter expert on loading, the `Loader` class should indeed feature an impressive array of loading related skills. In this light, it's not surprising that `Loader` should work in collaboration with a subject matter expert on HTTP requests, which is what the `URLRequest` class is. More than just a fancy way of describing file locations, `URLRequest` objects have the potential to manage an HTTP request's header, its method (GET versus POST), its POST data, MIME content type, and so on.

This sort of rich granularity is echoed throughout the ActionScript 3.0 API. For example, in the previous code exercise, the event handler was associated with the `Loader.contentLoaderInfo` property of the `myLoader` instance. As it happens, this property points to an instance of yet another class, `LoaderInfo`, which specifically manages byte data and other information about SWF files and image files. This class's skill set paves the way for the `bytesLoaded` and `bytesTotal` properties used by the progress event handler. Again, each step is categorized neatly.

This sort of approach wasn't unheard of, by the way, in older versions of ActionScript. It just wasn't as prevalent. The `TextFormat` class, for example, compartmentalizes formatting from the text fields it collaborates with (relevant code in bold).

```
// ActionScript 2.0
var tf:TextField = this.createTextField("sampleText", ¬
    0, 10, 50, 100, 20);
tf.selectable = false;
tf.autoSize = "center";

var styling:TextFormat = new TextFormat();
styling.font = "Blackadder";
```

```
styling.color = 0xBA1424;
styling.letterSpacing = 1.5;

tf.setNewTextFormat(styling);
tf.text = "Cooperation!";
```

For good measure, here are another two examples that show how ActionScript 3.0 expands on this sort of helpful compartmentalization.

In ActionScript 1.0 and 2.0, the MovieClip class featured a handful of methods collectively known as the Drawing API. You could reference a movie clip directly by its instance name and invoke, say, lineTo() and curveTo() to draw shapes at runtime. In ActionScript 3.0, this same Drawing API has been reallocated to a more suitable Graphics class, which is now associated with movie clips by way of the MovieClip.graphics property:

```
// ActionScript 2.0
myClip.lineTo(300, 200);

// ActionScript 3.0
myClip.graphics.lineTo(300, 200);
```

In ActionScript 3.0, the Sound class collaborates with three new classes—Sound Channel, SoundTransform, and SoundMixer—to manage audio-related functionality. These duties were previously consigned to the Sound class alone. Previously, the concept of sound channels was managed by a non-intuitive association between a Sound instance and a movie clip. In order to separate audio into individual "channels," you had to feed individual movie clip instance names to each use of the new Sound() constructor. It was an easy procedure to miss, and developers often wondered why adjusting the volume of one Sound instance affected the volumes of others. Now, the improved, decentralized functionality calls on specialized companion classes as needed.

```
// ActionScript 2.0
var mySound:Sound = new Sound();
mySound.loadSound("music.mp3", true);
mySound.setVolume(50);
mySound.stop();

// ActionScript 3.0
var mySound:Sound = new Sound();
mySound.load(new URLRequest("music.mp3"));

var myChannel:SoundChannel = mySound.play();
var myTransform:SoundTransform = myChannel.soundTransform;

myTransform.volume = 0.5;
myChannel.soundTransform = myTransform;
myChannel.stop();
```

By delegating functionality to numerous classes, the new API keeps its objects lean and focused. `MovieClip` instances are no longer burdened with loading tasks or the Drawing API, but all the same, are easily associated with companion classes that handle those duties. The concept goes even further: if you want some of the basic characteristics of a movie clip but don't need internal animation—that is, if you don't need to shuttle around a movie clip's playhead with `gotoAndPlay()`—then you now have the option of using the `Sprite` class instead, which doesn't carry the overhead of a timeline. Ultimately, this makes your tools more refined, giving you functionality that suits the object at hand, and leaving the extra tasks to other objects.

Obsolete Code

Waking up in a hotel room can sometimes be disorienting. You might reach for your glasses or a cup of water that, at home, is always right where you expect: at pillow height on the nightstand. Of course, hotel rooms are temporary. Soon enough, a red-eye flight takes you back to your humble abode, where the comforts of familiarity snuggle their way back into your daily routine.

No so with obsolete code! Unless you're involved specifically with legacy systems, where you know users are locked in to an older version of Flash Player, you'll have to leave certain once-familiar paradigms in the dust. Some of these ways have been deprecated for many versions of Flash, which means the term in question was officially frowned upon at some point because it was likely to be removed in the future. With ActionScript 3.0, that theoretical future has finally arrived. The ActionScript 2.0 Migration table provides an exhaustive list of features that ActionScript 3.0 no longer supports, but the following collection provides a summary of many common—yet no longer usable—practices.

on()/onClipEvent()

It is no longer possible to attach event handlers directly to objects, such as movie clips, buttons, and components. This is a significant change, because `on()` and `onClipEvent()` have been popular for years. Using direct attachment, you could previously program a button to respond to a mouse click, for example, by selecting the button symbol on the stage, opening the Actions panel, and then typing something like this:

```
on (release) {
  // Desired code here
}
```

This was optional as recently as ActionScript 2.0—an alternate approach to referencing event handlers by instance name. In ActionScript 3.0, the object in question *must* have an instance name, which is what uniquely identifies that symbol or component as something ActionScript can speak to. In contrast, direct attachment didn't require instance names because the intended recipient of your instruction was self-evident.

You can supply an instance name to an object by selecting it on the stage, and then typing the instance name into the Property inspector. Assuming an instance name myButton, here's how ActionScript 3.0 associates the occurrence of a mouse release with a function to be trigged by that occurrence:

```
myButton.addEventListener(MouseEvent.MOUSE_UP, function);
```

If you think of the Timeline as a grid, this code appears in a frame script that aligns vertically in the same "column"—the same frame—as the button it refers to. The term *function* in the previous line of code refers to an actual function definition, such as the following arbitrarily named mouseUpHandler():

```
myButton.addEventListener(MouseEvent.MOUSE_UP, ¬
    mouseUpHandler);

function mouseUpHandler(evt:MouseEvent):void {
    // Desired code here
}
```

The evt parameter refers to an instance of the MouseEvent class, which features numerous useful properties you can optionally reference inside the function. To find out what events are available for a button symbol, look up the SimpleButton class in the ActionScript 3.0 Language and Components Reference. Click the "Show Inherited Events" hyperlink in the Events section, and take your pick. One of these is mouseUp, and if you click on that, the Help panel shows that the mouseUp event belongs to the MouseEvent class and is referenced with the MouseEvent.MOUSE_UP constant. (A constant is simply a variable whose value doesn't change. Many classes store properties and events as constants in this way. By using the constant, instead of the string "mouseUp", you gain the benefit of code coloring to show you've entered the right code.) In the same way, the MovieClip class entry indicates what events are available for movie clips, the ComboBox class shows events for the ComboBox component, etc.

 The practical examples in Part IV of this book go into greater detail on event handling, including keyboard events (responding to keystrokes) and optional aspects like event bubbling.

getProperty()/setProperty()/tellTarget()

These functions still show up in hundreds of online tutorials, but they're no longer supported. Ever since ActionScript 1.0, their purpose has been simplified by dot notation. Consider a movie clip symbol with the instance name *myClip*. To set its width using `setProperty()`, you would refer to the instance name like this:

```
setProperty(myClip, _width, 200);
```

The updated approach is much easier on the eye (note the change from `_width` to `width`):

```
myClip.width = 200;
```

attachMovie()/attachSound()

The procedure for pulling assets from the library at runtime has changed. It still requires linkage information, but instead of a linkage identifier, Action-Script 3.0 requires a *linkage class*, which is designated by the same Symbol Properties dialog box you're used to. Right-click (Ctrl-click) on an asset in the library, and then choose Properties. When the dialog box opens, click the Advanced button if it's showing. This expands the Symbol Properties dialog box to its full extent. Select Export for ActionScript, and then enter a name into the Class field, as shown in Figure 3-1 (note that the Identifier field is disabled).

Rather than invoking `attachMovie()` or `attachSound()` on a related `MovieClip` or `Sound` instance, the library asset is attached by way of the `new` operator:

```
var mc:myClip = new myClip();
```

Visual objects, like movie clips and graphics, are then added to the display list, which manages a SWF file's visual objects:

```
addChild(mc);
```

 For more information on this process, see Chapter 8, and the practical examples in Part IV of this book.

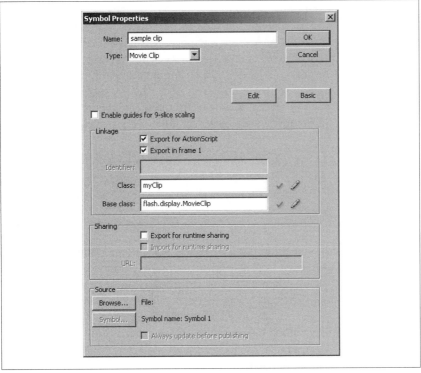

Figure 3-1. Specifying linkage properties

createEmptyMovieClip()/duplicateMovieClip()/createTextField()

In similar fashion, the `MovieClip` and `TextField` classes can now be instantiated directly with the `new` operator. In both cases, the resultant objects must be added to the display list.

```
// ActionScript 2.0
var mc:MovieClip = this.createEmptyMovieClip("myClip", 0);

// ActionScript 3.0
var mc:MovieClip = new MovieClip();
mc.name = "myClip"; // traditional instance name
addChild(mc);
```

In the ActionScript 2.0 version, the `MovieClip.createEmptyMovieClip()` method is invoked on a timeline with the global `this` property, but that could be replaced with any valid movie clip reference, which would then become the immediate parent of the new `MovieClip` instance. The Property-inspector–style instance name (the string `"myClip"`) is a required parameter, as is the second parameter, depth, which here happens to be `0` (the lowest depth). Because `createEmptyMovieClip()` returns a movie clip reference, the new instance can be referred to in subsequent code either by the *myClip* instance name or the mc variable.

In the ActionScript 3.0 version, depth is handled automatically (no depth parameter is required) and the Property-inspector–style instance name is optional, as the new object can, in any case, be referenced by the mc variable.

eval()

The `eval()` function crops up often in legacy code and in many online tutorials. In older ActionScript, it was used to evaluate expressions as variables, properties, or objects. When a variable or property name was evaluated, its value was returned. When an object name or reference was evaluated, a new reference to that object was returned. One typical use of `eval()` was to iterate through sequentially named movie clip instances using a `for` loop. Here, three movie clips with the instance names *mc0*, *mc1*, and *mc2* are conveniently set to a horizontal position of 200 all at once:

```
// ActionScript 2.0
for (var i:Number = 0; i < 3; i++) {
    eval("mc" + i)._x = 200;
}
```

While `eval()` is no longer available in ActionScript 3.0, the bracket notation approach to the same task, using the array access operator (`[]`), still works:

```
// ActionScript 3.0
for (var i:int = 0; i < 3; i++) {
    this["mc" + i].x = 200;
}
```

Bracket notation requires that an object reference precede the array access operator. In this case, the object reference is `this`, which refers to the timeline in which these movie clips appear. If the three movie clips were nested inside the timeline of another movie clip with the instance name *container*, then the same ActionScript 3.0 `for` loop would look like this:

```
for (var i:int = 0; i < 3; i++) {
    container["mc" + i].x = 200;
}
```

You can iterate through movie clips with an object reference, in which a variable points to a given `MovieClip` instance, or by Property-inspector–style instance name (that is, the `MovieClip._name` property in ActionScript 2.0 and the `MovieClip.name` property in ActionScript 3.0). In ActionScript 3.0, array access operator iteration through `MovieClip.name` property values only succeeds when those instance names are provided by hand using the Property inspector. The `MovieClip.name` property *indicates* the movie clip's instance name, but is not synonymous with it, as was the case with ActionScript 2.0's `MovieClip._name` property. If you prefer to iterate through `MovieClip.name` values generated by code, make sure to use the `DisplayObjectContainer.getChildByName()` method to locate those `name` values in the display list later:

```
for (var i:int = 0; i < 3; i++) {
    var mc:MovieClip = new MovieClip();
    mc.name = "mc" + i;
    this.addChild(mc);
}

for (i = 0; i < 3; i++) {
    mc = MovieClip(this.getChildByName("mc" + i));
    mc.graphics.lineStyle(3, 0xFF0000);
    mc.graphics.lineTo(0, 20);
    mc.x = 20 * i;
    // Locates dynamically generated movie clips
    // by name property and draws a short vertical
    // line in each
}
```

You can alternately use the `DisplayObjectContainer.getChildAt()` method to locate display objects by their index number in a given display list. Both of these methods can be invoked on the main timeline or on movie clips because the `MovieClip` class inherits from `DisplayObjectContainer`. Note, however, that the return value of both methods is typed as `DisplayObject`. For this reason, you may need to cast the return value as `MovieClip`, as shown in the previous example (`MovieClip(object)` or `object as MovieClip`)—otherwise the compiler will not let you to reference `MovieClip`-specific members, such as `currentFrame` or `scenes`.

Major Syntax and Structure Changes

The overwhelming majority of ActionScript's native classes are now arranged into packages, and packages must be imported into class files to be used. This importing is accomplished by way of the `import` directive, like this:

```
import fl.controls.CheckBox;
import flash.display.MovieClip;
import flash.events.MouseEvent;
```

Lines like these tell the compiler exactly which classes are meant by any subsequent references to `CheckBox`, `MovieClip`, and `MouseEvent` in your code. After all, you might very well be using the Adobe-supplied CheckBox component, but you could just as easily be using some third-party user interface component, whose package might be `com.niftystuff.CheckBox`. The `import` directive clarifies any ambiguity by setting the record straight from the beginning.

If, by chance, you intend to use two distinct classes that share the same name, you must precede each reference with the fully qualified package for clarity. Otherwise, the class name alone is sufficient:

```
import com.niftystuff.CheckBox;
import fl.controls.CheckBox;
import flash.display.MovieClip;

var cb1:com.niftystuff.CheckBox = new com.niftystuff.¬
    CheckBox();
var cb2:fl.controls.CheckBox = new fl.controls.CheckBox();
var mc:MovieClip = new MovieClip();
```

When appearing in class files, `import` directives are generally positioned immediately inside the package declaration:

```
package {
    import flash.display.MovieClip;
    public class SampleClass {
        public function SampleClass() {
            // Constructor code here
        }
    }
}
```

This practice makes any imported classes available to the whole package. If placed inside the class declaration, the imports are available only to the class:

```
package {
    public class SampleClass {
        import flash.display.MovieClip;
        public function SampleClass() {
            // Constructor code here
        }
    }
}
```

In frame scripts, `import` directives must appear once in each frame used.

Importing and Packages

If you're already familiar with importing, you won't discover anything new with the technique; it's just that in writing ActionScript 3.0 classes, you'll find that your blocks of `import` statements are more crowded than they used to be.

The ECMAScript specification defines a set of core functionality that, in ActionScript 3.0, appears as a small collection of top-level classes, listed under the All Packages→Top Level classes topic in the ActionScript 3.0 Language and Components Reference. There are only a couple dozen of these, which include such customary classes as `Array`, `Function`, `Math`, and `Object`. These classes are readily available, without importing, in custom classes and timeline code alike. The rest, comprising hundreds of other classes, including the Flash Player API (all the features unique to the Flash Player runtime) necessitate imports when used in custom classes. Fortunately, you need only a single import per referenced class. That is, importing `flash.text.TextField` once in a custom class lets you create as many text fields as you like in that class.

Though you don't encounter it as often in timeline code, the `import` directive is valid only for the frame in which it's placed. If you import a class inside a script on frame 1 and wish to use the same class in frame 5, then you have to import the referenced class again in frame 5. This step is necessary because, in ActionScript 3.0, timeline frames are effectively treated as methods of the `MovieClip` instance they belong to—methods of the default `MainTimeline` document class. Just as imports inside a class declaration are available only to that class, but not that class's package, imports inside a method are available only to that method.

In addition to the top-level classes, the ActionScript 3.0 packages hierarchy has three main branches: `flash`, `adobe`, and `fl`. Of these, the `flash` and `adobe` packages have a sort of "backstage pass" when referenced in timeline code: none of them requires the `import` directive when used in frame scripts. The `flash` packages consist of the Flash Player API and encompass most of the traditional Flash classes like `MovieClip`, `TextField`, and `SimpleButton` (button symbols). The `adobe` package contains functions and classes used to automate the authoring tool. These correspond to the Flash JavaScript application programming interface (JavaScript API)—also known as JSFL—outlined in the Extending Flash section in the documentation. The JavaScript API lets you run batch scripts on large volumes of FLA files and even create new panels and tools. The other main branch, `fl`, does require imports in frame scripts and tends to involve components, so not only do you need one `import` directive for each referenced type of component, you also need a copy of that component in the FLA file's library. Remember, custom classes always require imports when dealing with packaged classes that ship with the Flash authoring tool.

ActionScript 2.0 provided a sneak peek of the thorough package hierarchy currently in effect. The mx packages (mainly components) were fairly analogous to the current fl packages, and some of the flash packages were available for Flash Player 8, including flash.filters, flash.display for the Bitmap Data class, and flash.geom for a handful of geometry-related classes like Matrix, Point, and Rectangle.

Namespaces

Namespaces give you a way to control access to properties and methods in custom classes. ActionScript 2.0 had only two built-in namespaces: the access control specifiers public and private, which affected (and still affect) the availability of class members to outside code. ActionScript 3.0 increases this number to four by introducing protected and internal. These built-in specifiers work only in class files, and must precede class, property, and method declarations:

```
package {
    public class SampleClass {
        private var numValue:Number;
        public function SampleClass() {
            // Constructor code here
        }
    }
}
```

By default, ActionScript 2.0 members belonged to the public namespace unless specified otherwise. In ActionScript 3.0, this has changed to internal, which lets class members be accessed by any code in the same package. Members specified as protected are available only to the class that defines them, and to any subclasses of that class. Members specified as private are available only to the defining class, and public members are accessible to any outside code.

Developers now have the option to create custom namespaces to further manipulate object access. This is possible with class access control specifiers and useful when employed in advanced scenarios. On the other hand, namespaces can be a stumbling block if they unexpectedly sneak up on you. In ActionScript 3.0, this can happen with loaded XML data.

In XML, namespaces, when present, are specified with an xmlns attribute. Consider the XML example introduced in Chapter 1—but with one key difference: the presence of a namespace indicating a hypothetical music service (namespace in bold):

```
<?xml version="1.0" encoding="iso-8859-1"?>
<library xmlns:albums="http://www.adobe.com/albumlistings/">
    <artist name="The Beatles">
```

```
<album name="Abbey Road">
    <track title="Come Together" />
    <track title="Something" />
    <track title="Maxwell's Silver Hammer" />
    <track title="Oh! Darling" />
    <track title="Octopus's Garden" />
    <track title="I Want You (She's So Heavy)" />
    <track title="Here Comes the Sun" />
    <track title="Because" />
    <track title="You Never Give Me Your Money" />
    <track title="Sun King" />
    <track title="Mean Mr. Mustard" />
    <track title="Polythene Pam" />
    <track title="She Came in Through the Bathroom Window" />
    <track title="Golden Slumbers" />
    <track title="Carry That Weight" />
    <track title="The End" />
    <track title="Her Majesty" />
</album>
    </artist>
</library>
```

Numerous XML sources feature this sort of identifying data, such as iTunes playlists, blog RSS feeds, and even XHTML documents. ActionScript 2.0 ignored XML namespaces, but in ActionScript 3.0, XML namespaces cascade from parent elements to their children. In this case, for example, the `<library>` element's `xmlns` attribute is applied automatically to the remaining elements in the document.

At this point, tracing all `<track>` elements displays the following output:

```
var myXML:XML = new XML();
var xmlLoader:URLLoader = new URLLoader();
xmlLoader.load(new URLRequest("cds.xml"));
xmlLoader.addEventListener(
    Event.COMPLETE,
    function(evt:Event):void {
        myXML = XML(evt.target.data);
        trace(myXML..track);
    }
);
// Displays:
// <track title="Come Together"
//     xmlns:albums="http://www.adobe.com/albumlistings/"/>
// <track title="Something"
//     xmlns:albums="http://www.adobe.com/albumlistings/"/>
// <track title="Maxwell's Silver Hammer"
//     xmlns:albums="http://www.adobe.com/albumlistings/"/>
// ...
```

Note the presence of the `albums` namespace as an attribute of each `<track>` element, even though the original XML only shows this attribute for the `<library>` element. Why is this a problem? The tricky part is that XML namespaces aren't required to have an identifier, such as the one shown (`albums`). Note the lack of the `albums` identifier in this revision:

```
<?xml version="1.0" encoding="iso-8859-1"?>
<library xmlns="http://www.adobe.com/albumlistings/">
```

At this point, a trace of all `<track>` elements comes back with nothing at all. In fact, you can't see *any* of the elements now, because the namespace has no identifier.

To address this issue, you can use the new `Namespace` class:

```
var myXML:XML = new XML();
var xmlLoader:URLLoader = new URLLoader();
xmlLoader.load(new URLRequest("cds.xml"));
xmlLoader.addEventListener(
    Event.COMPLETE,
    function(evt:Event):void {
        myXML = XML(evt.target.data);
        var ns:Namespace = new Namespace("http://¬
            www.adobe.com/albumlistings/");
        trace(myXML..ns::track);
    }
);
```

Here, an arbitrarily named variable, `ns`, is declared and set to an instance of the `Namespace` class, whose constructor function receives the namespace *Uniform Resource Identifier* (URI) specified in the `xmlns` attribute. This allows `ns` to be used as a prefix for subsequent element references, by way of the `::` operator (`myXML..ns::track`).

If you don't know the URI beforehand, you can use the `XML.namespace()` method to retrieve it:

```
var ns:Namespace = new Namespace(myXML.namespace());
trace(myXML..ns::track);
```

Data Types and Typing

Before ActionScript 3.0, the default value of declared, but uninitialized, objects was always `undefined`, even if strongly typed:

```
// ActionScript 2.0
var b:Boolean;
trace(b);    // Displays: undefined

var str:String;
trace(str); // Displays: undefined

var d:Date;
trace(d);    // Displays: undefined

var a:Array;
```

```
trace(a);    // Displays: undefined

var n:Number;
trace(n);    // Displays: undefined
```

Due to the more memory-efficient nature of objects in ActionScript 3.0, this has changed. Now, the special undefined value applies only to variables that are untyped, such as var n (that is, declared, but not typed and not given an initial value). As a recommended best practice, objects should be strongly typed as a rule, so that the compiler will request only the minimum system memory required for each object. The default value of variables now depends on the corresponding data type:

```
// ActionScript 3.0
var b:Boolean;
trace(b);    // Displays: false

var str:String;
trace(str); // Displays: null

var d:Date;
trace(d);    // Displays: null

var a:Array;
trace(a);    // Displays: null

var n:Number;
trace(n);    // Displays: NaN (Not a Number)

var i:int;
trace(i);    // Displays: 0
```

Clearly, code that may have compared values to undefined in the past will no longer behave as expected. Even comparisons to null can no longer be assumed as useful, because some data types default to other values.

```
var someValue:Number;
if (someValue == undefined || someValue == null) {
    // In ActionScript 3.0, someValue is none of these
}
```

The upshot is that a theme discussed earlier in this chapter is bolstered yet again, that of programming with purpose. In ActionScript 3.0, in a more fundamental way than ever, each type of object has its own characteristics and consumes its own unique portion of system resources. This variety elicits an attention to detail that, with practice, leads to better programming. ActionScript 3.0 is the chess coach that encourages you to consider your move before even touching a piece. That's good advice!

Additional ActionScript 3.0 Resources

ActionScript 3.0 is an extensive subject, more so than any of its forerunners. An exhaustive exploration is beyond the scope or focus of this book, but additional resources are certainly available. For a solid foundation, consider *Learning ActionScript 3.0: A Beginner's Guide* (O'Reilly), by Rich Shupe and Zevan Rosser. For hundreds of ready-to-use solutions to real-world problems, consider the *ActionScript 3.0 Cookbook* (O'Reilly), by Joey Lott, Darron Schall, and Keith Peters. For a comprehensive overview of the language, consider *Essential ActionScript 3.0* (O'Reilly), by Colin Moock, which steps through ActionScript 3.0 in a thorough 900+ pages.

The Adobe Developer Connection website features a constantly rotating assortment of free articles and tutorials written by top community experts. Each of Adobe's developer tools has its own entry point, and relevant URLs for ActionScript include the following:

> *http://www.adobe.com/devnet/actionscript/*
> *http://www.adobe.com/devnet/flash/*
> *http://www.adobe.com/devnet/flex/*
> *http://www.adobe.com/devnet/air/*

Trevor McCauley has been working with Flash since 2000, a passion that eventually led to his being hired by Adobe. Trevor is an avid developer, trainer, writer, and conference speaker on topics related to Flash. His "ActionScript 3 Tip of the Day" thread at *http://kirupa.com* (*http://www.kirupa.com/forum/showthread.php?t=223798*) became something of a legend after the release of Flash CS3 and continues to help developers make the transition from old to new. He also provides free tutorials and sample files at his website, *http://senocular.com* (*http://www.senocular.com/flash/tutorials.php*).

CHAPTER 4

Exploring the Benefits of Using ActionScript 3.0

It has been said, and generally agreed, that in spite of how funny it would make a person look, two heads are better than one. The point of this adage, of course, is that collaboration can be a remarkably productive venture. Flash Player 10 promotes this ideal thanks to its two *virtual machines*, the software modules inside Flash Player that execute ActionScript programs. Until Flash Player 9, only a single virtual machine was necessary. It handled (and still handles) everything code-related from the very beginnings of ActionScript to the formal *object-oriented programming* (OOP) paradigm introduced with ActionScript 2.0. The architectural changes and improvements introduced with Action-Script 3.0, however, were substantial enough in Flash Player 9 to warrant a new virtual machine specifically optimized for the new language.

This new module, named *ActionScript Virtual Machine 2* (AVM2), works independently of the previous player codebase. It was unveiled in a prerelease version of Flash Player 9, originally slated as Flash Player 8.5. (There was no commercial release of Flash Player 8.5; in the final public release, its version number shipped as 9.) Legacy support is still handled by the previous codebase, now renamed *ActionScript Virtual Machine 1* (AVM1) and remains as a companion module inside Flash Players 9 and 10 to support backward compatibility. Meanwhile, AVM2 ushers ActionScript 3.0 into an arena of increased performance, efficiency, and an internal consistency that makes the language easier for newcomers to learn. In this way, both old and new code are able to function with maximum efficiency and performance.

In addition to benefiting from two heads, so to speak, Flash Player 10 encourages another nuance on the concept of collaboration: that of adherence to standards. Because other Flash Platform development tools rely on the same ECMAScript specification as Flash CS4, your work in ActionScript 3.0 leads directly to portability among other Adobe technologies, such as Flex and

Adobe Integrated Runtime (AIR), formerly codenamed Apollo. Learn Action-Script 3.0 in terms of the Flash authoring tool, and you already have a leg up on building online and desktop-based Rich Internet Applications (RIAs) and occasionally connected desktop applications.

Performance

In Adobe benchmarks, ActionScript 3.0 has been shown to increase application performance by an order of magnitude. This means that even complex programs can potentially execute with 10 times the speed and efficiency of ActionScript 2.0. That's the sort of impressiveness that rivals a juggler with flaming bowling pins—who is also spinning plates, while riding a unicycle on a tightrope with no net. To be sure, some of this improvement results from enhancements to the Flash Player runtime itself, from successively better rendering with each release, the advent of bitmap caching in Flash Player 8, and hardware acceleration in Flash Player 9.0.115.0. Ultimately, though, performance depends on how well your code is written, on adherence to recommended best practices, and the boost of being executed on AVM2.

In early 2005, a participant in the Flash ActionScript support forum posed a question about using ActionScript to render something called the Mandelbrot set, which is one of the most popular examples of a series of infinitely complex geometric shapes called fractals. Chances are good you've seen the Mandelbrot set depicted on progressive rock album covers, as the underlying mechanism for computer-generated (CG) effects like realistic mountain terrains, or even as the printed pattern on a handful of bowties at a programming convention. The initial view of this geometric set, seen in Figure 4-1, is defined by a complicated mathematical formula. This trait makes it a good candidate for showcasing the speed increases of ActionScript 3.0, as the code discussed in 2005 can be compared side by side with a modern interpretation.

In fact, you can re-create a version of the original SWF file yourself and evaluate its performance against an ActionScript 3.0 version on your own computer.

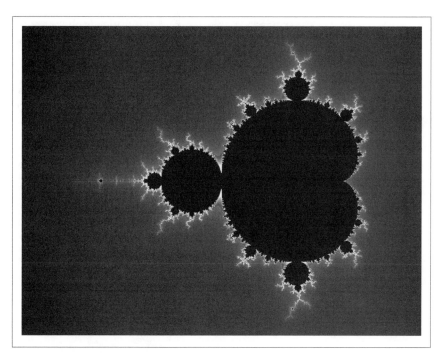

Figure 4-1. The Mandelbrot set

1. Create a new ActionScript 2.0 FLA file. Use the Property inspector to set
   the document's dimensions to **340** pixels by **240** pixels and the background
   color to **#000000** (black). Type the following code into frame 1 of a script
   layer:

```
var startTime:Number = getTimer();

var image:MovieClip = this.createEmptyMovieClip("mcImage", 0);
image._x = 240;
image._y = 120;

var colors:Array = new Array(
    0x000000, 0x0E0E0E, 0x1C1C1C, 0x2A2A2A, 0x383838,
    0x464646, 0x555555, 0x636363, 0x717171, 0x7F7F7F,
    0x8D8D8D, 0xB9B9B9, 0xAAAAAA, 0xB8B8B8, 0xC6C6C6,
    0xD4D4D4, 0xE2E2E2, 0xF0F0F0, 0xFFFFFF
);
var k:Number = -120;
var zArr:Array = new Array();

var myTimer:Number = setInterval(drawLine, 1);
```

This step sets up a startTime variable, which metaphorically clicks a stopwatch into action. This variable is compared to the getTimer() function again at the end, which then displays total elapsed seconds. The image variable holds a reference to a movie clip, which is used as a canvas on which the Drawing API plots a series of line segments that represent the Mandelbrot set. The colors variable points to an array of color values used during the drawing, k and zArr are used in the fractal calculation, and myTimer is eventually used to halt the repeated triggering of a custom drawLine() function, as looped once every millisecond by the setInterval() function.

2. Next comes the drawLine() function, which is the brain of the whole operation. Type the following code after the existing ActionScript code:

```
function drawLine():Void {
    var j:Number = 0;
    var x:Number = 0;
    var y:Number = 0;
    var n:Number = 0;
    var zAbs:Number = 0;
    for (j = -240; j <= 100; j++) {
        x = 0;
        y = 0;
        n = 0;
        do {
            n++;
            zArr = f(x, y, j / 100, k / 100);
            x = zArr[0];
            y = zArr[1];
            zAbs = zArr[2];
            if (n >= 20) {
                break;
            }
        } while (zAbs <= 4);
        if (zAbs > 4) {
            image.lineStyle(1, colors[n], 100);
            image.moveTo(j, k - 1);
            image.lineTo(j, k);
        }
    }
    k++;
    if (k >= 0) {
        clearInterval(myTimer);
        duplicate();
    }
}
```

For the sake of this demonstration, it doesn't matter if the Mandelbrot formula seems clear as mud. Just count on it that the magic happens inside the do..while statement, one of whose lines calls a custom f() function. The line segments are drawn by the calls to lineStyle(), moveTo(), and lineTo(), and the final if statement decides when to stop the setInterval() loop by calling clearInterval(), then completing the mirror image of the drawing with a call to the custom duplicate() function.

3. Here are the final short blocks of code, the f() and duplicate() functions. Type the following code after the existing ActionScript code. Note that the last line of the duplicate() function uses trace() to report the elapsed time to the Output panel.

```
function f(x:Number, y:Number, a:Number, b:Number):Array {
    var rPart:Number = x * x - y * y + a;
    var iPart:Number = 2 * x * y + b;
    return new Array(rPart, iPart, rPart * rPart + iPart * iPart);
}
function duplicate():Void {
    var flip:MovieClip = image.duplicateMovieClip("mcFlip", 1);
    flip._yscale = -100;
    flip._y -= 2;
    trace((getTimer() - startTime) / 1000);
}
```

4. Select Control→Test Movie to see your handiwork (Figure 4-2).

Special thanks to Keith Gladstien, PhD, MD (*http://www.kglad.com/*), for permission to reprint a version of his code in this book. See Keith's website for additional exploration of the Mandelbrot set in Flash.

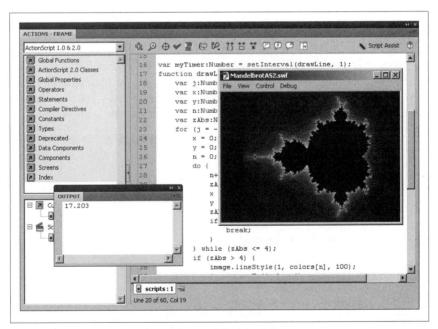

Figure 4-2. An ActionScript 2.0 rendering of the Mandelbrot set

Your own performance results may vary, depending on your computer's power and speed. You may even want to test repeatedly and take an average of elapsed times, remembering that results will vary for individual users who view your published content. You'll clearly see the sequential improvement when you configure the publish settings for this FLA file among various versions of Flash Player (File→Publish Settings→Flash→Version) Table 4-1 shows the averaged results of one such series of tests.

Table 4-1. Speed of Mandelbrot set as rendered in various versions of Flash Player

Flash Player version	ActionScript version	Elapsed time (in seconds)
Flash Player 6	ActionScript 2.0	21.847
Flash Player 7	ActionScript 2.0	15.225
Flash Player 8	ActionScript 2.0	13.729
Flash Player 9	ActionScript 2.0	10.338
Flash Player 9	ActionScript 3.0	2.853
Flash Player 10	ActionScript 2.0	15.557 *
Flash Player 10	ActionScript 3.0	6.387 *

* At the time of writing, Flash Player 10 actually performed more slowly than Flash Player 9. This should be addressed before Flash is publicly released.

Updating the Code to ActionScript 3.0

To experience the Mandelbrot set on your own in a matter of 2 to 3 seconds, save your current file as *MandelbrotAS3.fla*, and then complete the following steps. Great care has been taken to maintain the overall structure of this code, so that it parallels the ActionScript 2.0 version approximately line for line.

1. Configure the FLA file's publish settings for Flash Player 9 or 10 (File→Publish Settings→Flash→Version), and then change the Action-Script version to ActionScript 3.0.

2. Update the existing code as follows (changes in are bold):

```
var startTime:int = getTimer();

var image:Sprite = new Sprite();
image.x = 240;
image.y = 120;
addChild(image);

var colors:Array = new Array(
    0x000000, 0x0E0E0E, 0x1C1C1C, 0x2A2A2A, 0x383838,
    0x464646, 0x555555, 0x636363, 0x717171, 0x7F7F7F,
    0x8D8D8D, 0xB9B9B9, 0xAAAAAA, 0xB8B8B8, 0xC6C6C6,
```

```
        0xD4D4D4, 0xE2E2E2, 0xF0F0F0, 0xFFFFFF
);
var k:int = -120;
var zArr:Array = new Array();

var myTimer:Timer = new Timer(1, 0);
myTimer.addEventListener(TimerEvent.TIMER, drawLine);
myTimer.start();
```

This time, the int data type is used in cases where numerical values are integers, simply because int values consume a smaller memory footprint than Number values. Similarly, image is set to an instance of the Sprite class, rather than MovieClip, because Sprite is perfectly adequate—it supports the necessary Drawing API—and it's the smaller data type. In this case, the timer mechanism is an instance of the Timer class.

3. Here's the updated version of the drawLine() function. Update the existing function to look like this:

```
function drawLine(evt:TimerEvent):void {
    var j:int = 0;
    var x:Number = 0;
    var y:Number = 0;
    var n:int = 0;
    var zAbs:int = 0;
    for (j = -240; j <= 100; j++) {
        x = 0;
        y = 0;
        n = 0;
        do {
            n++;
            zArr = f(x, y, j / 100, k / 100);
            x = zArr[0];
            y = zArr[1];
            zAbs = zArr[2];
            if (n >= 20) {
                break;
            }
        } while (zAbs <= 4);
        if (zAbs > 4) {
            image.graphics.lineStyle(1, colors[n], 100);
            image.graphics.moveTo(j, k - 1);
            image.graphics.lineTo(j, k);
        }
    }
    k++;
    if (k >= 0) {
        myTimer.stop();
        duplicate();
    }
}
```

Not a whole lot changes, as you can see. The function now accepts a parameter, as required by the `TimerEvent` class, and its return value is changed from `Void` to the lowercase `void`. Appropriate `Number` types are changed to `int`, and the Drawing API is now routed through a `Graphics` instance, as referenced by the `Sprite.graphics` property. Rather than `clearInterval()`, the timer is halted by way of the `Timer.stop()` method.

4. Finally, here are the ActionScript 3.0 versions of the `f()` and `duplicate()` functions. Update the last blocks of code to look like this:

```
function f(x:Number, y:Number, a:Number, b:Number):Array {
    var rPart:Number = x * x - y * y + a;
    var iPart:Number = 2 * x * y + b;
    return new Array(rPart, iPart, rPart * rPart + iPart * iPart);
}
function duplicate():void {
    var bmpData:BitmapData = new BitmapData(340, 120, true, 0x000000);
    var mat:Matrix = new Matrix(1, 0, 0, 1, 240, 120);
    bmpData.draw(image, mat);
    var bmp:Bitmap = new Bitmap(bmpData);
    bmp.scaleY = -1;
    bmp.y = 238;
    addChild(bmp);
    swapChildren(bmp, image);
    trace((getTimer() - startTime) / 1000);
}
```

The `f()` function doesn't change at all. Since ActionScript 3.0 no longer supports the equivalent of `MovieClip.duplicateMovieClip()`, the `duplicate()` function requires a few more lines than its ActionScript 2.0 counterpart. Here, the `BitmapData` class is used to take a snapshot of the pixels drawn into the `image` sprite. These pixels are drawn into a `Bitmap` object, and then flipped to provide the mirror image. Because the line segments are drawn into the upper-left quadrant of the sprite—that is, left of 0 in the x-axis and above 0 in the y-axis—a matrix object is used to reposition the pixels into the lower-right quadrant (240 pixels over and 120 pixels down).

5. Select Control→Test Movie to see the increased rendering speed. As an added bonus, note that rendering occurs even more quickly when the `image` sprite is added to the display list only after the Mandelbrot calculations are made. Add two slashes to line 6 of Step 2 to comment it out:

```
var image:Sprite = new Sprite();
image.x = 240;
image.y = 120;
//addChild(image);
```

and then insert the same line into the `duplicate()` function of Step 4.

```
function duplicate():void {
    var bmpData:BitmapData = new BitmapData(340, 120);
    var mat:Matrix = new Matrix(1, 0, 0, 1, 240, 120);
    bmpData.draw(image, mat);
    var bmp:Bitmap = new Bitmap(bmpData);
    bmp.scaleY = -1;
    bmp.y = 238;
    addChild(image);
    addChild(bmp);
    swapChildren(bmp, image);
    trace((getTimer() - startTime) / 1000);
}
```

This step can shave off an additional second from the total elapsed time. Thanks again to Keith Gladstien, PhD, MD (*http://www.kglad.com/*) for input.

Efficiency

Imagine a warehouse with numerous and greatly varied products: everything from Fabergé eggs to collectible trading cards to garden rakes. In order to make shipping very easy, the warehouse manager has stocked a limited range of cardboard box sizes; in fact, all their dimensions are the same, one size fits all. As hoped for, everything is indeed easy to pack. The rakes fit into the boxes just fine, and so do the eggs and cards—it's just that anything smaller than a rake also needs several bucketsful of Styrofoam peanuts. For small shipments, this arrangement isn't so bad, but the trading cards happen to belong to a collectible franchise named Pokémon. One of these days—and the phenomenon will seem to explode overnight—several thousand customers are going to order individually wrapped packs of cards within the span of one week. When that happens, a vein will start to throb on the manager's forehead. Obviously, the packaging for these cards will take up more room than necessary —considerably more—and it may not be possible to fit all the required boxes on the shipping dock.

Thanks mainly to the addition of runtime types in ActionScript 3.0, Flash Players 9 and 10 can generally avoid this sort of scenario. To continue the somewhat loose analogy, you can think of runtime types as a well-organized assortment of custom-fitted cardboard boxes. Because the boxes aren't any larger than they need to be, storing them becomes a relatively efficient endeavor. In the real world, AVM2 is capable of requesting, or *allocating*, only the system memory it needs to create the objects called for by the various classes used in your code. Not only that, but the hierarchy of native ActionScript 3.0 classes has been considerably reorganized to take better advantage of a tiered system of complexity.

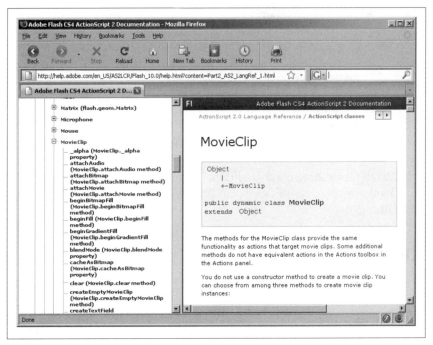

Figure 4-3. In ActionScript 2.0, the MovieClip class isn't compartmentalized

A quick look at the MovieClip class illustrates this principle, though the same notion applies to most other ActionScript 3.0 classes. First, consider the ActionScript 2.0 implementation of MovieClip. Consulting the ActionScript 2.0 Language Reference in the onboard documentation, you'll find that the family tree for the MovieClip class is remarkably small. This class inherits from the Object class alone (Figure 4-3), which is the base class upon which all classes are established.

This characteristic means the ActionScript 2.0 version of the MovieClip class carries practically all its own baggage. As often as not, this makes it heavier than it needs to be from the standpoint of system resources. If you want a visual object whose movement you can program around the stage, MovieClip is generally the most appropriate choice in ActionScript 2.0. All you really need for this sort of movement is a pair of properties that relate to the movie clip's x and y coordinates. The ActionScript 2.0 MovieClip class delivers the _x and _y properties right to your fingertips—but you also get a number of properties you don't really need in this situation, such as _currentframe and _total frames (you won't be using the movie clip's timeline), in addition to timeline-related methods like play(), stop(), gotoAndPlay(), and so on. Even worse, the ActionScript 2.0 version of MovieClip includes a method for loading external assets (loadMovie()), and several more for drawing shapes (lineStyle(),

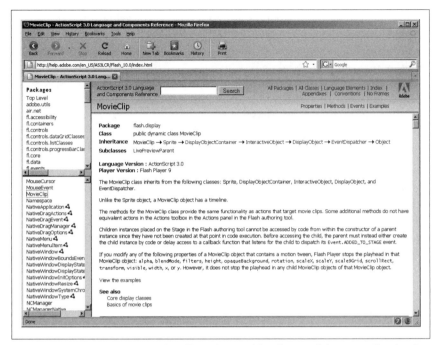

Figure 4-4. In ActionScript 3.0, the efficiently tiered family tree of the MovieClip class lets you control the size of the object you need

moveTo(), lineTo(), curveTo(), and others). These additional class members add to the overall weight of every MovieClip instance, even if you don't use them.

In ActionScript 3.0, the MovieClip class acquires most of its functionality from the Sprite class (Figure 4-4). In fact, movie clips *are* sprites; they're just sprites with timelines. In turn, the Sprite class inherits most of its functionality from DisplayObjectContainer, which inherits most of its features from InteractiveObject, then DisplayObject, EventDispatcher, and finally Object— each type getting progressively simpler toward the parent side and taking up a smaller footprint of system memory.

If you don't need the overhead of a timeline, use Sprite for your programmatic animation. It has x and y properties, but isn't encumbered by currentFrame or totalFrames properties, nor by the aforementioned timeline- or drawing-related methods. The Sprite class still lets you draw shapes—which means the ActionScript 3.0 MovieClip class does as well—but this set of functionality is deferred to the new Graphics class, and is associated with a given sprite or movie clip by way of its graphics property. Loading duties are separated altogether, and are the new Loader class's responsibility.

By strongly typing your variables and function return values in ActionScript 3.0, you give explicit instructions to the compiler to pack its goods into the sort of cardboard boxes that fit like a glove. Strong typing requires nothing more than a colon (:) and data type name.

```
var intergerValue:int = 1;
var nonIntegerValue:Number = 1.2;
var aSprite:Sprite = new Sprite();

var someFunction():void {
    // function code here
}
```

It's true that variables and function return values could be strongly typed in ActionScript 2.0, and doing so was useful: the practice facilitated authoring tool assistance like code hinting, and provided more comprehensive error warnings at compile time—but compile time is where the benefits ended. Once a SWF file is produced, AVM1 loses any remembrance of an object's type. AVM2 remembers.

Consistency

Ironically, one of ActionScript 3.0's most elegant aspects is a potential stumbling block to longtime Flash developers, only because, as the adage goes, old habits die hard. Flash pioneers will remember when on() and onClipEvent() were not only the most popular ways to handle button and movie clip events, they were the *only* way. If you wanted to repeatedly trigger a custom function or simply a handful of instructions, you could associate your intentions with, say, the enterFrame event of a particular movie clip symbol. You could select the symbol, open the Actions panel—which was then temporarily linked to that symbol—and then type something like this:

```
onClipEvent(enterFrame) {
    // responsive code here
}
```

If you wanted to handle another event, you would use the same onClipEvent() function (the same formatting), in cahoots with that other event. Both event handlers were attached to the object in question:

```
onClipEvent(enterFrame) {
    // responsive code here
}
onClipEvent(release) {
    // mouse-related code here
}
```

When Flash MX hit the scene a few years later, the same basic concept took on a new alternative procedure, which was optional. In this other approach, event handling code could be attached to frames instead of directly to objects. This meant the desired recipient of your instructions—a movie clip, button, or the like—now needed an instance name, otherwise ActionScript would have no idea which object you were talking to. Instance names were usually provided by way of the Property inspector, but could also be determined by code. In the new format, dot notation provided the necessary association (here, the instance name is *myClip*):

```
myClip.onEnterFrame = function():Void {
    // responsive code here, inside
    // an anonymous function literal
}
myClip.onRelease = aNamedCustomFunction;
function aNamedCustomFunction():Void {
    // mouse-related code here, inside
    // a named function definition
}
```

The dot notation approach brought with it a number of benefits that often went unnoticed.

- Finer grained control
  - 11 button events, versus the previous 8
  - 18 movie clip events, versus the previous 9
- Easier maintenance, because code could be stored in a single frame, rather than scattered among potentially dozens of objects
- More flexibility, as events could be assigned, deleted, and changed programmatically

As new versions of Flash Player continued to bring new functionality, two additional event handling mechanisms entered the developer's lexicon: an addListener() method, used by such classes as Stage, MovieClipLoader, Key, and Mouse, and an addEventListener() method, used by ActionScript 2.0 components. Both of these new formats worked in a similar way, requiring an Object instance to act as liaison between the object in question and the methods defined by its class. The two could even share the same listener object:

```
var listener:Object = new Object();
listener.onKeyUp = keyUpHandler;
listener.click = clickHandler;

function keyUpHandler():Void {
    // keyboard-related code here
}
function clickHandler(evt:Object):Void {
    // button component code here
}
```

```
Key.addListener(listener);
myComponentButton.addEventListener("click", listener);
```

Because these additions happened over subsequent releases of the Flash authoring tool, longtime developers could add them piecemeal to their skill sets, but you can easily see how a newcomer might be mystified by so many choices.

In ActionScript 3.0, event handling has very nearly been consolidated into a single consistent approach, similar to the one used by ActionScript 2.0 components. In fact, the only exception happens with the NetStream class, and even then, only when you need to respond to video metadata or cue points. The exception still makes use of an Object instance, and shares many elements of the listener mechanisms in ActionScript 2.0 (exception cases in bold):

```
var nc:NetConnection = new NetConnection();
nc.connect(null);
var ns:NetStream = new NetStream(nc);
videoPlayer.attachNetStream(ns);

var listener:Object = new Object();
listener.onMetaData = metaDataHandler;
listener.onCuePoint = cuePointHandler;

function metaDataHandler(evt:Object):void {
    // meta data code here
}
function cuePointHandler(evt:Object):void {
    // cue point code here
}

ns.client = listener;
ns.play("someVideoFile.flv");
```

Everything else uses the new EventDispatcher.addEventListener() method, which is inherited by all classes capable of dispatching events. Inheritance provides this event listening method in the same way it provides Sprite methods (and other functionality) to the MovieClip class, as touched on in the section entitled "Efficiency" on page 93 of this chapter. Events of all of these objects—movie clips, buttons, components, text fields, the stage, sounds, programmatic tweens, instances of the new Timer class, and more—are handled the same way far and wide.

```
// Assuming instances of MovieClip, TextField, and Tween ...
myClip.addEventListener(Event.ENTER_FRAME, enterFrameHandler);
myTextField.addEventListener(Event.SCROLL, scrollHandler);
myTween.addEventListener(TweenEvent.MOTION_FINISH,¬
    motionFinishHandler);

function enterFrameHandler(evt:Event):void {
    // responsive code here
}
```

```
function scrollHandler(evt:Event):void {
    // scroll-related code here
}
function motionFinishHandler(evt:TweenEvent):void {
    // tween-related code here
}
```

 For additional examples of ActionScript 3.0 event handling, see the section "Creating DragParrot, a Sample Class File" on page 33 in Chapter 2; the section "ActionScript Can No Longer Be Attached to Objects" on page 117 in Chapter 5; and the practical examples in Part III and Part IV of this book.

In addition to bringing together a consistent event handling model, Action-Script 3.0 unifies the approach employed to instantiate objects. In previous versions of ActionScript, you could easily create, for example, an array, string, or generic Object instance. The new statement neatly took care of it:

```
var a:Array = new Array();
var s:String = new String();
var o:Object = new Object();
```

Of course, some objects, such as these, had optional shortcut constructors (and still do):

```
var a:Array = [];
var s:String = "";
var o:Object = {};
```

but in either case, the construction of the desired object was a tidy process.

For other ActionScript 2.0 classes, notably MovieClip and TextField, it wasn't so graceful. Instantiation of these objects required an existing MovieClip instance (often the main timeline, often referred to with this), to use the createEmptyMovieClip() and createTextField() methods:

```
var mc:MovieClip = this.createEmptyMovieClip("myClip", ¬
    this.getNextHighestDepth());
var tf:TextField = this.createTextField("myTextField", ¬
    this.getNextHighestDepth(), 0, 0, 100, 22);
```

As these objects were created, the MovieClip instance on which these methods were invoked became the immediate parent of the new movie clip or text field. In the code shown, this parent is the main timeline, via this, but any movie clip instance name would do, in which case the referenced movie clip would become the new object's parent. Once it was established, you couldn't change this parent/child relationship.

In ActionScript 3.0, even movie clips and text fields can be constructed with the new statement:

```
var mc:MovieClip = new MovieClip();
var tf:TextField = new TextField();
```

At this point, the mc and tf variables are bona fide instances of their respective classes. The movie clip can be drawn into with the Drawing API, positioned and animated over time. You can assign the text field plain text or HTML formatted text, and so on. When either object is ready for display, it can be added to the display list of any descendant of the DisplayObjectContainer class, which includes the main timeline, movie clips, sprites, and any class that supports the addChild() method. In this way, you can reparent visual objects in ActionScript 3.0 as often as you like.

 For more information on the display list concept, see the practical examples in Part IV of this book.

Standards and Portability Among Other Technologies

If your Flash development has led you into parallel work with HTML/ XHTML, CSS, and JavaScript, you may already be familiar with the benefits of adherence to standards. The stakes in web development differ from those in Flash, because web developers have to make sure their content displays and behaves nearly the same—or, ideally, exactly the same—across a potentially sizeable number of browsers. This can be a sublimely challenging task, but the effort is reduced when browser manufacturers acknowledge and uphold the specifications on which these languages and technologies are based.

In contrast, Flash Player provides, for the most part, a single consistent runtime across any browser or operating system that supports the ActiveX control or plug-in. In the world of Flash development, the discipline involved in adhering to standards has already been taken care of. Adobe has leveraged this cohesive approach to let Flash developers step into the realms of Flex and AIR with relative ease. How? Because all of these tools rely on the same ActionScript 3.0 language, even though Flex and AIR support additional features.

Flex (*http://www.adobe.com/products/flex/*) is a highly productive, free open source platform for building and maintaining expressive web applications. The Flex framework, which includes dozens of visual layout components, user interface components, and data classes for connection to databases and web services, is written in ActionScript 3.0. This means that even though the Flex API contains new functionality, it operates with the same principles of performance, efficiency, and consistency demonstrated earlier in this chapter. Though its output overlaps with the sort of applications traditionally associated with Java or the .NET platform, Flex runs on ActionScript 3.0. If your interests lead you in the direction of Rich Internet Applications (RIAs), you'll find that your barrier to entry is significantly reduced when you choose Flex as your path.

The Adobe Integrated Runtime (AIR) (*http://www.adobe.com/products/air/*) lets Flash, Flex, and Dreamweaver developers use their existing skills to build applications that deploy to the desktop. AIR integrates elements of the WebKit browser engine (used by Safari), Flash Player 10, and Acrobat to provide a rich environment for combining the benefits of traditional web technologies like HTML, CSS, and JavaScript with the multimedia aspects of Flash and the PDF file format. AIR also works with the SQLite database management system. Even among these varied avenues, ActionScript 3.0 provides a familiar apparatus for channeling the unique strengths of each into a unified user experience.

ActionScript and the Flash CS4 Authoring Tool

Part II explores using the new paradigms of ActionScript 3.0 as they pertain to the Flash CS4 authoring tool. These chapters walk you through the Actions panel, help you decide when to use frame scripts as opposed to class files, and how to rethink the `on()`/`onClipEvent()` approach to event handling. You'll learn about the benefits of a document class and how to work with linkage changes, and see examples of how to dynamically attach movie clips, bitmap images, audio files, and fonts at runtime.

By the time you're through, you'll also be able to convert timeline animation into ActionScript (and then manipulate and reuse that code); use, skin, and style user interface components; work beyond the built-in component set, including some of the missing data components; and troubleshoot your code in the debugging workspace when things go awry.

Chapter 5, *Creating and Working with Code*

Chapter 6, *Creating a Document Class*

Chapter 7, *Working with Library and Linkage Changes*

Chapter 8, *Copying Motion as ActionScript 3.0*

Chapter 9, *Using ActionScript 3.0 Components*

Chapter 10, *Making Up for a Reduced Component Set*

Chapter 11, *Debugging and Troubleshooting*

Creating and Working with Code

Chapter 2 introduced the idea that ActionScript can be associated with a FLA file in more ways than one. Your approach is typically contingent on the complexity of a project and the manner in which certain visual effects are achieved. For example, you might be involved in a project that contains numerous timeline animations—think in terms of an interactive corporate mascot, whose responsiveness depends on a collection of canned manual tweens. This may require at least some code in selected keyframes of the animated timeline(s) in question. On the other hand, your project might consist of nothing more than a custom video player, in which case every asset could appear inside a single frame, and possibly be generated entirely with code. In this latter case, most or all of your ActionScript might be stored outside the authoring tool altogether.

In a nutshell, ActionScript 3.0 code can be placed in:

- Keyframes of a movie clip timeline, often the main timeline

- External code snippets, which are external text files with an *.as* extension, formatted just like keyframe code and brought into a timeline with the `include` directive

- Custom classes, which are also external text files with an *.as* extension, but structured with the `package` definition and `class` definition keywords and referenced by a timeline with the `import` directive

In ActionScript 2.0, you could also attach code directly to objects—not just to keyframes, but to the "surface" of movie clip symbols, buttons, and components—by way of the Actions panel or the Behaviors panel. ActionScript 3.0 no longer supports this ability. In fact, the Behaviors panel is disabled when a FLA file's publish settings are configured for ActionScript 3.0. The implications of this change are discussed in the section "Exploring New Features in the Actions Panel and Script Windows," later in this chapter.

Although you can use third-party script editors in conjunction with Flash CS3 Professional (see Chapter 2), the Actions panel is likely your most convenient first stop when it comes to timeline code. This is true for the simple reason that timeline code is physically attached to a FLA file's keyframes, so its placement requires the authoring tool regardless of where the code is created. For relatively simple projects, it takes less effort to type your ActionScript directly into the Actions panel than to continuously swap between the authoring tool and another editor. If you find yourself getting cramped in the Actions panel, especially in complex projects, that might be a nudge to consider moving your code to external files, possibly formatting them as custom classes. An example of this is shown in the section "Associating FLA Files to AS Files" in this chapter.

Thinking in Terms of the Timeline

When you use the Actions panel, keep in mind that your code operates under the auspices of a *timeline metaphor*, a workflow immediately familiar to Flash designers and people who work with video editing software. During authoring, the Timeline and Motion Editor provide a draggable playhead (Figure 5-1) that manages the display of visual elements present in a given frame (that is, in a given moment of time). As you drag the playhead manually along a timeline, you can watch as each keyframe updates the visual display, often in conjunction with motion tweens and shape tweens. At runtime, a SWF file proceeds in the same manner, executing ActionScript as the playhead enters any keyframe that contains code.

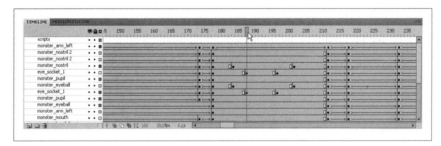

Figure 5-1. The Timeline playhead triggers both code and display updates

 Only the Timeline works in conjunction with the Actions panel. The Motion Editor is strictly designed for visual content.

In fact, ActionScript takes higher priority than visual updates. When Flash Player encounters a keyframe, it first executes any ActionScript it finds, and only then updates the display. This distinction is subtle, but important. Consider the following example, in which a for loop is mistakenly used to update the position of a movie clip with the instance name *myClip*:

```
// Incorrect code
for (var i:int = 0; i < 50; i++) {
    myClip.x += 2;
}
```

The expression inside this loop, myClip.x += 2, increments the x property of *myClip* by 2 pixels on each turn. This may give the impression that *myClip* will inch to the right in 2-pixel steps, traveling a total of 100 pixels over time, but that isn't what actually happens. In practice, the movie clip jumps immediately to the right—the full distance. Why? When the playhead enters this frame, Flash Player executes the for loop first, all in one go, and only then updates the visual elements of the frame, including *myClip*. By the time that update happens, the value of x has already been increased to 100.

To successfully animate this movement with ActionScript, you could use an Event.ENTER_FRAME handler, which triggers its instructions every time the playhead enters a frame. This action happens even when the playhead has been halted with a stop() method (think of the playhead as an idling engine that rotates even when the car is standing still).

```
myClip.addEventListener(Event.ENTER_FRAME, slideClip);

function slideClip(evt:Event):void {
    if (myClip.x < 100) {
        myClip.x += 2;
    } else {
        myClip.removeEventListener(Event.ENTER_FRAME, ¬
            slideClip);
    }
}
```

In this revision, the x property of myClip is incremented only once per frame entry. The if statement removes the event listener, which has been triggering slideClip(), when x reaches 100.

In another approach, you could use the Tween class and one of the many easing classes located in the same fl.transitions package:

```
import fl.transitions.Tween;
import fl.transitions.easing.*;

var tw:Tween = new Tween(myClip, "x", Strong.easeInOut, ¬
    0, 100, 1.5, true);
```

This time, the related classes must be imported. The first line brings in Tween, and the second line brings in all the classes of the easing package in one swoop, thanks to the wildcard character (*): Regular, Strong, Elastic, Bounce, Back, and None. A variable is declared—here, tw—and instructions are given by way of a series of parameters. Again, *myClip* is moved along its x-axis, using a combination strong ease in/ease out. The starting position is 0, and the destination is 100. Here, the tween lasts 1.5 seconds (the final parameter, true, interprets the previous parameter in terms of seconds, rather than frames).

Thanks to looping mechanisms like Event.ENTER_FRAME and Tween, a single frame of ActionScript can perform animation that might otherwise span hundreds or even thousands of frames. This can be a tremendous advantage, but even so, certain scenarios demand an artist's touch.

Figure 5-2 shows an interactive cartoon character, Grotto, created by Chris Georgenes (*http://mudbubble.com/*). Grotto "sleeps" until the user "disturbs" him by moving the mouse cursor over his massive form. If the user chooses not to, the animation simply loops and Grotto slumbers on.

The required programming isn't especially difficult, but it can become over-complicated if forced into a single frame. Here, the movie clip's instance name, appropriately enough, is *grotto*:

```
grotto.addEventListener(Event.ENTER_FRAME, slumber);
function slumber(evt:Event):void {
    if (grotto.currentFrame == 129) {
        grotto.gotoAndPlay(1);
    }
    if (grotto.currentFrame == grotto.totalFrames) {
        grotto.stop();
    }
}

grotto.addEventListener(MouseEvent.MOUSE_OVER, wake);
function wake(evt:MouseEvent):void {
    grotto.gotoAndPlay(174);
}
```

Two event handlers run the show here. First, an Event.ENTER_FRAME handler checks the MovieClip.currentFrame property of *grotto* to see if that movie clip's current frame equals 129, which happens to be a good place to loop the playhead. If currentFrame indeed equals 129, *grotto* is instructed to play again from frame 1 of its own timeline, which loops the sleeping sequence. Second, a MouseEvent.MOUSE_OVER handler breaks out of this loop by sending *grotto* directly to frame 174, which leads to frames in which the monster opens his eyes. Back in the Enter.ENTER_FRAME handler, if currentFrame equals the total number of frames in that timeline—in other words, if the full animation has run its course—*grotto* is instructed to stop.

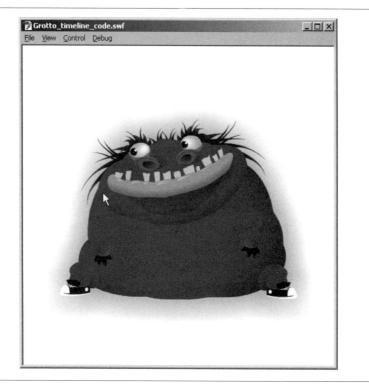

Figure 5-2. An interactive character responding to the mouse cursor ("Grotto" character created by Chris Georgenes, http://mudbubble.com, used with permission)

This code's problem is that the `Event.ENTER_FRAME` handler incessantly triggers the custom `slumber()` function. At a default frame rate of 24 frames per second (fps), `slumber()` would be executed approximately every 42 milliseconds! As it turns out, this particular FLA file has a frame rate of 30fps, which makes the situation even worse. In spite of all this triggering, the value of `currentFrame` meets the criteria for action on only two possible frames. Clearly, this code isn't as efficient or easy to work with as it could be!

Here's another approach.

By adding a few short lines of code to keyframes in the *grotto* timeline, you can drop the convoluted event handler altogether, leaving only the `MouseEvent.MOUSE_OVER` handler:

```
grotto.addEventListener(MouseEvent.MOUSE_OVER, wake);
function wake(evt:MouseEvent):void {
    grotto.gotoAndPlay(174);
}
```

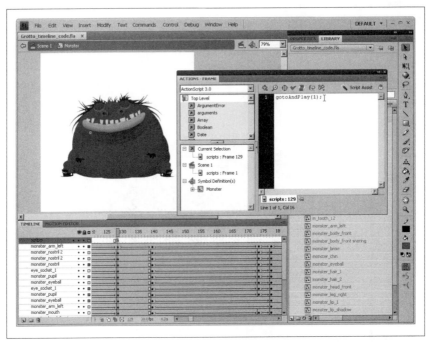

Figure 5-3. The selected frame determines where the Actions panel attaches its code ("Grotto" character created by Chris Georgenes, http://mudbubble.com, used with permission)

That's the same wake() function as before; no changes. Meanwhile, the functionality previously managed by the Event.ENTER_FRAME handler is now provided by two effortless frame scripts in the *grotto* timeline:

```
// In frame 129 of the grotto movie clip:
gotoAndPlay(1);
```

```
// In frame 810 of the grotto movie clip:
stop();
```

To attach ActionScript to a desired frame, simply select that frame in the Timeline, and then add a new keyframe (Insert→Timeline→Keyframe). With the keyframe selected, open the Actions panel, and then start typing, as shown in Figure 5-3. If the Actions panel is already open, it automatically updates to point to the selected keyframe.

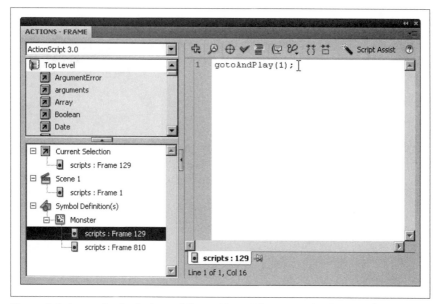

Figure 5-4. A tree view in the lower left provides quick access to keyframe code

ActionScript can be attached to any keyframe of any layer, but this practice often leads to confusion, as code may become lost among potentially hundreds of keyframes and layers. As a best practice, Adobe recommends that, when code is present, you should place it in a dedicated scripts layer at the top of any timeline. This action puts code keyframes in immediate view. Most developers name this layer `scripts` or `actions`, but the name doesn't matter as long as it descriptively distinguishes the layer.

Note that the lower-left corner of the Actions panel (Figure 5-4) offers a hierarchical tree view of coded keyframes in the main timeline (Scene 1), as well as coded keyframes in the timelines of movie clip symbols. In this case, only one symbol exists (the animated character named Monster in the library—*grotto* is the instance name), but additional symbols would be just as easy to locate in this area. You can select frames either by clicking a keyframe of the Timeline or, for quicker access, clicking one of the tree view nodes. At bottom-center, a pushpin icon lets you open the scripts of more than one frame at a time.

That discussion covers the basics of how to attach code to keyframes. The actual writing of code happens in the Script pane on the right side, which is

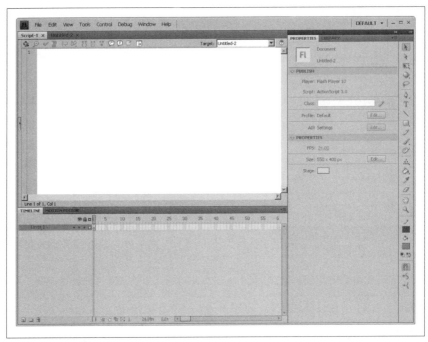

Figure 5-5. Script windows, which edit external ActionScript file, are displayed as tabbed documents

handier than ever thanks to a number of enhancements introduced in Flash CS3 and still present in Flash CS4.

New Features in the Actions Panel and Script Windows

When a FLA file is configured for ActionScript 3.0, the Flash authoring tool provides two interfaces for writing code: the Actions panel and Script windows. You use the Actions panel, available under Window→Actions, for creating and editing code attached to timeline keyframes, as seen earlier in this chapter.

Script windows are used for creating and editing code stored in external ActionScript files. Just like FLA files, Script windows are displayed as tabbed documents rather than in a panel. As Figure 5-5 shows, the selection of a Script window temporarily disables authoring tool panels, which become active again when a FLA file is selected. To open a Script window, select File→New→ActionScript file, or open an existing ActionScript file.

The features of both the Actions panel and Script windows overlap considerably. Flash professionals will already be familiar with the features carried over

Figure 5-6. The Actions panel toolbar

from previous versions of the authoring tool, but to cover the bases, the next sections provide a brief overview of existing features before launching into the new items.

Actions Panel

Figure 5-6 shows the Actions panel's toolbar, whose buttons are described from left to right.

- **Add a New Item to the Script:** Provides a list of the full ActionScript 3.0 *application programming interface* (API). Select and click to add properties, methods, and events to the current position of the cursor in the Script pane.

- **Find:** Opens a Find and Replace dialog box.

- **Insert a Target Path:** Opens an Insert Target Path dialog box with a tree view of targettable objects, such as movie clips, text fields, buttons, and components, by instance name. Select the desired target, and then click OK to add the target path to the current position of the cursor in the Script pane.

- **Check Syntax:** Provides guidance for some—but not all—syntax errors. This feature is not as thorough as the compiler errors, compiler warnings, and runtime errors discussed in Chapter 11.

- **Auto Format:** Formats Actions panel code according to user preferences set using Edit→Preferences→Auto Format (Flash→Preferences→Auto Format). Erroneous code can't be formatted, so this button acts as a kind of secondary syntax checker.

- **Show Code Hint:** Displays a tooltip with expected parameters when the cursor is positioned immediately after a method call's first parenthesis.

- **Debug Options:** Adds and removes breakpoints, and clears all breakpoints. Breakpoints are discussed in detail in Chapter 11.

- **Show/Hide Toolbox:** Shows and hides the Actions panel's left side.

- **Script Assist:** Isn't covered in this book, as the feature isn't especially useful with ActionScript 3.0.

- **Help:** Opens the onboard documentation in a browser.

The following is erroneous code which the Check Syntax button failed to catch:

```
var num:int = 1;
var num:int = 2;
```

In ActionScript 3.0, variables can't be declared more than once in the same scope. If you run the syntax checker against these two lines, you get a message saying, "This script contains no errors," which is misleading. The syntax checker also misses capitalization errors, such as `tracE()` or `trAce()`, and is dependable only in terms of gross structural syntax. For confident testing, watch the Compiler Errors panel during the compile process.

Collapsible code sections

As of Flash CS3, the Actions panel supports collapsible code sections, a practice known as *code folding*. This feature lets you temporarily condense one or more lines of text into a stand-in button, which helps reduce clutter in long or complex passages of code. The collapsed button displays the first few characters of the folded text for easy identification (see Figure 5-7). Line numbering is properly accounted for. Hovering over the button causes a tooltip to display a longer excerpt of the folded text, and double-clicking expands the code to its original state. Collapsed sections can be nested, and are saved with the FLA file, so they're remembered when you close and reopen the authoring tool.

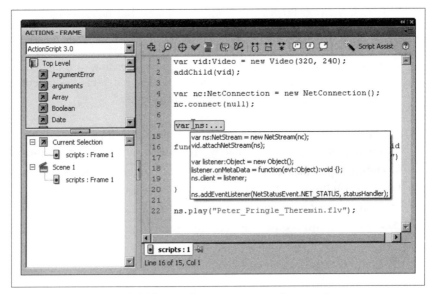

Figure 5-7. Collapsed code folds into a button you can easily expand

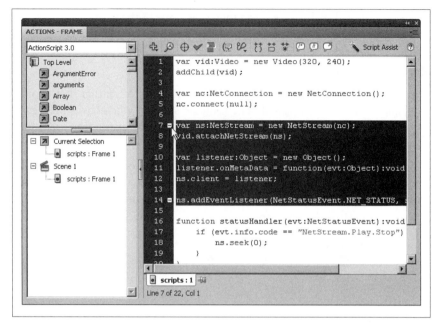

Figure 5-8. Selecting code displays a pair of minus (Windows) or arrow (Mac) icons

To collapse a section of code, use the mouse or arrow keys to select a number of adjacent lines. A pair of minus icons (Windows) or arrow icons (Mac) appear to the left of the selection (Figure 5-8). You have the following options for collapsing the code:

- Click one of the minus or arrow icons.
- Click the 🔆 Collapse Between Braces button in the Actions panel toolbar.
- Click the 🔆 Collapse Section button in the Actions panel toolbar. Holding Alt while clicking collapses code outside the selection.
- Right-click (Ctrl-click) the selection, and then choose one of the collapse-related options:
  - Collapse Between Braces doesn't require a selection, and folds text between two curly braces ({}) when the cursor is positioned between such braces.
  - Collapse Selection folds the current selection.
  - Collapse Outside Section folds everything but the current selection.

To expand a previously collapsed section of code, choose any of the following:

- Double-click the folded text, which looks like a button.

- Right-click (Ctrl-click), and then select one of the expand options.
- Click the ⁂ Expand All button in the Actions panel toolbar.

Shortcuts for quickly adding and removing code comments

Now you can handle code commenting with a few clicks, rather than typing. This may seem like a marginal benefit, like a sprinter who shaves his legs to gain a few seconds, but every little bit helps. For every distraction cast aside, you gain additional time and focus spent on actual coding.

Commenting lets you add instructional notes to your code that are ignored by the compiler. You have two ways to comment. A line comment is designated by two slashes (//) in a given line, and affects only the line in which it appears:

```
// This handles the NET_STATUS event ...
function statusHandler(evt:NetStatusEvent):void {
    if (evt.info.code == "NetStream.Play.Stop") {
        removeChild(vid); // Removes video from
                          // the display list
    }
}
```

Note that a line comment can begin before or after executable code.

A block comment is also designated by a special character sequence, /* ... */, only this time, everything between those characters is affected:

```
/*
This handles the NET_STATUS event ...
function statusHandler(evt:NetStatusEvent):void {
    if (evt.info.code == "NetStream.Play.Stop") {
        removeChild(vid);
    }
}
*/
```

 Developers often use both block and line comments during troubleshooting to temporarily isolate regions of code.

You can certainly type these character sequences by hand, but using the new shortcuts will save you time. To comment out a region of code, use the mouse or arrow keys to select a number of adjacent lines. At this point, you have two options, either of which will do:

- Right-click (Ctrl-click) the selection, and then choose one of the comment-related options:
  - Apply /* */ Comment wraps the selection in a block comment

- Apply // Comment precedes each line in the selection with double slashes; if no selection is made, the double slashes appear wherever the cursor is positioned
- Click the 🗩 Apply block comment button or the 🗩 Apply line comment button in the Actions panel toolbar.

To uncomment a region of code, choose any of the following:

- Select the comment, right-click (Ctrl-click), and then choose Remove Comment
- Click the 🗩 Remove Comment button in the Actions panel's toolbar.

Script Windows

Figure 5-9 shows a Script window's toolbar. Of the buttons shown, every one performs exactly as described in the section "Actions Panel." The only difference is that Script windows don't feature a Script Assist button. Instead, they display a Target drop-down menu, which was introduced in Flash CS3.

Figure 5-9. A Script window toolbar

The Target drop-down list becomes active when one or more FLA files are open in addition to the current script document. The drop-down list displays each of the open FLA files and lets you specify which one should be compiled in concert with the current script document (when using Control→Test Movie or Debug→Debug Movie).

ActionScript Can No Longer Be Attached to Objects

In the earliest days of ActionScript, code could be attached directly to objects in much the same way it can be attached to frames. You can't attach code in the same manner in ActionScript 3.0. Direct attachment to objects was made possible by two functions, on() and onClipEvent(), which were supported as recently as ActionScript 2.0. In fact, these functions are still available in Flash CS4, but only when a FLA file's publish settings are configured for versions of ActionScript other than 3.0.

This change has a potentially significant impact on certain traditional Flash developer workflows. For example, the Behaviors panel replies on the on() and onClipEvent() functions for many of its behaviors. Because these functions are no longer supported, the Behaviors panel is disabled in FLA files that use the language's latest version.

If you were a fan of the Behaviors panel but find yourself wanting or needing to work in ActionScript 3.0, keep your chin up! The secret to this panel is that it's nothing more than a ghostwriter. It writes ActionScript, and so can you. Obviously, some uses of the Behaviors panel are more involved than others, but here's an investigative effort into reproducing some functionality by hand.

1. Create an ActionScript 3.0 FLA file. In the Timeline, rename the default layer to **information**. Use the Text tool to create a static text field with a paragraph of stand-in text, as shown in Figure 5-10.

2. Convert the text field to a movie clip symbol, and then give it the instance name *mcInfo* in the Property inspector.

3. Double-click the movie clip to enter its timeline. Select frame 2 in the timeline, and then add a keyframe. This action duplicates the text field in frame 1. Update the text field in frame 2 with different stand-in text.

4. Select Edit→Edit Document to return to the main timeline. Add a new layer, and then name it **buttons**. In the new layer, use one of the drawing tools to draw a shape, and then convert the shape to a button symbol. Drag a second instance of this button from the Library to the same new layer, as shown in Figure 5-11.

   If this were an ActionScript 2.0 FLA file, you could use the Behaviors panel to attach a prewritten code template to each button, instructing it to display its corresponding text field by sending *mcInfo* to the relevant keyframe. Instead, you're going to see how easy it can be to write this sort of ActionScript 3.0 by hand.

5. Use the Property inspector to give both button symbols an instance name. For this demonstration, use btnLeft and btnRight. Add a new layer to the main timeline for your code. Select frame 1 of this new layer, and then enter the following code into the Actions panel:

   ```
   mcInfo.stop();

   btnLeft.addEventListener(MouseEvent.CLICK, leftHandler);
   function leftHandler(evt:MouseEvent):void {
       mcInfo.gotoAndStop(1);
   }

   btnRight.addEventListener(MouseEvent.CLICK, rightHandler);
   function rightHandler(evt:MouseEvent):void {
       mcInfo.gotoAndStop(2);
   }
   ```

The first line tells *mcInfo* to stop where it is (frame 1), which displays the first text field. The remaining two code blocks associate mouse-related event handlers to the button symbols, using the same structure seen elsewhere throughout this chapter. Button symbols are defined by the `SimpleButton` class, which, like `MovieClip`, inherits functionality from the `EventDispatcher` class, including `addEventListener()`. This method partners an event with a custom function, as shown. Because this code appears in the same frame as the assets to which it refers, the playhead has no problem wiring up all the parts when it enters this frame during playback.

> For more information on the new event handling model, see Chapter 4, and the practical examples in Part III and Part IV of this book.

6. Select Control→Test Movie to verify that the buttons correctly update *mcInfo*.

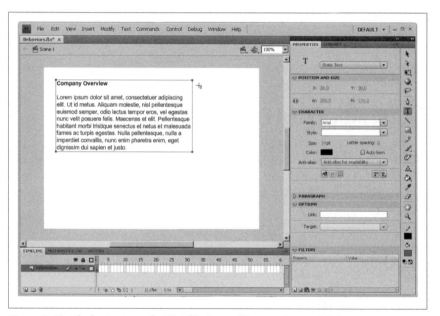

Figure 5-10. The beginnings of a FLA file that will be wired up with behaviors

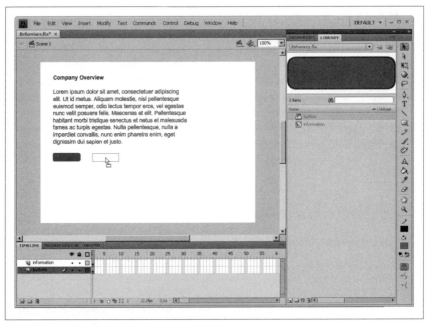

Figure 5-11. Dragging a second button into position

Setting ActionScript Preferences

Working with ActionScript in the Flash authoring tool is a customizable experience. You have several places to set your preferences, discussed in the following sections. Some of these preferences pertain to the appearance of code in the Actions panel and Script windows, while others affect the way Action-Script is compiled.

Preferences Dialog Box

Select Edit→Preferences (Flash→Preferences) to open the authoring tool's general Preferences dialog box. This dialog box influences Flash CS4 across the board, from ActionScript to the drawing tools, text characteristics, and how graphic assets are imported from other applications.

ActionScript

In the Preferences dialog box's Category list area, select ActionScript to review and edit ActionScript preferences (Figure 5-12).

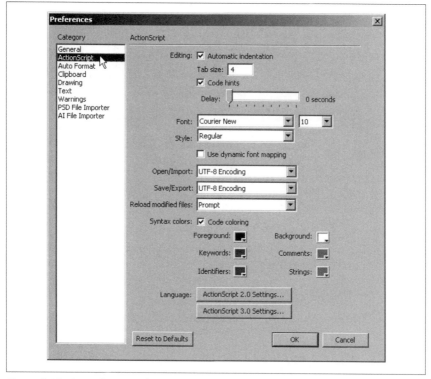

Figure 5-12. ActionScript preferences

Most of these settings affect the appearance of code in the Actions panel and Script windows, including font face and size, the tab size for optional automatic indentation, and configurable syntax colors for optional code coloring. You can toggle code hinting here, and delay tooltips for code hinting in quarter-second increments from 0 to 4 seconds.

The ActionScript 3.0 Settings button manages source and library path settings for built-in and custom class packages, as well as SWC files (components built in Flash or Flex) that bundle ActionScript and/or visual assets. Clicking this button opens a dialog box named ActionScript 3.0 Advanced Settings, with four areas to specify file paths (Figure 5-13).

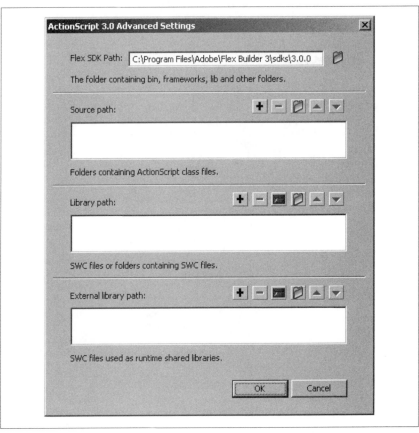

Figure 5-13. The ActionScript 3.0 Advanced Settings dialog box manages Source and Library path settings

- **Flex SDK Path:** Only necessary when a FLA file collaborates with assets from the Flex framework. Without such collaboration, Flash documents ignore this field. By default, this path points to a file named *flex.swc*, installed with Flash CS4, but you can change this path to a different location of the Flex Software Development Kit (SDK)—such as the install folder for Flex Builder 3, for example—if you prefer.

- **Source Path:** In Flash CS3, this setting was formerly configured with two paths: a dot (.) indicating the FLA file's current folder, and *$(AppConfig)/ActionScript 3.0/Classes*, which pointed to the built-in, or *intrinsic*, classes native to ActionScript 3.0. In Flash CS4, these paths are located in a per-FLA dialog box discussed in the "Flash Publish Settings" on page 124 of this chapter. Because these paths are now located elsewhere, this setting is empty in this dialog box. You can optionally add paths to custom classes, including third-party code distributed as AS files, by clicking the ⊞ Add New Path button, and then clicking the 🗁 Browse to Path button.

- **Library Path:** Developers can distribute their ActionScript as AS files or SWC files. The difference is primarily that the SWC format can hold numerous files—including the subfolders that represent package structures —in a single archive, like ZIP or SIT files. This provides a degree of protection because a SWC's contents are self-contained. If you want FLA files to use third-party code stored in SWC files, click the ⊞ Add New Path button, and then click the 🖿 Browse to SWC File button to point to a SWC file or the 🗁 Browse to Path button to point to a folder of SWC files.

- **External Library Path:** This setting follows the same concept as Library Path, but for SWC files that contain visual or audio assets for use as runtime shared libraries. This provides developers a way to re-use elements stored in a central location, which is useful in team settings.

The Source Path setting, also known as a *classpath setting*, tells the compiler where to look for corresponding AS files when classes are referenced in ActionScript 3.0 code. If you write a custom class file (touched on later in this chapter), you can safely compile when your AS file is located in the same folder as the FLA file that uses it. You'll soon realize, however, how handy it is to keep a full library of custom class files within reach. This is where the Source Path setting becomes useful.

In Windows, for example, you might keep a folder named *ActionScript 3.0 Classes* inside your *My Documents* folder. If you have a library of custom sound classes arranged in a package called `com.loudmouth.sound`, it means your *ActionScript 3.0 Classes* folder contains a subfolder named *com*, which in turn contains nested subfolders *loudmouth* and *sound*, which finally contain the custom class files in question. Adding the location of *My Documents\Action Script 3.0 Classes* to your Source Path setting lets you reference these custom classes in the same manner as built-in classes. For example, to reference any class inside the `com.loudmouth.sound` package, you could use the `import` directive like this: `import com.loudmouth.sound.*`. After this line, classes in the custom package can be referenced by class name alone, just like the built-in `MovieClip` class.

Auto Format

In the Preferences dialog box's Category list area, select Auto Format to review and edit formatting preferences for ActionScript (Figure 5-14).

A handful of checkboxes let you specify your styling choices for ActionScript code. A text area gives you a visual preview.

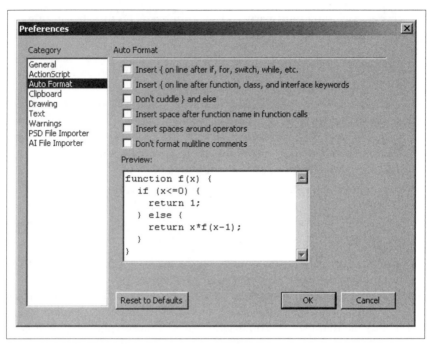

Figure 5-14. Auto Format preferences for ActionScript

The Auto Format feature is best suited for frame scripts. Using it with external class files often formats that code incorrectly, sometimes rendering it unusable.

Flash Publish Settings

With an ActionScript 3.0 FLA file open, select File→Publish Settings→Flash→Settings to open a FLA-file–specific equivalent to the Action-Script 3.0 Advanced Settings dialog box (Figure 5-15) discussed earlier. This dialog box offers one of the two locations to specify a FLA file's *document class* (see Chapter 6 for details), as well as source and library path settings that may be pertinent to only the document at hand. Notice the dot (.) entry in the Source Path tab. The Library path tab contains the default path *$(AppConfig)/ActionScript 3.0/libs*, which points to the Flash CS4 intrinsic files for Action-Script 3.0. You can specify additional classpaths and SWC files as described in the "ActionScript" subsection of the "Preferences Dialog Box" on page 120 earlier in this chapter.

By default, when classes are compiled into a SWF file, these classes are exported into frame 1. In most cases this is appropriate, but advanced developers may choose to override this setting by changing the frame number displayed.

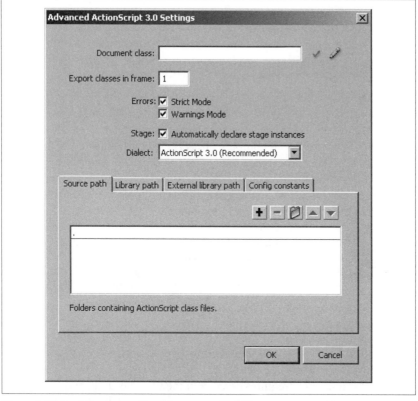

Figure 5-15. Preferences specific to the current FLA file

You can toggle Strict mode and Warnings mode here. These two affect the volume of guidance sent to the Compiler Errors and Output panels during compiling (see Chapter 11 for details).

The "Automatically declare stage instances" setting pertains to class files that refer to assets in a companion FLA file—assets that have already been given instance names on the stage. Technically, these instance names should be declared as properties in the class definition, but because they already exist as instance names on the stage, declaring them as properties can cause a conflict at compile time. You can omit these declarations in the class file as long as this checkbox is selected.

The Dialect drop-down list determines which flavor of ActionScript the compiler uses. As discussed in Chapter 1, ActionScript 3.0 is an implementation of the ECMA-262 specification. As it happens, ActionScript is stricter than the specification requires. While ECMAScript allows for prototype-based inheritance, the ActionScript dialect does not. Advanced developers who wish to make use of this feature may set the dialect to ECMAScript, but the recommended default is ActionScript 3.0, which lets SWF files perform more efficiently due to the omission of prototype-related infrastructure.

Associating FLA Files with AS Files

At the beginning of this chapter, ActionScript was described as something that can be written in external files as well as keyframes. When stored outside a FLA file, ActionScript is saved as a simple text file with an *.as* extension, such as *commonFunctions.as*. In complex projects especially, it often makes sense to store ActionScript in external files. You can organize script files into code libraries for common re-use, easily searched, and edited with any simple text editor or a Script window of the Flash authoring tool. For an overview on a selection of external script editors, see Chapter 2.

 When a FLA file is published, its ActionScript is "baked in" to the compiled SWF file. This is roughly analogous to the way the layers in Photoshop PSD file are no longer available in an exported JPG. It is important to understand that FLA files must be republished when external code is updated.

External ActionScript can be referenced by a FLA file in four ways: as a snippet, brought into Flash with the `include` directive; as a class, referenced by the timeline with the `import` directive and instantiated in keyframe code; as a document class, which requires no code in the FLA file at all; and finally, as a linkage class. These last two options are covered in Chapter 6 and Chapter 7, respectively.

To see how AS files can improve workflow efficiency, consider the following keyframe ActionScript, which displays and loops the video content shown in Figure 5-16.

```
var vid:Video = new Video(320, 240);
addChild(vid);

var nc:NetConnection = new NetConnection();
nc.connect(null);

var ns:NetStream = new NetStream(nc);
vid.attachNetStream(ns);

var listener:Object = new Object();
listener.onMetaData = function(evt:Object):void {};
ns.client = listener;

ns.addEventListener(NetStatusEvent.NET_STATUS, ¬
    statusHandler);
```

```
function statusHandler(evt:NetStatusEvent):void {
    if (evt.info.code == "NetStream.Play.Stop") {
        ns.seek(0);
    }
}

ns.play("Peter_Pringle_Theremin.flv");
```

Figure 5-16. Keyframe coded video content (performance by Peter Pringle, http://PeterPringle.com, used with permission)

If you want a series of videos, each as a separate SWF file in its own HTML document, you can copy the original FLA file as often as necessary. Only the final line would need to be updated, in order to point to a different FLV file. This approach works in a pinch, but if the functionality changes—for example, the video should now rewind and pause, rather than loop—additional code must be revised in each separate FLA file. To avoid this, you can begin to *abstract* your code—that is, lift the reusable portion for general application— by consolidating the repetitive elements into a single script file. This way, the whole series of FLA files can then look to the same external code for instructions.

Code Snippets

The Actions panel gives you an export feature that facilitates the creation of code snippets. Just click the panel's menu, as shown in Figure 5-17, and then select Export Script. This action opens a Save As dialog box that lets you save the code content of the selected frame as an AS file.

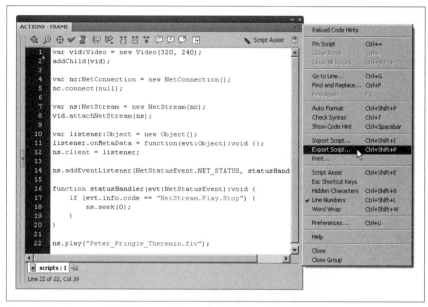

```
ACTIONS - FRAME
                                                        Script Assist
 1    var vid:Video = new Video(320, 240);
 2    addChild(vid);
 3
 4    var nc:NetConnection = new NetConnection();
 5    nc.connect(null);
 6
 7    var ns:NetStream = new NetStream(nc);
 8    vid.attachNetStream(ns);
 9
10    var listener:Object = new Object();
11    listener.onMetaData = function(evt:Object):void ();
12    ns.client = listener;
13
14    ns.addEventListener(NetStatusEvent.NET_STATUS, statusHand
15
16    function statusHandler(evt:NetStatusEvent):void {
17        if (evt.info.code == "NetStream.Play.Stop") {
18            ns.seek(0);
19        }
20    }
21
22    ns.play("Peter_Pringle_Theremin.flv");

 scripts : 1
Line 22 of 22, Col 39
```

Menu items shown:

Reload Code Hints	
Pin Script	Ctrl+=
Close Script	Ctrl+-
Close All Scripts	Ctrl+Shift+-
Go to Line...	Ctrl+G
Find and Replace...	Ctrl+F
Find Again	F3
Auto Format	Ctrl+Shift+F
Check Syntax	Ctrl+T
Show Code Hint	Ctrl+Spacebar
Import Script...	Ctrl+Shift+I
Export Script...	Ctrl+Shift+P
Print...	
Script Assist	Ctrl+Shift+E
Esc Shortcut Keys	
Hidden Characters	Ctrl+Shift+8
✔ Line Numbers	Ctrl+Shift+L
Word Wrap	Ctrl+Shift+W
Preferences...	Ctrl+U
Help	
Close	
Close Group	

Figure 5-17. Exporting keyframe code to an external script file

To use this external file, delete the existing keyframe code—all but the last line, in this case—and then use the `include` directive:

```
include "VideoPlayback_scr.as";
ns.play("Peter_Pringle_Theremin.flv");
```

Because the AS and FLA files are in the same folder, only the script's file name is necessary. For files in separate locations, include the full file path between the quotation marks after the `include` directive.

In ActionScript 2.0, the `include` directive was preceded by the pound sign—`#include`—and the line that contained it could not end with a semicolon. In ActionScript 3.0, the pound sign is gone and the semicolon is optional, but recommended.

At this point, only the two lines shown are necessary in each separate FLA file, where the second line will be updated to point to the corresponding FLV file. At compile time, the `include` directive effectively pastes the content of *Video Playback_scr.as* into the keyframe, as if it had never been exported. The benefit to your workflow is that any change made to the AS file is now updated automatically in each companion FLA file as it's recompiled.

Classes

Custom classes potentially give you an even greater sense of abstraction. Just as built-in classes define native objects like MovieClip, TextField, Array, and the like, custom classes define custom objects that can be just as useful. The structure of classes requires a package and class declaration. Class properties are declared near the top, and import directives are required for every additional class referenced in the code. Class code is saved as simple text, with the same file name as the class itself. In this case, the file name would be *VideoPlayback.as* because the class itself is called VideoPlayback.

```
package {

    import flash.display.MovieClip;
    import flash.events.NetStatusEvent;
    import flash.media.Video;
    import flash.net.NetConnection;
    import flash.net.NetStream;

    public class VideoPlayback {

        private var _vid:Video;
        private var _nc:NetConnection;
        private var _ns:NetStream;
        private var _listener:Object;

        public function VideoPlayback(timeline:MovieClip, ¬
                file:String) {
            init(timeline, file);
        }
        private function init(timeline:MovieClip, ¬
                file:String):void {
            _vid = new Video(320, 240);
            timeline.addChild(_vid);

            _nc = new NetConnection();
            _nc.connect(null);

            _ns = new NetStream(_nc);
            _vid.attachNetStream(_ns);

            _listener = new Object();
            _listener.onMetaData = function( ¬
                    evt:Object):void {};
            _ns.client = _listener;

            _ns.addEventListener(NetStatusEvent.NET_STATUS, ¬
                    statusHandler);

            _ns.play(file);
        }
        private  function statusHandler( ¬
```

```
        evt:NetStatusEvent):void {
        if (evt.info.code == "NetStream.Play.Stop") {
            _ns.seek(0);
        }
    }
  }
}
```

To use this class, delete all of the existing keyframe code and use the `import` directive instead:

```
import VideoPlayback;
new VideoPlayback(this, "Peter_Pringle_Theremin.flv");
```

Note the lack of quotation marks and file extension: you're importing a class this time, not a text file. After this line, the custom class can be instantiated with the `new` keyword, just like any built-in class. This includes the possibility of parameters, as shown. If the AS and FLA files are in the same folder, the `import` directive is optional, provided that the FLA file's Source Path setting includes the dot (.) entry discussed in the "Flash Publish Settings" on page 124 of this chapter.

At this point, each separate FLA file needs only the two lines shown, where a custom `VideoPlayback` object manages the video content when you give it a target timeline and the file path of an FLV file. Any change to the class is automatically updated for each companion FLA file as it's recompiled.

Using Script Assist

The concept of Script Assist has existed in many versions of the Flash authoring tool, and has evolved over the years. Prior to Adobe's acquisition of Macromedia, Flash MX developers encountered a similar feature in an Actions panel preference setting for Normal Mode versus Expert Mode. Think of Script Assist as a built-in form of on-the-job training that can potentially expand your overall understanding of the ActionScript 3.0 API. Just be advised, Script Assist can also be a very tedious tool, so its usefulness depends largely on your personal learning preferences. This feature temporarily sets the Actions panel's Script pane as read-only, and gives you an alternative approach to adding, removing, and editing code.

Consider a FLA file with three movie clip symbols already on the stage. Each symbol has a unique instance name: *mcA*, *mcB*, and *mcC*. In this hypothetical scenario, you would like to program the second symbol, *mcB*, to respond to a mouse click that sends the current webpage to a new URL. In order to use Script Assist in this endeavor, it helps to mentally enter into a research-oriented

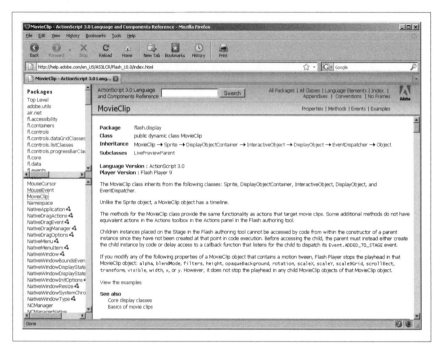

Figure 5-18. The onboard documentation, displaying the MovieClip class entry

state of mind. Why? Because using Script Assist is a bit like forgoing the highway (typing is faster!) in favor of numerous back roads. You'll need a map.

These three symbols are movie clips, which means they're instances of the MovieClip class. Your first stop, then, may very well be the onboard documentation, in order to consult the MovieClip class entry of the ActionScript 3.0 Language and Components Reference (Figure 5-18). Classes define objects, and you can effectively think of class entries as Owner's Manuals for the object in question. Entries typically cover one or more of the following categories, depending on the functionality of the class: *properties*, which describe the object's characteristics; *methods*, which describe what the object can do; and *events*, which describe what the object can react to.

In this scenario, you'd like to program *mcB* to respond to a mouse click, so you scroll the Events heading to see if this goal is even possible with movie clips. Under the Events heading, make sure to click the Show Inherited Events hyperlink to unveil events that the MovieClip class inherits from other classes in its family tree. Sure enough, supported events include click, mouseUp, and other mouse-related responses.

In order to associate an event with a function, you need *mcB* to actually *do* something; namely, to make the event/function association. The things an

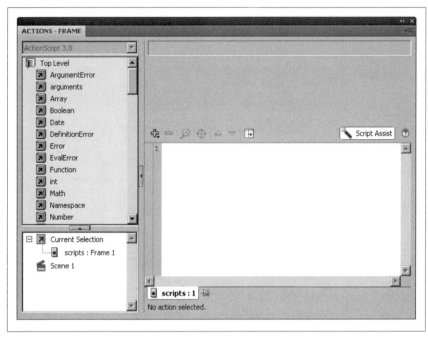

Figure 5-19. Script Assist changes the Actions panel's Script pane

object can do are called methods, so you scroll to the Public Methods heading and, this time, click the Show Inherited Methods hyperlink. The `MovieClip` class supports an `addEventListener()` method inherited from the `EventDispatcher` class. Click the `EventDispatcher` hyperlink to learn that this class belongs to the `flash.events` package. Now it's time to use this information.

When selected, the Actions panel's Script Assist button changes the Script pane as shown in Figure 5-19. The area at the bottom is no longer editable by direct typing, so the `addEventListener()` method must be assigned to *mcB* with the ⊕ "Add a new item to the script" button. Remember, movie clips inherit from `EventDispatcher`, which resides in the `flash.events` package. Clicking the blue plus icon leads you to the desired method by way of a series of submenus: flash.events→EventDispatcher→Methods→addEventListener.

Selecting this method updates the Script pane as shown in Figure 5-20. At this point, clicking into the Object input field activates the ⊕ "Insert a target path" button, which you can use to build a reference to *mcB* by way of a dialog box (you could alternately type `mcB` directly into the Object input field). Note that the `flash.events.EventDispatcher` package has been automatically imported. Strictly speaking, this isn't necessary for every class referenced in keyframe code, but its presence doesn't hurt anything.

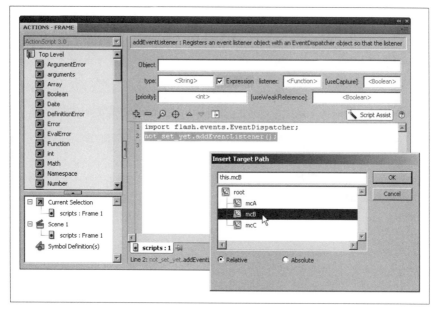

Figure 5-20. Using the "Insert a target path" button to build an object reference

Each input field indicates the particular sort of input it needs. The type and listener fields, for example, represent the first two parameters required by the addEventListener() method: a string and a function, respectively. The remaining parameters are set between brackets—for example, [useCapture]—which tells you the remaining parameters are optional.

As you researched earlier in the onboard documentation, movie clips support a click event, which is displayed as a hyperlink in the documentation. Clicking that hyperlink shows that the click event belongs to the MouseEvent class, and should be referenced as the CLICK constant. Now you can type MouseEvent.CLICK into the type input field. As you do, Script Assist continues to build the addEventListener() expression in the non-editable bottom region of the Script pane. In this way, you may continue to supply parameters, such as a custom clickHandler reference in the listener field (Figure 5-21).

Sometimes Script Assist is, frankly, not worth the effort. To actually write the clickHandler() function you just referenced, you would have to click the blue plus icon again to add a new expression. This time, the choice would be Language Elements→Statements, Keywords & Directives→definition keyword→function, which is arguably unintuitive, even for a seasoned programmer. After choosing "function", you'd see the Script pane update as shown in Figure 5-22, and you could again fill out the input fields in the Script pane's upper half.

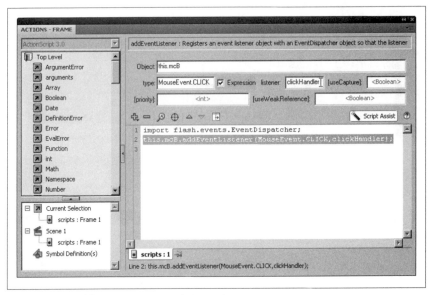

Figure 5-21. Building expressions with Script Assist

You might just find it easier to deselect the Script Assist button at this point, and then type in the remaining code by hand:

```
function clickHandler(evt:MouseEvent):void {
    var url:URLRequest = new URLRequest("http://www.domain.com/");
    navigateToURL(url);
}
```

The choice is yours.

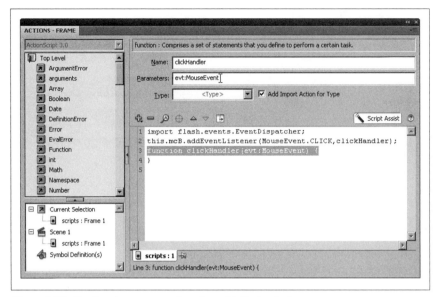

Figure 5-22. Configuring a custom function with Script Assist

CHAPTER 6

Creating a Document Class

Flash CS4 Professional lets you associate a *document class* with your FLA file. The document class is an optional class definition that controls the main timeline, and is constructed when the main timeline initializes. If you choose not to provide your own document class, then Flash generates one for you in documents configured for ActionScript 3.0. The choice is yours, which means you can migrate to this new feature at your own pace. As a note of encouragement, you won't find anything unusual in FLA files with automatically generated document classes. The main timeline operates and feels the same as it used to. You can still put frame scripts where you like; it's just that the main timeline has taken on a more formalized structure behind the scenes.

In FLA files with a custom document class, the main timeline can be programmed to offer additional functionality in a way that feels built-in. You could, for example, create a document class with a `pauseFrame()` method, something that pauses the timeline for a given number of seconds, then lets it continue. (This suggestion is demonstrated later in this chapter.) Thanks to the document class, using the new `pauseFrame()` method becomes as hassle-free as using `stop()` or `gotoAndPlay()`: just type it into whatever frame script meets your needs. This addition to the Flash workflow is useful in team environments where designer and developer disciplines may not overlap, because it allows for complete separation of assets from code. It hasn't always been so easy.

Shortly after the introduction of ActionScript 2.0 in Flash MX 2004 (version 7 of the authoring tool), developers began to experiment with bona fide class files. This was the introduction of external text files capable of defining new data types—flexible, portable, custom objects that could be used in the same way as familiar native objects, such as `Array`, `Date`, and `Math`. It wasn't long before a new breed of Flash developer emerged: adventurous coders whose every goal involved the reduction of the main timeline to a single frame. From a programming standpoint, the traditional jumble of nested timeline code had been artfully curtailed into the minimalist beauty of a Zen garden. This was a completely new way to program in Flash, and could justly be described as revolutionary.

The best part was, designers who chose to could happily continue writing frame scripts where needed. Meanwhile, developers could pursue their own passions away from timelines and drawing tools. For developers coming from other backgrounds, such as Java or C#, the new paradigm made Flash more comfortable, because it came closer to matching their own workflow in which an application of any complexity begins with a single entry point, a class usually named Main.

In spite of such improvements, these ActionScript trailblazers had to halt one step shy of their ultimate ambition. Until Flash CS3, you couldn't associate the main timeline directly with an entry point class file. That first and only keyframe had to have, at minimum, a single line of code to kick start the application. Something like this:

```
var application:Main = new Main();
```

Or even simpler:

```
new Main();
```

This single line of code may not seem like much of a hindrance, but keep in mind, Flash is a unique authoring environment in that it appeals equally to both artists and coders. Some Flash users prefer not to touch ActionScript at all, even if it's only one line. Now they don't have to, because every last shred of code can be saved in a simple text file external to the FLA file.

You have two ways to attach a document class to a FLA file: the Property inspector and the Publish Settings dialog. Here's a look at both.

1. Create a new ActionScript 3.0 FLA file, and then save it as *SampleDocClass.fla*.

2. Create a new ActionScript file, and then save it as *MainMovie.as* in the same folder as *SampleDocClass.fla*.

3. Type the following code in *MainMovie.as*:

```
package {
    import flash.display.Sprite;
    import flash.events.Event;
    public class MainMovie extends Sprite {
        var sp:Sprite;
        // constructor
        public function MainMovie() {
            init();
        }
        private function init():void {
            sp = new Sprite();
            sp.graphics.beginFill(0x0099FF, 1);
```

```
                sp.graphics.drawRect(-50,-50,100,100);
                sp.graphics.endFill();
                sp.x = 100;
                sp.y = 100;
                addChild(sp);
                addEventListener(Event.ENTER_FRAME, rotateSquare);
            }
            private function rotateSquare(event:Event):void {
                sp.rotation += 5;
            }
        }
    }
```

4. Save your changes, and then return to *SampleDocClass.fla*. To prove there's nothing up anyone's sleeve, select Control→Test Movie, and note the blank SWF file. The document class has not yet been assigned. Close the SWF file.

5. In your work area, click the Stage or pasteboard. This action updates the Property inspector to reflect the properties of the FLA document itself. Open the Property inspector, and then type the name of the document class, `MainMovie`, into the Document class field, as shown in Figure 6-1. Note that the *.as* file extension is omitted: this isn't the name of the file, but rather of the class itself.

6. Select Control→Test Movie again. This time, you see a rotating blue square —without any ActionScript actually in the FLA file.

7. Close the SWF file, and then, in the Property inspector, click the Profile area's Edit button to open the Publish Settings dialog box (you can also open this box by selecting File→Publish Settings). Select the Flash tab, and then click the Settings button next to the Script drop-down list. This action opens the Advanced ActionScript 3.0 Settings dialog, as shown in Figure 6-2.

    Notice that the Document class field is already filled in, because you previously entered it in the Property inspector. If you change or remove it here, it's also changed or removed in the Property inspector, and vice versa.

8. Click the green checkmark next to the Document class field. You see an alert box that verifies the location of *MainMovie.as*. Click the pencil icon, and Flash switches the active document from *SampleDocClass.fla* to *Main Movie.as*, opening it if necessary. The Property inspector also features a pencil icon that does the same thing.

In the previous example, the FLA and AS files are located in the same folder. Generally, this arrangement makes the most sense for document classes, though strictly speaking you can place a document class wherever you like. For example, in a team environment, you may have a number of commonly

Figure 6-1. Assigning a document class with the Property inspector

used code libraries arranged into *packages*. Packages are a logical organization of classes, arranged in hierarchical folders that are often stored in a centralized location. Hypothetically, your company's in-house classes might be referenced in packages such as `com.companyname.utilies`, `com.companyname.graphics`, and the like.

If your document class resides in a package structure, you must provide the fully qualified namespace to that document class, in either the Class field of the Property inspector or the Advanced ActionScript 3.0 Settings dialog box. If *MainMovie.as* was located inside a folder named *companyname*, located in turn inside a folder named *com*, the full namespace would be `com.company name.MainMovie`. In most cases, however, the document class corresponds to the specific requirements of the FLA file, and therefore resides in the same folder for easy access. The document class may very well depend on any number of additional classes, including shared code libraries in other packages. In order to make use of those classes, the document class must reference them with `import` directives as needed.

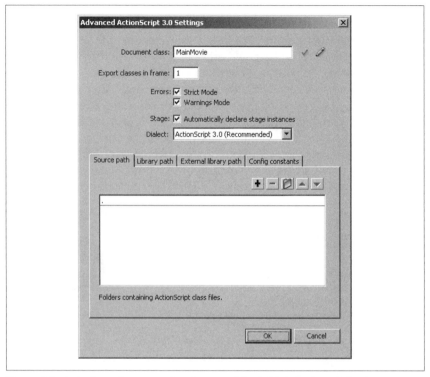

Figure 6-2. Assigning a document class by way of the Publish Settings dialog box

 For more information on the `import` directive, see the "Major Syntax and Structure Changes" on page 77 in Chapter 3 and the "Associating FLA Files with AS Files" on page 126 in Chapter 5.

A document class must extend either the `Sprite` class or `MovieClip` class, depending on the application's needs. If the document class controls the main timeline with `MovieClip` methods such as `gotoAndPlay()` or `gotoAndStop()`, or if the main timeline has frame scripts—in other words, if the main timeline needs to behave like a movie clip—the document class must extend `MovieClip`.

In the *MainMovie.as* example, the only methods used, `addChild()` and `addEventListener()`, are supported by the smaller `Sprite` class, so extending `Sprite` is sufficient. Because `MovieClip` extends `Sprite`, movie clip objects benefit from all the functionality available to sprite objects, but have the additional overhead of a timeline. In order to save memory and possibly increase performance, it's best to have your document class extend as small a base class as possible.

For an example that requires `MovieClip`, consider the following document class, `CompanyTemplate`, which could prove useful in a workflow for banner ad designers. One of the perennial questions on the Adobe support forums involves temporarily pausing, and then resuming the main timeline. While you can certainly add filler keyframes to extend the timeline, this manual approach quickly becomes tedious when numerous pauses are needed, especially in FLA files with high frame rates. To make matters worse, revisions can potentially mean the painstaking removal of extra frames, which can be difficult in timelines with dozens of layers. Wouldn't it be great if something like a `pauseFrame()` method were built into the language? A document class makes it so:

```
package {
    import flash.display.MovieClip;
    import flash.events.TimerEvent;
    import flash.utils.Timer;
    public class CompanyTemplate extends MovieClip {
        private var _timer:Timer;
        // constructor
        public function CompanyTemplate() {
            _timer = new Timer(1000, 1);
            _timer.addEventListener(TimerEvent.TIMER, ¬
                resumeFrame);
        }
        // Pause frame
        public function pauseFrame(seconds:Number):void {
            stop();
            _timer.delay = seconds * 1000;
            _timer.start();
        }
        // Resume frame
        private function resumeFrame(evt:TimerEvent):void {
            play();
        }
    }
}
```

This class's methods, `pauseFrame()` and `resumeFrame()`, employ the `stop()` and `play()` methods of the `MovieClip` class, which means `CompanyTemplate` must extend `MovieClip` in order to go about its business.

A `Timer` instance is declared as the private `_timer` property, which is then instantiated in the constructor function and associated with the `resumeFrame()` method. The `pauseFrame()` method is conveniently called from any number of frame scripts in main timeline. It halts the timeline via `MovieClip.stop()`, and then sets the `Timer.delay` property of `_timer` to a value in seconds provided by the frame script. Because the `delay` property expects milliseconds, the incom-

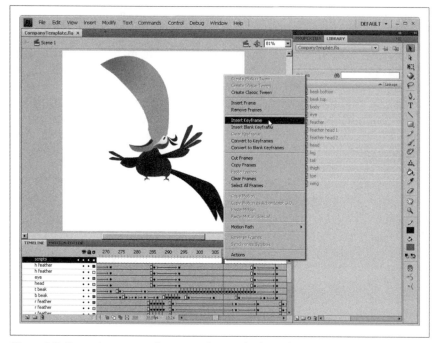

Figure 6-3. Preparing to use a document class method in a frame script

ing `seconds` parameter is multiplied by 1,000. At this point, `_timer` is told to begin its work, which is to eventually call `resumeFrame()`—but all this complexity is neatly tucked away for designers who simply want to pause the main timeline with a simple line of code.

> There's a reason why the `_timer` property is preceded by an underscore. By popular convention, many developers set private properties apart by the using this punctuation. This was a source of potential conflict in ActionScript 2.0, because many built-in properties formerly featured underscores for unrelated reasons. Their removal in ActionScript 3.0 eliminates this confusion.

To use this document class, save it as *CompanyTemplate.as*, associate it with a FLA file as described earlier, and then add a keyframe where desired (Figure 6-3).

Use the Actions panel and enter, for example, `pauseFrame(5);`, which pauses the chosen frame for 5 seconds, and then resumes. Because the `CompanyTemplate` class is associated with the main timeline—in fact, *is* the main timeline at runtime—the `pauseFrame()` method executes as naturally as `stop()`, `play()`, or any other `MovieClip` method.

Company-wide technical policies of any stripe can be managed in this way for whole teams of designers/developers, who needn't be bothered with the underlying mechanics of the custom functionality. As policies and requirements change, the document class can be updated without interrupting the workflow of the team members who use it. Because the document class imports other classes as needed, the complexity of its custom features isn't tied to a single class file.

CHAPTER 7

Working with Library and Linkage Changes

Like its forerunner, ActionScript 3.0 supports the attachment of library assets at runtime, but the mechanics have changed. The only class methods that now contain the word "attach" relate to connecting the SWF file to an external device, such as `NetStream.attachCamera()`, which lets the user transmit webcam input. You don't find familiar methods like `MovieClip.attachMovie()` and `Sound.attachSound()` anywhere, so how can you access the library now at runtime? The answer's gratifyingly elegant, and even in its simple approach, ActionScript 3.0 gives you more elaborate options than before.

Linkages Now Reference Classes

Prior to ActionScript 3.0, you could optionally assign library assets a *linkage identifier* in the Library panel. This procedure provided a unique label for the chosen asset, so that you could single it out at runtime when needed, and pull it to the stage. Linkage identifiers are still possible in Flash CS4 Professional when a FLA file is configured for an older version of ActionScript. To access an asset's linkage properties, right-click (Ctrl-click) the asset as shown in Figure 7-1, and then select Properties.

Selecting Properties opens the Symbol Properties dialog box, whose Linkage area is initially the same for documents configured for any version of Action-Script. The Export for ActionScript checkbox is enabled, but nothing else in that area is enabled (Figure 7-2).

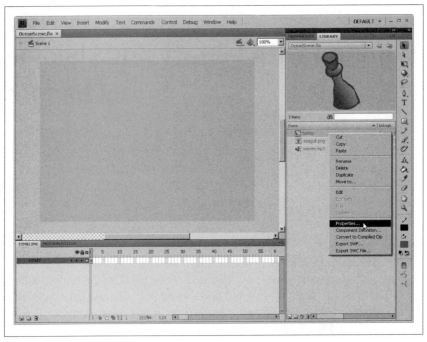

Figure 7-1. Right-click (Ctrl-click) an asset to access its linkage properties

The difference arrives when you select that Export for ActionScript checkbox. In ActionScript 2.0 documents, the Identifier field is enabled and automatically populated with the selected asset's library name (Figure 7-3). The Class field is enabled for optional association with a custom class file—you don't need this for garden variety attaching—and the Base class field is disabled, because it applies only to ActionScript 3.0. Finally, the Export in first frame checkbox is enabled and automatically selected.

The identifier name is technically unrelated to the asset's library name, and you can change it to another name, if desired.

ActionScript 2.0 presents numerous ways to attach assets at runtime, but the variety isn't always a blessing. Too many choices can make the syntax hard to remember. The MovieClip and Sound classes, for example, support attachMovie() and attachSound() methods, respectively, to attach movie clips and audio files from the library. Image files, such as JPEGs, GIFs, and PNGs, require the BitmapData.loadBitmap() method. Fonts are referenced by linkage

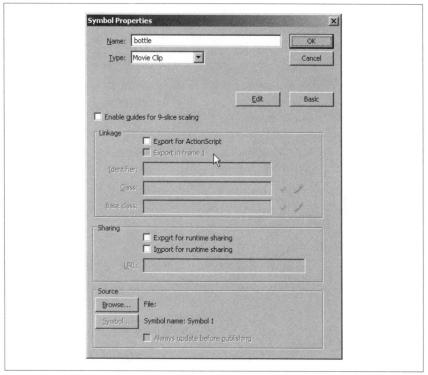

Figure 7-2. The initial state of the Symbol Properties dialog box

identifier in instances of `TextFormat` or `StyleSheet`. Oddly, button symbols can't be attached unless converted to movie clips.

In contrast, ActionScript 3.0 unifies these mechanisms into a single approach, and supports every sort of asset a library can hold, other than graphic symbols. In an ActionScript 3.0 FLA file, checking Export for ActionScript enables a different set of input fields in the Symbol Properties dialog box, as shown in Figure 7-4.

This time, the linkage Identifier field is disabled and the asset's name has automatically been supplied for the Class field instead. The Base class field is enabled and automatically populated with an appropriate related class (this `bottle` asset happens to be a movie clip symbol, and the base class is set to the fully qualified package `flash.display.MovieClip`).

This configuration seems to indicate that ActionScript 3.0 linkage requires a custom class. In truth, it does; but the authoring tool lends a hand by writing this class for you. If you click OK at this point, then you see an alert that tells you as much (Figure 7-5). Select the "Don't warn me again" checkbox if you

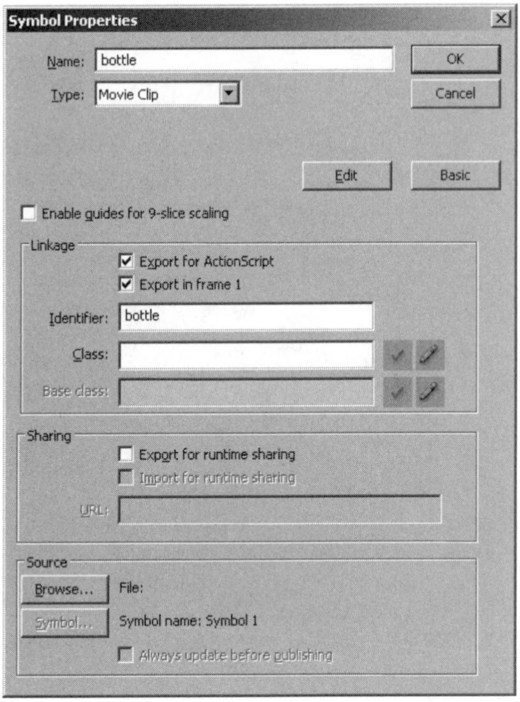

Figure 7-3. Linkage properties in ActionScript 1.0 and 2.0 documents

prefer not to see this warning every time you supply linkage properties to a library asset. Click OK to acknowledge the alert.

In the FLA file illustrated, the asset in question is a drawing of a half-submerged bottle, which has been converted to a movie clip symbol. The library name of this asset is "bottle," which provides the default class name. When the SWF file is compiled, a custom `bottle` class is written on your behalf that extends `MovieClip`, which means you can "attach" the bottle asset by instantiating it and adding it to the display list. For example, you could declare a variable named `asset`, strongly type it as `bottle`, and set it to a new instance of the `bottle` class like this:

```
var asset:bottle = new bottle();
```

Because the `bottle` class extends `MovieClip`, it supports all the features defined by that class, including `x`, `y`, `width`, and `height` properties. To center this asset, you could use the following two new lines:

```
var asset:bottle = new bottle();
asset.x = (stage.stageWidth / 2) - (asset.width / 2);
asset.y = (stage.stageHeight / 2) - (asset.height / 2);
```

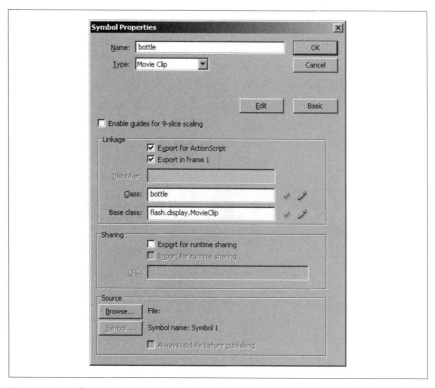

Figure 7-4. Linkage properties in ActionScript 3.0 documents

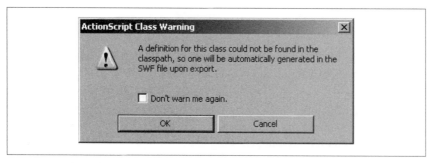

Figure 7-5. The authoring tool gives a warning before writing the linkage class

Keep in mind that, like any visual object in ActionScript 3.0, the bottle instance must be added to the display list in order to be seen (shown in bold):

```
var asset:bottle = new bottle();
asset.x = (stage.stageWidth / 2) - (asset.width / 2);
asset.y = (stage.stageHeight / 2) - (asset.height / 2);
addChild(asset);
```

Now, the SWF file shows the attached movie clip symbol (Figure 7-6).

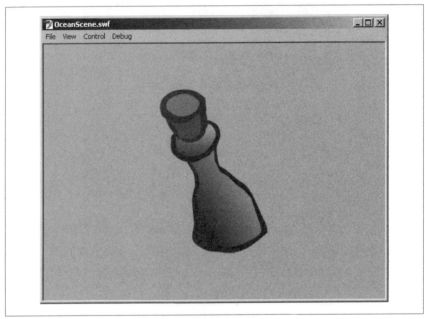

Figure 7-6. A library asset attached at runtime

Naming Classes

By longstanding convention, class names begin with a capital letter. If the class name is composed of more than one word, this convention is applied to each word and spaces are removed, which is why, for example, "movie clip" becomes MovieClip. Though perfectly acceptable from a technical standpoint, advanced programmers may cringe at a class named bottle, so to stay consistent with recommended best practices, you may want to rename your linkage classes accordingly. In this case, the change would be Bottle, and the instantiation would changes as follows:

```
var asset:Bottle = new Bottle();
```

If your asset's library name happens to contain spaces—for example, "floating bottle"—the authoring tool removes those spaces for you, suggesting `floatingbottle` as your class name, in which case the manual change to `FloatingBottle` not only defers to convention but also makes the class name easier to read.

In addition to spaces, many other characters are not allowed in class names. Like variables, class names can't begin with a number or any punctuation other than an underscore (_) or dollar sign ($). If your library asset happens to include invalid characters, you see the warning shown in Figure 7-7 when you click OK in the Symbol Properties dialog box.

Figure 7-7. Class names must contain valid characters

Specifying a Base Class

In most cases, you can stick with the base class supplied automatically for you in the Base class field of the Symbol Properties dialog box. The authoring tool is smart enough to recognize the file format of the associated asset and, for example, suggests the following base classes for various types of assets:

- `flash.display.MovieClip`: movie clip symbol
- `flash.display.SimpleButton`: button symbol
- `flash.display.BitmapData`: image files (JPEG, GIF, PNG, BMP, TIFF, and so on)
- `flash.media.Sound`: audio files (MP3, WAV, AIFF, and so on)
- `flash.text.Font`: font files

 In the case of images and audio, Flash supports more file formats for importing than it does for the loading of external files.

If a movie clip symbol contains only one frame and no nested multiframe assets, then it effectively meets the criteria of a sprite, and you may change its base class accordingly (Figure 7-8). By extending the `Sprite` class, your asset avoids the slight memory overhead of the `MovieClip` class.

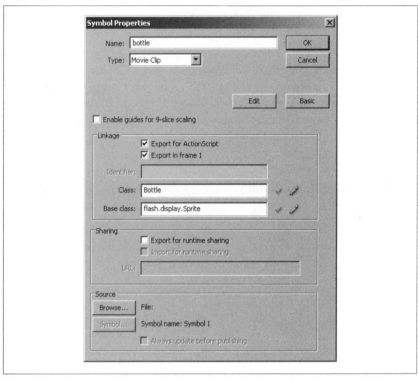

Figure 7-8. Simple, one-frame movie clip symbols may be configured to extend Sprite

Writing a Custom Class

If you like, you can write your own class to provide additional functionality for an attached asset. Custom classes must extend the same base class displayed in the Symbol Properties dialog box.

To make the submerged bottle drift back and forth, for example, you could write something like the custom `FloatingBottle` class that follows, which extends `Sprite`:

```
package {
    import flash.display.Sprite;
    import flash.events.Event;
    public class FloatingBottle extends Sprite {
        private var _driftCounter:Number;
        // constructor
        public function FloatingBottle() {
            _driftCounter = 0;
            addEventListener(Event.ENTER_FRAME, drift);
        }
        private function drift(evt:Event):void {
            _driftCounter += 0.12;
```

```
            this.x += Math.cos(_driftCounter) * 2;
        }
    }
}
```

In this case, the Class field in the Symbol Properties dialog box must be set to FloatingBottle and the Base class must be set to flash.display.Sprite, as shown in Figure 7-9.

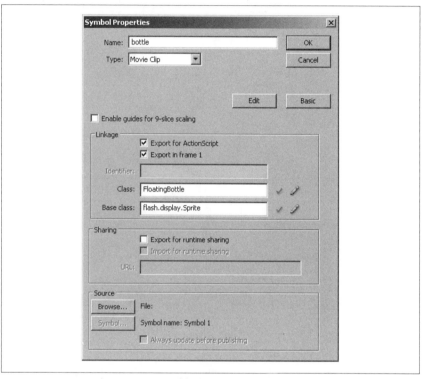

Figure 7-9. Custom classes are entered by hand

The actual class file, *FloatingBottle.as*, must appear in same folder as the FLA file if no package is provided in the Class field. If your class file exists elsewhere, be sure to include its package information in the Symbol Properties dialog box.

 For more information on packages, see the section "Importing and Packages" on page 78 in Chapter 3 and Figure 5-12 in Chapter 5.

To verify that the custom class is available, in the Symbol Properties dialog box, click the green checkmark button next to the Class field. Doing so gives

you a message that tells where the class was found or that one will be automatically generated upon export. The pencil button opens the associated class
file in a Script window of the authoring tool (Figure 7-10). No warning is given
for custom classes when you click the OK button, because the authoring tool
doesn't have to write a class for you.

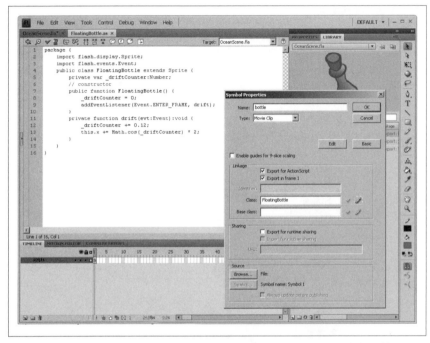

Figure 7-10. The pencil button next to the Class field opens the associated class file

The instantiation of assets based on custom classes is no different from those
with automatically generated classes. The following lines attach the same bottle library asset, positioning it slightly lower than the center of the stage. This
time, the bottle drifts back and forth because a frame loop repeatedly executes
the `drift()` method of the `FloatingBottle` class.

```
var fb:FloatingBottle = new FloatingBottle();
fb.x = (stage.stageWidth / 2) - (fb.width / 2);
fb.y = ((stage.stageHeight / 2) - (fb.height / 2)) + 50;
addChild(fb);
```

Recognizing the Associated Class

Because each type of asset represents its own class, instantiation must follow
the rules that normally pertain to that class. A seagull photo imported into the

library as *seagull.png* represents the `BitmapData` class. Assuming a default (automatically written) class is set as `Seagull` in the Symbol Properties dialog box, the asset can be added to the stage in conjunction with the `Bitmap` class, as is true of any `BitmapData` instance:

```
var sg:Seagull = new Seagull(150, 286);
var bmp:Bitmap = new Bitmap(sg);
addChild(bmp);
```

The `BitmapData` constructor function requires a width and height, here obtained from the Bitmap Properties dialog box for this asset. Right-click (Ctrlclick) an asset in the library, and then select Properties to open this dialog box. Notice, in Figure 7-11, that linkage properties are also available from this dialog box.

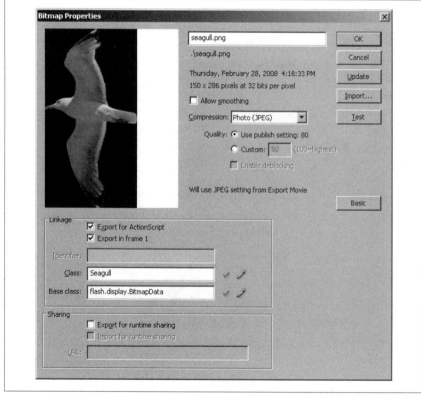

Figure 7-11. Bitmap dimensions can be obtained from the Bitmap Properties dialog box (seagull photo by Patrick Nijhuis, used with permission)

In this case, the `bmp` variable points to an instance of the `Bitmap` class, which features `x` and `width` properties, just like movie clips. To position the image before adding it to the display list, simply configure the desired properties (new code in bold).

```
var sg:Seagull = new Seagull(150, 286);
var bmp:Bitmap = new Bitmap(sg);
bmp.x = stage.stageWidth - bmp.width;
addChild(bmp);
```

An audio file imported into the library as *waves.mp3* represents the Sound class. Assuming a default (automatically written) class is set as Waves in the Symbol Properties dialog box, the asset can be instantiated the same as any Sound instance:

```
var wv:Waves = new Waves();
wv.play();
```

With FloatingBottle, Seagull, and Waves attached to the SWF file at runtime, the SWF looks like Figure 7-12. (You'll just have to trust that the bottle's drifting, and roaring ocean waves are audible.)

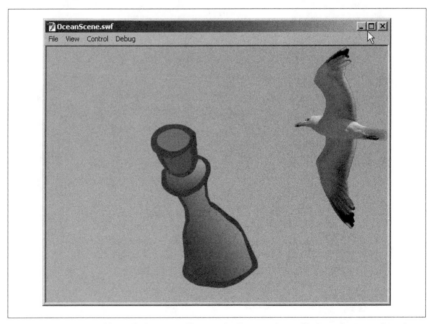

Figure 7-12. A SWF file with dynamically attached assets (seagull photo by Patrick Nijhuis, used with permission)

Attaching Fonts

One of the benefits of designing in Flash, as opposed to traditional HTML, is that SWF files can embed fonts. While you don't need ActionScript to use embedded fonts, you can certainly instantiate text fields dynamically and format them with instances of the TextFormat or StyleSheet classes, which, in turn, can reference fonts stored in the library.

To embed a font and make it available to ActionScript 3.0, use the following steps:

1. Create a new FLA file, and, inside the Library panel, right-click (Ctrl-click), and then select New Font, as shown in Figure 7-13. You can also make this selection from the panel menu in the upper right (just below the X that closes the panel).

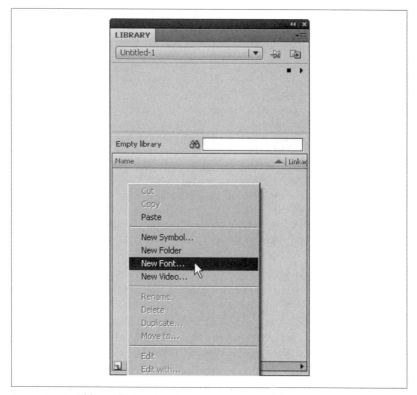

Figure 7-13. Adding a font to the library

This opens a Font Symbol Properties dialog box (Figure 7-14) that lets you select an installed font and give it a name. The name you give can differ from the font's actual name; in fact, because different versions of the font (**bold**, *italic*, and so on) must be included as separate assets, you may find it useful to provide a name that indicates the style used. The content of the Name field becomes the asset's library name. If you click the Advanced button, you can already assign linkage information in this step; otherwise, proceed to Step 2.

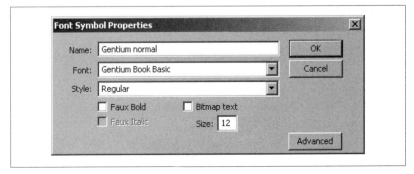

Figure 7-14. Importing a font to the library

 When including font variants, make sure to select the desired variant in the Style drop-down. Faux variants are often available—such as Faux Bold, shown—when the actual variant is not installed on the computer that publishes the SWF file. Bitmap text refers to bitmapped fonts, which are not composed of vector shapes. Most fonts are vector-based, and as such scale cleanly. By choosing Bitmap text, you rasterize vector font outlines, which means they do not scale cleanly. The Size field pertains only to bitmapped fonts, so it makes no difference what value it reads for vector fonts.

2. Once imported, the font appears in the library with a representative "A" icon. Right-click (Ctrl-click) the asset, and then choose Properties, just as when assigning linkage to any other asset. In the Font Symbol Properties dialog box, click the Advanced button if necessary. Select Export for ActionScript, and then provide a meaningful class name, such as GentiumNormal, as shown in Figure 7-15. Verify that the base class is flash.text.Font. Click OK to exit the dialog box. Embedding is complete!

3. Select frame 1 in the main timeline, and then type the following Action-Script into the Actions panel:

```
var gentium:GentiumNormal = new GentiumNormal();

var fmt:TextFormat = new TextFormat();
fmt.font = gentium.fontName;
fmt.size = 32;
```

An arbitrarily named variable, gentium, is declared and set to an instance of the GentiumNormal class defined in the Font Symbol Properties dialog box in Step 2. Remember, this linkage class extends Font, so the gentium object supports all the functionality defined by the Font class. Next, another variable, fmt, is set to an instance of the TextFormat class. The operative line is where the font property of the TextFormat instance (fmt) is set to the fontName property of the gentium instance.

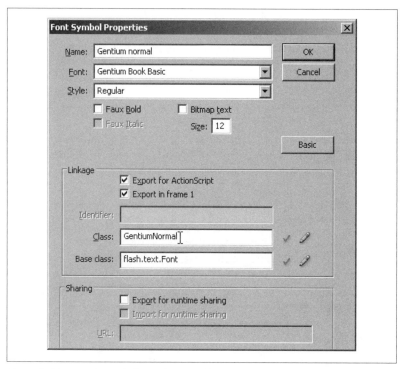

Figure 7-15. Providing a linkage class to a font

4. To use this formatting object with text field, add the following code after the existing ActionScript:

```
var myTextField:TextField = new TextField();
myTextField.autoSize = "left";
myTextField.embedFonts = true;
myTextField.defaultTextFormat = fmt;
myTextField.text = "Lorem ipsum dolor sit amet.";
addChild(myTextField);
```

A third variable, myTextField, is declared and set to an instance of the TextField class. The operative lines show the embedFonts property set to true and the defaultTextFormat property set to the TextFormat instance (fmt) created in Step 3. The TextField class also supports a setTextFormat() method to format text already displayed in a text field, but the `defaultTextFormat` property sets the default formatting. The `setTextFormat()` method works like this:

```
regularText.text = "Lorem ipsum dolor sit amet."
regularText.setTextFormat(fmt);
```

and can be constrained to individual characters with additional parameters.

 Gentium is an elegant, effectively open source typeface designed by Victor Gaultney and freely released under the SIL Open Font License (*http://scripts.sil.org/OFL*). Files for Windows, Mac, and Linux are available for download at *http://scripts.sil.org/Gentium_download* and *http://scripts.sil.org/Gentium_basic*.

5. Alternatively, you can format text using Cascading Style Sheets (CSS) markup, either stored in an external CSS file or defined directly in ActionScript. Add the following new lines after the existing code:

```
var css:StyleSheet = new StyleSheet();
css.setStyle("p", {fontFamily:gentium.fontName, fontSize:32});
css.setStyle("a", {textDecoration:"underline"});
```

Here, an arbitrarily named variable, `css`, is declared and set to an instance of the `StyleSheet` class. In the next two lines, the `StyleSheet.setStyle()` method is invoked on `css` to declare two new styles: a p *element selector*, which affects all `<p>` HTML elements, and an a element selector, which affects all `<a>` HTML elements. (The HTML in this example refers to a text field, rather than the HTML document that would theoretically embed this SWF file.)

The `setStyle()` method accepts two parameters: a string representing the element to stylize, and an object to define the style's properties. In this case, the object is declared with curly braces ({}) as a shortcut to bypass the expression `new Object()`. The `fontFamily` property is set to `gentium.fontName`, just as the `TextFormat.font` property was set in Step 3.

 The `StyleSheet` class is especially useful for formatting hyperlinks, but it supports only a small subset of the actual CSS specification, just as Flash text fields support only a small subset of the HTML specification. See the `StyleSheet` class entry in the ActionScript 3.0 Language and Components Reference for full details.

6. Here's a second text field to illustrate use of the StyleSheet instance. Add the following code after the existing ActionScript:

```
var webText:TextField = new TextField();
webText.autoSize = "left";
webText.embedFonts = true;
webText.styleSheet = css;
webText.htmlText = "<p>Lorem ipsum dolor ¬
    <a href='http://www.oreilly.com/'>sit amet</a>.</p>";
webText.y = 52;
addChild(webText);
```

This time, the text field's styleSheet property is set to the css instance created in Step 5, and its htmlText property is set to an HTML-formatted string, including <p> and <a> elements.

7. Select Control→Test Movie to see both text fields display a message with the embedded Gentium font (Figure 7-16).

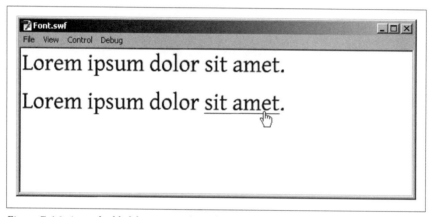

Figure 7-16. An embedded font in simple and HTML-formatted text

CHAPTER 8

Copying Motion as ActionScript 3.0

Flash CS4 Professional features an interesting tool, introduced in Flash CS3, that helps bridge the gap between programmed and timeline-based animation. Available from the Timeline panel, this feature facilitates collaboration between designers and developers by converting timeline tweens and keyframe settings into ActionScript 3.0 code, and sometimes a flexible XML-based format used by the new `Animator` class. The ActionScript involved is generated automatically. This feature lets a designer use traditional animation techniques, complete with motion guides and easing, to provide sophisticated motion templates that a developer can harness to program animation for any number of additional objects, even in separate FLA files.

Copying Motion

Imagine a project in which three photos are each required to respond visually to a mouse click. The photos are expected to start small, and then increase in size and rotate slightly while easing to a stop. Ideally, this motion should include a bit of blur along the y-axis. The developer assigned to this project is perfectly comfortable writing the necessary ActionScript, but doesn't have a stylistic sense of how the motion should ultimately be conveyed. Conversely, the designer on this project is thoroughly comfortable finessing the motion, but doesn't know the first thing about code. How can these team members combine their efforts?

The clear answer is to make use of the authoring tool's Copy Motion as ActionScript 3.0 feature, which can capture the following characteristics of a motion tween:

- Position
- Scale
- Skew

- Rotation
- Transformation point
- Color
- Blend mode
- Orientation to path
- Scale
- Cache as bitmap setting
- Frame labels
- Motion guides
- Custom easing
- Filters

Flash CS4 now gives you two distinct tweening models. The new approach, which works in conjunction with the new Motion Editor panel, generates property arrays of motion tween data on a frame-by-frame basis. The old approach—familiar to longtime Flash users and now known as a *classic tween*—translates keyframe data alone into an XML format that's less dense, relatively speaking, and easier to modify by direct code manipulation.

Because the Copy Motion as ActionScript 3.0 feature is a marriage of timeline- and code-based tweening, this chapter pays tribute to the wedding rhyme "something old, something new," and picks the best of both worlds to achieve its goal.

In this imaginary team setting, the designer gets the project rolling—for starters, with the new tweening model—and then hands off the motion data to the developer. You can follow along by playing both roles.

1. In a new ActionScript 3.0 FLA file, use the Rectangle tool to draw an approximately 300 × 400 pixel rectangle on the stage.

2. Convert the rectangle to a movie clip symbol named **standin**, with its registration point in the center, and then position it just above the lower middle edge of the stage. Use the Free Transform tool to resize the movie clip to approximately 25 percent of its actual size (Figure 8-1).

3. In the Timeline, select frame 20, and then add a new frame (Insert→Timeline→Frame) to produce a span of frames. Flash's new tweening model creates property keyframes for you. Right-click (Ctrl-click) anywhere inside the span of frames, and then select Create Motion Tween. This action sets the current layer apart as a Motion Tween layer, so you can take advantage of the new Motion Editor panel to configure tween characteristics.

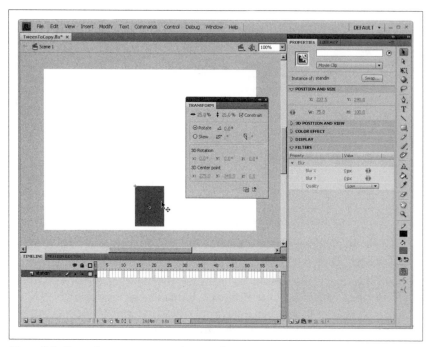

Figure 8-1. Preparing to create a motion template

4. Select frame 20. This step indicates your intent to apply changes to that frame. Now select the movie clip, and then use the Free Transform tool to resize the movie clip's dimensions to approximately 80 percent. Make sure to rotate the rectangle as described in the hypothetical project requirements (for example, apply a 15-degree rotation) and reposition the movie clip up toward the top of the stage.

5. Open the Motion Editor panel by clicking its tab or selecting Window→Motion Editor. Note the three hot text values along the bottom-left corner (Figure 8-2). Hover over these to see a tooltip of their names: Graph Size, Expanded Graph Size, and Viewable Frames. These hot text values adjust the settings of the property graphs inside the Motion Editor panel. Click and hold over the number for Viewable Frames. While holding down the mouse button, slide the mouse left and right to adjust the number. As you do, note that the number of visible frames in the Motion Editor panel's graphs update to match. Set the Viewable Frames value to 20, to show the full number of frames in your tween span.

6. Scrub the playhead—that is, drag the playhead back and forth—to assess your work. As you do, note that a yellow diamond appears in the graphs' Keyframe column when the playhead encounters a property keyframe.

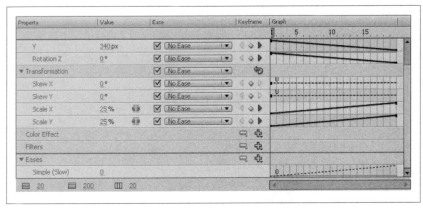

Property	Value	Ease	Keyframe	Graph
				5 10 15
Y	340 px	☑ No Ease ▾	◁ ◇ ▶	
Rotation Z	0°	☑ No Ease ▾	◁ ◇ ▶	
▼ Transformation		☑ No Ease ▾		
Skew X	0°	☑ No Ease ▾	◁ ◇ ▶	
Skew Y	0°	☑ No Ease ▾	◁ ◇ ▶	
Scale X	25%	☑ No Ease ▾	◁ ◇ ▶	
Scale Y	25%	☑ No Ease ▾	◁ ◇ ▶	
Color Effect				
Filters				
▼ Eases				
Simple (Slow)	0			

Figure 8-2. Investigating the Motion Editor panel

This is an ◉ Add or Remove Keyframe button, which does what its name describes. Drag the playhead to frame 1.

7. Scroll vertically if necessary to locate the Filters. Click the ⬚ Add Color, Filter, or Ease button, and then select Blur. Change the default Blur X and Blur Y values to 0, and then drag the playhead to frame 13. Add a keyframe to the Blur Y row by clicking the Add Keyframe button or right-clicking (Ctrl-clicking) the curve and choosing Add Keyframe from the context menu. Change the Blur Y value to 40 at this new keyframe. Finally, drag the playhead to frame 20, add another keyframe to the Blur Y row, and then, in that last keyframe, change the Blur Y value to 0 again.

8. Select the Timeline—not in the Motion Editor panel, but the panel labeled Timeline—and then click the Motion Tween layer to select it. Use the Property inspector's Ease hot text to apply an ease of 100. If you like, scrub the playhead again or press Enter (Return) to preview the animation with the easing. When you're satisfied, right-click (Ctrl-click) inside the span of frames, and then select Copy Motion as ActionScript 3.0.

At this point, the authoring tool has copied some text to the clipboard on your behalf, so be careful to avoid selecting Edit→Copy or otherwise replacing the clipboard contents.

You may now remove your designer hat.

Applying Motion to Other Objects

With your motion data copied to the clipboard, it's time to don your developer hat and put that data to use.

1. Create a new ActionScript 3.0 FLA file. In the Timeline, select frame 1, and then open the Actions panel as if to type some code. Instead, paste the contents of the clipboard. You should now see a considerable amount of ActionScript in the Actions panel. The actual code pasted depends on the tweens you made in your role as designer, but you should see something like the following:

```
import fl.motion.AnimatorFactory;
import fl.motion.MotionBase;
import flash.filters.*;
import flash.geom.Point;
var __motion_standin_2:MotionBase;
if(__motion_standin_2 == null) {
    import fl.motion.Motion;
    __motion_standin_2 = new Motion();
    __motion_standin_2.duration = 20;

    // The following calls to addPropertyArray assign data values
    // for each tweened property. There is one value in the Array
    // for every frame in the tween, or fewer if the last value
    // remains the same for the rest of the frames.
    __motion_standin_2.addPropertyArray("x", [0,0,0,0,0,0,0,0,0,0,0,¬
        0,0,0,0,0,0,0,0,0,0]);
    __motion_standin_2.addPropertyArray("y", [0,-14.7562,-28.7166,¬
        -41.8812,-54.2425,-65.8156,-76.5852,-86.5591,-95.7297,¬
        -104.104,-111.683,-118.467,-124.454,-129.638,-134.026,¬
        -137.611,-140.408,-142.401,-143.598,-144]);
    __motion_standin_2.addPropertyArray("scaleX", [0.25,0.31,0.36,¬
        0.41,0.46,0.50,0.54,0.58,0.62,0.65,0.68,0.70,0.73,0.75,¬
        0.76,0.78,0.79,0.79,0.80,0.80]);
    __motion_standin_2.addPropertyArray("scaleY", [0.25,0.31,0.36,¬
        0.41,0.46,0.50,0.54,0.58,0.62,0.65,0.68,0.70,0.73,0.75,¬
        0.76,0.78,0.79,0.79,0.80,0.80]);
    __motion_standin_2.addPropertyArray("skewX", [0]);
    __motion_standin_2.addPropertyArray("skewY", [0]);
    __motion_standin_2.addPropertyArray("rotationConcat", [0,¬
        -1.53716,-2.99142,-4.36279,-5.65047,-6.85604,-7.97792,¬
        --9.01691,9.9722,-10.8446,-11.6341,-12.3407,-12.9644,¬
        -13.5044,-13.9616,-14.335,-14.6263,-14.834,-14.9587,¬
        -15.0005]);

    // This call to initFilters supplies the Motion with an Array
    // of the fully-qualified class names of the filters in the
    // target's DisplayObject.filters list, in the same order and
    // indices.
    __motion_standin_2.initFilters(["flash.filters.BlurFilter"],¬
        [0]);

    // The following calls to addFilterPropertyArray assign data
    // values for each tweened filter's properties.
    __motion_standin_2.addFilterPropertyArray(0, "blurX", [0]);
    __motion_standin_2.addFilterPropertyArray(0, "blurY", [0,¬
        6.48999,12.63,18.42,23.8567,28.9467,33.6833,38.07,36.3943,¬
```

```
              30.08,24.3657,19.2514,14.7371,10.8286,7.52001,4.81715,¬
          2.70857,1.20572,0.302858,0]);
       __motion_standin_2.addFilterPropertyArray(0, "quality",¬
          [BitmapFilterQuality.LOW]);

       // Create an AnimatorFactory instance, which will manage
       // targets for its corresponding Motion.
       var __animFactory_standin_2:AnimatorFactory = new AnimatorFactory(¬
          __motion_standin_2);

       // Call the addTarget function on the AnimatorFactory
       // instance to target a DisplayObject with this Motion.
       // __animFactory_standin_2.addTarget(<instance name goes here>);
    }
```

Note a number of important aspects here:

- Several import directives in the first few lines, which let you use the AnimatorFactory class and other related classes
- The declaration of a __motion_standin_2 variable (the actual variable name may vary), which is at first set to an instance of the MotionBase class, and later to a Motion instance
- Numerous lines of automatically generated motion-related Action-Script (these are the tween property arrays)
- A call to the AnimationFactory.addTarget() method, invoked on an instance named __animFactory_standin_2 (again, the actual variable name may vary)

2. On its own, this pasted code can't produce anything visual. It expects a DisplayObject instance, which means you have to provide one. Select File→Import→Import to Library, and then locate three image files approximately 300 × 400 pixels apiece.

3. Create a new layer in the timeline, and then drag each image to the stage. Convert each image to a movie clip symbol. Use the Free Transform tool to resize each movie clip to 25 percent of its actual size, and then arrange the movie clips as shown in Figure 8-3.

 The MovieClip class inherits functionality from DisplayObject, so movie clip symbols meet the needs of the AnimatorFactory class, which expects a DisplayObject instance.

4. Select the movie clip on the left, and then give it the instance name *photo1*. Return to the Actions panel, and then uncomment the last line of code by removing the leading double slashes (change shown in bold).

```
// Call the addTarget function on the AnimatorFactory
// instance to target a DisplayObject with this Motion.
__animFactory_standin_2.addTarget(<instance name goes here>);
```

Replace the expression <instance name goes here> with the instance name
photo1.

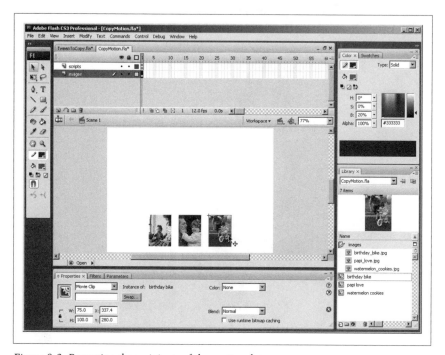

Figure 8-3. Preparing the recipients of the motion data

5. Select Control→Text Movie to compile the SWF file. Thanks to the Copy
   Motion as ActionScript 3.0 feature, the left movie clip now mimics the
   animation created in a separate FLA file by the designer (Figure 8-4).

So far, so good! The designer created a motion template with all the subtlety
that comes from a manual approach. The developer then applied that motion
to another object—including changes in position, scale, rotation, and blur—
with very little effort. In this exercise, the motion data happened to be copied
and pasted in the same authoring environment, but bear in mind, the pasted
code is nothing more than text. The designer could just as easily have sent the
motion data in an email message.

This is a useful start, but the property arrays in the generated code are fairly
unwieldy. Consider the array for the y property.

```
__motion_standin_2.addPropertyArray("y", [0,-14.7562,-28.7166,¬
    -41.8812,-54.2425,-65.8156,-76.5852,-86.5591,-95.7297,¬
    -104.104,-111.683,-118.467,-124.454,-129.638,-134.026,¬
    -137.611,-140.408,-142.401,-143.598,-144]);
```

Figure 8-4. Programmed animation, accomplished automatically

Those values represent a frame-by-frame snapshot of the destination `DisplayObject` instance's vertical movement. Which of those values represents the keyframe at frame 13? What if any of these values needs to be changed by hand in the code? These questions don't have easy answers!

In the remainder of this chapter, you'll see how the developer can tweak this animation by having the designer export it as automatically generated XML. The developer can then edit the XML and even revise the ActionScript to make the animation more responsive. The trick is to use classic tweens.

Going Retro for the Sake of XML

It doesn't take long to redo the animation using classic tweens.

---

1. Return to your motion template FLA file. In the Timeline, right-click (Ctrl-click) the layer with the Motion Tween, and then select Remove Tween.

2. Select frame 20, and then insert a keyframe (Insert→Timeline→Keyframe). In frame 20, resize the rectangle movie clip to 80 percent, rotate it, and reposition it toward the top of the stage. Right-click (Ctrl-click) anywhere between frames 1 and 20, and then select Create Classic Tween. In the Ease area of the Property inspector, make sure the Rotate drop-down displays Auto and the Scale checkbox is selected. Apply an Ease value of 100.

3. Select frame 13 and insert a keyframe. Select the movie clip and, using the Filters area of the Property inspector, add a blur and set the Blur Y property to 40. Scrub the playhead, if you like, to preview your work.

4. At this point, you have three keyframes in your span of frames. The first two keyframes have classic tweens applied. Carefully select all frames but the last keyframe—that is, all frames that have a tween—and then right-click (Ctrl-click) and select Copy Motion as ActionScript 3.0. When you do, Flash prompts you with the dialog box shown in Figure 8-5. Type **photo1,** and then click OK to close the dialog box.

Figure 8-5. With classic tweens, Copy Motion as ActionScript 3.0 prompts for an instance name

 At this point, again, the authoring tool has copied text to the clipboard on your behalf. Be careful to avoid selecting Edit→Copy or otherwise replacing the clipboard contents.

5. Return to the FLA file with the three photos. Delete the existing Action-Script, and then replace it by pasting the current contents of the clipboard. As before, your own generated code may vary from what is shown here. Nonetheless, it'll look something like this:

```
import fl.motion.Animator;
var photo1_xml:XML = <Motion duration="20" xmlns="fl.motion.*"
    xmlns:geom="flash.geom.*" xmlns:filters="flash.filters.*">
    <source>
        <Source frameRate="24" x="275.95" y="334.5" scaleX="1.001"
```

```
                scaleY="1" rotation="0" elementType="movie clip"
                symbolName="standin">
                <dimensions>
                    <geom:Rectangle left="0" top="0" width="83.95"
                        height="108.95"/>
                </dimensions>
                <transformationPoint>
                    <geom:Point x="0.4997022036926742"
                        y="0.5002294630564479"/>
                </transformationPoint>
            </Source>
        </source>

        <Keyframe index="0" tweenSnap="true" tweenSync="true">
            <tweens>
                <CustomEase>
                    <geom:Point x="0.4502575506968478" y="0"/>
                    <geom:Point x="0.7075778422117028"
                        y="0.6092627089536725"/>
                </CustomEase>
            </tweens>
            <filters>
                <filters:BlurFilter blurX="0" blurY="0" quality="1"/>
            </filters>
        </Keyframe>

        <Keyframe index="12" tweenSnap="true" tweenSync="true"
            x="-11.399999999999977" y="-104.44999999999999"
            scaleX="2.451548451548452" scaleY="2.453" rotation="-11.3">
            <tweens>
                <CustomEase>
                    <geom:Point x="0.29906669248852413"
                        y="0.5760325983121745"/>
                    <geom:Point x="0.6150788560295106" y="1"/>
                </CustomEase>
            </tweens>
            <filters>
                <filters:BlurFilter blurX="0" blurY="40" quality="1"/>
            </filters>
        </Keyframe>

        <Keyframe index="19" x="-15" y="-137.95"
            scaleX="2.9180819180819184" scaleY="2.921" rotation="-15">
            <filters>
                <filters:BlurFilter blurX="0" blurY="0" quality="1"/>
            </filters>
        </Keyframe>
    </Motion>;

    var photo1_animator:Animator = new Animator(photo1_xml, photo1);
    photo1_animator.play();
```

Don't worry if that looks like just as much code as before. There are a number of important changes this time.

- Only a single `import` directive in the first line, which allows use of the `Animator` class

- The declaration of a `photo1_xml` variable, set to an instance of the `XML` class and populated with a lengthy XML document (the motion tween data)

- The declaration of a `photo1_animator` variable in the next-to-last line, set to an instance of the `Animator` class and presented with two parameters: the XML instance `photo1_xml`, and the instance name `photo1`, as supplied by the designer

- A call to the `Animator.play()` method, invoked on `photo1_animator`

How is this more useful than data gathered from the new tweening model? It all depends on whether or not you plan to edit frame properties in the code. In this case, the XML represents snapshots of merely the keyframes. In contrast, the other approach flooded you with 20 snapshots of every frame in the tween span. Here, there are only three, and because they're keyframes, you can type in your changes and let Flash interpolate the in-between values for you.

Editing the Default XML

Fast-forward half a week. The designer's out sick today, but that doesn't stop the team lead from letting you know (in a panic!) that the animation needs to be adjusted. The blur effect is a tad heavy, says the client, and the rotation needs to lean ever so slightly more to the left. Surely this is an easy fix, right?

As it turns out, the answer's yes.

1. In the three photos FLA file, open the Actions panel again, and then take another look at the XML. The basic structure looks like this (with most of the information removed for the sake of brevity):

```
<Motion attributes omitted >
    <source>
        // elements omitted
    </source>

    <Keyframe attributes omitted >
        // elements omitted
    </Keyframe>

    <Keyframe attributes omitted >
        // elements omitted
    </Keyframe>

    <Keyframe attributes omitted >
        // elements omitted
```

```
        </Keyframe>
    </Motion>;
```

The <source> element, and its children, describe the default state of the
original stand-in rectangle. The remaining sibling elements, <Keyframe>,
and their children, represent the three keyframes used in the designer's
FLA file, frames 1, 13, and 20. This adjustment's goal is to reduce the blur
effect slightly—that's in the second <Keyframe> element—and increase the
rotation by a smidgeon—that's in the third.

2. Obviously, your personal adjustments will vary depending on the exact
   nature of your own XML, so feel free to experiment. One possibility might
   look like this (operative changes in bold):

```
<Keyframe index="12" tweenSnap="true" tweenSync="true"
    x="-11.399999999999977" y="-104.44999999999999"
    scaleX="2.451548451548452" scaleY="2.453" rotation="-11.3">
    <tweens>
        <CustomEase>
            <geom:Point x="0.29906669248852413"
                y="0.5760325983121745"/>
            <geom:Point x="0.6150788560295106" y="1"/>
        </CustomEase>
    </tweens>
    <filters>
        <filters:BlurFilter blurX="0" blurY="20" quality="1"/>
    </filters>
</Keyframe>

<Keyframe index="19" x="-18" y="-137.95"
    scaleX="2.9180819180819184" scaleY="2.921" rotation="-15">
    <filters>
        <filters:BlurFilter blurX="0" blurY="0" quality="1"/>
    </filters>
</Keyframe>
```

In the first of the listed <Keyframe> elements, the blurY attribute of a nested
<filters> element has been changed from 40 to 20. In the second, a
rotation attribute has been changed from –15 to –18.

 It's worth noting that the index attributes of these <Key
frame> elements don't match the frame numbers of the
actual keyframes in the timeline: they're behind by one
number apiece. This discrepancy occurs because the
<Keyframe> elements start their counting from 0, rather
than 1. So the XML version of frame 13 is listed as 12,
and the XML version of frame 20 listed as 19.

3. Select Control→Test Movie to see the updated visuals.

Editing the Default ActionScript

Now that the animation satisfies the customer, it's time to make the photos respond to mouse clicks.

1. To let each movie clip respond separately to ActionScript instructions, each symbol needs its own unique instance name. Select each move clip in turn, and then use the Property inspector to give them the instance names *photo1*, *photo2*, and *photo3*.

2. Open the Actions panel one last time, and then comment out the final two lines of the existing code:

```
//var photo1_animator:Animator = new Animator(photo1_xml, ¬
    photo1);
//photo1_animator.play();
```

3. Type the following new ActionScript after the commented code:

```
photo1.buttonMode = true;
photo1.addEventListener(MouseEvent.CLICK, clickHandler);
photo2.buttonMode = true;
photo2.addEventListener(MouseEvent.CLICK, clickHandler);
photo3.buttonMode = true;
photo3.addEventListener(MouseEvent.CLICK, clickHandler);

var photo1_animator:Animator = new Animator(photo1_xml, ¬
    photo1);

function clickHandler(evt:MouseEvent):void {
    photo1_animator.rewind();
    photo1_animator.target = evt.target as MovieClip;
    photo1_animator.play();
}
```

The first six lines configure each movie clip in the same way. Setting the `Sprite.buttonMode` property to `true` causes the mouse pointer to change from the default arrow to the cursor used for hyperlinks when the mouse hovers over each movie clip (this is possible because the `MovieClip` class inherits functionality from `Sprite`). The `EventDispatcher.addEventLis tener()` method associates each movie clip with a custom `clickHandler()` function in response to mouse clicks (possible because the `MovieClip` class also inherits from `EventDispatcher`).

The `clickHandler()` function is executed any time one of the movie clips is clicked.

Figure 8-6. Responsive animation, programmed with very little custom code

The `clickHandler` function does three tasks:

- Invokes `rewind()` on the most recent animation, as represented by the `photo1_animator` instance (this resets an enlarged image to its original state)
- Sets the `target` property of `photo1_animator` to the selected (clicked) movie clip symbol, by way of the `MouseEvent.target` property (to assure `photo1_animator` that its new target is indeed a movie clip, the reference is cast as a movie clip with the `as` operator)
- Invokes `play()` on the newly targeted `photo1_animator` instance, which sets the most recently clicked movie clip in motion

4. Select Control→Test Movie to experience the updated interactivity (Figure 8-6).

Be aware that the XML generated by the Copy Motion as *ActionScript* 3.0 feature is influenced by three XML namespaces:

- `xmlns="fl.motion.*"`
- `xmlns:geom="flash.geom.*"`
- `xmlns:filters="flash.filters.*"`

These namespaces must be accounted for if you intend to navigate these XML elements with ECMAScript for XML (E4X) syntax. For more information, see the section "Namespaces" on page 80 in Chapter 3.

CHAPTER 9

Using ActionScript 3.0 Components

It's entirely possible, of course, to produce Flash content without ActionScript. Even if not interactive, such content typically bears the visual distinction of compelling custom artwork, which is why the Flash authoring tool has appealed to designers and developers alike for years. When ActionScript does enter the equation, the creative possibilities extend even further, occasionally venturing into territory that, in recent years, has become the mainstay of Flex; namely, Rich Internet Applications (RIAs). When you develop content that requires sophisticated user input—for example, when input text fields aren't enough, and you need radio buttons, combo boxes, and the like—the Components panel becomes your genie in a bottle. The Flash CS4 Professional ActionScript 3.0 component set, introduced in Flash CS3, is easier to skin and use, and performs more efficiently, than ever before.

Overview of the Component Set

Out of the box, the Components panel (Window→Components) offers a handy number of predesigned *components*—often informally called *widgets* or *controls*—that provide a wide range of features without the need for complicated programming. In ActionScript 3.0 documents, these components are divided into two categories: User Interface (UI) and Video, as seen in Figure 9-1. The UI group contains numerous components comparable to HTML `<form>` elements, such as `CheckBox`, `RadioButton`, `ComboBox`, and `Button`. The `Button` component differs from button symbols in that you can select and deselect it to switch it on and off, it has a built-in disabled state, and shares other features consistent with the component set as a whole. This group also contains useful components that have no equivalent in HTML, such as `ColorPicker`, `NumericStepper`, and `TileList`.

The Video group contains the `FLVPlayback` component, used to deploy video files in Flash with drag-and-drop ease; the `FLVPlaybackCaptioning` component,

Figure 9-1. The Components panel, showing User Interface and Video components

which facilitates captioning for foreign language subtitles and the hearing impaired; and numerous video-specific user interface components, such as a standalone play button, mute button, and volume control slider.

Increased Performance and Reduced File Size

The UI and Video components have been rewritten from the ground up in ActionScript 3.0, which lets them benefit from the same performance enhancements recounted throughout this book (in particular, see Chapter 4). This also means you can't mix and match the components with those that were written for ActionScript 2.0. Fortunately, the Components panel automatically updates its choices depending on the version of ActionScript selected for the current FLA file. If you start in one version of ActionScript, add components to the stage or library, and then change the FLA file's publish settings to ActionScript 3.0—or vice versa—you'll see warning messages when you try to compile the SWF file, and the compile will fail.

The performance improvement for ActionScript 3.0 components is substantial and can be demonstrated with a simple **for** loop, using practically the same code for a side-by-side comparison between ActionScript 2.0 and 3.0 components.

1. Create a new ActionScript 2.0 FLA file, and then open the Components panel. Drag a copy of the ComboBox component to the stage. Use the Property inspector to give this component the instance name myComboBox.

2. Select frame 1 in the Timeline, and then open the Actions panel. Enter the following ActionScript 2.0 code:

```
var startTime:Number = getTimer();

for (var i:Number = 0; i < 50000; i++) {
    myComboBox.addItem({label:i, data:i});
}

trace((getTimer() - startTime) / 1000);
```

In this code, a startTime variable performs the ActionScript equivalent to starting a stopwatch. A for loop increments a numeric variable, i, from 0 to 49,999, which populates the ComboBox instance with 50,000 label/data pairs. Finally, the "stopwatch" is halted, and the result is converted to seconds and displayed in the Output panel.

3. Select Control→Test Movie to review the length of time it takes your SWF file to display. *Be prepared to wait several seconds!* Your actual elapsed time may vary, depending on the speed of your computer, but in one series of tests, the code in Step 2 executes in 6.337 seconds.

The following steps demonstrate an equivalent test using the ActionScript 3.0 version of the same component.

4. Create a new ActionScript 3.0 FLA file, and then drag a copy of the ComboBox component to the stage. Give it the instance name myComboBox.

5. Select frame 1 in the Timeline, and then enter the following ActionScript 3.0 into the Actions panel:

```
var startTime:int = getTimer();

for (var i:int = 0; i < 50000; i++) {
    myComboBox.addItem({label:i, data:i});
}

trace((getTimer() - startTime) / 1000);
```

This code is almost identical. In fact, the only change is the numeric variable typing, from Number to int.

6. Select Control→Text Movie to review the new elapsed time. Again, your actual results may vary, but in one series of tests, the ActionScript 3.0

version of this same component displayed in 1.419 seconds, which is a remarkable increase in speed.

In addition to working more efficiently, the components tend to add significantly less weight to SWF files than their ActionScript 2.0 counterparts. Table 9-1 shows a comparison of the components shared by both languages.

Table 9-1. File sizes contributed by ActionScript 2.0 components versus ActionScript 3.0 components (only shows components shared by both languages)

Component	AS 2.0 file size	AS 3.0 file size
Button	27KB	15KB
CheckBox	28KB	15KB
ComboBox	56KB	35KB
DataGrid	59KB	40KB
Label	23KB	14KB
List	48KB	29KB
Loader (now named UILoader)	27KB	15KB
NumericStepper	29KB	18KB
ProgressBar	26KB	16KB
RadioButton	29KB	16KB
ScrollPane	39KB	22KB
TextArea	40KB	21KB
TextInput	25KB	15KB
UIScrollBar	34KB	18KB
FLVPlayback	35KB	57KB

It's important to realize that these file sizes aren't cumulative. In both Action-Script 2.0 and 3.0, each component shares its common framework with other components in the component set for that language. The biggest penalty comes with the first component's file size; additional components add only a small increase because they share most of the programming framework already provided by the first component. For example, the combined weight of the ActionScript 3.0 versions of Button and CheckBox is only 17KB—not the 30KB you might expect—which is only 2KB more than either component alone.

Feature Changes

In ActionScript 2.0 documents, components are generally stored in the Library as discrete entities. In ActionScript 3.0 documents, the introduction of even a single component creates a new library folder named Component Assets. This

Figure 9-2. The same three components displayed in the libraries of an ActionScript 2.0 document (left) and an ActionScript 3.0 document (right)

folder contains movie clip symbols used by the components' skins, and must not be deleted unless respective components are purposefully removed from the FLA file (skinning is discussed in greater detail in the sections "Styling Components with Code" and "Skinning Components Manually" in this chapter). Figure 9-2 shows the same three components—Button, CheckBox, and ComboBox—as dragged into an ActionScript 2.0 FLA file (left side) versus an ActionScript 3.0 FLA file (right side). Note the Component Assets folder on the right, and note also that the ActionScript 3.0 version of ComboBox carries with it a copy of List and TextInput, whose respective weights are already included in the total file size for ComboBox.

You can configure all components in the Component Inspector panel (Window→Component Inspector), as shown in Figure 9-3. Just select the component on the stage and arrange the settings as you please. In ActionScript 3.0 documents, the Bindings and Schema tabs of the Component Inspector panel are clickable, but their panes are disabled, as they apply only to data components, which are not compatible with ActionScript 3.0.

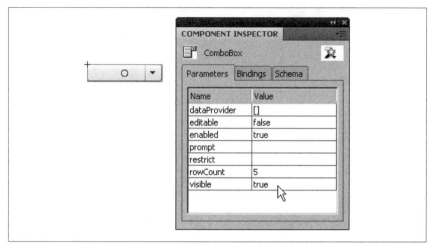

Figure 9-3. ComboBox component parameters, as displayed in the Component Inspector panel

Because of the general event handling changes in ActionScript 3.0, the components are programmed somewhat differently from the ActionScript 2.0 set. For details, see the section "Changes in Writing Code for Components" on page 188 later in this chapter.

Although it has an *application programming interface* (API) and can be fully programmed like any other component, the ActionScript 3.0 `FLVPlayback` component has been updated so that its composition can be customized without any need for code.

1. Create a new ActionScript 3.0 FLA file, and then open the Components panel. Drag a copy of the `FLVPlayback` component to the stage. No instance name is necessary. Save this file as *CustomVideo.fla*, because you're going to use it again later in this chapter.

2. Select the Component Inspector panel, and then ensure that the **skin** property is set to **None**. You don't need a skin in this case, because in the next step you'll be supplying a pair of individual skin elements to customize video playback features.

3. Drag a copy each of the `PausePlayButton` and `SeekBar` components, and position them on the stage wherever you prefer. If you like, change the dimensions of the FLA file to match the surface area taken up by these components. None of the components requires instance names.

4. With the `FLVPlayback` component selected, use the Component Inspector panel to set the **source** property to an FLV file, as shown in Figure 9-4. Click OK to close the Content Path dialog box.

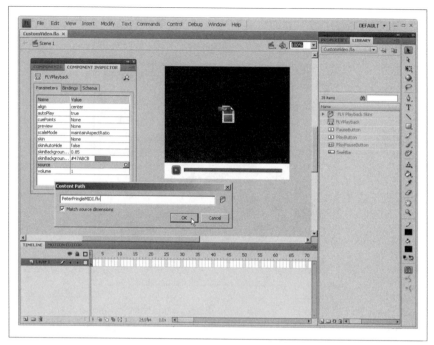

Figure 9-4. Customizing the FLVPlayback component without code

5. Select Control→Test Movie to verify that the `PausePlayButton` and `Seek Bar` components do indeed control video playback, even without the use of ActionScript or instance names (Figure 9-5).

New and Removed Components

Flash CS3 introduced six components for use in ActionScript 3.0 documents that remain available in Flash CS4: `ColorPicker`, `Slider`, `TileList`, `FLVPlaybackCaptioning`, `CaptionButton`, and `FullScreenButton`. These components are demonstrated in the section "Changes in Writing Code for Components" on page 188 later in this chapter. In conjunction with these additions, a number of previously available components have been removed, which only happens when a FLA file is configured for ActionScript 3.0. The removed items consist of the non-visual data components, including `XMLConnector` and `Web ServiceConnector`; the media components, superseded in Flash 8 by `FLVPlayback`; and the following UI components: `Accordion`, `Alert`, `DateChooser`, `Date Field`, `Menu`, `MenuBar`, `Tree`, and `Window`.

Figure 9-5. The FLVPlayback component and video-related UI components collaborate, even without ActionScript (theremin performance by Peter Pringle, http://PeterPringle .com, used with permission)

 The media components are actually intended for ActionScript 1.0 but still function in ActionScript 2.0 documents. They are not, however, compatible with ActionScript 3.0.

The full list of authoring tool components for ActionScript 2.0 and 3.0 is shown in Table 9-2, Table 9-3, Table 9-4, and Table 9-5.

Table 9-2. Data components available with Flash CS4 Professional

Component	AS 2.0	AS 3.0
DataHolder	X	
DataSet	X	
RDBMSResolver	X	
WebServiceConnector	X	
XMLConnector	X	
XUpdateResolver	X	

Table 9-3. *Media components available with Flash CS4 Professional*

Component	AS 2.0	AS 3.0
MediaController	X	Superseded by FLVPlayback
MediaDisplay	X	Superseded by FLVPlayback
MediaPlayback	X	Superseded by FLVPlayback

Table 9-4. *User Interface components available with Flash CS4 Professional*

Component	AS 2.0	AS 3.0
Accordion	X	
Alert	X	
Button	X	X
CheckBox	X	X
ColorPicker		X
ComboBox	X	X
DataGrid	X	X
DateChooser	X	
DateField	X	
Label	X	X
List	X	X
Loader	X	X (renamed UILoader)
Menu	X	
MenuBar	X	
NumericStepper	X	X
ProgressBar	X	X
RadioButton	X	X
ScrollPane	X	X
Slider		X
TextArea	X	X
TextInput	X	X
TileList		X
Tree	X	
UIScrollBar	X	X
Window	X	

Table 9-5. Video components available with Flash CS4 Professional

Component	AS 2.0	AS 3.0
FLVPlayback	X	X
FLVPlaybackCaptioning		X
BackButton	X	X
BufferingBar	X	X
CaptionButton		X
ForwardButton	X	X
FullScreenButton		X
MuteButton	X	X
PauseButton	X	X
PlayButton	X	X
PlayPauseButton	X	X
SeekBar	X	X
StopButton	X	X
VolumeBar	X	X

 For details on how to work around many of the missing components in ActionScript 3.0 documents, see Chapter 10.

Changes in Writing Code for Components

Thanks to the improved event-handling model in ActionScript 3.0, writing code for the component set is as straightforward as any of the event handling examples illustrated in other chapters of this book. Like movie clip symbols and button symbols, components inherit from the `EventDispatcher` class, which means they all support the `addEventListener()` method that lets you associate an event with a custom function that responds to that event. The similarity among the following examples underscores the consistency inherent throughout the ActionScript 3.0 API. These examples demonstrate how to use the UI components that weren't available in versions of the authoring tool prior to Flash CS3.

Until you get familiar with a particular component, your first step in programming one should always be to consult its class entry in the ActionScript 3.0 Language and Components Reference, available at a moment's notice from the documentation (Window→Help), which opens in a browser window. A

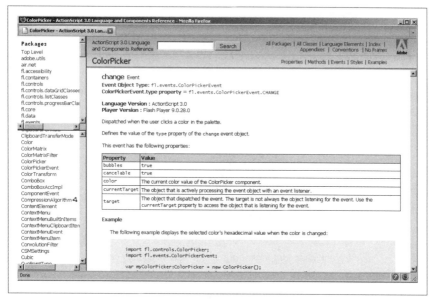

Figure 9-6. The ColorPicker component documentation

class entry's Events summary, in particular, lets you know immediately what events a component supports, as well as what data type the event belongs to. For example, the ColorPicker class entry features a **change** event. Clicking on the hyperlink for this event indicates that the event is referenced by way of the ColorPickerEvent class, as seen in Figure 9-6.

All the components reveal their secrets in this way, so you can easily program them. In all cases, the parameters shown in the Component Inspector panel correspond to properties of the component's class. Properties may be configured in the panel, with ActionScript, or a combination of both.

ColorPicker

The ColorPicker component displays a clickable color chip that expands into a configurable color palette that lets you select a color or type in a color (Figure 9-7). Assuming a ColorPicker component on the stage with the instance name myColorPicker and a movie clip with the instance name myMovieClip,the following ActionScript handles the selection of a color from the component's configurable color palette:

```
import fl.events.ColorPickerEvent;

var myColor:ColorTransform = new ColorTransform();

myColorPicker.addEventListener(ColorPickerEvent.CHANGE, ¬
```

```
        changeHandler);
    function changeHandler(evt:ColorPickerEvent):void {
        myColor.color = myColorPicker.selectedColor;
        myMovieClip.transform.colorTransform = myColor;
    }
```

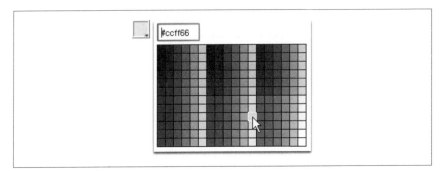

Figure 9-7. The ColorPicker component allows the user to specify colors

The ColorPickerEvent class must be imported, even in a frame script, because it isn't part of the flash package. A myColor variable is declared and set to an instance of the ColorTransform class, waiting to be used in response to a change event from the component. The operative code here is the addEventListener() method, which associates the ColorPickerEvent.CHANGE event constant with a custom changeHandler() function.

The changeHandler() function sets the color property of the myColor instance to the currently selected color, and is then assigned to the colorTransform property of a movie clip with the instance name *myMovieClip*. All DisplayObject objects, including movie clip symbols and sprites, support color transformation in this way.

The color palette of the ColorPicker component is fully customizable, and can display up to 1,024 colors. To have the myColorPicker instance display red, white, and blue, simply assign an array of hexadecimal values to the ColorPicker.colors property:

```
    myColorPicker.colors = new Array(0xFF0000, 0xFFFFFF, 0x0000FF);
```

Slider

The Slider component provides a slider with a draggable knob that optionally snaps to a configurable range of values (Figure 9-8).

As Figure 9-9 indicates, the Slider component can be displayed horizontally, but is easily set to a vertical orientation by a change to the direction parameter (the first entry in the Name column). Numerous other parameters are availa-

Figure 9-8. The Slider component lets users select from a range of values

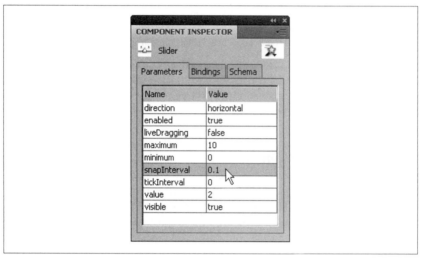

Figure 9-9. The Slider component parameters

ble. The `liveDragging` parameter determines how often `Slider` dispatches its change event. When `liveDragging` is set to `true`, `SliderEvent.CHANGE` is dispatched while the knob is dragged, as often as the `Slider.value` property updates. When set to `false`, the `SliderEvent.CHANGE` event is dispatched only when you release the knob.

The `maximum` and `minimum` parameters define the component's range of selectable values, and `snapInterval` determines the rate at which snapping should occur. The `tickInterval` parameter determines the distribution of visible tick marks, and `value` determines the starting position of the knob.

 According to the `Slider` class documentation, a `snapIn terval` value of 0 is supposed to mean continuous dragging, but this isn't what actually happens. In a range from 0 to 10, a `snapInterval` value of 1 snaps the knob to the values 0, 1, 2, 3, etc. A value of 5 snaps the knob to the values 0, 5, and 10. To achieve continuous dragging, enter a very small value, such as 0.1.

The following ActionScript shows the `Slider` component as a volume slider, assuming its range is set from 0 to 1. The volume setting is taken from the `Slider.value` property (see code in bold):

```
import fl.events.SliderEvent;

var mySound:Sound = new Sound();
mySound.load(new URLRequest("sampleSong.mp3"));
var myChannel:SoundChannel = mySound.play();
var myTransform:SoundTransform = new SoundTransform();

mySlider.addEventListener(SliderEvent.CHANGE, changeHandler);
function changeHandler(evt:SliderEvent):void {
    myTransform.volume = mySlider.value;
    myChannel.soundTransform = myTransform;
}
```

A `Sound` instance is associated with a `SoundChannel` instance, which makes it available to volume transformations. Here again, the actual event handler is very simple: the `SliderEvent.CHANGE` event is associated with a custom `changeHandler()` function, which invokes the `Slide.value` property on the `mySlider` instance in order to update the `volume` property of a `SoundTransform` instance that, in turn, updates the volume of the `Sound` instance.

TileList

The `TileList` component is comparable in some ways to an HTML table or a simplified version of the `DataGrid` component. In a nutshell, it provides a grid of rows and columns to display images (Figure 9-10).

Figure 9-10. The TileList component displays a grid of images

Like the Slider component, the properties of TileList are easy to configure in the Component Inspector panel (Figure 9-11). The columnCount and rowCount parameters determine the number of columns and rows in the grid, respectively, while columnWidth and rowHeight determine their dimensions. The direction parameter specifies whether images progress sequentially across or down the grid before wrapping. Scrolling is configured with scroll Policy parameter, which you can set to auto, on, or off.

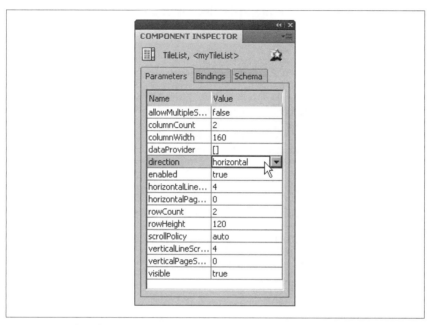

Figure 9-11. The TileList component parameters

The following ActionScript produces the 2 by 2 grid shown in Figure 9-10:

```
myTileList.addItem({label:"Sandmen", source:"sandmen.jpg"});
myTileList.addItem({label:"Braids", source:"braids.jpg"});
myTileList.addItem({label:"Jumping", source:"jumping.jpg"});
myTileList.addItem({label:"Crazy", source:"crazy.jpg"});

myTileList.addEventListener(Event.CHANGE, changeHandler);

function changeHandler(evt:Event):void {
    trace(myTileList.selectedItem.label);
}
```

Note that the change event for this component comes directly from the Event class, which means no import directive is necessary in frame scripts that handle TileList events.

FLVPlaybackCaptioning and CaptionButton

Video subtitles and captions have been possible for several releases of Flash, but until the `FLVPlaybackCaptioning` component, introduced in Flash CS3, they required custom programming. In ActionScript 3.0 documents, you can now add captioning to your videos without code. You do need an XML document that adheres to the World Wide Web Consortium's (W3C) specification for TimedText (TT) documents (*http://www.w3.org/AudioVideo/TT/*). The `CaptionButton` component selects and deselects captioning. Here's an example of a TimedText XML document:

```xml
<?xml version="1.0" encoding="iso-8859-1"?>
<tt xmlns="http://www.w3.org/2006/04/ttaf1"
    xmlns:tts="http://www.w3.org/2006/04/ttaf1#styling">
<head>
    <styling>
        <style id="1" tts:textAlign="left"
            tts:fontFamily="Arial" />
        <style id="2" tts:textAlign="center"
            tts:fontFamily="Arial" />
    </styling>
</head>
<body>
    <div>
        <p begin="00:00:09.50" dur="1000ms" style="1">
            Okay, action!</p>
        <p begin="00:00:11.00" dur="2800ms" style="2">
            Twinkle, twi ... le</p>
        <p begin="00:00:15.50" dur="1500ms" style="1">
            Okay, action!</p>
        <p begin="00:00:17.50" dur="4600ms" style="2">
            Twink ... le ... tink [hiccup]!  Oh!</p>
        <p begin="00:00:22.75" dur="2100ms" style="1">
            Okay, action!</p>
        <p begin="00:00:25.75" end="00:00:29.25" style="2">
            Twinkle, twinkle, little star</p>
        <p begin="00:00:29.75" end="00:00:32.50" style="2">
            how I wonder what you are</p>
        <p begin="00:00:33.00" end="00:00:36.00" style="2">
            bup bup bup ... world so high,</p>
        <p begin="00:00:36.50" end="00:00:39.00" style="2">
            like a diamond in the sky,</p>
        <p begin="00:00:39.50" end="00:00:40.00" style="2">
            Oh!</p>
        <p begin="00:00:41.25" end="00:00:41.75" style="2">
            Oh dear.</p>
        <p begin="00:00:42.25" end="00:00:43.25" style="1">
            Action!</p>
        <p begin="00:00:43.50" end="00:00:47.00" style="2">
            [sproing! sproing! sproing!]</p>
        <p begin="00:00:48.00" end="00:00:53.00" style="2">
            How I wonder what you are.  Bup!</p>
```

```
<p begin="00:00:54.00" end="00:00:55.50" style="2">
    Buh buh buh, oh ...</p>
<p begin="00:00:56.00" end="00:00:57.00" style="2">
    Buh buh, oh ...</p>
<p begin="00:00:57.50" end="00:00:58.50" style="2">
    Nooo!</p>
    </div>
    </body>
    </tt>
```

Note that a `<styling>` element, nested in the `<head>` element, allows for the declaration of styles—here, left- and center-alignment—that can be referenced by an id attribute later in the body of the document. Note, also, the alternate ways to specify the duration of a caption, including collaborative begin and dur attributes, such as begin="00:00:09.50" dur="1000ms", and collaborative begin and end pairings, such as begin="00:00:25.75" end="00:00:29.25". Once a TimedText document is prepared, the process of captioning is trivial.

Drag a copy of the FLVPlayback and FLVPlaybackCaptioning components to the stage. Neither component needs an instance name. FLVPlaybackCaptioning becomes invisible at runtime. Position it where you like.

Use the Component Inspector panel to configure the skin parameter of the FLVPlayback component to None or to one of the skins with the word "Under" in the name, like SkinUnderPlaySeekCaption (this is important because skins with "Over" in the name obscure the captioning text field). Set the source parameter to a video file that correlates with the TimedText document.

Select the FLVPlaybackCaptioning component, and then set its source parameter to the location of the TimedText document, as shown in Figure 9-12.

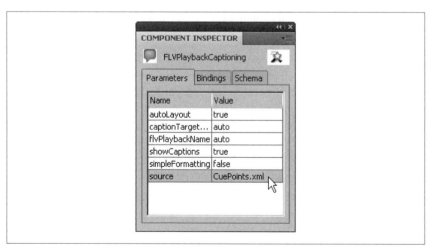

Figure 9-12. Configuring the source parameter

Figure 9-13. The FLVPlaybackCaptioning component provides video captions without ActionScript ("Andréa" character created by Chris Georgenes, http://mudbubble.com, used with permission)

At runtime, captions are automatically transferred from XML format to visual display, as seen in Figure 9-13. The `CaptionButton` component is built-in to any skin whose name contains the word "Caption" and allows the user to select and deselect captions. If no skin is selected, captions are displayed by default. The `CaptionButton` component can also be used on its own, apart from any skin, in the same manner described in the FLVPlayback exercise in the "Feature Changes" on page 182 of this chapter.

FullScreenButton

The `FullScreenButton` component exists as a built-in element of several of the provided skins for the `FLVPlayback` component, as well as a standalone component used with `FLVPlayback`. Ultimately, the `FullScreenButton` component is just a button that invokes the `FLVPlayback.enterFullScreenDisplayState()` method. To demonstrate its use, you have to view the SWF file and video content in a properly configured browser window.

1. Open the *CustomVideo.fla* file created in this chapter's "Feature Changes" on page 182, and then resave it as *FullScreenButton.fla*.

2. Open the Components panel, and then drag a copy of the `FullScreenButton` component to the stage. No instance name is necessary.

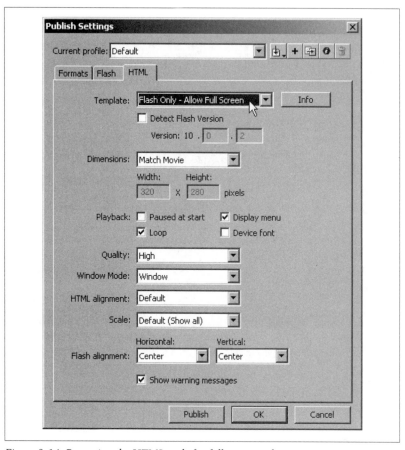

Figure 9-14. Preparing the HTML code for full-screen video

3. Select File→Publish Settings→HTML, and then change the Template drop-down list to "Flash Only - Allow Full Screen," as shown in Figure 9-14.

The selection of this template automatically inserts crucial lines of code in the HTML that embeds the SWF file, although the addition can certainly be made by hand. If you prefer to work manually, you have to add a new `<param>` element inside the existing `<object>` element to explicitly permit full-screen viewing (new code in bold):

```
<object><param name="allowFullScreen" value="true" />
```

then add a corresponding attribute to the companion `<embed>` element:

```
<embed src="FullScreenButton.swf" ... other attributes ...
    allowFullScreen="true" ... />
```

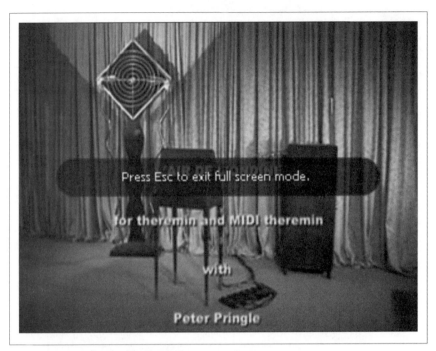

Figure 9-15. A video displayed in full-screen mode

These additions must be mirrored in the JavaScript function that appears in the same HTML document.

4. Select File→Publish Preview→HTML to launch the SWF file in a browser. Click the `FullScreenButton` component to see the video display in full-screen mode (Figure 9-15). Press the Esc key at any time to exit full-screen mode.

   Note that during full-screen mode, the video UI controls are hidden from view. This happens because the `FLVPlayback.fullScreenTakeOver` property is set to `true` by default.

5. Close the SWF file. Select the `FLVPlayback` component on the stage, and then use the Property inspector to name it `myFLVPlayback`. Select frame 1 in the Timeline, and then open the Actions panel. Enter the following code:

   ```
   myFLVPlayback.fullScreenTakeOver = false;
   ```

6. Select File→Publish Preview→HTML once again to launch the SWF file in a browser. Note that this time, the components remain visible in either mode (Figure 9-16).

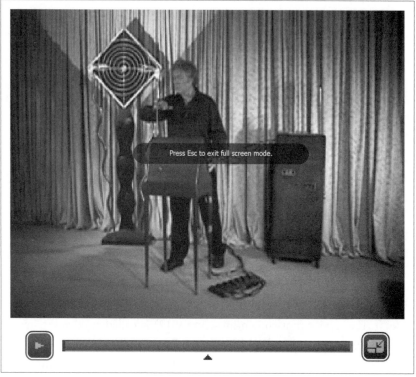

Figure 9-16. A video in full-screen mode with video UI components (theremin performance by Peter Pringle, http://PeterPringle.com, used with permission)

Changing the Appearance of Components

The standard look and feel of the ActionScript 3.0 component set can be freely changed, a procedure called *styling* or *skinning*, depending on how you go about it.

Styling Components with Code

The `StyleManager` class lets you reference special styling properties—called styles—for each component. For example, in the Help menu's ActionScript 3.0 Language and Components Reference, if you consult the class entry for the `Button` component, you find that in addition to Public Properties, Public Methods, and Events summaries, the `Button` class also features a summary for Styles, as seen in Figure 9-17. Make sure to always click "Show Inherited Styles" to see them all.

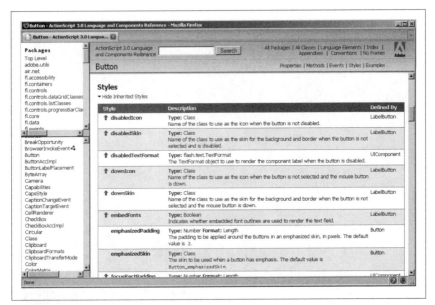

Figure 9-17. Style properties of the Button class

One of these styles (not shown in Figure 9-17) is called `textFormat`, which makes a quick and useful demonstration of two `StyleManager` methods.

1. Create an ActionScript 3.0 FLA file, and then open the Components panel. Drag a copy of the `Button` and `CheckBox` components to the stage.

2. Select frame 1 in the Timeline, and then open the Actions panel. Enter the following code:

```
import fl.managers.StyleManager;
import fl.controls.Button;
import fl.controls.CheckBox;

var myTextFormat:TextFormat = new TextFormat();
myTextFormat.size = 26;

StyleManager.setStyle("textFormat", myTextFormat);
```

The `StyleManager`, `Button`, and `CheckBox` classes must be imported, even in frame scripts, because none of these classes belongs to the `flash` package. A `myTextFormat` variable is declared and set to an instance of the `TextFormat` class, and then has its `size` property set to 26. Finally, the static `StyleManager.setStyle()` method is invoked, with `"textFormat"` as the first parameter, and the `myTextFormat` instance as the other. The `"textFormat"` parameter is a string that refers to the `textFormat` style that both of these components happen to share.

3. Select Control→Test Movie to experience a font size that's too large for the current dimensions of the components (Figure 9-18), showing that the setStyle() method applies styling to all components in a document that feature the textFormat style.

Figure 9-18. Component text formatting changed with ActionScript

4. Close the SWF file, and then return to the Actions panel. Update the existing ActionScript so that it looks like this (changes in bold):

```
import fl.managers.StyleManager;
import fl.controls.Button;
import fl.controls.CheckBox;

var myTextFormat1:TextFormat = new TextFormat();
myTextFormat1.size = 26;

var myTextFormat2:TextFormat = new TextFormat();
myTextFormat2.size = 8;

StyleManager.setStyle("textFormat", myTextFormat1);
StyleManager.setComponentStyle(Button, "textFormat", ¬
    myTextFormat2);
```

This time, two TextFormat instances exist. The first one, as before, is fed into the StyleManager.setStyle() method, and updates the textFormat style of both components. The second one, which was configured with a smaller font size, is fed into the StyleManager.setComponentStyle() method, which accepts one additional parameter; namely, the class name of one of the components, Button. This second method overrides the global formatting established by the setStyle() method, because it calls out a particular component type by name.

5. Select Control→Test Movie again to verify that the Button component now has a much smaller font size (Figure 9-19).

6. Close the SWF file again. You've seen how to affect the styling of all components in a document, and you've also seen how to affect the styling of all of one *type* of component. The final way to stylize components is to invoke the UIComponent.setStyle() method, which is inherited by each

Figure 9-19. Formatting focused on one specific type of component

component individually. Select the `CheckBox` component, and then use the Property inspector to give it the instance name **myCheckBox**. Return again to the Actions panel, and then update the existing code so it looks like this (changes in bold):

```
import fl.managers.StyleManager;
import fl.controls.Button;
import fl.controls.CheckBox;

var myTextFormat1:TextFormat = new TextFormat();
myTextFormat1.size = 26;

var myTextFormat2:TextFormat = new TextFormat();
myTextFormat2.size = 8;

var myTextFormat3:TextFormat = new TextFormat();
myTextFormat3.size = 12;

StyleManager.setStyle("textFormat", myTextFormat1);
StyleManager.setComponentStyle(Button, "textFormat", ¬
    myTextFormat2);
myCheckBox.setStyle("textFormat", myTextFormat3);
```

A third `TextFormat` instance has been added, this one routed specifically to the `myCheckBox` instance, via its inherited `UIComponent.setStyle()` method. The original size-26 formatting is still in effect, but the `Button` component overrides it, thanks to its more specifically honed `myTextFormat2` instance. Here, the `CheckBox` component also overrides it, thanks to its *even more specifically honed* `myTextFormat3` instance.

7. Select Control→Test Movie one last time to verify that the `CheckBox` component now features a practically normal-sized font (Figure 9-20).

The `textFormat` style isn't the only property available, of course. Many components feature an `icon` style, for example, that lets you incorporate a small image into the component's display. Consult the class entry of the component(s) in question, and have fun experimenting!

Figure 9-20. Formatting focused on one specific instance of a component

Skinning Components Manually

It goes without saying that some design choices are more successful when implemented manually. Changing the actual make-up of a component's skin —that is, redrawing or manipulating the actual movie clips that comprise a component's features—is called skinning, and from a designer's standpoint, it couldn't be any more intuitive than the following steps.

1. Create a new ActionScript 3.0 FLA file, and then open the Components panel. Drag a copy of the Button component to the stage.

2. Double-click the Button component on the stage, just as you would to edit in place any movie clip symbol. Doing so opens the component into an "exploded view" that reveals each element of its default skin, as seen in Figure 9-21.

3. Double-click the representation of the over state to enter the timeline of that element. Most component skins take advantage of 9-slice scaling, as seen in Figure 9-22. The dashed lines indicate which portions of the image will scale when resized and which portions won't. In Figure 9-22, the corner regions maintain their present aspect ratios, while the top, bottom, and sides stretch as necessary.

4. Individual component skins may vary, but you'll typically find a number of timeline layers already in place. Here, these include layers named highlight and fill. Carefully select the content of these layers, and then delete it. Select the Paint Bucket tool, choose a markedly different fill color, such as pink, and then click inside the border layer stroke to fill the rounded rectangle.

5. Select Edit→Edit Document to return to the main timeline. Drag another copy of the Button component from the Library to the stage.

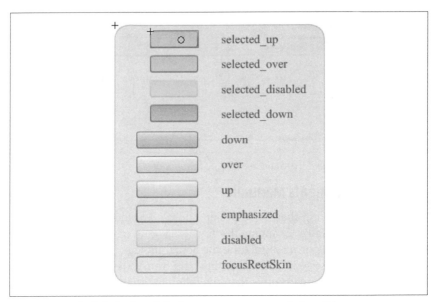

Figure 9-21. The default skin of the Button component, ready for editing

6. Select Control→Test Movie, and then move your cursor over and away from both Button components to verify that their over states have visually changed.

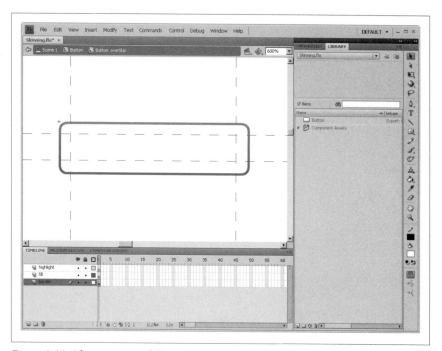

Figure 9-22. The over state of the Button component, showing 9-slice scaling lines

CHAPTER 10

Making Up for a Reduced Component Set

In spite of the component improvements discussed in Chapter 9, the overall number of components in the Flash authoring tool has been reduced for ActionScript 3.0 FLA files. The data components, in particular, have been removed completely and now belong to the Flex framework. A handful of user interface (UI) components, such as `Accordion`, `Tree`, and `Window`, are also absent.

 See Table 9-2 through Table 9-5 in Chapter 9 for a full list of new and removed components.

These components are still available for ActionScript 2.0 documents, but the Components panel adjusts its contents based on a FLA file's publish settings (File→Publish Settings→Flash→Script). Even if you start in an ActionScript 2.0 document, and then add components to the Library panel and change your publish settings, you will only see error messages when you compile. Components designed for different versions of ActionScript can't be mixed in the same FLA file. This chapter discusses a number of ways to work around (or work without) Flash components no longer supported in ActionScript 3.0.

Working Without Data Components in ActionScript 3.0

The data components in ActionScript 2.0 offered a panel-based interface for configuring sophisticated data interactions among UI components and even external data sources, such as XML documents and databases. In a sense, they provided a more complex, but similar apparatus to the Script Assist feature of the Actions panel, best suited to older ActionScript. Developers who routinely work with complex data binding are generally going to find a more comfortable workflow in Flex Builder 3, which is specifically geared toward Rich Internet Application (RIA) development. You may, however, encounter the occasional need for some of these features in the Flash authoring tool. The following sections discuss the implementation of a pair of popular data components in ActionScript 2.0, and then recommend a replacement workflow for Action-Script 3.0 documents.

Creating an XMLConnector Scenario in ActionScript 2.0

In ActionScript 2.0, one of the XMLConnector component's uses was to load, parse, and use XML data to populate UI components. During this process, a copy of the DataBindingClasses component (Window→Common Libraries→Classes) was automatically added to the library, which facilitated nearly codeless *data binding* among components; that is, components could be configured to influence the data content and visual display of other components automatically. You could do this with barely any use of ActionScript, but the process was fairly involved and required a well organized bit of fiddling among tabs of the Component Inspector panel, as demonstrated in the following example. Although the XMLConnector component was potentially helpful to designers, you can reproduce the functionality illustrated here with relatively little effort in ActionScript 3.0. One approach is discussed immediately after the ActionScript 2.0 version.

1. Create a new ActionScript 2.0 FLA file, and then save it as *XMLConnector.fla*. In the Timeline, rename the default layer to **scripts,** and then add a new layer named **components**.

2. Open the Components panel. With the components layer selected, drag a copy of the XMLConnector component to the stage. It doesn't matter where you position this component, because, like all data components, it becomes invisible at runtime. Select the XMLConnector component, and then use the Property inspector to give it the instance name **xmlConn**.

3. Drag a copy of the ComboBox and TextInput components to the stage. Give the ComboBox component the instance name **myComboBox**, and the TextInput component the instance name **myTextInput**.

4. Create a new XML document in the same folder as *XMLConnector.fla,* and then save the new document as *cds.xml* (this is the same file used in Chapter 1, so you may copy that one, if you like). The contents of this XML file should read as follows:

```
<?xml version="1.0" encoding="iso-8859-1"?>
<library>
```

```
<artist name="The Beatles">
    <album name="Abbey Road">
        <track title="Come Together" />
        <track title="Something" />
        <track title="Maxwell's Silver Hammer" />
        <track title="Oh! Darling" />
        <track title="Octopus's Garden" />
        <track title="I Want You (She's So Heavy)" />
        <track title="Here Comes the Sun" />
        <track title="Because" />
        <track title="You Never Give Me Your Money" />
        <track title="Sun King" />
        <track title="Mean Mr. Mustard" />
        <track title="Polythene Pam" />
        <track title="She Came in Through the Bathroom Window" />
        <track title="Golden Slumbers" />
        <track title="Carry That Weight" />
        <track title="The End" />
        <track title="Her Majesty" />
    </album>
</artist>
</library>
```

5. Select xmlConn, and then open the Component Inspector panel (Window→Component Inspector). Select the Parameters tab, and then enter **cds.xml** as the value of the URL parameter. Set the direction parameter to receive, as shown in Figure 10-1. This associates the XMLConnector component with the *cds.xml* document.

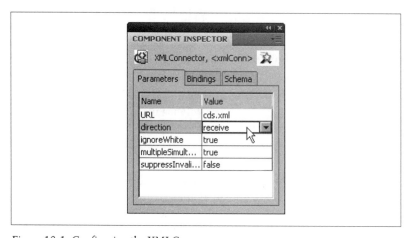

Figure 10-1. Configuring the XMLConnector component

6. Select the Component Inspector panel's Schema tab. Select the existing results schema, and then click the far right ⊞ arrow button to browse for the *cds.xml* document (Figure 10-2).

Figure 10-2. Establishing the XML for the results schema

7. When the XML document is displayed in the Schema tab, notice the results→library→artist→album→track node, as shown in Figure 10-3. This node represents the numerous <track> elements of the XML document, which are going to be displayed by the ComboBox component.

8. Select the myComboBox instance. In the Component Inspector panel, select the Bindings tab, and then click the ✛ button to add a binding. This opens the Add Binding dialog box. Select dataProvider, and then click OK to close the dialog box. In the Bindings tab, double-click the bound to parameter to open the Bound To dialog box.

9. In the Bound To dialog box, as shown in Figure 10-4, select XMLConnector, <xmlConn> on the left (this is the xmlConn instance) and the deeply nested track node on the right, as noted in Step 7. Click OK to close the dialog box. This action automatically adds the DataBindingClasses component to the library.

10. At this point, the myComboBox instance is associated with the <track> elements of the XML document, thanks to the XMLConnector component. Now you just need a trigger. Select frame 1 of the scripts layer, and then open the Actions panel. Type the following ActionScript:

```
xmlConn.trigger();
```

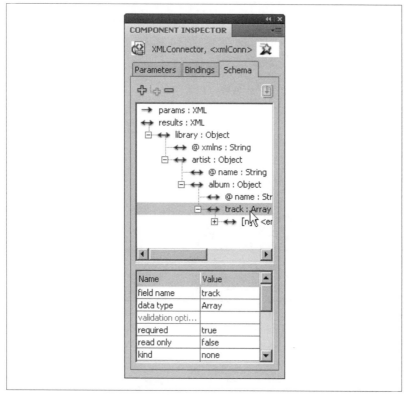

Figure 10-3. Selecting the <track> elements of the XML document

Select Control→Test Movie to confirm that the ComboBox component displays the names of the tracks from The Beatles' *Abbey Road* album (Figure 10-5).

11. To demonstrate data binding between the ComboBox and TextInput components, close the SWF file, and then continue with a few additional steps. Select the myTextInput instance, and then return to the Component Inspector panel's Bindings tab. Click the ✚ button to open the Add Binding dialog box. You see one choice for text, which refers to the TextInput.text property of the component (the text it displays). Select the text binding, then click OK to close the dialog box.

12. In the Bindings tab, double-click the bound to parameter to open the Bound To dialog box. As shown in Figure 10-6, select ComboBox, <myComboBox> on the left, and selectedItem on the right, which refers to the ComboBox.selectedItem property of the myComboBox instance.

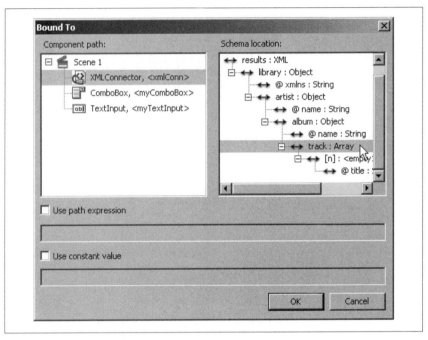

Figure 10-4. Binding the ComboBox component with the XMLConnector component

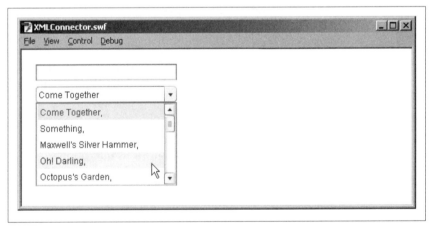

Figure 10-5. A ComboBox component displaying data from an XML file

13. Turn on the "Use path expression" checkbox, and then enter the expression **title**, as shown in Figure 10-6. This associates the **title** property of the currently selected item in the ComboBox—namely, a **<track>** element's

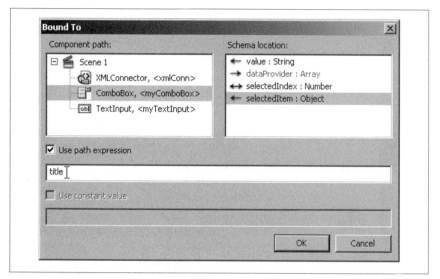

Figure 10-6. Binding the TextInput component with the ComboBox component

title attribute—with the TextInput.text property of the myTextInput instance. Click OK to close the dialog box.

14. Select Control→Test Movie to confirm that the TextInput component updates automatically to display the current value of the ComboBox component.

Recreating an XMLConnector Scenario in ActionScript 3.0

ActionScript 3.0 has no data components to recreate the XMLConnector, but you can reproduce the features just described in ActionScript 3.0 with surprisingly little code. It's a matter of loading the XML document and responding to a couple pertinent events.

1. Create a new ActionScript 3.0 FLA file, and then name it *XMLConnector Mimic.fla*. Rename the default layer in the Timeline to **scripts,** and then add a new layer named **components**.

2. With the components layer selected, open the Components panel, and then drag a copy of the ComboBox and TextInput components to the stage. Give the ComboBox component the instance name **myComboBox,** and the TextInput component the instance name **myTextInput**.

3. Select frame 1 of the scripts layer, and then open the Actions panel. Enter the following code:

```
var myXML:XML = new XML();
var xmlLoader:URLLoader = new URLLoader();
```

```
xmlLoader.load(new URLRequest("cds.xml"));
xmlLoader.addEventListener(Event.COMPLETE, completeHandler);

function completeHandler(evt:Event):void {
    myXML = XML(evt.target.data);
    var len:int = myXML..track.length();
    for (var i:int = 0; i < len; i++) {
        myComboBox.addItem({label:myXML..track[i].@title});
    }
    myComboBox.addEventListener(Event.CHANGE, changeHandler);
}

function changeHandler(evt:Event):void {
    myTextInput.text = myComboBox.selectedLabel;
}
```

In the first four lines, the variable myXML is declared and set to an instance of the XML class. Another variable, xmlLoader, is set to a URLLoader instance and used to request the *cds.xml* document. Finally, the Event.COMPLETE event, which indicates that the XML document has loaded, is associated with a custom completeHandler() function.

The completeHandler() function parses the XML document, and routes its contents to the myXML instance. Using ECMAScript for XML (E4X) syntax, the remainder of this function uses a for loop to repeatedly invoke ComboBox.addItem() on the myComboBox instance in order to supply it with labels. Finally, the Event.CHANGE event constant is associated with a custom changeHandler() function, which updates the TextInput.text property of the myTextInput instance.

 See the section "Namespaces" on page 80 in Chapter 3, for more detailed information on E4X and the navigation of XML documents.

4. Select Control→Test Movie to confirm that the ComboBox component correctly displays track information that the TextInput component updates automatically to display the current value of the ComboBox component. Compare the ActionScript 2.0 and 3.0 SWF files for this exercise, and you'll see that the ActionScript 3.0 SWF file weighs less than half of its companion's file size.

Creating a WebServiceConnector Scenario in ActionScript 2.0

Web services provide an XML-based mechanism for data exchange by way of a protocol called Simple Object Access Protocol (SOAP), (*http://www.w3.org/ TR/soap12-part0/*), whose specification is maintained by the World Wide Web Consortium (W3C), the same body responsible for the HTML specification.

SOAP messages can be consumed with the ActionScript 2.0 `WebServiceConnec tor` data component.

1. Create a new ActionScript 2.0 FLA file, and then name it *WebServiceComponent.fla*. In the Timeline, rename the default layer to **scripts**, and create a new layer named **component**.

2. With the **component** layer selected, open the Components panel, and then drag a copy of the `WebServiceConnector` component to the stage. Use the Property inspector to give the component the instance name **wsConn**.

3. Open the Web Services panel (Window→Other Panels→Web Services). Unfortunately, this panel is active only in ActionScript 2.0 documents, but it provides a handy way to check what methods are available from any number of Web services, in addition to what parameters those methods expect. Click the Define Web services button (a blue globe) to open the Define Web Services dialog box. In this dialog box, click the ⊕ button to add a new Web service URL. Enter *http://www.w3schools.com/webservi ces/tempconvert.asmx?WSDL*, and then click the OK button to close the dialog box. This action updates the Web Services panel (Figure 10-7) to show the name of a particular Web service provided by *http://w3schools .com*, `TempConvert`, which features two methods. Open the `params` node beneath `FahrenheitToCelsius()` to see that a single string parameter is expected: a value in Fahrenheit, to be converted to Celsius.

4. With the `WebServiceConnector` component selected, open the Component Inspector panel, and then set the `WSDLURL` parameter to *http://www .w3schools.com/webservices/tempconvert.asmx?WSDL*, the `operation` parameter to **FahrenheitToCelsius**, and the other two parameters to **true** (Figure 10-8). This action prepares the `wsConn` instance to use the `FahrenheitToCelsius()` method of the `TempConvert`Web service.

5. Select frame 1 of the **scripts** layer, and then open the Actions panel. Type the following ActionScript:

```
wsConn.addEventListener("result", resultHandler);
wsConn.params = ["451"];
wsConn.trigger();

function resultHandler(evt:Object):Void {
    trace(evt.target.results);
};
```

This associates the `WebServiceConnector.result` event with a custom `resultHandler()` function that traces the value returned by the Web service. The `WebServiceConnector.params` property of the `wsConn` instance is set to an `Array` instance (the square brackets, [], are a shorthand for the expression `new Array()`). In honor of Ray Bradbury's novel *Fahrenheit 451*,

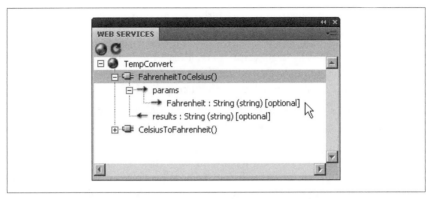

Figure 10-7. Reviewing Web service methods in the Web Services panel

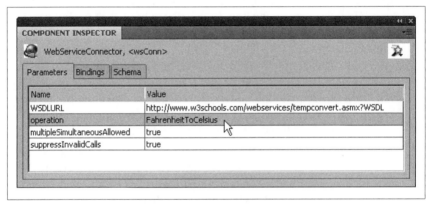

Figure 10-8. Preparing to consume a publicly available Web service

the string "451" is provided as the sole value of the params array. Some methods receive numerous parameters, would be added in a comma-delimited list. Finally, the WebServiceConnector.trigger() method nudges the wsConn instance into action.

6. Select Control→Test Movie to confirm that the value 232.777777777778 (the Celsius value for 451 degrees Fahrenheit) appears in the Output panel. In the menu bar of the SWF file, select View→Bandwidth Profiler to see that the file weighs 40KB.

Recreating a WebServiceConnector Scenario in ActionScript 3.0

No ActionScript 3.0 equivalent to WebServiceConnector ships with the authoring tool, but a free third-party extension, written by Pieter Michels (*http://www.wellconsidered.be/*), neatly fits the bill. Pieter kindly granted permission

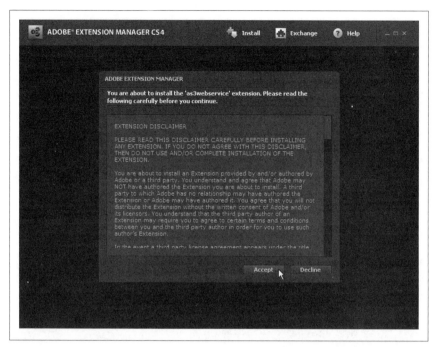

Figure 10-9. Agreeing to the standard Adobe Extension Manager disclaimer

for the use of his extension in conjunction with this book. His `WebService` component extension, available at *http://www.wellconsidered.be/blog/as3-web service-component/*, provides three Web service–related classes, demonstrated in this exercise.

To reproduce the `WebService` connector feature in ActionScript 3.0, you need to download Pieter Michels' WebService Component extension from *http://www.wellconsidered.be/blog/as3-webservice-component/*. When the download is complete, unpack the ZIP archive, and then double-click the *wellconsidered_ws.mxp* file to open it in the Adobe Extension Manager (Figure 10-9). Click the Accept button, and then click the OK button to see the extension included among your list of extensions, which will vary from the one depicted.

Make sure the new extension is turned on by ensuring the checkbox in the Enabled column is selected in the On/Off column (Figure 10-10).

Shut down the Flash authoring tool, and then launch it again so that the extension is activated at startup.

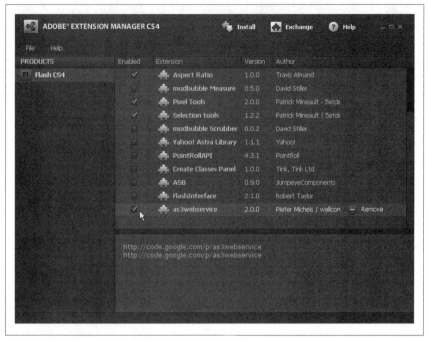

Figure 10-10. The WebService component extension, installed and active

1. Create a new ActionScript 3.0 FLA file, and then name it
   WebServiceExtension.fla. Rename the default layer in the Timeline to
   scripts.

2. Open the Components panel and note that a new folder, named
   wellconsidered, is now available. Open this new folder, and then drag a
   copy of the `Operation`, `OperationEvent`, and `WebService` components to the
   library. These provide a virtual `be.wellconsidered.services` package for
   three classes corresponding to the three components in the library. These
   classes will be referenced in the ActionScript in Step 3.

3. Select frame 1 of the **scripts** layer, and then open the Actions panel. Type
   the following code:

```
import be.wellconsidered.services.WebService;
import be.wellconsidered.services.Operation;
import be.wellconsidered.services.events.OperationEvent;

var ws:WebService = new WebService("http://www.w3schools.com/¬
    webservices/tempconvert.asmx?WSDL");

var op:Operation = new Operation(ws);
op.FahrenheitToCelsius("451");
```

```
op.addEventListener(OperationEvent.COMPLETE, completeHandler);
function completeHandler(evt:OperationEvent):void {
    trace(evt.data);
}

op.addEventListener(OperationEvent.FAILED, failedHandler);
function failedHandler(evt:OperationEvent):void {
    trace(evt.data);
}
```

After the required classes are imported, a `ws` variable is declared and set to an instance of the custom `WebService` class, which is fed the URL of the `TempConvert` Web service as a parameter. An `op` variable is set to an instance of the custom `Operation` class, which is associated with the `ws` instance. The remote `FahrenheitToCelsius()` method is invoked on the `op` instance, and passed in the string `"451"` parameter.

Finally, two events are associated with respective custom functions: the `OperationEvent.COMPLETE` event is triggered when the `Operation` instance receives data from the Web service, in which case the value 232.777777777778 is sent to the Output panel; if the Web service is unavailable, or some other error occurs, then the `OperationEvent.FAILED` event may be handled to gracefully deal with the situation.

4. Select Control→Text Movie to verify that the Web service communication succeeds. In the file menu of the SWF file, select View→Bandwidth Profiler to see that the file weighs a mere 6KB.

ActionScript 2.0 Components in ActionScript 3.0 SWF Files

Even though you can't include ActionScript 2.0 components in ActionScript 3.0 FLA files (and vice versa), an interesting detour lets you load ActionScript 2.0 SWF files at runtime by ActionScript 3.0 SWF files. Intercommunication between such SWF files is possible by way of the native `LocalConnection` and `ExternalInterface` classes. Renowned Flash guru Grant Skinner (*http://gskin ner.com/*) offers a set of free classes named `SWFBridge`, written in ActionScript 2.0 and 3.0, to facilitate this communication. In this way, ActionScript 2.0 components, such as `Accordion` and `DateField`, can be incorporated into an ActionScript 3.0 workflow.

Download Grant's classes from *http://www.gskinner.com/blog/archives/2007/ 07/swfbridge_easie.html*. When the download is complete, unpack the ZIP archive, and then decide on a folder in which to store the files used for the following exercise. The `SWFBridge` classes are organized into a `com.gskinner.utils` package, so make sure to create corresponding *com/gskinner/utils* subfolders inside your chosen exercise folder. Place the *SWFBridgeAS2.as* and *SWFBridgeAS3.as* files into the *utils* subfolder before continuing.

 You can also store these classes in separate folders, such as a repository of routinely accessed ActionScript 2.0 and 3.0 classes, as long as you configure your global classpath settings to be aware of those locations. See Chapter 5 for more details.

1. Create a new ActionScript 2.0 FLA file and name it *ContentAS2.fla*. Rename the default layer in the Timeline to **scripts,** and then create a new layer named **components**.

2. With the `components` layer selected, open the Components panel, and then drag a copy of the `Accordion` and `DateField` components to the left side of the stage. Use the Property inspector to give the `Accordion` component the instance name **myAccordion,** and the `DateField` component the instance name **myDateField**.

3. To provide some content for the `myAccordion` instance, use the Create New Symbol dialog box (Insert→New Symbol) a few times to create two or three movie clip symbols. In turn, double-click each symbol in the library to enter its timeline. Use the drawing tools to draw a few shapes to distinguish each symbol, or import a unique graphic file into each symbol. When finished, right-click (Ctrl-click) each symbol in the library, and then select Properties. Select the Export for ActionScript checkbox to provide a unique linkage identifier for every symbol.

4. Select the `myAccordion` instance. In the Component Inspector panel, double-click to configure the `childLabels`, `childNames`, and `childSymbols` parameters to correspond to movie clip symbols created in Step 3. For example, if you have three movie clips that contain photos of a child building snowmen in the sand, showing off her braids, and jumping, you might configure the `childLabels` parameter with descriptive labels like `Sandmen`, `Braids`, and `Jumping`, as seen in Figure 10-11. The `childNames` *parameter* refers to yet-to-be-created instance names for these symbols, so you might use *mcSandmen*, *mcBraids*, and *mcJumping*. Finally, `childSymbols` refers to the symbols' linkage identifiers, so you might use `sandmen`, `braids`, and `jumping`.

5. Select Control→Test Movie to verify that the `Accordion` component displays your content, as seen in Figure 10-12. Click from pane to pane to switch from one movie clip to the next.

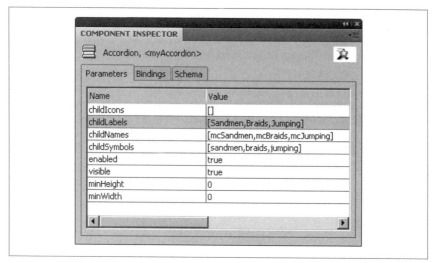

Figure 10-11. Preparing the Accordion component

Figure 10-12. Verifying the Accordion component

6. Close the SWF file. Select frame 1 of the scripts layer, and then open the Actions panel. Enter the following ActionScript:

```
import com.gskinner.utils.SWFBridgeAS2;

var myBridge:SWFBridgeAS2 = new SWFBridgeAS2("connectionID", this);
```

The SWFBridgeAS2 class is imported, and a myBridge variable is declared, and set to a instance of the SWFBridgeAS2 class. This variable will manage the *bridge* of communication between this SWF file and the host Action-Script 3.0 SWF file that'll eventually load it. Two parameters are provided to the myBridge instance: an arbitrarily named connection identifier ("connectionID"), and a reference to the current SWF file (this).

Continue entering the following code:

```
function selectSegment(segment:Number):Void {
    myAccordion.selectedIndex = segment;
}
```

Here, a custom selectSegment() function selects which pane of the Accordion component to display, by setting the Accordion.selectedIndex property of the myAccordion instance to an incoming parameter, segment. The ActionScript 3.0 SWF file that loads this file at runtime will trigger this function.

Enter the remainder of the ActionScript 2.0 code:

```
var accListener:Object = new Object();
accListener.change = accChangeHandler;
myAccordion.addEventListener("change", accListener);
function accChangeHandler(evt:Object):Void {
    myBridge.send("notifyComboBox", evt.target.selectedIndex);
}

var dfListener:Object = new Object();
dfListener.change = dfChangeHandler;
myDateField.addEventListener("change", dfListener);
function dfChangeHandler(evt:Object):Void {
    myBridge.send("notifyTextInput", evt.target.selectedDate);
}
```

These two blocks of code do practically the same thing. In each case, a listener variable is declared, and set to an instance of the Object class. These listener objects act as event handling stand-ins on behalf of the myAccordion and myDateField instances. Each listener is associated with the change event of its corresponding component, set to trigger a companion function that sends a message to the forthcoming ActionScript 3.0 SWF file by way of the myBridge instance.

Each event handler invokes the SWFBridgeAS2.send() method on the myBridge instance, and tells the ActionScript 3.0 SWF file what to do. For example, when the user changes the `myAccordion` instance, it uses the `myBridge` instance to trigger a function in the ActionScript 3.0 SWF file by way of the string reference `"notifyComboBox"`, passing a parameter whose value is the number of its own index.

7. Select Control→Test Movie again to update the ActionScript 2.0 SWF file.

8. Create a new ActionScript 3.0 FLA file, and then name it *ContentAS3.fla*. Rename the default layer in the Timeline to **scripts**, and create a new layer named **components**.

9. With the `components` layer selected, open the Components panel, and then drag a copy of the `ComboBox` and `TextInput` components to the stage. Use the Property inspector to give the `ComboBox` component the instance name **myComboBox**, and the `TextInput` component the instance name **myTextInput**. Arrange these components on the right side of the stage, in order to make room for the ActionScript 2.0 SWF file.

10. Select the `myComboBox` instance. In the Component Inspector panel, double-click to configure the `dataProvider` parameter to correspond to the movie clip symbols displayed by the `Accordion` instance in the ActionScript 2.0 SWF file. For example, click the ✚ button to add a new entry. In the new entry, change the `label` field to `Sandmen`, and the `data` field to `0`. Add a second new entry. In the second new entry, change the `label` field to `Braids` and the `data` field to `1`. Create a third new entry. In the third new entry, change the `label` field to `Jumping`, and the `data` field to `2`.

11. Select frame 1 of the `scripts` layer, and then open the Actions panel. Type the following ActionScript 3.0:

```
import com.gskinner.utils.SWFBridgeAS3;

var myBridge:SWFBridgeAS3 = new SWFBridgeAS3("connectionID", this);
```

So far, the code's nearly identical. The ActionScript 3.0 version instantiates its own `myBridge` variable, only this time the variable's set to an instance of the `SWFBridgeAS3` class. The `"connectionID"` parameter here matches the one specified in the ActionScript 2.0 file, which opens a single channel of communication between the two SWF files.

Continue entering the following code:

```
var myLoader = new Loader()
myLoader.load(new URLRequest("contentAS2.swf"));
addChild(myLoader);
```

Here, a `Loader` instance loads the ActionScript 2.0 SWF file and adds it to the display list.

Continue with the following code:

```
function notifyComboBox(num:int):void {
    myComboBox.selectedIndex = num;
}

function notifyTextInput(str:String):void {
    myTextInput.text = str;
}
```

These functions define the behavior of the notifications sent by the ActionScript 2.0 SWF file, whose event handlers trigger `notifyComboBox()` and `notifyTextInput()` by way of the string references `"notifyComboBox"` and `"notifyTextInput"` (see Step 6).

Continue entering the remaining code, which sends a message to the ActionScript 2.0 SWF file, using the by-now familiar `SWFBridge.send()` method:

```
myComboBox.addEventListener(Event.CHANGE, changeHandler);

function changeHandler(evt:Event):void {
    myBridge.send("selectSegment", evt.target.selectedIndex);
}
```

12. Select Control→Test Movie to experience the collaboration between ActionScript 2.0 and 3.0 SWF files. Note that selecting various panes in the `Accordion` component updates the `ComboBox` component in the host SWF file, and vice versa. Note also that various selections of the `Date Field` component update the `TextInput` component in the host SWF file (Figure 10-13).

For alternatives to `SWFBridge`, experiment with the free ActionScript Bridge component by Jumpeye, available at *www.JumpeyeComponents.com/Flash -Components/Various/ActionScript-Bridge-91/*, and FlashInterface, by Robert Taylor, available at *www.flashextensions.com/products/flashinterface.php*.

Exploring Third-Party UI Components

Numerous third-party companies have developed components for Flash, some of which require licensing fees and some of which are free. A Google search on "ActionScript 3.0 Flash components" will lead you to a number of component repositories, as well as tutorials to help you create your own. Here is an example of two ready-made component providers.

Figure 10-13. Collaboration between ActionScript 2.0 and 3.0 SWF files, thanks to Grant Skinner's SWFBridge classes

Yahoo! ASTRA Components

The Yahoo! Developer Network (*http://developer.yahoo.com/*) offers a number of ActionScript 3.0 UI components under the BSD free software license, as part of a Flash component set (*http://developer.yahoo.com/flash/astra-flash/*) called ASTRA. Components are installed with the Adobe Extension Manager and closely match the API, syntax, and library folder structure of the built-in ActionScript 3.0 component set. ASTRA components include:

- `AutoComplete`: provides a list of suggestions from a supplied dataset based on the characters entered by the user
- `AlertManager`: manages the queuing of alert windows
- `AudioPlayback`: conceptually similar to `FLVPlayback`, but for audio files
- `BarChart`, `ColumnChart`, `LineChart`, and `PieChart`: display tabular data in various graphical representations

- Menu and MenuBar: ActionScript 3.0 versions of the native ActionScript 2.0 equivalents
- TabBar: facilitates switching among various application states
- Tree: an ActionScript 3.0 version of the native ActionScript 2.0 equivalent

Here's a quick demonstration of the Yahoo! ASTRA TabBar component.

1. Download the ASTRA component set from *http://developer.yahoo.com/flash/astra-flash/*. When the download completes, unpack the ZIP archive, and then double-click the *Astra.mxp* file to open it in the Adobe Extension Manager. Follow the steps described for installing Pieter Michels' Web-Service component extension earlier in this chapter (see the "Recreating a WebServiceConnector Scenario in ActionScript 3.0" on page 216). Shut down the Flash authoring tool, and then launch it again so that the extension is activated at startup.

2. Create a new ActionScript 3.0 FLA file, and then open the Components panel. Drag a copy of the TabBar component from the Yahoo! folder to the stage. Use the Property inspector to give this component the instance name **myTabBar**.

3. Select the myTabBar instance. In the Component Inspector panel, double-click to configure the dataProvider parameter. In the Values dialog box that opens, click the ✚ button to add a new entry. In the new entry, change the label field to **Home**, and the data field to **home**. Add a second new entry. In the second new entry, change the label field to **About Us**, and the data field to **about us**. Create a third new entry. In the third new entry, change the label field to **Contact Us**, and the data field to **contact us**. Set the autoSizeTabsToTextWidth parameter to **true** to ensure that the labels expand to fit their content.

4. In the Timeline, select frame 1, and then open the Actions panel. Enter the following code:

```
import com.yahoo.astra.fl.events.TabBarEvent;

myTabBar.addEventListener(TabBarEvent.ITEM_CLICK, clickHandler);

function clickHandler(evt:TabBarEvent):void {
    trace(evt.item.data);
}
```

Here, an `import` directive makes the `TabBarEvent` class available to this frame script. The `myTabBar` component instance is referenced by instance name and associated with a custom `clickHandler()` function to handle the `TabBarEvent.ITEM_CLICK` event. Inside the `clickHandler()` function, a `trace()` function references the `data` property of the currently selected tab, and sends its value to the Output panel. In actual practice, you might use the expression `evt.item.data` inside a call to `gotoAndPlay()`, to send the timeline to a frame label associated with the selected tab.

5. Select Control→Test Movie to verify that tab selection sends corresponding values to the Output panel.

 This syntax is from the Astra Library Documentation (*http://developer.yahoo.com/flash/astra-flash/classrefer ence/*), which thoroughly covers the full ASTRA API.

Jumpeye Components

Jumpeye offers a wide variety of attractive ActionScript 3.0 UI components for sale on its website: *www.JumpeyeComponents.com/Flash-Components/*. Components include:

- Accordion Panel V3: provides horizontal and vertical multipane selection, like the native ActionScript 2.0 Accordion component, but much more powerful and configurable
- Loader Pro: loads images or animations, both from the library or external files, with visual transitions
- Color Picker Pro: provides robust color picking capability with a variety of user interfaces
- Thumbnail Slider: loads images and displays them as a scrollable thumbnail carousel
- ToolTip 2007 Pro: provides highly configurable tool tips when the user hovers over designated areas
- Numerous additional audio/video, menu, and transition effects components

As a gift to readers of this book, Jumpeye has offered a special coupon code that lets you download its Accordion Panel V3 component free of charge. Read on to see how to cash in, and check out the quick demonstration.

1. Create a user account on the Jumpeye Components website. Navigate to the Accordion Panel V3 webpage (*www.JumpeyeComponents.com/Flash -Components/User-Interface/Accordion-Panel-V3-40/*). Click the Add to Shopping Cart button.

2. On the Shopping Cart page, enter this coupon code into the field titled "Enter your discount coupon number here":

   e0a5a7f2573beb2171da4b38f1j13058

3. Click the Check button. This action refreshes the web page to indicate a full discount. Click the Check Out button. Verify your customer information, and then click the Post Your Order button. When the web page refreshes, click the hyperlink that says, "Go to download page." Download the component.

4. When the download is complete, unpack the ZIP archive, and then double-click the *AccordionPanelV3AS3.mxp* file to open it in the Adobe Extension Manager. Follow the steps described for installing Pieter Michels' WebService component extension earlier in this chapter (see the "Recreating a WebServiceConnector Scenario in ActionScript 3.0" on page 216). Shut down the Flash authoring tool, and then launch it again so that the extension is activated at startup.

5. Open the *accordion_panel.fla* file included with the download. Note that a copy of the component already exists on the stage, and has the instance name accordionPanel.

6. In the Parameters panel, note that the xmlPath parameter already shows the value acc_panel.xml. This parameter points to an XML document included with the other sample files from the ZIP archive. Open the XML document to see its contents:

```
<?xml version="1.0" encoding="UTF-8"?>
<component name="Accordion Panel v3">
<data childStyle="style1">
<item title="Jumpeye"    contentPath="images/img1.jpg"/>
<item title="Working"    contentPath="images/img2.jpg"/>
<item title="Drawing"    contentPath="images/img3.jpg"/>
<item title="On meeting" contentPath="images/img4.jpg"/>
<item title="Having fun" contentPath="images/img5.jpg"/>
</data>
</component>
```

These XML nodes give you a straightforward way to let the component know what content to display.

7. Select Control→Test Movie to verify that clicking on headings displays the corresponding pane.

8. Delete one of the `<item>` nodes in the XML document, and then save the file. In the Flash authoring tool, select Control→Test Movie again to verify that the corresponding pane is no longer present.

 The full Jumpeye Accordion Panel V3 API is available in the AccordionPanelV3.pdf file included with the ZIP archive.

CHAPTER 11

Debugging and Troubleshooting

Debugging Is a Good Thing

Murphy's Law may be pessimistic, but at some point for all of us, the adage rings true: If something can go wrong, it will. Despite your best intentions, the SWF files you produce will sooner or later perform in unexpected ways. Maybe an audio clip will fail to play or a button will get stuck in its rollover state. In complex situations, the likelihood of a Murphyism is bound to increase, especially in projects comprised of numerous ActionScript classes or SWF files. This all makes perfect sense, of course. Complexity means a developer has to keep more in mind while working. Humans simply have a limit to the number of details they can juggle at once, so the occasional particulars get overlooked. The cause of unexpected behavior is usually the result of an error in the developer's logic, though certainly other factors may come into play. An external asset, such as a JPEG file, might be missing from the server; a needed database might be inaccessible; perhaps a typo has crept into the code. The challenge in all these cases is straightforward. Once a SWF file is compiled, the timeline and all vestiges of ActionScript are gone. Assets and programming code have been compiled into bytecode, which is effectively indecipherable to the eye— and unchangeable.

How, then, can a developer see what's going on, other than to experience the error(s) directly and make minimally informed guesses? The answer hinges on debugging, which is a skill, and ultimately a way of thinking, that will help you tremendously in your Flash endeavors. Fortunately, Flash CS4 Professional features a number of updated debugging tools. Some of these work just fine for documents configured for ActionScript 2.0, but the most beneficial improvements appear with ActionScript 3.0.

Testing Your ActionScript 3.0 Code

Programmers tend to learn a famous motto early on, especially when the teacher isn't a book or mentor, but rather a challenging experience. There's nothing like a fiasco to make a learning point stick, especially when you have to stay late at the office to fix it! The motto goes like this: Test early, test often. This bears repeating. Test early, test often.

This motto is a good one because it keeps you from getting ahead of yourself. If you type 100 lines of code, either in a keyframe or class file, and only test at that point ... well, you're taking a pretty big risk. If your ActionScript has errors, the issue (or issues) might stem from any one (or more) of those 100 lines. To be sure, some errors do cause chain reactions, so you really can't guarantee that you'll see only a handful of errors at once. Sometimes you'll see dozens. Ideally, though, you'll want to grind through as few simultaneous errors as possible. Testing early and testing often helps keep those numbers down.

Compiler Errors

You can perform testing, in its most basic form, by the simple act of running a SWF file in the Flash authoring tool (Control→Test Movie, or Control→Test Scene). If invalid code causes the compiler concern, it alerts you by sending an announcement to the Compiler Errors panel. This alert occurs without any effort on your part. In fact, errors brought to light in this way are the sort that keep a SWF file from compiling in the first place, so a user never sees this category of errors.

The Compiler Errors panel gives you a brief description of each error, and lets you know where to find it, including relevant asset names and scene, layer, frame, and line numbers. For more information on this panel, see the section "Exploring the Compiler Errors Panel" on page 240 later in this chapter.

The Flash authoring tool lets you configure the degree to which the Compiler Errors panel displays its messages. This is determined by a pair of *modes* called Strict Mode and Warnings Mode, which can be set on a per-FLA file basis under File→Publish Settings→Flash→Settings.

You can get a full list of ActionScript 3.0 compiler errors from the built-in documentation (search "compiler errors"), or on-line at the Adobe online Help Resource Center:

http://help.adobe.com/en_US/AS3LCR/Flash_10.0/compi lerErrors.html

Some errors appear only when you compile in Strict Mode (enabled by default). Strict mode is determined by the *presence* of a check mark under File→Publish Settings→Flash→Settings→Strict Mode.

Compiler Warnings

Once a SWF file compiles, it is finally capable of trying to carry out the instructions you've given it. Even so, your technically valid code may not be written according to the recommended best practices of Adobe. As an example, consider type declaration, which is optional in ActionScript 3.0. It's possible and valid to declare variables without including a post colon suffix:

```
// type declared
var worthANickel:int = 5;

// type not declared
var worthADime = 10;
```

However, omitting the type declaration keeps you from benefiting from ActionScript 3.0's improved efficiency in Flash Player 9 and higher. For example, in ActionScript 3.0, the int type (a 32-bit signed integer) takes up less system memory than the Number type (a 64-bit double precision non-integer). If you choose to refrain from explicitly specifying a variable's data type, Flash has no choice but to request as much memory as it reasonably can, on the chance that the variable might be a string, a date, or some other object that requires more RAM. For this reason alone, although type declarations are not required, they're definitely a good idea. Compiler warnings provide a good reminder of recommended best practices like this one, and they also appear in the Compiler Errors panel.

In addition, some of these warnings are geared toward developer education. Certain programming concepts, sometimes specific to ActionScript, seem intuitive right away, while others may sink in only after months of experience. For example, the default value of many data types is null; that is, variables that have been declared and include type declarations but have not yet been assigned a value.

```
var str:String;
trace(str); // Displays: null
```

```
var d:Date;
trace(d); // Displays: null

var mc:MovieClip;
trace(mc); // Displays: null
```

If you compare any of these to `null` with an `if` statement, the expression evaluates to `true`:

```
var str:String;
if (str == null) {
    trace("default value is null");
} else {
    trace("default value is something else");
}
// Displays: default value is null
```

If you're new to Flash programming, you might assume that the default value for all data types is `null`, but as it turns out, instances of `Boolean`, `int`, `uint`, and `Number` are by default `false`, `0`, `0`, and `NaN` (Not a Number), respectively.

In the following example, the comparison of the default value of a Boolean to `null` is actually interpreted as `false`:

```
var b:Boolean;
if (b == null) {
    trace("default value is null");
} else {
    trace("default value is something else");
}
// Displays: default value is something else
```

In practice, this means your ActionScript might not always behave as you had intended. Many compiler warnings help steer you in the right direction.

Finally, a number of compiler warnings relate specifically to ActionScript 2.0–3.0 migration issues. You may consider these Help docs migration warnings a collection of freebie insider tips!

 A full list of ActionScript 3.0 compiler warnings can be obtained from the built-in documentation (search "compiler warnings"), or online at the Adobe online Help Resource Center:

> *http://help.adobe.com/en_US/AS3LCR/Flash_10.0/compilerWarnings.html*

Note that some warnings appear only when you compile in Warnings Mode (enabled by default). Warnings mode is determined by the presence of a check mark in File→Publish Settings→Flash→Settings→Warnings Mode.

Runtime Errors

Runtime errors occur, by definition, at runtime—in other words, after a SWF file has passed the rounds of compiler errors and warnings. Because of this, runtime errors are often a bit harder to track down than the sort described earlier. After all, the ActionScript involved has already passed the test: it's valid, and has already been converted to bytecode. At that point, the scenes, layers, and line numbers shown in compiler errors and warnings are effectively meaningless. For this reason, notifications of runtime errors do not (cannot!) provide an X-marks-the-spot treasure map to erroneous ActionScript. In fact, the code itself might actually be just fine. The culprit may well be a malformed external file. Don't let that alarm you, though. While not as precise as compiler errors and warnings in terms of location, runtime error messages do try to show where they originated.

Figure 11-1 shows an example error in which a SWF file attempts to load an XML document that provides file data for a slideshow. In this case, the ActionScript is correct; it's the XML that contains an error (one of the elements, <slide>, is missing its matching end-tag, </slide>). Because this SWF file is being tested in the Flash authoring tool, the runtime error is displayed in the Output panel.

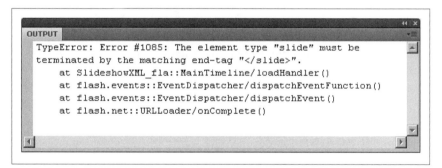

Figure 11-1. A runtime error, displayed in the Output panel

Helpfully, this message indicates that the trouble happened during the execution of a function named `loadHandler()` in the main timeline, as seen in the first line that starts with the word "at." Further hints—the mention of `EventDispatcher` and `URLLoader/onComplete()`—suggest that `loadHandler()` is an event handler. These are all signposts that should at least give you a head start as you re-examine your source files. Given the error's description, "the element type 'slide' must be terminated...," and the hints on where to look, you have considerably more information to go on than in previous versions of Flash, which provided only compiler errors and warnings.

To a certain extent, runtime errors are only as helpful as your naming conventions and coding practices. For example, the ActionScript that loads the XML in Figure 11-1 might look something like this:

```
var myXML:XML = new XML();
var xmlLoader:URLLoader = new URLLoader();
xmlLoader.load(new URLRequest("slideshow.xml"));
xmlLoader.addEventListener(Event.COMPLETE, loadHandler);
```

That last line of code associates a custom function, `loadHandler()`, with an `Event.COMPLETE` event. This event is dispatched when the `xmlLoader` instance finishes loading the *slideshow.xml* file. The `loadHandler()` function might look like this:

```
function loadHandler(evt:Event):void {
    myXML = XML(evt.target.data);
    myComboBox.dataProvider = new DataProvider(myXML);
}
```

There's certainly nothing wrong with that function—it's valid ActionScript—but because the error message mentions `loadHandler()` by name, you know where to find it in the source file's frame script. The lack of any obvious errors in the function itself may nudge you into looking at the XML file, where the error actually occurs.

In this scenario, the warning message's guidance is helpful because `loadHandler()` is defined as a *named function*. This event handler might just as well have been written as a *function literal*, also known as an *anonymous function*, in which the function's code appears directly as a parameter of `addEventListener()` (changes in bold):

```
var myXML:XML = new XML();
var xmlLoader:URLLoader = new URLLoader();
xmlLoader.load(new URLRequest("slideshow.xml"));

xmlLoader.addEventListener(
    Event.COMPLETE,
    function (evt:Event):void {
        myXML = XML(evt.target.data);
        myComboBox.dataProvider = new DataProvider(myXML);
    }
);
```

If so, the runtime error inevitably becomes less clear, simply because the event handler function no longer has a name.

```
TypeError: Error #1085: The element type "slide" must be
    terminated by the matching end-tag "</slide>".
    at MethodInfo-392()
    at flash.events::EventDispatcher/dispatchEventFunction()
    at flash.events::EventDispatcher/dispatchEvent()
    at flash.net::URLLoader/onComplete()
```

This time, the function formerly known as `loadHandler()` is referenced as `MethodInfo-392()`. Cryptic? Perhaps. The compiler automatically assigns a name to the anonymous function. Ultimately, everything must have a reference, so Flash does what it needs to in order to keep track of the instructions you've given it. Bear this trait in mind as you program, and avoid anonymous functions if you want to improve the clarity of your error messages.

 A full list of ActionScript 3.0 runtime errors can be obtained from the built-in documentation (search "run-time errors"), or online at the Adobe online Help Resource Center:

> *http://help.adobe.com/en_US/AS3LCR/Flash_10.0/runti
> meErrors.html*

Note that runtime errors appear regardless of your settings for compiler errors and warnings, located under File→Publish Settings→Flash→Settings.

Reviewing Improvements in Debugging Over ActionScript 2.0

So far, you've seen a number of ways in which Flash communicates problems without you having to take any action (other than to address the errors, of course!). But true problem solving, at minimum, is an interactive process. Ideally, it's proactive. The remainder of the chapter fleshes out the Compiler Errors panel in greater detail, and introduces additional debugging tools that require input from you, ranging from the simplest—the humble `trace()` function—to the improved debug workspace.

Don't Underestimate trace()

The `trace()` function bears some similarity to good old low-tech paper sticky notes. Regardless of how powerful (and portable) PDAs and cell phones have become, replete with programmable reminders, alarms, and automated email dispatches, nothing beats the convenience of those stick-anywhere yellow notes. They're lightweight, informative, and reusable. Likewise, the `trace()` function makes a terrific and uncomplicated tool.

In short, the `trace()` function sends information to the Output panel. The information it sends is entirely up to you. Doing so is as easy as passing an expression to the function as a parameter. To ensure that a button is responding to mouse clicks, for example, you might pass in a simple confirmation string.

```
myButton.addEventListener(MouseEvent.CLICK, onClick);
function onClick(evt:MouseEvent):void {
    trace("This button is working!");
}
```

Of course, you're not limited to strings. The `trace()` function is great for bringing all sorts of things to light, from the current value of a custom variable to the contents of an XML node; from the position of a movie clip (for example, the `MovieClip.x` property) to an object's data type when used with the `is` operator.

```
var s:Sprite = new Sprite();
trace(s is Sprite); // Displays true
trace(s is Number); // Displays false
```

Be aware that `trace()` always outputs a string, no matter what expression you feed it. When passed any object, the function essentially invokes the `Object.toString()` method defined for that object (remember, all objects in ActionScript inherit from the `Object` class, which means all objects have a `toString()` method).

So, has anything changed for this elementary debugging tool in ActionScript 3.0? The answer is yes, even though it's a small update. Sometimes it's the little things that can make your day! The `trace()` function now accepts multiple parameters, separated by commas. If you're heavily into using `trace()`, this can save you a degree of typing.

```
var n:Number = 42;
var b:Boolean = true;
var d:Dictionary = new Dictionary();
trace(n, b, d); // Displays 42 true [object Dictionary]
```

In previous versions of ActionScript, the same output would have required a bit of string wrangling:

```
trace(n + " " + b + " " + d);
// Displays the same, but tedious to type
```

 Trace statements display only when enabled. This situation occurs when two settings in the Flash authoring tool are in agreement. The checkbox under File→Publish Settings →Flash→Omit trace actions must be deselected. Also, the Output panel's filter level must be set to Verbose. The filter level is available under the Output panel's ▾☰ menu in the upper-right corner (beneath the X that closes the panel).

Runtime Errors Displayed in Flash Player 9 and Higher

Runtime errors are available only in ActionScript 3.0, which means they're available only as of Flash Player 9. Returning to the example shown earlier

(Figure 11-1), if the same SWF file is embedded in an HTML document and viewed in a browser, the error message appears in a dialog box presented to the user, as shown in Figure 11-2. In ActionScript 2.0 or 1.0, something like this would likely have failed silently—meaning, the user may have seen partial elements of the user interface, but none of the slideshow photos. In fact, in such a scenario, it might not even be absolutely clear that something has gone wrong. The website may simply come across as incomplete or abandoned. ActionScript 3.0 fixes that. Because runtime errors are visually obvious—that dialog box is hard to miss!—the developer sees and addresses errors before the SWF file goes public.

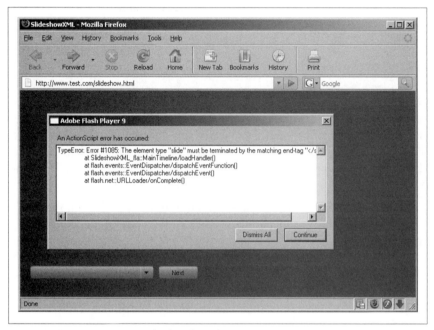

Figure 11-2. A runtime error, displayed in a browser

 To see runtime errors in a browser, as demonstrated in Figure 11-2, you must have a debug version of Flash Player 9 or higher installed. Debugging is introduced in the "Debug Vs. Release Players" on page 25 of Chapter 2 and explored further in this chapter.

Exploring the Compiler Errors Panel

The Compiler Errors panel gives you a remarkably direct road map to errors and warnings related to the process that compiles FLA source files to published SWF files. If multiple errors or warnings are found, the Compiler Errors panel displays one line item per message, as shown in Figure 11-3.

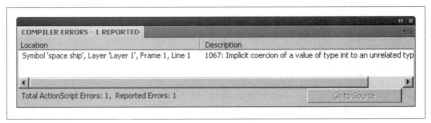

Figure 11-3. The Compiler Errors panel, showing three frame script errors

Notice that the Compiler Errors panel gives you quite a bit of information. The panel's tab reports the number of errors found (three, in this case). The status bar at the bottom of the panel duplicates this information for convenience. Three columns inside the panel dictate where to locate the problem (these are the Location and Source columns; only Location appears in Figure 11-3) and a detailed summary of the error (the Description column).

The Location column provides the scene, layer, frame, and line number of the offending code, which is incredibly useful for files whose ActionScript is distributed among numerous keyframes or class files. The Source column shows the line of code itself. In cases where code has been placed inside the nested timeline of a movie clip symbol, the Location column mentions that symbol by name, and then the layer, frame, and line number, as before. In Figure 11-4, an error occurs in the scripts layer of a movie clip symbol whose library name is "space ship."

COMPILER ERRORS - 1 REPORTED

Location	Description
Symbol 'space ship', Layer 'Layer 1', Frame 1, Line 1	1067: Implicit coercion of a value of type int to an unrelated typ

Total ActionScript Errors: 1, Reported Errors: 1   Go to Source

Figure 11-4. Errors in nested movie clip scripts revealed

In this scenario, it doesn't matter what scene or layer the symbol appears in—several instances might, in fact, appear in many places. Likewise, it doesn't

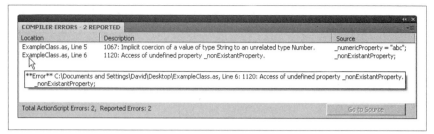

Figure 11-5. A tooltip with the full content of an error entry

matter if any of the symbol's instances has been given an instance name in the Property inspector, as only the original asset in the library needs correction.

When erroneous ActionScript has been placed in external class files instead of keyframes, the Location column states the name of the ActionScript file, and then the line number. If at any time the panel seems too cramped, bring your mouse pointer over a line item, as shown in Figure 11-5. This brings up a tooltip that displays the full content of all three columns.

To copy the content of the Description or Source column to the clipboard, right-click (Ctrl-click) the desired line item and select the appropriate option from the context menu. You'll also find an option for clearing all the panel's line items (Clear) and for jumping to the location of the actual line of Action-Script (Go to Source). The latter moves the playhead automatically to the relevant keyframe, opens the Actions panel if necessary, and highlights the guilty line number. This happens even in nested movie clip timelines, in which case the movie clip symbol is opened in the Symbol Editor from the library. If the code is in an ActionScript class file, then Flash jumps to the relevant line, opening the AS file if necessary.

This line jumping is a remarkable productivity booster and can also be activated by the Go to Source button in the lower-right corner of the panel, which becomes enabled when you click a line item to select it. In fact, this feature is so welcome, there's even a third way to trigger it: simply double-click the desired line item.

Using the Compile Errors Panel to Open Code

Double-clicking a Compiler Errors panel line item is the quickest route to accessing and fixing problematic code. Here's a quick example.

1. In a new ActionScript 3.0 FLA file, use the Rectangle tool to draw a small shape anywhere on the Stage.

2. Convert the shape to a movie clip symbol, and then double-click the symbol to enter its timeline.

3. Inside the symbol's timeline, add a new layer named **scripts**. Add a keyframe in frame 15 of the `scripts` layer, and then open the Actions panel. Type the following invalid ActionScript:

```
var shouldBeNumeric:Number = "But this is a string.";
```

4. Choose Edit→Edit Document to return to the main timeline.

5. Choose Control→Test Movie to see an implicit coercion error in the Compiler Errors panel.

6. Close the Actions panel. Double-click the error in the Compiler Errors panel to see Flash reopen the Actions panel and jump automatically to the correct line number of frame 15 of the movie clip symbol's timeline.

Interpreting and Understanding Errors

Admittedly, the numbers assigned to compiler errors, warnings and runtime errors aren't self-explanatory. Compiler errors range from 1000 to 1209, warnings from 1009 to 3607, and runtime errors from 1000 to 2157. The numbers are completely arbitrary (at least, to non-Adobe employees), so you can't easily group them by some pattern or mnemonic device, such as, "Ah, those 1-800 phone numbers are the toll free ones." While you may eventually find yourself recognizing the numbers of a handful of your own pet errors, the bottom line is that you'll want to pay attention to their descriptions. As a note of encouragement, even if the numeric assignments don't have much inherent meaning, they're great for using as search terms at the Adobe website, Google, and your favorite tech blogs.

These errors and warnings are listed in the ActionScript 3.0 Language Reference (search Help for "compiler errors," "compiler warnings," and "run-time errors"). Skim through the documentation's Code Message heading for any of these terms, and you'll see that for the most part, the messages themselves are fairly straightforward. True, not all of them necessarily make sense when they occur. That trait is demonstrated later in this chapter with "Compiler Error: 1037: Packages cannot be nested." But even that message comes together after an explanation, and a fair number of errors and warnings feature a Description heading in the same table that shows the Code Message heading. The content of that Description column, when it does appear, may overlap with the Description column of the Compiler Errors panel. Even so, it often elaborates, including code samples.

One of the most helpful things you can bear in mind when interpreting errors and warnings is that ActionScript 3.0 is an object-oriented language—this version more so than any other. The ActionScript 3.0 Language and Components Reference is neatly organized into a structure that matches the hierarchy

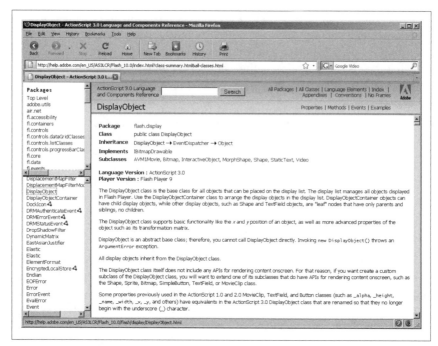

Figure 11-6. A class listing in the ActionScript 3.0 Language Reference

of the *application programming interface* (API) of Flash itself; in other words, in a structure that matches the very composition of the language. If an error or warning mentions a class file you don't think you're using, look up that class and investigate its placement in the class hierarchy (essentially a family tree). You might, for example, see a compiler error concerning the DisplayObject class, even though you suspect the issue is related to a button symbol. As Figure 11-6 shows, the DisplayObject class listing, like all class listings, shows a collection of hyperlinks just below the main heading.

These links include Package, Inheritance, and Subclasses. The Package heading tells what major branch of the API this class belongs to (in this case, the flash.display package). The Inheritance heading tells what classes this class inherits from. Here, it's easy to see that all DisplayObject objects are also instances of EventDispatcher—they feature all the functionality of that class, plus functionality of their own—and are also instances, ultimately, of the Object class. The Subclasses heading tells what classes further extend this class by inheriting from it. In this hypothetical scenario, you're looking for something that seems like a button, because your hunch tells you a button symbol is at fault. Of the choices shown, InteractiveObject seems like the best bet. Certainly, it won't always be this easy, but be sure to always let your fingers do the walking through the documentation.

The documentation is the closest resource and often the quickest way to find your bearings. Clicking `InteractiveObject` brings you to the listing for that class, whose own Subclasses heading includes an entry called `SimpleButton`, which in fact is the class that defines button symbols.

> The authoring tool includes Help content that is installed locally on your hard drive. If you don't have an Internet connection, you're not entirely out of luck, but the local content is limited to the Using Flash book and the ActionScript 3.0 Language and Components Reference. For anything outside of that, including ActionScript 2.0 reference documentation, you do need to be online.

Identifying Common Errors and What They Mean

Coming from any level of ActionScript 2.0 experience, you may find yourself "stuck" with old habits that were perfectly fine before, perhaps even recommended best practices. New syntax changes things. Some changes are relatively obvious, because they get abundant coverage in the Adobe Developer Connection (*http://www.adobe.com/devnet/*); the improved ActionScript 3.0 event handling model comes to mind. Other changes may show up on your doorstep at midnight unannounced, pushing their way past you to the fridge, thanking you in advance for a place to crash—through mouthfuls of your last leftover pizza. Here's a list of some of most common gate-crashers.

Be careful where you type your code

Many of the ActionScript 3.0 guides on the market—and in fact, most of the code samples in the ActionScript 3.0 Language Reference—are written in class format, complete with `package` and `class` declarations. When such code is typed or pasted into a keyframe, you see the following compiler error:

```
Compiler Error: 1037: Packages cannot be nested.
```

This error happens because every ActionScript 3.0 SWF file is associated with a default *document class* (see Chapter 6), which can be optionally overridden by a custom class. This means the SWF file's code already exists inside a package automatically. The introduction of a second (seemingly original) package declaration in timeline code causes those two packages to be nested, which isn't allowed.

To test sample code that's formatted as a class, make sure to set it as the document class of your FLA file or create an instance of it in your timeline code:

```
var codeSample:ExampleCode = new ExampleCode();
```

Alternatively, though it may take more effort, you can "lift" the relevant code sample from its class trappings by removing the package and class declarations and any exclusively class-related elements, such as public and private member attributes, converting constants to variables, and the like.

Here's an example that lets you test a code sample from the ActionScript 3.0 Language Reference in a timeline keyframe. This example is taken directly from the Graphics.moveTo() method listing:

```
package {
    import flash.display.Sprite;
    import flash.display.CapsStyle;
    import flash.display.LineScaleMode;
    public class Graphics_moveToExample extends Sprite {
        public function Graphics_moveToExample():void {
            graphics.lineStyle(3, 0x990000, 0.25, false, ¬
                LineScaleMode.NONE, CapsStyle.SQUARE);
            graphics.moveTo(10, 20);
            graphics.lineTo(20, 20);
            graphics.moveTo(30, 20);
            graphics.lineTo(50, 20);
            graphics.moveTo(60, 20);
            graphics.lineTo(80, 20);
            graphics.moveTo(90, 20);
            graphics.lineTo(110, 20);
            graphics.moveTo(120, 20);
            graphics.lineTo(130, 20);
        }
    }
}
```

As written, you can't test this ActionScript from a keyframe. It must be saved as an ActionScript (.as) file named *Graphics_moveToExample.as* in the same folder as a new ActionScript 3.0 FLA file. The FLA file's document class must be set to Graphics_moveToExample, as explained in Chapter 6.

The point of this sample code is to demonstrate the moveTo() method, which is simple enough to illustrate and actually use in a timeline setting. Note that this class extends Sprite, which means that when used as a document class, it treats the main timeline as a Sprite instance. Because the Sprite class and MovieClip class share the same family tree, both inherit a graphics property from DisplayObject. This means that even the default document class—that is, the absence of a custom document class (just a plain old FLA file)—can be used for this example. Contrast the previous package-based code with the following pared-down revision:

```
function Graphics_moveToExample():void {
    graphics.lineStyle(3, 0x990000, 0.25, false, ¬
        LineScaleMode.NONE, CapsStyle.SQUARE);
    graphics.moveTo(10, 20);
    graphics.lineTo(20, 20);
```

```
    graphics.moveTo(30, 20);
    graphics.lineTo(50, 20);
    graphics.moveTo(60, 20);
    graphics.lineTo(80, 20);
    graphics.moveTo(90, 20);
    graphics.lineTo(110, 20);
    graphics.moveTo(120, 20);
    graphics.lineTo(130, 20);
}
Graphics_moveToExample();
```

The package and class declarations are gone. The import statements are gone. The constructor function, along with its public attribute, has been removed. What remains is the part that actually demonstrates the moveTo() method. If you paste the revised version in frame 1 of a new ActionScript 3.0 FLA file and test the movie, you see a dashed line in the upper-left corner of the stage. The dashed line occurs because lineTo() draws while moveTo() merely moves the pen.

Remember to omit property underscores

Years ago, most of the familiar movie clip getter/setter properties were preceded by an underscore (MovieClip._x, _y, _width, _height, _currentframe, and so on). As ActionScript matured and new properties were introduced, the underscore was omitted for the new properties (MovieClip.hitArea, scale9Grid, forceSmoothing, and so on). This led to a perplexing situation for newcomers, as it wasn't apparent without longtime experience why some properties had the underscore and others didn't. It was simply a matter of a historical change in convention. This scenario was frustrating for seasoned developers new to Flash because, by widely held convention (even in other programming languages), private class members are often preceded with an underscore to set them apart—yet the MovieClip getter/setter properties, and also those of the TextField class and others, were public.

In ActionScript 3.0, the underscore has been dropped across the board as a relic of the past. Still, you may find that your fingers automatically type mc._width when you actually mean mc.width.

```
// Assumes a movie clip symbol with the instance name mcBox
mcBox._x = 400; // Displays compiler warning
```

If you do, then you see a compiler warning when the compiler is configured for Warnings Mode:

```
Compiler Warning: 1058: Migration issue: The property _x is no
longer supported. Use the DisplayObject.x property instead.
```

You may also see an error in the Output panel:

```
ReferenceError: Error #1056: Cannot create property _x on flash.display.Sprite.
```

Don't be thrown by the mention of `DisplayObject` or `Sprite`: the `MovieClip` class is a descendent of both classes (its full pedigree is `DisplayObject→InteractiveObject→DisplayObjectContainer→Sprite→MovieClip`). Just drop the underscore and the warning goes away:

```
mcBox.x = 400; // Updates movie clip's horizontal position
```

Referencing movie clip's parent requires explicit conversion (casting)

Imagine a relatively simple movie, such as a banner ad or corporate presentation. The main timeline moves from frame to frame, then halts—thanks to a keyframe `stop()` call—and waits for a nested movie clip in that frame to display an animation of its own. The last keyframe of the nested movie clip tells the main timeline to continue again by issuing a call to `MovieClip.play()` in the following manner:

```
// Last keyframe of a movie clip symbol in the main timeline
this.parent.play();
```

That seems like a straightforward exercise, but in ActionScript 3.0 it generates a potentially confusing compiler error when the compiler is configured for Strict Mode.

```
Compiler Error: 1061: Call to a possibly undefined method play
    through a reference with static type flash.display: ¬
    DisplayObjectContainer.
```

How is `MovieClip.play()` an undefined method, much less static? As it turns out, the problem here is nothing more than a confusion of data type. From the point of view of the movie clip's timeline code, the expression `this.parent` thinks it's referencing a `DisplayObjectContainer` instance, and that particular class appears too early in the `MovieClip` inheritance chain to feature a `play()` method. Movie clip symbols *are* instances of `DisplayObjectContainer`, but additional inheritance eventually gives them the properties, methods, and events featured in the `MovieClip` class.

To nudge ActionScript 3.0 in the right direction, use the **as** operator or relevant class function—in this case, `MovieClip()`—to explicitly convert, or cast, the reference:

```
// Last keyframe of a movie clip symbol in the main timeline
(this.parent as MovieClip).play();
```

Or:

```
MovieClip(this.parent).play();
```

In some cases, the **as** operator is the only real choice for casting. Date(*someValue*) doesn't convert to the Date data type, but instead behaves the same as new Date.toString(). Array(*someValue*) behaves the same as new Array(*someValue*), which sets a new array to the length specified by a numeric parameter.

Variables can be declared only once per timeline or class

In ActionScript 2.0, you could declare a variable in one frame, then declare it again in another (or even the same) frame, or declare the variable more than once in a class file. In fact, re-declaring a variable was a handy way of clearing it out and starting fresh. It tended to happen in one particular circumstance, especially: for statements. Due to the strict nature of ActionScript 3.0, the following pair of for statements generates a compiler error because the variable i has been declared more than once in the same scope.

```
for (var i:int = 0; i < someUpperLimit; i++) {
    // loop code here
}
// Displays compiler error
for (var i:int = 0; i < someArray.length; i += 2) {
    // loop code here
}
Compiler Error: 1151: A conflict exists with definition
    variable name in namespace internal (or relevant namespace).
```

A compiler warning can also be generated by this issue.

```
Compiler Warning: 3596: Duplicate variable definition.
```

To fix these multiple declarations, drop the **var** definition keyword in the second (or any subsequent) update of the value of the previously declared variable (change in bold):

```
for (var i:int = 0; i < someUpperLimit; i++) {
    // loop code here
}
for (i = 0; i < someArray.length; i += 2) {
    // loop code here
}
```

Undeclared timeline variables cannot be referenced

In a common practice ActionScript 2.0 timeline code, an if statement could be used to check for the existence of a variable. If the variable hadn't yet been declared, or hadn't yet been given a value, a reference to it returned null or undefined, which resolved to false in an if statement. People often used this technique for checking variables passed into the SWF file from external code, such as JavaScript, as with FlashVars.

In ActionScript 3.0, any reference to an undeclared variable generates a compiler error when the compiler is configured for strict mode.

```
if (someUndeclaredVariable) { // Displays compiler error
    // variable exists
} else {
    // variable does not exist
}
```

Or:

```
// Displays compiler error
if (someOtherUndeclaredVariable != null) {
    // variable exists
} else {
    // variable does not exist
}
```

Generates an error:

```
Compiler Error: 1120: Access of undefined property variable name.
```

To avoid this error, precede the variable with the this expression keyword, which causes Flash to interpret the variable as a class property. In ActionScript 3.0, after all, the main timeline is associated with a default document class (see Chapter 6), which can be overridden by a custom class. In either case, timeline variables are ultimately class properties. The inclusion of this reminds the compiler of that point and keeps the compiler error at bay.

Properties and methods cannot be referenced from a null reference

Related closely to the previous example, ActionScript 3.0 generates a runtime error if you try to reference properties or methods of an object that hasn't yet been given a value. (In the previous example, it was a reference to the variable or object itself that caused a compiler error.)

```
var aNullObject:Object; // Declared, but not given a value
if (aNullObject.someProperty) { // Runtime error
    // property exists
} else {
    // property does not exist
}
```

Results in the error:

```
TypeError: Error #1009: Cannot access a property or method
of a null object reference.
```

Note that the variable (an Object instance) does exist, but doesn't yet contain the property referenced, someProperty. To avoid the runtime error, use the logical AND operator (&&) to test for the object first:

```
var aNullObject:Object; // Declared, but not given a value
if (aNullObject && aNullObject.someProperty) {
```

```
    // property exists
} else {
    // property does not exist
}
```

Or use a `try..catch..finally` block:

```
var aNullObject:Object;
try {
    if (aNullObject.aProperty) {
        // property exists
    }
} catch (e:Error) {
    // property does not exist
    trace("Caught error: " + e);
} finally {
    // trace("bad reference!");
}
```

Troubleshooting

How do you eat an elephant? One bite (or maybe one byte!) at a time. This adage has been a gentle encouragement since Lao Tzu first rendered it as The journey of a thousand miles begins with one step. In short, and in terms of programming, it speaks to breaking down large problems into smaller components, and then repeating the process until the first step (or first bite) becomes clear. In development environments, that first step, no matter how long the journey, tends to be easier when it's small. Remember, testing early and testing often helps to keep you from getting overwhelmed.

When you do encounter an error or warning you truly can't make heads or tails of, your situation is ready for troubleshooting. Troubleshooting is a "divide and conquer" approach to problem solving, in which your main aim as a developer is to isolate potential sources of the trouble at hand and, by a process of elimination, find the actual causes and fix them. The `trace()` statement, mentioned earlier in this chapter, is a good entry point into the troubleshooting process. Two other tools, the Compiler Errors panel and Output panel, are just as important and may be the instruments that alerted you to the trouble in the first place. The most powerful tool in your arsenal is the mechanism that lets you see into a SWF file's inner workings at runtime. It's called the *debugging workspace*, and it's only available for ActionScript 3.0 documents.

Using the Enhanced Debugging Workspace

FLA documents configured for ActionScript 2.0 and earlier do have a debugging tool, but it exists as a fairly cramped environment, packed into a single panel called the ActionScript 2.0 Debugger panel (Figure 11-7).

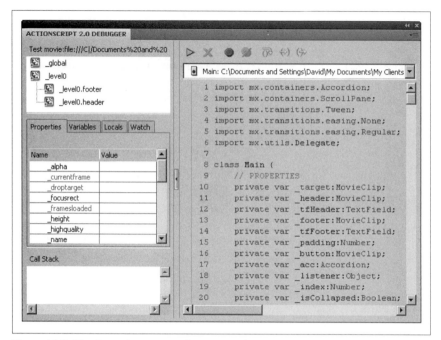

Figure 11-7. The ActionScript 2.0 Debugger panel

To be sure, the old panel is no slouch. It does get the job done. In addition, it's your only choice if your document's Publish Settings are configured for anything other than ActionScript 3.0 (see File→Publish Settings→Flash). In contrast, using the updated workspace is like stepping from an office cubicle into a swank conference lounge. Its panels are separate, which means you'll find plenty of elbow room, and the panels can be collapsed, expanded, and rearranged like those of any other workspace (Figure 11-8).

Using the new debugger is relatively easy, but you should be aware of a few changes before diving into an example.

For better or worse, the ActionScript 2.0 Debugger panel's introspective tree view is no longer available in the new workspace. This is unfortunate, because the tree view was a useful discoverability tool. In addition, two file menu selections in the debug version of Flash Player have disappeared for SWF files published in ActionScript 3.0. Those selections were List Objects and List Variables, each of which sent a text-based snapshot to the Output panel of the objects and variables resident in memory at the time the selections were made. The closest approximation now for the List Objects and List Variables selections is the new public describeType() function, found in the flash.utils package.

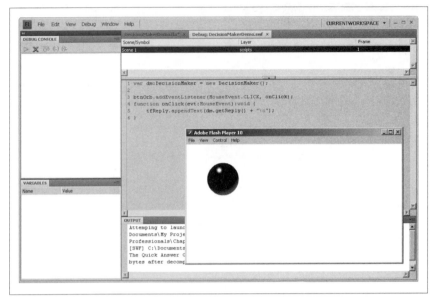

Figure 11-8. The debugging workspace

Use a `trace()` statement to display the results to the Output panel in XML format:

```
trace(describeType(objectReference));

// In timeline code, for example, the following
// provides a data dump of the timeline:
trace(describeType(this));
```

 The option for the SWF files in tabs preference is located under Edit (Flash)→Preferences→General→Workspace→Open test movie in tabs. ActionScript 3.0 SWF files are displayed in windows only during debugging, but may be displayed in tabs during normal testing.

Using the Debugger Workspace

In ActionScript 3.0 FLA files, debugging is possible only with documents that actually contain ActionScript. That trait may seem self-evident, but the ActionScript 2.0 Debugger panel can be displayed regardless of the presence or absence of code. If you select Debug→Debug Movie for a codeless ActionScript 3.0 file, you see an alert box warning: "You cannot debug this SWF because it does not contain ActionScript." Can't argue with that.

To demonstrate the debugging environment, you need a bit of code. The slightest smattering will do.

1. In a new ActionScript 3.0 FLA file, select frame 1 in the Timeline, and then open the Actions panel. Type the following minimal ActionScript:

```
trace("Just a bit of code.");
```

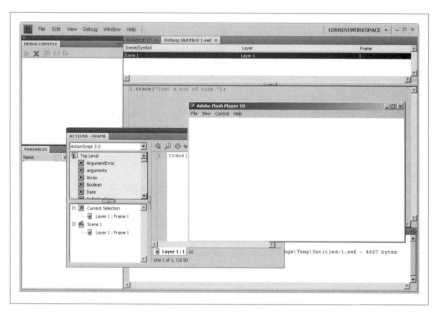

Figure 11-9. A very basic debugging session

2. Select Debug→Debug Movie to enter the debugging workspace. Note the empty Debug Console panel and Variables panel on the left side (Figure 11-9). These panels are empty for a reason, which will be covered shortly. The SWF file itself appears in the debug version of Flash Player, just off center in the figure. The Actions panel may or may not be present, but if so, any changes you make will require a new debug session. The area just below the document tabs, near the top on the right, indicates that ActionScript has been found in Scene 1, Layer 1, Frame 1. In cases where ActionScript appears in several scenes or frames, this area of the debugging workspace displays each of those locations as a clickable line item. The largest pane, middle-right and behind the other content, shows the code for the currently selected frame or, if an AS file is open, the code in the script file whose tab is selected.

This is another change from the older debugger. In the ActionScript 2.0 Debug panel, as debugging starts, the panel waits for you to choose which script(s) to examine, including external AS files, which needn't be open when debugging starts. Any classes that are referenced with import statements, in keyframe or external files, are made available in a list box. In the new workspace, AS files must be opened prior to debugging if you wish to examine their contents before debugging begins.

Finally, the Output panel appears at the bottom right (obscured, here) and behaves as it does during authoring.

3. End the debugging session by any of the following methods: close Flash Player, close the SWF file's tab in the Flash authoring environment, or, in the Debug Console panel of the workspace, click the red X.

Breakpoints

In order to get the most out of a debugging session, you need to add breakpoints. A breakpoint is a special toggle that lets you pause the execution of code inside a SWF file. Breakpoints are easy to add, both to timeline or external ActionScript. Just locate the desired line number, and then click to the left of it, in the gutter, until a red circle appears (Figure 11-10).

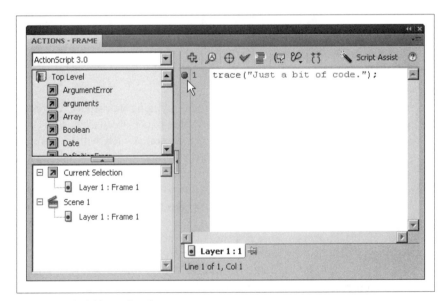

Figure 11-10. Adding a breakpoint

To remove a breakpoint, click the red circle to make it disappear. Alternatively, you can right-click (Ctrl-click) to the left of a line and select Toggle Breakpoint from the context menu, which adds or removes a red circle. To remove all breakpoints at once, select Remove Breakpoints in This File. Flash CS4 is smart enough to remember your breakpoints even after you close the authoring tool, whether they appear in timeline or class code. You may add as many breakpoints as you wish. In the next few steps, you'll learn how they work.

1. Continuing with the same FLA file, use the Actions panel to add a breakpoint to the left of line 1, which contains the `trace()` function.

2. Select Debug→Debug Movie to re-enter the debugging workspace. Note the difference among the panels: Flash Player no longer shows, because it hasn't yet opened (the breakpoint in the first line of code has halted the movie). In addition, both the Debug Console panel and the Variables panel now display information, as seen in Figure 11-11 (click the + sign or arrow triangle inside the Variables panel to open the nodes shown).

In the upper left, the Debug Console panel displays an interesting bit of information in an area known as the *call stack*: `Untitled_fla::MainTimeline/frame1`. The call stack shows the currently executing method, in an ordered list of all methods under execution. Here, the list displays only one item because only one method is executing. Unless you associate a FLA file with a custom document class (see Chapter 6), an automatic document class is assigned by default. This class is named `MainTimeline`, and keyframe scripts are considered methods of that class, which explains the `MainTimeline/frame1` reference, functionally equivalent to the more familiar syntax `MainTimeline.frame1()`. In complex movies, you may see many entries in the call stack, as potentially numerous methods call each other, and then remove themselves as execution completes.

The Variables panel displays the properties of the object currently in scope, which is still `MainTimeline`. Click the + sign or arrow triangle next to the word `this`, and you see the familiar properties of the `MovieClip` class, which is the data type of the main timeline in this scenario. The values of these properties reflect the current state of the main timeline as movie clip. The `currentLabels` property, for example, is an empty array, because the main timeline hasn't been given any frame labels. The x and y properties are 0 and 0, because the main timeline is inherently positioned in the stage's upper-left corner.

 The expressions after some properties, for example (@120aec1), are hexadecimal representations of their addresses in memory.

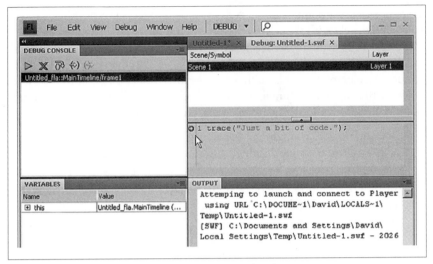

Figure 11-11. The debugger workspace, halted on a breakpoint

3. In the Debug Console panel, click the green arrow button. Two things happen when you do: first, Flash Player appears; second, the Output panel displays the trace() message, "Just a bit of code." The buttons along the top of the Debug Console panel let you control the playback of your breakpoints (Figure 11-12).

The green arrow resumes normal play of the SWF file until the next breakpoint is encountered. The red X closes the current debugging session. The remaining three arrow buttons let you Step Over, Step In, and Step Out of your breakpoints.

- **Step Over** causes the debugger to move to the very next line of code and pause, as though it has encountered a breakpoint. By clicking this button repeatedly, you can step through your code line by line, keeping an eye on the Variables panel to see how values change.

- **Step In** jumps to any function or method referenced on the current breakpoint, and then steps through the code of that function or method line by line.

- **Step Out** moves the debugger immediately to the exit point of the current function or method, typically where the function or method returns a value.

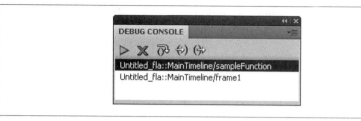

Figure 11-12. Debug Console panel buttons, with a new method in the call stack

Stepping Through a Debugging Example

Here's a slightly more complex—but still very simple—example that demonstrates the Debug Console panel and Variables panel in action.

1. In a new ActionScript 3.0 FLA file, use the Oval tool to draw a small shape in the stage's upper-left. Convert the shape to a movie clip symbol, and then use the Property inspector to give it the instance name *btnOrb*.

2. Use the Text tool to add a text field to the right of the movie clip. Use the Property inspector to make sure this text field is set to Dynamic Text, has a width and height of approximately 300 pixels, is set to Multiline, and has the instance name **tfReply**.

3. Create a new layer, and then name it **scripts**. Save the FLA file as *DecisionMakerDemo.fla*.

4. Create a new ActionScript file, and then save it as *DecisionMaker.as*.

5. Type the following code into the ActionScript file:

```
package {
    public class DecisionMaker {
        private var _replies:Array;
        public function DecisionMaker() {
            _replies = new Array("Yes", "You betcha", "No", ¬
                "No Way", "Maybe");
        }
        public function getReply():String {
            return _replies[getRandomMessage()];
        }
        private function getRandomMessage():int {
            var count:int = _replies.length;
            var float:Number = Math.random() * count;
            var index:int = Math.ceil(float);
            return index;
        }
    }
}
```

This ActionScript defines a class, `DecisionMaker`, that answers yes/no questions. The code contains an error that'll be spelled out in the debugging workspace.

6. Save *DecisionMaker.as,* and then return to *DecisionMakerDemo.fla.* In frame 1 of the `scripts` layer, type the following ActionScript:

```
var dm:DecisionMaker = new DecisionMaker();

btnOrb.addEventListener(MouseEvent.CLICK, onClick);
function onClick(evt:MouseEvent):void {
    tfReply.appendText(dm.getReply() + "\n");
}
```

7. Select Control→Test Movie to test the movie.

8. When the SWF file opens in Flash Player, click the "orb" button several times to populate the dynamic text field with replies. Occasionally, you should see "null" among the answers, as shown in Figure 11-13.

9. Close Flash Player.

10. A breakpoint would be useful, but where should it go? The "orb" button clearly works, because text does appear when the button is clicked, so the FLA file shouldn't need a breakpoint. Return to *DecisionMaker.as* and add a breakpoint to line 7 (the first line of the `getReply()` definition).

11. Select Debug→Debug Movie to enter the debugging workspace. Click the "orb" button in Flash Player. Note that Flash stops at the breakpoint (you may have to drag Flash Player aside to see the panels you're interested in). The call stack in the Debug Console panel now shows two methods (Figure 11-14) because the `onClick()` function in the timeline has called the `getReply()` method in the class file.

    The Variables panel now shows properties of the current object, the `DecisionMaker` instance, which features a `_replies` array with five elements, 0 through 4, and a `length` property of 5.

12. Click the Step Over button, and watch the small yellow arrow move from the breakpoint in line 7 to the next line. Click the Step In button to enter the `getRandomMessage()` method referenced in that line. The call stack updates with a third method—the one you just entered—and the Variables panel now displays the three variables declared in the `getRandomMessage()` method: `count`, `float`, and `index`.

13. Click the Step Over button again. The yellow arrow moves to line 11. Continue clicking Step Over to advance to line 12, 13, and onward. The `count` variable updates to 5, the `float` variable to a random number, and so on. You will eventually exit the function through the `return` statement, at which point Flash Player proceeds as usual, until it encounters another

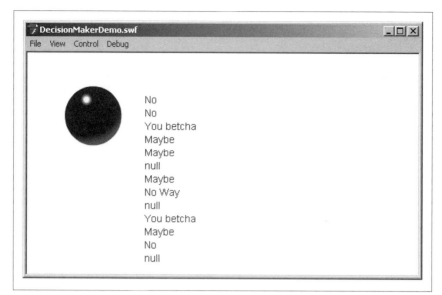

Figure 11-13. A simple application in need of troubleshooting

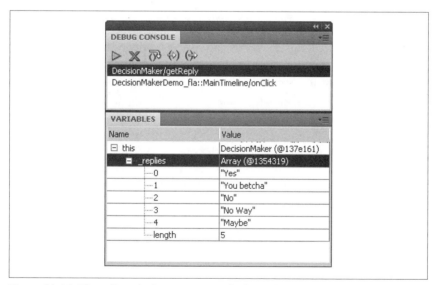

Figure 11-14. The call stack showing two methods, with properties of the current scope below

breakpoint. The green arrow (Continue) button also returns Flash Player to a normal execution flow.

If nothing jumps out at you, then you may have to repeat the process a few times. This is the patient discipline of a good troubleshooter. The clues really are right in front of you.

Eventually, you see the `float` variable get assigned a number greater than 4, which gets rounded up to 5 and assigned to the `index` variable in line 13. The trouble with 5 in this scenario is that the `_replies` property, an `Array` instance, has a total of five elements. Arrays start their count at zero, as shown in the Variables panel in step 12, which displayed elements 0 through 4. There is no element 5. Aha!

The cause of that occasional number 5 is the `Math.ceil()` method in line 13, which always rounds up. Change that method to this (change in bold):

```
var index:int = Math.floor(float);
```

`Math.floor()` always rounds down, which ensures that `index` is always a number between 0 and 4.

Debugging Remotely

Flash is a medium designed for the Web. Even with the advent of the Adobe Integrated Runtime (AIR), it's safe to say that most Flash content is currently displayed in a browser—and browsers don't feature the Flash debugging workspace. In spite of this inevitable gap, you can bridge published SWF files past their browser host environments in order to communicate with the Flash authoring tool. The process is called remote debugging.

To allow Flash CS4 to remotely debug a SWF file, you need to indicate your intent by selecting the checkbox at File→Publish Settings→Flash→Permit debugging. Adding that checkmark enables a Password input field (Figure 11-15) intended to let you password protect a SWF file to ensure that only you can debug it. Unfortunately, this password field is only supported by ActionScript 2.0 documents. The Permit debugging option saves breakpoints and other debug information into the compiled SWF file, which can increase file size. In light of this, when it's time for deployment, you may want to disable remote debugging and perhaps enable Omit trace actions in the same preferences dialog box.

With remote debugging enabled, select Debug→Begin Remote Debugging Session→ActionScript 3.0. The debugging workspace appears, and the Output panel displays the message "Waiting for Player to connect...". At this point, launch the SWF file in a browser and then right-click (Ctrl-click) and select Debugger. You need a debug version of the Flash Player ActiveX control or plug-in for this to work, as described in the next section (you may also use the

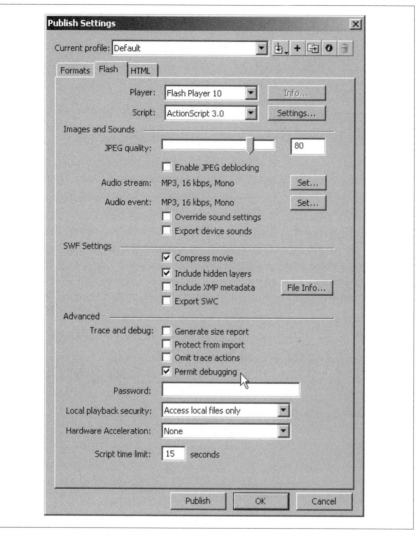

Figure 11-15. Configuring a SWF file for remote debugging

debug version of the standalone Flash Player). The SWF file connects with the authoring tool and debugging continues as before.

Logging trace() Statements from a Browser

The Flex documentation has a trick that explains how to configure the debug version of Flash Player to log `trace()` statements to a local text file. Fortunately, it works for Flash too, and it doesn't involve the debugging workspace. In order to make use of this technique, you'll have to install the debug version of Flash Player as an ActiveX control or plug-in. You can find the necessary files within the installation folder of Flash CS4:

- Windows: *C:\Program Files\Adobe\Adobe Flash CS4\Players\Debug*
- Mac: */Applications/Adobe Flash CS4/Players/Debug/*

These files are also available from the Adobe website:

http://www.adobe.com/support/flashplayer/downloads.html

1. Uninstall your current version of Flash Player with the uninstall file here: *http://www.adobe.com/support/flashplayer/downloads.html#uninstaller*

2. Close all your browsers, and then launch the desired installation file. The one with "ActiveX" in the filename is for Internet Explorer; the one with "Plugin" is for other browsers in Windows, such as Firefox; the one with "UB" is for Mac. For convenience, you may want to use one browser for debugging and one for normal viewing. You know the debug version has been properly installed when you right-click (Ctrl-click) a SWF file in the relevant browser: the context menu has a new option named Debugger.

3. Create a new text file named *mm.cfg* in the following location:
   - Windows: *C:\Documents and Settings\<user name>\mm.cfg*
   - Mac: */Library/Application Support/Adobe/mm.cfg*

   Add the following content to *mm.cfg*, and then save the file:

   ```
   ErrorReportingEnable=1
   TraceOutputFileEnable=1
   MaxWarnings=0
   ```

4. If you're on a Windows machine, you'll have to perform the following additional steps:

   1. On the Desktop, right-click on My Computer, and then, from the context menu, select Properties.

   2. In the System Properties dialog box, select the Advanced tab, and then click the Environment Variables button.

   3. In the User variables area (not the System variables area), click the New button, add the following new variable, and then click OK:
      - Variable name: HOMEDRIVE
      - Variable value: C:\

   4. Click the New button again, add the following new variable, and then click OK:
      - Variable name: HOMEPATH
      - Variable value: C:\Documents and Settings\<user name>

5. Click OK until the remaining dialog boxes are closed.

6. Restart your computer.

At this point, when you view a SWF file in a browser that has the debug version of Flash Player installed, any `trace()` statements in that SWF file are written to a text file named *flashlog.txt*. This text file is cleared and restarted each time you view the SWF file in a new browser session. The location of *flashlog.txt* used to be configurable, but this changed with version 9.0.28.0 of Flash Player. The current location is:

- Windows: *C:\Documents and Settings\<user name>\Application Data\Mac romedia\Flash Player\Logs\flashlog.txt*
- Mac: *<user name>:Library:Preferences:Macromedia:Flash Player: Logs:flashlog.txt*

 Alessandro Crugnola wrote a Firefox extension called FlashTracer that reads from *flashlog.txt*. This free extension is available at *http://www.sephiroth.it/firefox/*.

How Do I?

Part III begins a new look at ActionScript, focusing on how you accomplish a task? This part of the book is presented cookbook-style—a concise look at a problem, solution, and discussion for each of several issues. This format lets you hone in on syntax and methodology in easily digestible recipes.

Part III starts off by highlighting the Graphics class, formerly the Drawing API. Reviewing this material at the outset lets you explore the remainder of the book topics using code-only solutions. Then you'll learn the most significant changes introduced by ActionScript 3.0, the new display architecture and event model. Next, you'll discover new ways of using text for display and interactivity. Finally, you'll concentrate on input/output processes, including sending and loading XML, and variables, as well as loading images, external SWF files, sound, and video.

Chapter 12, *How Do I Draw with Code?*

Chapter 13, *How Do I Work with the Display List?*

Chapter 14, *How Do I Work with Events?*

Chapter 15, *How Do I Work with Text?*

Chapter 16, *How Do I Work with XML?*

Chapter 17, *How Do I Work with External Assets?*

How Do I Draw with Code?

12.0 Introduction

In addition to importing assets, or creating them in the Flash authoring environment, you can include assets in your projects by drawing them dynamically with ActionScript at runtime. Much of the last half of this book will take advantage of this approach to minimize the number of custom assets required, and let you generate content exclusively with code. For that reason, this section starts off with a brief introduction to drawing with code.

A code-only approach doesn't easily offer the artistic range afforded if you can use imported or hand-drawn assets, but significant tradeoffs include increased flexibility and reduced file size. Indeed, an entirely new creative horizon becomes available with code-generated art, and using ActionScript combined with previously created assets is, of course, the best of both worlds.

You have two primary methods of drawing with code: manipulating vectors with the Graphics class, and manipulating pixels with the BitmapData and/or related classes. This chapter will primarily focus on the former, but will also discuss a few simple pixel-based techniques, such as bitmap caching and basic filters.

 To effectively demonstrate some of the concepts in this chapter, you need to use a display object or two. Part I and Part II of this book covered the creation and use of display objects throughout, and you'll look at some of those concepts again in Chapter 13. For clarity, however, the first recipe in this chapter reviews the process of creating a display object into which you can draw, since you need a display object for the subsequent recipes.

12.1 Creating a Display Object Dynamically

Problem

You want to create a display object that will serve as an empty canvas for drawing.

Solution

Use the new keyword to create an instance of a class that is part of the DisplayObject class hierarchy, and then add it to the display list.

Discussion

Display objects and the display list are covered in more detail in Chapter 13. However, in case you haven't yet read the first half of this book, you'll find it handy now if you know just enough about the display list to create an empty display object to serve as a canvas on which you can draw with code. The combination of creating a new display object and drawing on it with the techniques discussed here lets you create code-only movie clips, sprites, buttons, and more.

All display objects can be created using the new keyword. The following two examples create a movie clip and sprite, respectively:

```
var mc:MovieClip = new MovieClip();
var sp:Sprite = new Sprite();
```

Neither the movie clip nor the sprite, however, is ever visible to the user unless you add them to the display list. To add a display object to the display list, use the addChild() method. The following, for example, adds the previously created sprite to the display list:

```
addChild(sp);
```

In this scenario, the sprite would be visible because you added it to the display list, but the movie clip would not be visible. (So far, the sprite has no content but is still technically viewable as an empty canvas. The remainder of this chapter will show how to draw into the sprite.) The movie clip, however, cannot be seen even if it already has content, until you add it to the display list.

See Also

"13.2 Creating a New Display Object" on page 286 for more information on creating a display object.

12.2 Referencing an Object's Graphics Property

Problem

You want to efficiently reference the `graphics` property of a display object, such as a sprite or the main timeline, to use as the target for vector-based drawing.

Solution

Store a reference to the `graphics` property in a variable.

Discussion

To draw with vectors, you must first reference the `graphics` property of a display object. Then you can access the methods and properties of the `Graphics` class, which is responsible for dynamic vector drawing. You can reduce code length and improve performance by storing a reference to the property in a variable, and using that variable thereafter where you would otherwise have referenced the property directly.

If you want to draw into a display object, for example, such as the sprite `sp` you created in "12.1 Creating a Display Object Dynamically" on page 268, you can reference its `graphics` property like so:

```
var g:Graphics = sp.graphics;
```

Thereafter, you need only refer to `g` when using a method or property of the `Graphics` class. You can also reference the `graphics` property of the main timeline with the following:

```
var g:Graphics = this.graphics;
```

This line of code assumes you are writing the script in the main timeline, so the `this` keyword refers to the correct display object: the main timeline itself.

 While it's a matter of personal coding preference, drawing directly on the main timeline isn't usually as useful as being able to contain your drawing in a display object you can manipulate later.

12.3 Defining a Line Style

Problem

You want to specify the appearance of a line you wish to draw.

Solution

Use the `lineStyle()` method of the `Graphics` class to define line attributes.

Discussion

The last line of the following code block sets any lines subsequently drawn into the display object `sp` to be of 1-pixel thickness and blue in color. The line settings for the `Graphics` object `g` remain in effect until changed or reset.

```
var sp:Sprite = new Sprite();
addChild(sp);
var g:Graphics = sp.graphics;
g.lineStyle(1, 0x0000FF);
```

The first parameter is `thickness`, a pixel value, with 0 being a hairline. The second parameter is the `color` of the line.

You also have additional optional parameters that closely mimic the Property inspector settings. These parameters include `alpha`, `pixelHinting` (also called stroke hinting, a Boolean to determine if the lines are drawn on the whole pixel), `scaleMode` (to determine if and how lines are scaled when the parent container is scaled), `caps` (specifying type of line end cap used), `joints` (specifying type of joint type used), and `miterLimit` (determining how sharp corners appear).

If you want to clear everything previously drawn into the display object, you can use the `clear()` method of the `Graphics` class. However, because a line isn't drawn when a pixel thickness isn't specified, you can also clear just the line attributes by passing no parameters to the `lineStyle()` method.

```
g.lineStyle();
```

See Also

"12.6 Defining a Fill Style" on page 273 for a demonstration of using multiple `lineTo()` commands to create a triangle.

12.4 Drawing a Line

Problem

You want to draw a line from point A to point B.

Solution

Use the `moveTo()` and `lineTo()` methods of the `Graphics` class.

Discussion

Drawing a line works the same way it does with pen and paper. First, you place your pen at the first point of the line. If you don't take this first step in Flash, the line begins at the origin (0, 0) of the display object, such as the registration point of a parent sprite or even the top-left corner of the Flash stage. Also like pen and paper, combining `moveTo()` and `lineTo()` method calls in your scripts lets you draw complex shapes without creating one continuous line.

To draw a line on the stage from point (100, 100), to point (300, 100), use the following code:

```
var g:Graphics = this.graphics;
g.lineStyle(1, 0x0000FF);
g.moveTo(100,100);
g.lineTo(300,100);
```

In most cases, you have greater control if you draw into a container display object so you can easily manipulate your sprite or movie clip as a whole. When drawing onto the sprite or movie clip, the registration point of assets drawn into the display object is (0, 0), regardless of the display object's x and y co-ordinates on the stage, because the drawn assets inside are relative to the display object's coordinate space, not that of the stage. So, you're better off achieving the previous goal of drawing a line on the stage from (100, 100) to (300, 100) by drawing a line from (0, 0) to (200, 0), and positioning the display object.

```
var sp:Sprite = new Sprite();
addChild(sp);
sp.x = sp.y = 100;
var g:Graphics = sp.graphics;
g.lineStyle(1, 0x0000FF);
g.lineTo(200,0);
```

In this case, because you want the line to begin from the relative origin point of (0, 0), you can omit the moveTo() method call.

To demonstrate the ease with which you can now manipulate the drawn assets as a whole, the following line will rotate the container sprite 45 degrees, thus rotating the line inside.

```
sp.rotation = 45;
```

See Also

"12.6 Defining a Fill Style" on page 273 for a demonstration of using multiple lineTo() commands to create a triangle.

12.5 Drawing a Curve

Problem

You want to draw a curve from point A to point B.

Solution

Use the curveTo() method of the Graphics class.

Discussion

Drawing a curve is similar to drawing a line, in that a curve is drawn from the current drawing point to a new point. However, the curveTo() method adds a third point, called a control point or handle, to shape the curve. ActionScript creates curves that use one control point for two points. This trait is in contrast to many drawing applications, such as Adobe Illustrator, which uses one or more control points for every point.

Placing the control point is an important part of determining the shape of your curve. For example, consider turning the line from "12.4 Drawing a Line" on page 271 into a concave arc, resembling a smile. To pull the curve down in the middle, you might select a control point halfway between and below the two end points. Therefore, if the line spans from (0, 0) to (200, 0), one possible choice for a control point is (100, 100). These x and y coordinates are passed to the curveTo() method as the first and second arguments, while the destination or end point x and y coordinates are the last two arguments of the method.

```
var sp:Sprite = new Sprite();
addChild(sp);
sp.x = sp.y = 100;
var g:Graphics = sp.graphics;
g.lineStyle(1, 0x0000FF);
g.curveTo(100, 100, 200, 0);
```

Omitting `moveTo()` in the code sets the first point at (0, 0), or the sprites registration point. The final result is a curve that starts at (0, 0), ends at (200, 0), but is curved through a control point of (100, 100).

12.6 Defining a Fill Style

Problem

You want to fill a drawn shape with a color.

Solution

Use the `beginFill()` and `endFill()` methods of the `Graphics` class.

Discussion

In "12.3 Defining a Line Style" on page 270, you learned how to define a line style, but even a closed line has no fill without specifying a fill style. The `beginFill()` method specifies a color and opacity to fill any shapes drawn until you call the `endFill()` method.

When you use a fill, if drawn shapes aren't closed (meaning the line does not end at its starting point), the shapes are closed for you. To demonstrate this effect, the following code draws a complete triangle even though the instruction that draws the last side of the triangle is commented out (to prevent it from drawing). If you remove the `beginFill()` and `endFill()` instructions from this code, then you see only the two lines specified, because the fill process is no longer auto-closing the shape.

```
var sp:Sprite = new Sprite();
addChild(sp);
sp.x = sp.y = 100;
var g:Graphics = sp.graphics;
g.lineStyle(2, 0xFF0000);
g.beginFill(0x0000FF, 1);
g.moveTo(0, -50);
g.lineTo(50, 50);
```

```
g.lineTo(-50, 50);
//g.lineTo(0, -50);
g.endFill();
```

12.7 Drawing a Rectangle

Problem

You want to draw a rectangle.

Solution

Use the drawRect() method of the Graphics class.

Discussion

ActionScript 3.0 has added a few methods to draw geometric shapes, removing
the need to build them with multiple line segments. Creating a rectangle is as
easy as calling drawRect(), passing in the rectangle's x and y location, followed
by height and width.

```
var sp:Sprite = new Sprite();
addChild(sp);
sp.x = sp.y = 100;
var g:Graphics = sp.graphics;
g.lineStyle(1, 0x0000FF);
g.drawRect(0, 0, 100, 60);
```

All primitives in this chapter, except for a circle, are drawn down and to the
right of the x and y coordinates specified. When drawing into a parent container, as in this example, this trait results in a registration point at the upper-
left corner of the shape. To draw this rectangle around its center point, offset
the x and y values passed into drawRect() by half the width and half the height,
respectively. The following substitute line makes the rectangle center-aligned
within its parent container, sp.

```
g.drawRect(-50, -30, 100, 60);
```

12.8 Drawing a Rectangle with Rounded Corners

Problem

You want to draw a rectangle with rounded corners.

Solution

Use the `drawRoundRect()` method of the `Graphics` class.

Discussion

This variance on `drawRect()` requires a fifth parameter that represents the diameter of a circle used to round off the rectangle's corners. The last line of the following code creates a 100 × 60 pixel rectangle with rounded corners that have a radius of 15.

```
var sp:Sprite = new Sprite();
addChild(sp);
sp.x = sp.y = 100;
var g:Graphics = sp.graphics;
g.lineStyle(1, 0x0000FF);
g.drawRoundRect(0, 0, 100, 60, 15);
```

The fifth parameter requires a diameter, rather than a potentially more intuitive radius, to easily support the optional sixth parameter. Instead of specifying only a diameter to build the rectangle's corners, you can also specify a height and width, constructing your corner from an ellipse. This method gives you more granular control over the corner shapes. The following substitute line, for example, uses an ellipse with a width of 30 and a height of 50 to create its corners.

```
g.drawRoundRect(0, 0, 100, 60, 30, 50);
```

You can also use the under-documented method `drawRoundRectComplex()` that requires eight parameters. The first four are, again, the x, y, width, and height of the rectangle. The last four, however, are the diameters of each corner circle, in the order of upper-left, upper-right, lower-left, lower-right. The following substitute line for the previous example would create a tab shape, with a straight bottom edge, and two rounded top corners:

```
g.drawRoundRectComplex(0, 0, 100, 40, 20, 20, 0, 0);
```

See Also

"12.7 Drawing a Rectangle" on page 274 for drawing a rectangle and "12.9 Drawing a Circle" on page 276 for drawing a circle.

12.9 Drawing a Circle

Problem

You want to draw a circle.

Solution

Use the `drawCircle()` method of the `Graphics` class.

Discussion

In addition to x and y starting coordinates, drawing a circle requires only one additional argument value: the radius of the circle (half its diameter, or width/ height). The following code creates a circle that is 40 × 40 pixels by using a radius of 20.

```
var sp:Sprite = new Sprite();
addChild(sp);
sp.x = sp.y = 100;
var g:Graphics = sp.graphics;
g.lineStyle(1, 0x0000FF);
g.drawCircle(0, 0, 20);
```

The circle is drawn differently. Instead of drawing with its origin at the upper-left corner of the shape, as is true with other primitives, the circle's origin is its center. To draw a circle that's below and to the right of its parent container's registration point, you must offset the x and y coordinates by the amount used for the circle's radius. The following substitute line aligns the circle to the top-left corner of the sprite.

```
g.drawCircle(20, 20, 20);
```

You can also draw an ellipse using the `drawEllipse()` method. Rather than accepting a radius as its third parameter, it accepts a width and height as parameters three and four, just like `drawRect()`. Also like drawing a rectangle, the default registration point of the ellipse is the upper-left corner (in contrast to the `drawCircle()` method's default center registration point). Substituting the following for the `drawCircle()` instruction in the prior example draws an ellipse that is 100 pixels wide and 50 pixels tall.

```
g.drawEllipse(0, 0, 100, 50);
```

See Also

"12.7 Drawing a Rectangle" on page 274 for drawing a rectangle and "12.8 Drawing a Rectangle with Rounded Corners" on page 274 for drawing rectangle with rounded corners.

12.10 Creating a Gradient Fill

Problem

You want to create a gradient fill to replace solid colors when filling drawn shapes.

Solution

Use the beginGradientFill() and endFill() methods of the Graphics class.

Discussion

To create a gradient fill, you must first understand its component parts. First is the type of gradient: linear or radial. Next is a set of *parallel arrays* (arrays with an equal number of objects in the same order) that represent up to 15 colors in the gradient. These arrays contain the color values themselves, their alpha values, and the amount of the total gradient each color is meant to occupy, respectively. Finally, an optional matrix can be used to rotate, scale, skew, or offset the location of the gradient. Here is the gradient fill creation segment:

```
var gradType:String = GradientType.LINEAR;
var colors:Array = [0x000000, 0x000000];
var alphas:Array = [1, 0];
var ratios:Array = [0, 255];
var matrix:Matrix = new Matrix();
matrix.createGradientBox(100, 100, 0, 0, 0);
```

The color values use standard hexadecimal notation. The alpha values are expressed in decimal notation of percent values between 0 and 1. However, the ratio of color quantity, is expressed as an increasing set of numbers between 0 and 255, representing their position along the gradient.

An equally spaced two-color gradient, such as this example uses, is created using the two extreme values of 0 and 255. Both colors are full at the ends of the gradient, and mix together in the middle. Adding another equally spaced third color would require a ratio array of 0, 127, and 255. Finally, to skew a gradient toward one dominant color, you might use a ratio array of 0 and 127.

This would show the first color in one third of the gradient and mix over to the second color that occupied two thirds of the gradient.

The last part of creating a gradient is the optional matrix to manipulate its position, scale, and angle. You create the matrix with the standard use of the new keyword, but editing it can get complex. Fortunately, you have a special method of the Matrix class specifically for this purpose, createGradient Box(). The eponymous method accepts a width, height, rotation, horizontal translation, and vertical translation to manipulate the gradient for you.

This example uses a width and height that matches the size of the rectangle itself, and no horizontal or vertical translation is specified, so the full gradient is visible. With a rotation of 0, the gradient moves from first color to last color, in a left to right direction.

Finally, these values are passed into the beginGradientFill() method (used in place of the beginFill() method of prior recipes) in the order discussed: gradient type, color array, alpha array, ratio array, and matrix. The result is a smooth gradient from opaque black to transparent.

```
var sp:Sprite = new Sprite();
addChild(spMask);
sp.x = sp.y = 100;
var g:Graphics = sp.graphics;
g.beginGradientFill(gradType, colors, alphas, ratios, matrix);
g.drawRect(0, 0, 100, 100);
g.endFill();
```

12.11 Using a Drawn Shape as a Dynamic Mask

Problem

You want to mask a display object with another display object created at runtime.

Solution

Draw the mask using the Graphics class, and then use the mask property of shape, sprite, and movie clip display objects.

Discussion

This recipe adds only one significant new line to material covered in previous recipes. However, due to subtle changes (variable names, size, and fill style), the complete code has been collected here. This example combines two sprites, one with a rectangle with a solid fill, and another with a rectangle with a gradient fill. The solid rectangle is on the bottom and is 300 pixels wide by 300 pixels tall. The top rectangle contains a gradient of 100 percent alpha black to 0 percent alpha black (transparent), and measures only 100 × 100 pixels.

The last line of this recipe is the important one. To use one display object to dynamically mask another, set the mask property of the *maskee*, to the *mask*.

```
var sp:Sprite = new Sprite();
addChild(sp);
var g:Graphics = sp.graphics;
g.lineStyle();
g.beginFill(0x000099, 1);
g.drawRect(0, 0, 300, 300);
g.endFill();

var gradType:String = GradientType.LINEAR;
var colors:Array = [0x000000, 0x000000];
var alphas:Array = [1, 0];
var ratios:Array = [0, 255];
var matrix:Matrix = new Matrix();
matrix.createGradientBox(100, 100, 0, 0, 0);

var spMask:Sprite = new Sprite();
addChild(spMask);
spMask.x = spMask.y = 100;
var gMask:Graphics = spMask.graphics;
gMask.beginGradientFill(gradType, colors, alphas, ratios, matrix);
gMask.drawRect(0, 0, 100, 100);
gMask.endFill();

sp.mask = spMask;
```

Note that this minimal approach supports only 1-bit masks. That is, any non-transparent pixel, no matter what the alpha value of that pixel, is considered opaque and part of the mask. This example uses a gradient that changes from 100 percent alpha to 0 percent alpha to emphasize that the alpha data has no effect, by default, on the mask.

However, 8-bit masks, or masks with varying degrees of alpha values, are supported when using bitmap caching, as seen in the next recipe.

See Also

"12.6 Defining a Fill Style" on page 273 and "12.10 Creating a Gradient Fill" on page 277 for how to create a solid or gradient fill, and see "12.12 Caching Vector as Bitmap" on page 280 for how to cache a bitmap.

12.12 Caching Vector as Bitmap

Problem

You want to use pixel-based effects on vector assets and/or attempt to increase performance of vector rendering.

Solution

Temporarily work with a visual asset as a bitmap, by temporarily storing bitmap representation of the asset.

Discussion

You need significant CPU processing power to composite and render moving vectors many times a second. In some cases, you can improve performance by treating the vector asset as a bitmap, behind the scenes. In simple terms, Flash Player takes a screenshot of the vector any time a major transformation, such as changes to rotation, alpha, or scale, occurs and composites the bitmap version rather than the vector asset itself.

Because the bitmap version is cached, you have no degradation of visual quality any time a major transformation occurs. However, the need to maintain an equivalent bitmap also means performance can actually worsen if you use this feature injudiciously. Therefore, bitmap caching is not recommended if the asset is rotating, scaling, or changing opacity frequently.

More directly, sometimes you need to temporarily convert a vector to bitmap to apply pixel-based effects, like filters and 8-bit masks. In some cases, this process is automatic, such as when you're applying a simple filter like a drop shadow. In other cases, you must explicitly enable the feature.

This recipe adds only two lines of code to the very end of the prior "12.11 Using a Drawn Shape as a Dynamic Mask" on page 278 to use a drawn shape as a dynamic mask. The repeated code has been omitted.

```
sp.cacheAsBitmap = true;
spMask.cacheAsBitmap = true;
```

By enabling bitmap caching for both the mask and maskee, both can be composited as bitmaps. Then you can use the gradient alpha values in the mask when displaying the underlying content.

See Also

"12.10 Creating a Gradient Fill" on page 277 for creating a gradient fill and "12.11 Using a Drawn Shape as a Dynamic Mask" on page 278 to use a drawn shape as a dynamic mask.

12.13 Applying a Simple Bitmap Filter

Problem

You want to apply simple bitmap filter effects to a display object, such as drop shadow, bevel, or blur.

Solution

Use one of the simple filter classes, including `DropShadowFilter()`, `BevelFilter()` or `BlurFilter()`.

Discussion

Applying simple filters to display objects is very easy for two reasons. First, the filter classes are easy to use and work similarly to the way the same filters are applied in the Flash authoring environment. Second, there is a built-in `filters` property in any display object that can have a filter applied, making it straightforward to set the property to the filters you wish to add.

Creating a filter follows the same pattern as most other instantiations in ActionScript 3.0, using the new keyword. Conveniently, the parameters for setting the values of the filter are all optional, and use default values if none are specified. This means that, at minimum, you can create filters using the following example format, which demonstrates the drop shadow and bevel filters:

```
var dsFilter:DropShadowFilter = new DropShadowFilter();
var bvFilter:BevelFilter = new BevelFilter();
```

You can apply the filters just as easily by setting the `filters` property of your display object. The `filters` property requires an array to let multiple filters be applied at the same time (such as applying both a bevel and a drop shadow). When applying only one filter, you need only pass a single-item array to the property. The following new script creates a filled rectangle, and applies a drop shadow effect:

```
var sp:Sprite = new Sprite();
addChild(sp);
sp.x = sp.y = 100;
```

```
var g:Graphics = sp.graphics;
g.lineStyle(1, 0x000099);
g.beginFill(0x0000FF, 1);
g.drawRect(0, 0, 100, 60);
g.endFill();

var ds:DropShadowFilter = new DropShadowFilter();
sp.filters = [ds];
```

If you wanted to apply both a drop shadow filter and a bevel filter, the last block of code would read:

```
var ds:DropShadowFilter = new DropShadowFilter();
var bv:BevelFilter = new BevelFilter();
sp.filters = [ds, bv];
```

To manipulate a filter's settings, you can use different optional settings for each filter. The first batch of settings for the drop shadow filter are relatively intuitive numerical values, in this order: distance offset (pixels), angle (degrees), color (in hexadecimal notation), alpha (decimal percent range, 0–1), extent of blur in the x direction, extent of blur in the y direction, strength (the amount of color applied and degree of spread), and quality (how many times the filter's applied). The last batch of options are three Booleans that represent the special setting of this filter—whether or not the shadow is cast inside the shape (to represent a "hole" in the canvas, for example), whether or not the underlying shadow is knocked out (revealing the canvas), and whether or not the object casting the shadow is hidden (leaving only the shadow).

So, if you want to create a lighter, softer shadow, cast down and to the left, you might substitute the previous filter instantiation with the following:

```
var ds:DropShadowFilter = new DropShadowFilter(5, 135, 0x000099, .5, 10, 10);
```

You can also change values after creating a setting by manipulating the desired property directly. You just have to remember to reapply the filters to the display object after any change. For example, revisit the filter setup at the beginning of this recipe:

```
var ds:DropShadowFilter = new DropShadowFilter();
sp.filters = [ds];
```

You could then change a specific setting, such as the angle, in the filter, and then reapply the filter to see your change in action. The following code changes the angle from the default 45 to 135:

```
ds.angle = 135;
sp.filters = [ds];
```

CHAPTER 13

How Do I Work with the Display List?

13.0 Introduction

The new display architecture is one of the two biggest ActionScript changes in version 3.0. (The other biggest change comes in the form of the new event model, which the next chapter covers.) In this chapter, you'll learn the basics of displaying content, which have been simplified over prior versions of ActionScript in a few ways.

To begin with, presenting visual assets to the user has become much more consistent. Previous ActionScript versions gave you a handful of different ways to display a movie clip, for example, and many more when factoring in the display of all types of visible assets. In ActionScript 3.0, however, all visual assets are displayed in the same general manner: create the asset (if necessary) using the new keyword, and then add it to the *display list*.

The display list is a type of linear array (although with its own access methods) of objects that the user can see. In simple terms, an empty SWF file has an empty display list, a SWF file with a single movie clip has a display list that contains one item, and so on. (More accurately, each SWF file includes the stage and main timeline at the root of the display list, but you can't remove these, and so they're not included as list indices.)

Although the display list can contain only objects with visual data, you can create such a display object without adding it to the display list. That is, a sound can't be a display object because you can't see it, but you can create a movie clip (which can be visible) without adding it to the display list.

You can hide a display object while it's in the display list (by manipulating its visible or alpha properties, or even moving it offstage or covering it up with another display object). You can also remove an item from the display list without removing it from memory, thereby making it invisible to the user. Remember, however, that if an object has a visual component, it's a display object and therefore can be included in the display list and, conversely, objects that are incapable of being seen by the user can't be display objects and therefore can't be included in the display list.

13.1 Choosing Which Type of Display Object to Use

Problem

You want to identify which kind of display object is best suited for a particular task.

Solution

Review the display object classes to determine which has the most useful set of properties, methods and/or events to satisfy your needs.

Discussion

Understanding the display list begins with looking at the classes that make up the collection of all objects that can be part of the display list, as seen in Figure 13-1. They originate with the `DisplayObject` class, which defines the basic properties, methods, and events all display objects share.

This chapter focuses on the most common display objects, but an overview of all the display list classes helps clarify their purposes. Begin on the left of Figure 13-1, with three eponymous classes.

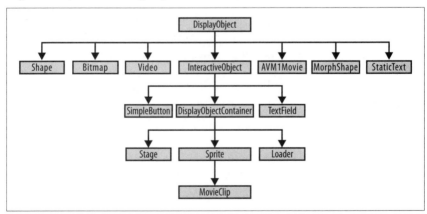

Figure 13-1. Hierarchy of display list classes

Shape is a lightweight class that requires very little memory and performance overhead because it has no timeline or mechanism for reacting to mouse events. The result of creating and drawing into a shape with ActionScript is the same as the element created when you draw a shape by hand in the Flash authoring environment. Accomplishing this with code is a new feature in ActionScript 3.0.

Bitmap and Video classes are used, as you might expect, to display bitmaps and videos spawned from ActionScript. Skipping for a moment to the right half of Figure 13-1, you find three classes that you're less likely to use directly. AVM1Movie references loaded SWF files created using ActionScript 1.0 or 2.0, MorphShape refers to timeline-based shape tweens, and StaticText refers to non-interactive text elements created in the Flash IDE. You can't create instances of these classes, but they're used as parent classes for other display objects.

Moving back to the center of the figure, InteractiveObject can't be instantiated directly, but is a parent class for all interactive elements in the display list. The third row of the figure contains SimpleButton, TextField (so, in ActionScript 3.0, you can create true buttons on the fly), and another parent class that can't be instantiated, DisplayObjectContainer. This latter class adds the ability for a display object to have children. While a bitmap couldn't contain a nested movie clip, for example, any child of the DisplayObjectContainer class can.

The Stage class can't be instantiated but does give you access to stage properties from any display object in the display list. Loader is used to load external display assets such as images and other SWF files, and Sprite is simply a movie clip without a timeline, provided for memory and performance optimization. Finally, MovieClip adds a timeline to Sprite, and the collection of display list classes is complete.

Choosing an appropriate display object depends largely on the task at hand. Some choices are clear, such as when dynamic bitmaps, videos, buttons, or text fields must be created, using their respective classes, or when external assets must be loaded into a Loader instance.

Others aren't as obvious, but will soon become second nature. Shape instances serve primarily as canvases for dynamically drawing assets using the Graphics class, as discussed in Chapter 12. Because shapes have no timeline or user event capabilities, they're best suited for drawing backgrounds and other objects that aren't interactive. Movie clips are useful for frame-based animations, just as in the Flash IDE, and sprites are optimal for ActionScript-based animations when you don't need a timeline, but you do need user events.

See Also

Chapter 12

13.2 Creating a New Display Object

Problem

You want to create an asset, such as a movie clip or sprite, which is derived from one of the `DisplayObject` classes.

Solution

Use the new keyword to create instances from scratch or from a Library linkage class.

Discussion

Creating any new display object is consistent throughout ActionScript 3.0, using the new keyword to spawn a new instance of the display object's class. Typically, you want to store that instance in a variable that's also typed to the display object's class, or a relevant parent class. The following examples show the creation of four different display objects, and their corresponding variable references with data typing.

```
var mc:MovieClip = new MovieClip();
var sp:Sprite = new Sprite();
var tf:TextField = new TextField();
var sh:Shape = new Shape();
```

Building on that consistency, you can also create an instance of a Library-based display object using the same syntax. The only difference is that instead of using one of Flash's built-in classes, you should use the name of the Library element's linkage class.

 For more information about using the Library and linkage classes, see Chapter 7.

In this next example, a Library movie clip has been given a linkage class of `Ball`. The syntax still uses the new keyword to create an instance of the class, and stores the instance in a variable typed with the same class.

```
var ballObj:Ball = new Ball();
```

If desired, you can also type the variable with a relevant parent display class. For example, the Library element may have originated as a movie clip and, when given the linkage class of `Ball`, extended `MovieClip` as its base class. You could type the new instance of the `Ball` class as `MovieClip`, `Sprite`, or `DisplayObject`. You could use any one of the following three possible lines. This example relates to casting display objects to different data types, which will be covered later in the chapter.

```
var ballObj:MovieClip = new Ball();
var ballObj:Sprite = new Ball();
var ballObj:DisplayObject = new Ball();
```

While you can work with display objects immediately after creating them, you can't see them until they're added to the display list. This topic is covered in the next recipe.

See Also

"13.3 Adding a Display Object to the Display List" on page 287 for adding a display object to the display list.

13.3 Adding a Display Object to the Display List

Problem

You want a display object to be visible to the user.

Solution

Use the `addChild()` method of the display object container's class to add the object to the display list.

Discussion

A display object must be in the display list if it's ever to be visible at runtime or be responsible for providing access to other display properties (such as a stage reference). This quality is independent of the `visible` or `alpha` property values of a display object, or other techniques for showing or hiding a visual asset.

The following script creates a new sprite and positions it at point (30, 30).

```
var sp:Sprite = new Sprite();
sp.x = sp.y = 30;
```

However, even though the sprite has x and y coordinates that are within the stage, you can't see it until it's added to the display list. The following method adds the specified display object to the top of the display list, regardless of the number of items already in the list.

```
addChild(sp);
```

The display list isn't just a linear array of display objects; it's also contiguous. That is, it can't have gaps between display objects. This is a device for automating and optimizing depth management, and eliminates the need for the `getNextHighestDepth()` method in prior versions of ActionScript. Rather than specifying an arbitrarily high depth number to be sure a new visual asset is on top of another, using `addChild()` automatically appends the display object to the end (top) of the display list.

Further, the list automatically adjusts itself to eliminate any gaps. If you remove an object from the display list (discussed later in this chapter), then all objects higher in the list automatically drop down. If you insert an object in a position lower than other objects in the list (also discussed later in this chapter), then the higher objects all bump up a position.

So far, the sprite has no content, but you can add visual data through the use of another display object. The following script segment creates a shape and draws into it a 40-pixel by 40-pixel yellow square.

```
var sh:Shape = new Shape();
var g:Graphics = sh.graphics;
g.lineStyle(1, 0x000000);
g.beginFill(0xFFFF00, 1);
g.drawRect(0, 0, 40, 40);
g.endFill();
```

Previously, the sprite was added to the main timeline but, in this case, the shape will be added to the sprite. Display objects can be added to other display objects, and the former become children of the latter.

```
sp.addChild(sh);
```

You can certainly draw directly into a sprite. However, in addition to demonstrating hierarchical, or nested, display objects, this emphasizes that not all display objects behave the same way. On its own, the shape couldn't function as an interactive element because it can't process mouse clicks, among other events. However, by adding the shape to a sprite, the shape can then, by extension, be clickable.

See Also

"13.1 Choosing Which Type of Display Object to Use" on page 284 for choosing a display object type, "13.4 Specifying the Depth of a Display Object" on page 289 for setting the depth of an object, "13.6 Removing a Display Object from the Display List" on page 292, for removing an object from a display list, and "13.9 Casting a Display Object from One Type to Another" on page 297 for recasting a display object type.

13.4 Specifying the Depth of a Display Object

Problem

You want to place a display object at a particular visual stacking depth, or swap the visual depths of two display objects.

Solution

Based on need, use the addChild(), addChildAt(), setChildIndex(), swapChildren(), or swapChildrenAt() methods of the display object container's class.

Discussion

You'll often find it helpful to alter the depths at which display objects reside. Consider, for example, an interactive jigsaw puzzle. To simulate a real-world puzzle experience, it helps to move the clicked piece to the top of the pile while dragging it to the puzzle board.

You have several ways to change the stacking order of display objects. The first is simply to add the same object to the display again. In the following code, a sprite (red, 0xFF0000) is added to the display list first, followed by a movie clip (blue, 0x0000FF). However, the first sprite is added to the display list again. Because it's the same object, it's automatically removed from its prior position and placed in its new position. As a result, the sprite moves to the top of the stacking order.

```
var sp:Sprite = new Sprite();
drawSquare(sp, 0xFF0000);
sp.x = sp.y = 20;
addChild(sp);

var mc:MovieClip = new MovieClip();
drawSquare(mc, 0x0000FF);
mc.x = mc.y = 40;
```

```
addChild(mc);

addChild(sp);

function drawSquare(obj:Object, col:uint):void {
    var g:Graphics = obj.graphics;
    g.beginFill(col, 1);
    g.drawRect(0, 0, 40, 40);
    g.endFill();
}
```

You also have more direct ways of placing a display object at a specific level. The addChildAt() method is a companion to addChild() but lets you dictate a destination depth for the display object. The method has two parameters: the object being placed, and the target depth. As with addChild(), the object on which this method is called dictates scope—the display list to which this child will be added. Omitting an object reference before the method adds the child to the current scope—the display list in which the omitted object resides.

For example, the following adds a library symbol, stored in the variable boxSp, to the bottom of the main timeline (the current scope) by specifying a depth of zero.

```
var boxSp:Sprite = new Box();
addChildAt(boxSp, 0);
```

For example, the following adds a display object to the main timeline (the current scope) because no target for addChild() is specified. In this case, it adds a library symbol, stored in the variable boxSp, to the bottom of the main time-line by specifying a depth of zero.

```
var boxSp:Sprite = new Box();
addChildAt(boxSp, 0);
```

If you wanted to add boxSp to the bottom of the child list of an existing display object container, such as the previously created movie clip mc, the syntax would follow the examples for addChild() and look like this:

```
mc.addChildAt(boxSp, 0);
```

See Also

"13.3 Adding a Display Object to the Display List" on page 287 for adding a display object to the display list.

13.5 Finding a Display Object

Problem

You need to create a reference to a display object, but you have access to only its name or position in the display list.

Solution

Use the getChildAt() or getChildByName() methods of the display object container's class.

Discussion

People often want to access a display object without already having a reference to the object in question. For example, you may want to generate an object's name by combining strings or accepting user input, or you may want to loop through all children of a container addressing each item by child index.

The first line of the following ActionScript block retrieves a reference to an object by using its name. The second shows how to reference the bottom-most display object (because it gets the display list child at depth zero).

```
var dispObj:DisplayObject = getChildByName("claire");
var dispObj2:DisplayObject = getChildAt(0);
```

Both these methods are really useful. The latter makes it possible to work with an object at any depth, even without knowing which object currently occupies that position in the display list. You virtually require the former when creating display objects with ActionScript because of a small change in the new version of the language.

In ActionScript 2.0, you could use a name that was added to a symbol instance with code to reference its properties or methods. That is, if you created an empty movie clip, you could assign it a name with ActionScript, and then use that name as a proper instance name as if it were applied in Flash's Property inspector.

In ActionScript 3.0, you can't do this any more. The string used for the instance's name property remains a string—a property value—and can't be evaluated as an object. The following code example illustrates this point. The first code segment creates, names, and positions a display object, and then adds it to the display list. The second segment traces the x coordinate of the display object, using its programmatically assigned name as an instance reference. The result is an error because the value of the name property isn't understood to be a proper object.

```
var sp:Sprite = new Sprite();
sp.name = "claire";
sp.x = 100;
addChild(sp);

trace(claire.x);
//yields error:
//1120: Access of undefined property claire.
```

The simple solution is to use the getChildByName() method to return a fully qualified object reference, as seen here:

```
var dispObj:DisplayObject = getChildByName("claire");
trace(dispObj.x);
//yields 100
```

See Also

"13.4 Specifying the Depth of a Display Object" on page 289, for setting the depth of the display object.

13.6 Removing a Display Object from the Display List

Problem

You want a display object to be hidden from view, unable to receive events, and/or disassociated from familial relationship with other display objects.

Solution

Use the removeChild() or removeChildAt() methods of the display object container's class to remove the object from the display list.

Discussion

You have a few ways to hide a display object, and more than one way to block events from reaching a display object. These tasks required a little thinking in prior versions of ActionScript, but are incredibly easy when using the display list. You just have to remove the display object in question from the display list.

The following line removes a display object sp from the scope in which the display object resides. Continuing the scenario shared by other recipes in this chapter, consider the sprite, sp, in the main timeline.

```
removeChild(sp);
```

As with addChild(), you can also invoke this method in another scope. The following, for example, removes a hypothetical nested movie clip mc from its parent sp.

```
sp.removeChild(mc);
```

Finally, just as you could add a child to a specific depth with addChildAt(), you can also remove a child from a specific depth. The following example removes the first child, or child at the lowest depth, of all nested display objects within sp.

```
sp.removeChildAt(0);
```

Note that none of these methods removes a child from memory. They all remove only the object in question from the display list. So you can temporarily remove a child from the display list and restore it later. If you want to remove a display object from memory as well, you can set it to null.

The following repeats the earlier example of removing sprite sp from the display list, but then also nullifies the sprite so it can be marked for removal from memory by the garbage collector.

```
removeChild(sp);
sp = null;
```

See Also

"13.3 Adding a Display Object to the Display List" on page 287 for adding a display object to the display list and "13.4 Specifying the Depth of a Display Object" on page 289 for setting the depth of a display object.

13.7 Working with Children of a Display Object Container

Problem

You want to determine if a display object has children or a particular child, or you want to disable the mouse events of all children.

Solution

Check to see if a display object is of type DisplayObjectContainer to see if it can have children. Use the numChildren property to determine if a display object container has children, or the contains() method to determine if a particular child of the container exists. Use the `mouseChildren` property to enable or disable mouse events for all children of a container.

Discussion

Every visible element is a display object but not all display objects are display object containers as shown in Figure 13-1. Neither shapes, bitmaps, nor videos, for example, are display object containers and, therefore, can't have children.

When trying to work with children of an object, it helps to avoid errors by first making sure that the object can have children. You do this by checking to see if the instance in question qualifies as a `DisplayObjectContainer` data type, using the `is` operator. This conditional traces a result if `mc` is a movie clip, because a movie clip is a display object container:

```
var mc:MovieClip = new MovieClip();

if (mc is DisplayObjectContainer) {
    trace("container");
}
```

You can use this technique to make sure that any properties or methods of a container are used without error. For example, the following code replaces the string in the previous `trace` statement with a use of the `numChildren` property to see how many children are nested within the movie clip:

```
if (mc is DisplayObjectContainer) {
    trace(mc.numChildren);
}
```

If you want to see if a particular child exists, you can use the `contains()` method. The following example traces a result only if a child reference `sp` is found inside the container `mc`.

```
var mc:MovieClip = new MovieClip();
var sp:Sprite = new Sprite();
mc.addChild(sp);
addChild(mc);

if (mc is DisplayObjectContainer) {
    if (mc.contains(sp)) {
        trace("sp found");
    }
}
```

Finally, it's handy to know how to prevent children of a display object from receiving mouse events. This will become more apparent when events are discussed in the next chapter, but consider this example. If you dynamically create a display object to serve as a button, and add to that object a text field child to serve as the button's label, then the text field reacts to the cursor and possibly trap mouse events when not wanted.

For example, you may not see the hand cursor responsible for indicating the presence of an interactive element and, depending on how you set up your file, the text field may prevent the button from reacting to a mouse click.

While you certainly want a text field to be able to react to the mouse at other times, the button label in this example shouldn't interfere with standard user interface design. In this case, it's handy to use the `mouseChildren` property of the button object to disable mouse events for all children.

To demonstrate this change, you need a little code for handling text and events before covering that material in greater detail in later chapters. For now, the ActionScript has been broken into four segments. The last two blocks set up the text and mouse event, respectively.

The first block creates a new sprite, draws a yellow rectangle inside, and adds the sprite to the display list. The second block contains two properties that illustrate the usefulness of `mouseChildren`. The `buttonMode` property tells Flash Player to treat the sprite as if it were a button, and display the desired hand cursor when rolling over the button. The commented line uses the `mouseChildren` property, and will be explained following the script.

```
var sp:Sprite = new Sprite();
var g:Graphics = sp.graphics;
g.beginFill(0xFFFF00, 1);
g.drawRect(0, 0, 100, 30);
g.endFill();
addChild(sp);

sp.buttonMode = true;
//sp.mouseChildren = false;

addLabel(sp);
function addLabel(obj:Sprite):void {
    var txtFrmt:TextFormat = new TextFormat();
    txtFrmt.size = 24;
    txtFrmt.align = TextFormatAlign.CENTER;

    var txtFld:TextField = new TextField();
    txtFld.width = 100;
    txtFld.height = 30;
    txtFld.text = "Label";
    txtFld.setTextFormat(txtFrmt);

    obj.addChild(txtFld);
}

sp.addEventListener(MouseEvent.CLICK, onClick);
function onClick(evt:MouseEvent):void {
```

```
        trace("button clicked");
    }
```

By default, `mouseChildren` is `true`, letting children of an object receive events. In this state, you'll notice that the cursor doesn't change from pointer to hand when rolling over the button. This is because the text field is the same size of the button, and is intercepting the cursor before it reaches the button. By uncommenting the `mouseChildren` line, thereby setting the property to `false`, no children of the sprite receive mouse events, and the button behaves normally.

See Also

"13.1 Choosing Which Type of Display Object to Use" on page 284.

13.8 Working with Parents of a Display Object

Problem

You want to refer to a parent or ancestor of a display object.

Solution

Use the `parent` property of the display object.

Discussion

You'll often need to reference a parent or ancestor—a parent's parent, or (informally) grandparent—of a display object. Accessing the parent of a display object is similar to working your way through a directory structure on your computer. Any parent of a display object also qualifies as a display object container by the mere fact that it has children. Moving up one level, so to speak, from child to container requires only the use of the `parent` property.

The following example revisits the red and blue squares from earlier recipes. The parent, or blue movie clip, is positioned at point (20, 20) in the main timeline. The child, or red sprite, is offset another 30 pixels in both the x and y directions. Since a display object's location is relative to its parent, querying the x location of the child returns a value of 30, but the x location of its parent is 20.

To check these results, the third block of this script traces the x coordinate of the sprite and its parent.

```
var mc:MovieClip = new MovieClip();
drawSquare(mc, 0x0000FF);
```

```
mc.x = mc.y = 20;
addChild(mc);

var sp:Sprite = new Sprite();
drawSquare(sp, 0xFF0000);
sp.x = sp.y = 30;
mc.addChild(sp);

trace(sp.x);
trace(sp.parent.x);

function drawSquare(obj:Object, col:uint):void {
    var g:Graphics = obj.graphics;
    g.beginFill(col, 1);
    g.drawRect(0, 0, 40, 40);
    g.endFill();
}
```

 This works without further qualification because the x property is available to both display objects and display object
containers. When you attempt to use a property or method
that isn't universally available, the ActionScript 3.0 compiler
may object and require additional information to handle the
request. You can see this in the next recipe.

See Also

"13.9 Casting a Display Object from One Type to Another" on page 297 for
casting a display object from one type to another.

13.9 Casting a Display Object from One Type to Another

Problem

You want to explicitly convert a display object from one type to another. Alternately, you receive a compiler error telling you that a property or method
you're trying to manipulate may be undefined due to a static reference to
DisplayObject or DisplayObjectContainer.

Solution

Cast the display object to the appropriate type, officially declaring its type for
the compiler.

Discussion

Casting is the process of explicitly changing an object from one data type to another. For example, you can change a string to an integer by casting it with int(). The following casts two strings, and traces the outcome of adding the resulting integers.

```
trace(int("1") + int("2"));
// 3
```

If the strings had not been cast to integers prior to using the plus (+) operator, the result would have been an execution that concatenated the strings "1" and "2" to get "12" rather than adding the two numbers 1 and 2 to get 3. You can also cast from one related display object type to another, and the following scenario is a good example of when this is required.

In the previous recipe, the parent property was used to query the x location of a parent container. This was possible because both the parent and child had an x property. However, quite often the ActionScript compiler is unsure whether or not a targeted parent has the requested property or method in its class.

For instance, a movie clip could be a child of a sprite, or a sprite could be a child of a movie clip. If you were to query a property that applied only to a movie clip, using nothing more than a passing reference to a display object's parent, the compiler wouldn't know the data type of the parent and, therefore, couldn't know if the property existed. Here's some example code:

```
var mc:MovieClip = new MovieClip();
drawSquare(mc, 0x0000FF);
mc.x = mc.y = 20;
addChild(mc);

var sp:Sprite = new Sprite();
drawSquare(sp, 0xFF0000);
sp.x = sp.y = 20;
mc.addChild(sp);

var totFr:int = sp.parent.totalFrames;
trace(totFr);

function drawSquare(obj:Object, col:uint):void {
    var g:Graphics = obj.graphics;
    g.beginFill(col, 1);
    g.drawRect(0, 0, 40, 40);
    g.endFill();
}
```

In this situation, you get an error that says something like this:

```
//1119: Access of possibly undefined property
totalFrames through a reference with static type flash.display:DisplayObjectContainer.
```

Briefly, `totalFrames` is a property of a movie clip but is missing from other types of display object containers (such as sprite). Without telling the compiler the parent is a movie clip, it throws an error.

The solution is to cast the parent as type `MovieClip`, just as the previous example cast from string to integer using `int()`.

```
var totFr:int = MovieClip(sp.parent).totalFrames;
trace(totFr);
```

Once the compiler explicitly knows this, it doesn't generate an error, and the script functions as intended.

See Also

"13.8 Working with Parents of a Display Object" on page 296 for working with the parents of display objects.

13.10 Changing the Parent of a Display Object

Problem

You want to move a child display object from one parent to another.

Solution

Use the `addChild()` method (or equivalent) and ActionScript 3.0's automatic display list management to re-parent the child on the fly.

Discussion

One of the display list's greatest qualities is the ability to change a display object's parent with very little effort. In the following setup, the sprite `sp` is a child of the movie clip `mc`. As a result, the sprite displays at point (50, 50), which is the location of `mc`.

```
var mc:MovieClip = new MovieClip();
mc.x = mc.y = 50;
addChild(mc);

var sp:Sprite = new Sprite();
var g:Graphics = sp.graphics;
g.beginFill(0xFF00FF, 1);
g.drawRect(0, 0, 40, 40);
```

```
g.endFill();
mc.addChild(sp);

var mc2:MovieClip = new MovieClip();
mc2.x = mc2.y = 150;
addChild(mc2);

//mc2.addChild(sp);
```

However, if you uncomment the last line of the script, **sp** is again added to the display list, but this time, as a child of **mc2**. Because the same display object reference is being added to the display list twice, the first occurrence is automatically removed from the list, and the object moves to become a child of **mc2**. Consequently, the sprite now displays at point (150, 150), the location of **mc2**.

Re-parenting on the fly has many benefits. Consider, for example, a drag-and-drop scenario where every time you drop an item onto a new parent, the item becomes a child of the drop target. You could easily use this setup to group objects, manipulate their properties as a single item, and even remove an entire group of objects from the display list, simply by altering one parent.

13.11 Referencing the Stage Through a Display Object

Problem

You want to work with properties, methods, or events related to the stage, using a display object as a point of reference.

Solution

Use the **stage** property of any relevant display object already in the display list.

Discussion

ActionScript 3.0 no longer has a ubiquitous reference to the stage. Instead, you typically access the stage through the **stage** property of a display object. For this to be possible, however, the display object must be a child of a display list.

The following attempt to query the stage frame rate generates an error because the **stage** property of the display object is null. You can see this directly by trying to trace the **stage** property itself, in the last line of this script block.

```
var sp:Sprite = new Sprite();
trace(sp.stage);
//null
```

```
trace(sp.stage.frameRate);
//TypeError: Error #1009: Cannot access a property
or method of a null object reference at main_fla::MainTimeline/frame1()
```

Once the display object is added to the display list, however, the **stage** property is valid, and no error occurs. The **stage** property also then correctly traces a reference to the **Stage** instance.

```
addChild(sp);
trace(sp.stage);
//[object Stage]

trace(sp.stage.frameRate);
//12
```

You most often encounter this issue when using classes, simply because it's easier to get a reference to the stage within a Flash timeline frame script. This is because the main timeline itself is automatically a part of the display list, and can reference the stage. However, this timeline-based example still illustrates the problem and, ideally, this will help you avoid null object reference errors when the stage is involved.

CHAPTER 14

How Do I Work with Events?

14.0 Introduction

The new event model is one of the biggest changes ActionScript 3.0 introduces. Gone are the event handlers of prior versions, such as `onRelease` or the more antiquated `on(release)` handler applied directly to symbol instances. The new model makes use exclusively of *event listeners*. In simple terms, event listeners are established to monitor for the occurrence of a particular event, and then execute a function when that event is received. Since listeners are required for all event processing, this chapter both explains and uses them extensively.

Even if you have experience with event listeners from prior versions of ActionScript (perhaps from use with components or objects for capturing key events), the event flow is quite different in ActionScript 3.0. Events can cascade down through the display list and bubble back up to the root of the file, allowing for advanced event handling. In line with the focus of this quick answer guide, this chapter covers the basic essentials of event processing, but provides an adequate overview to get you started.

14.1 Understanding Event Listeners

Problem

You want to understand the basic operation of an event listener.

Solution

Create an event listener and accompanying function to execute when a desired event is received.

Discussion

The first part of reacting to an event is to create an event listener. You do this by using the `addEventListener()` method, attaching the listener to the object that will be the event. Intermediate to advanced use of the event model suggests a variety of places to attach listeners, some of which this chapter demonstrates. This example, however, uses the direct approach, and attaches the listener to the interactive object that a user will click: a sprite referenced by `sp`.

```
sp.addEventListener(MouseEvent.CLICK, onClick);
```

The method requires two arguments. The first is the event for which the listener must listen. Typically, you use constants provided for this purpose but, as you'll learn later in this chapter, you can also use strings. In this case, a mouse click has been specified by using the `CLICK` event of the `MouseEvent` class.

The second argument is the name of the function you want to trigger when the event occurs. The function used as a listener function is like any other function except that listener functions *require* an argument, even though arguments in standalone functions are optional. This is because the event model is designed to pass on information about the event, the target of the event (the interactive element that was clicked, for example), which object the listener is attached to, and related information (such as stage locations, modifier key usage, and other data). Just like other arguments, a data type should be specified for the listener argument for type checking. The type provided should be the type of the event associated with the listener.

```
function onClick(evt:MouseEvent):void {
    trace("button clicked");
}
```

Here is an example script that shows a listener in action. When you click the red sprite, the `onClick()` listener function is triggered, and the string is traced to the Output panel. In later recipes in this chapter, you'll learn how to work with the item that the user clicked, and parse data from the argument.

```
var sp:Sprite = new Sprite();
drawSquare(sp, 0xFF0000);
sp.x = sp.y = 100;
sp.buttonMode = true;
addChild(sp);

sp.addEventListener(MouseEvent.CLICK, onClick);
function onClick(evt:MouseEvent):void {
    trace("sprite clicked");
}

function drawSquare(obj:Object, col:uint):void {
    var g:Graphics = obj.graphics;
    g.beginFill(col, 1);
```

```
        g.drawRect(0, 0, 40, 40);
        g.endFill();
    }
```

14.2 Capturing Mouse Events

Problem

You want to execute code when the user interacts with an element using the mouse, for example enlarging an object when rolling over it with the mouse.

Solution

Listen for one or more events from the MouseEvent class.

Discussion

In the previous recipe, you learned the basics of event listeners, using a mouse click as an example. This recipe demonstrates not only how to react to other mouse events, but also the ability to attach more than one listener to an object. This ability lets you perform different actions based on each event, even when interacting with the same object.

The following script excerpt works when interacting with a display object called sp. When rolling over the object, sp becomes 150 percent larger than its original size. When rolling out, sp returns to its original size.

```
sp.addEventListener(MouseEvent.MOUSE_OVER, onOver);
sp.addEventListener(MouseEvent.MOUSE_OUT, onOut);

function onOver(evt:MouseEvent):void {
    sp.scaleX = sp.scaleY *= 1.5;
}
function onOut(evt:MouseEvent):void {
    sp.scaleX = sp.scaleY = 1;
}
```

The code is very similar to the previous recipe's example. The event-related differences are that two listeners are used, each listens for a different event, and each calls a different function. In essence, the listener code has been doubled to account for the new listener set, but both listeners are attached to the same object.

The next script example uses separate mouse down and up events, in contrast to the use of the CLICK event, which triggers after the consecutive executions of both down and up events (forming a complete "click"). This script turns on object dragging when you click on a display object, and turns off dragging when you release the mouse over the display object.

A very important change in this script is the introduction of the **target** property seen in the onDown() function. This property, parsed from the listener function argument, contains the target that dispatched the event. Using this property, you can avoid hard-coding the object in the function.

For example, this script successfully drags either of two display objects, using only one set of functions. That is, relevant listeners are attached to each object, but both listeners reference the same functions. If the object being manipulated inside the functions were hard-coded, rather than identified through the event's **target** property, only the hard-coded object would move, regardless of which the user tried to drag.

```
var sp:Sprite = new Sprite();
drawCir(sp, 0x9900AA);
sp.x = sp.y = 100;
addChild(sp);

var sp2:Sprite = new Sprite();
drawCir(sp2, 0x00AA00);
sp2.x = sp2.y = 200;
addChild(sp2);

sp.addEventListener(MouseEvent.MOUSE_DOWN, onDown);
sp.addEventListener(MouseEvent.MOUSE_UP, onUp);

sp2.addEventListener(MouseEvent.MOUSE_DOWN, onDown);
sp2.addEventListener(MouseEvent.MOUSE_UP, onUp);

function onDown(evt:MouseEvent):void {
    evt.target.startDrag();
}
function onUp(evt:MouseEvent):void {
    stopDrag();
}

function drawCir(obj:Object, col:uint):void {
    var g:Graphics = obj.graphics;
    g.beginFill(col, 1);
    g.drawCircle(0, 0, 40);
    g.endFill();
}
```

A later recipe will improve upon this script by correctly reacting when the mouse is released outside the bounds of the display object.

See Also

"14.1 Understanding Event Listeners" on page 303 for understanding event listeners, "14.5 Using the target and currentTarget Event Properties" on page 310 for when to use `target` and `currentTarget` properties, and "14.6 Simulating a Mouse Up Outside Event" on page 311 for simulating a mouse up outside event.

14.3 Understanding Event Flow

Problem

You want a basic understanding of the flow of events in ActionScript 3.0.

Solution

Review the *capture*, *target*, and *bubbling* phases, with particular attention to the default use of target and bubbling phases.

Discussion

Events flow through a SWF file in a specified manner, and mechanisms exist to work with these events in multiple ways. For ease of discussion, this recipe will discuss the flow of a `MouseEvent.CLICK` event, and assume the user clicked on a movie clip that's nested inside another movie clip found in the main timeline. Looking at Figure 14-1, the movie clip clicked by the user is `mc2`, and is also labeled as "target."

When someone clicks the movie clip, the event actually starts at the stage and begins to move through the display list. It makes its way through the display objects until it encounters the object on which she clicked. This is the *target* of the event. Rather than stopping when it reaches the target, the event continues on its round trip journey back through the display list to the main timeline and stage.

The initial journey to, but not including, the target is the *capture phase* of the event model. The actual time spent with the target is the *target phase*, and the return journey back to the stage is the *bubbling phase*.

The capture phase is the period during which Flash Player is trying to identify the object that dispatched the event. Starting at the stage, the event moves through display objects until the target's found, at which point the phase ends. By default, the capture phase is not used. "14.14 Capturing an Event Before It

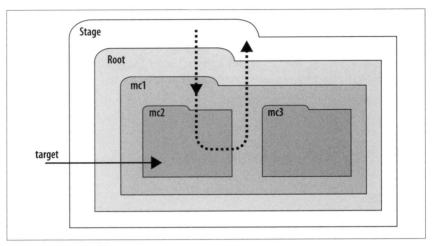

Figure 14-1. Event flow in ActionScript 3.0

Reaches Its Target" on page 326, "Using the Capture Phase," discusses turning on this phase.

The target and bubbling phases however, which listeners employ by default, are used in virtually every ActionScript 3.0 project. The importance of the target phase is probably fairly obvious. Briefly, Flash Player is processing a mouse click (for example) at the object on which the user clicked. This model is called the event-processing model in prior versions of ActionScript.

The bubbling phase brings new power to ActionScript. Using event bubbling, you can attach a listener to a parent object, and the desired event acts on all of its children. The next recipe demonstrates.

See Also

"14.4 Using Event Bubbling" on page 308 for event bubbling, and "14.14 Capturing an Event Before It Reaches Its Target" on page 326 for using the capture phase.

14.4 Using Event Bubbling

Problem

You want to simplify code and add power to event processing by capturing events as they move through the display list from one object to another.

Solution

Attach an event listener to a display object container and let event bubbling act on its children.

Discussion

In "14.2 Capturing Mouse Events" on page 305, the example script used a direct approach to event processing by attaching an event listener to each display object. This recipe includes a modified version of that example that takes advantage of event bubbling. You see two significant changes.

First, a display object container has been created, into which two circle sprites have been added. Second, instead of attaching a listener to each sprite, one listener is attached to the container. The default behavior to bubble events means that all its children can process the event.

```
var contnr:Sprite = new Sprite();
addChild(contnr);

var sp:Sprite = new Sprite();
drawCir(sp, 0x9900AA);
sp.x = sp.y = 100;
contnr.addChild(sp);

var sp2:Sprite = new Sprite();
drawCir(sp2, 0x00AA00);
sp2.x = sp2.y = 200;
contnr.addChild(sp2);

contnr.addEventListener(MouseEvent.MOUSE_DOWN, onDown);
contnr.addEventListener(MouseEvent.MOUSE_UP, onUp);

function onDown(evt:MouseEvent):void {
    evt.target.startDrag();
}
function onUp(evt:MouseEvent):void {
    stopDrag();
}

function drawCir(obj:Object, col:uint):void {
    var g:Graphics = obj.graphics;
    g.beginFill(col, 1);
    g.drawCircle(0, 0, 40);
    g.endFill();
}
```

Only the clicked circle is dragged (instead of the container and, therefore, both children) because only the target of the event is affected. The evt.target property always refers to the circle receiving the mouse down event.

See Also

"14.5 Using the target and currentTarget Event Properties" on page 310 for when to use target and currentTarget properties.

14.5 Using the target and currentTarget Event Properties

Problem

When parsing data from an event listener function argument, you want to know when to use the target and currentTarget properties.

Solution

Use target when you want to know which object is the recipient of the event, and use currentTarget when you want to know to which object the event listener is attached.

Discussion

In one regard, the distinction between the target and currentTarget is straight-forward. The object acted upon by the event (the button that's clicked, the sprite that's rolled over, etc.) is the target, while the object to which the listener is attached is the currentTarget. The two properties can refer to the same object when the event dispatcher is also the object with the listener. This circumstance is true when attaching a listener directly to a button, for example. Clicking on the button dispatches the mouse event (button is target), and the listener is attached to the button (button is currentTarget).

When to use each property, however, is not always clear. The following script demonstrates a draggable window metaphor. A window-like sprite is drawn and, within it, a drag bar is drawn. An event listener starts dragging on mouse down, stops dragging on mouse up, and is attached to the window sprite.

```
var window:Sprite = new Sprite();
drawRoundedRectangle(window, 0x000099, 200, 200);
window.x = window.y = 100;
addChild(window);

var dragBar:Sprite = new Sprite();
drawRoundedRectangle(dragBar, 0x000033, 200, 40);
window.addChild(dragBar);

window.addEventListener(MouseEvent.MOUSE_DOWN, onDown);
window.addEventListener(MouseEvent.MOUSE_UP, onUp);
```

```
function onDown(evt:MouseEvent):void {
    //evt.target.startDrag();
    evt.currentTarget.startDrag();
}
function onUp(evt:MouseEvent):void {
    stopDrag();
}

function drawRoundedRectangle(obj:Object, col:uint, ¬
        w:Number, h:Number):void {
    var g:Graphics = obj.graphics;
    g.lineStyle(1, col);
    g.beginFill(col, .5);
    g.drawRoundRect(0, 0, w, h, 20);
    g.endFill();
}
```

Attaching the listener to the window sprite means that any child of that display object container can process the mouse event. This outcome occurs because the default behavior (unchanged in this example) lets the children capture the event during bubbling.

The most common approach of using the target property within the listener function means that you can drag the container and any child within. This ability creates the unfortunate side effect of being able to drag the bar by itself, without dragging the window along with it. See this in action by switching between the two bolded lines in the onDown() function of this example (commenting out the line not in use).

As written, however, currentTarget is used in the function, so only the object to which the listener is attached can be dragged. As a result, dragging the window drags the window, and dragging the bar also drags the window.

14.6 Simulating a Mouse Up Outside Event

Problem

You want a means of insuring that mouse events occurring outside the bounds of a display object can be processed. However, ActionScript 3.0 has no equivalent to the onReleaseOutside event found in prior versions of ActionScript.

Solution

Add an additional listener to the stage responsible for reacting to mouse up events.

Discussion

In certain ActionScript 3.0 scenarios, such as drag-and-drop activities, an application can go awry due to the lack of a "mouse up outside" event. Consider the simple drag-and-drop example in "14.4 Using Event Bubbling" on page 308. If, while dragging one of the circle sprites in that example, you accidentally release the mouse button while the cursor is *not* over the same sprite, the dragging behavior doesn't cease. The sprite in question didn't receive the mouse up event required to execute the stopDrag() method. To stop the dragging, you must click on the sprite again to ensure that the mouse button is released over the sprite, and a mouse up event occurs.

Although earlier versions of ActionScript had a built-in event mechanism (onReleaseOutside) for this scenario, ActionScript 3.0 doesn't include this feature.

Instead, you must add a listener to the stage to receive the mouse up event (because the event doesn't occur at the display object). In most cases, you can even just associate the listener to the same function used by the display object listener. Only one line of code needs to be added to "14.4 Using Event Bubbling" on page 308, like the example shown here in bold, to achieve the desired result.

```
contnr.addEventListener(MouseEvent.MOUSE_DOWN, onDown);
contnr.addEventListener(MouseEvent.MOUSE_UP, onUp);

stage.addEventListener(MouseEvent.MOUSE_UP, onUp);
```

See Also

"14.4 Using Event Bubbling" on page 308 for event bubbling.

14.7 Capturing Frame Events

Problem

You want to use a recurring event to repeatedly trigger a function.

Solution

Use the Event.ENTER_FRAME event.

Discussion

A frame script is executed only once each time the Flash playhead enters a frame span. The playhead must leave the frame span and re-enter it again to execute the script a subsequent time. If, for example, you stop the playhead in a frame that contains a frame script, then that script doesn't behave as if it were in a frame loop executing continuously.

You can, however, use the Event.ENTER_FRAME event to repeatedly trigger a function. This event is available to sprites and movie clips (including the main timeline), and triggers as many times per second as dictated by the frame rate of your SWF file. The following example adds 10 degrees to the current rotation of a sprite, each time the event occurs.

```
var sp:Sprite;
drawSquare();

sp.addEventListener(Event.ENTER_FRAME, onLoop);

function onLoop(evt:Event):void {
    evt.target.rotation += 10;
}

function drawSquare():void {
    sp = new Sprite();
    var g:Graphics = sp.graphics;
    g.beginFill(0x000099, 1);
    g.drawRect(0, 0, 40, 40);
    g.endFill();
    sp.x = sp.y = 100;
    addChild(sp);
}
```

 It is very important to remove enter frame event listeners when you're no longer using them, as a later recipe will demonstrate. Not removing the listeners can prevent them from being collected by the garbage collector. This trait can be especially intrusive when the listener's in a SWF file that you wish to load into another SWF file. If the listener wasn't properly removed in the loaded content, it can prevent the loaded file from being unloaded.

See Also

"14.8 Improving Performance by Removing Event Listeners" on page 314 for removing event listeners.

14.8 Improving Performance by Removing Event Listeners

Problem

You want to remove any unused event listeners to reduce memory and performance overhead.

Solution

Use the `removeEventListener()` method to remove a specific event listener.

Discussion

As you might imagine, performing an unnecessary task repeatedly can waste resources. In the case of event listeners, both memory and performance are at risk if you don't remove unused listeners.

A listener is unnecessary when your application no longer needs to rely on it to capture an event. For example, if a button's never clicked, you still need its listener if the button *can be* clicked. That is, the need to react to that button click still remains, even if the button's not used. However, tasks that will no longer be needed can be eliminated upon the completion of an event. For instance, if your project contains a one-time load process, listeners for events such as progress, error checking, and load-complete can all be removed once the loading has concluded.

The bold lines in the following code can be inserted in the `onLoop()` function in the previous recipe. Assume this project design requires only that the rotation add 10 degrees per event, and then stop once the rotation reaches or exceeds 135 degrees. The rotation is stopped, therefore, by removing the event listener in a conditional within the listener function.

```
function onLoop(evt:Event):void {
    evt.target.rotation += 10;
    if (evt.target.rotation >= 135) {
        sp.removeEventListener(Event.ENTER_FRAME, onLoop);
    }
}
```

The `removeEventListener()` method requires arguments. You must specify the coupling of event and listener function that must be removed, because you can create multiple listeners for the same object that listen for the same event but trigger different functions, or that trigger the same function upon the occurrence of different events.

If you use any optional listener features, such as invoking the capture phase, setting event priority, or using weak references (all discussed in later recipes), you shouldn't include these parameters in the removal process. For example, the following hypothetical listener uses a weak reference, but the removal of that same listener does not include those same parameter values.

```
sp.addEventListener(Event.ENTER_FRAME, onLoop, false, 0, true);
sp.removeEventListener(Event.ENTER_FRAME, onLoop);
```

 Removing listeners is important for memory management and performance, but it's *crucial* when it comes to loading and unloading external assets. Enter frame event listeners that haven't been removed from a loaded SWF file, for example, prevent that SWF file from being unloaded at runtime.

See Also

"14.7 Capturing Frame Events" on page 312 for capturing frame events and "14.10 Capturing Stage Events" on page 317 through "14.12 Dispatching Your Own Events" on page 323 for optional event listener features.

14.9 Capturing Keyboard Events

Problem

You want to respond to keyboard input from the user.

Solution

Listen for the `KeyboardEvent.KEY_DOWN` event and parse keyboard input from the listener argument.

Discussion

Two example uses for Keyboard event listeners include attaching them to a text field, in which case they respond only when the text field has focus, or attaching them to the stage, which is ideal for navigation systems. The following script uses a listener to demonstrate a few methods and properties related to key events.

The first three lines of the `onKeyPressed()` function use the event `charCode` property to look for text input. The `charCode` property is the numeric value of a key found in the designated character set. (UTF-8 is the default character set.) A key with a corresponding text character returns a `charCode` greater than zero for each character. For example, lowercase *a* and uppercase *A* have different charCode values.

Using the String method fromCharCode()translates this number into a string value. Other keys, such as Tab, Backspace, arrow keys, and so forth, return a charCode of zero, letting you filter them out, if desired.

The remainder of the onKeyPressed() function is a navigation example, explained after the script.

```
var sp:Sprite;
drawSquare();

stage.addEventListener(KeyboardEvent.KEY_DOWN, onKeyPressed);
function onKeyPressed(evt:KeyboardEvent):void {
    if (evt.charCode > 0) {
        trace(String.fromCharCode(evt.charCode), "= char code", evt.charCode);
    }

    var shiftMod:int = 1
    if (evt.shiftKey) { shiftMod = 10 };

    if (evt.keyCode == Keyboard.RIGHT) {
        sp.x += shiftMod;
    } else if (evt.keyCode == Keyboard.DOWN) {
        sp.y += shiftMod;
    }
}

function drawSquare():void {
    sp = new Sprite();
    var g:Graphics = sp.graphics;
    g.beginFill(0x000099, 1);
    g.drawRect(0, 0, 40, 40);
    g.endFill();
    sp.x = sp.y = 20;
    addChild(sp);
}
```

The next two lines use the event shiftKey property to see if the Shift key is pressed. Starting with a value of 1, the value of shiftMod is changed to 10 only if shiftKey is true (meaning the Shift key is pressed). As a result, the sprite is moved 1 pixel at a time unless the Shift key is pressed, in which case the sprite is moved 10 pixels at a time.

The last conditional block checks the value of keyCode. The keyCode property returns a numeric value that corresponds to the value of a *key* on the keyboard, not a specific character on that key. For example, the *1* on a keypad and the *1* on the main keyboard return different keyCode values, but lowercase *a* and uppercase *A* return the same keyCode values.

You can use the keyCode property for things like navigation by comparing its value to constants of the KeyboardEvent class that stand for the arrow keys. In this recipe, the x-coordinate of the sprite sp is changed when the right arrow key is pressed, and the y-coordinate of sp is changed when the down arrow key is pressed.

14.10 Capturing Stage Events

Problem

You want to determine when the user resizes the stage, when the mouse leaves the stage, or when the user enters full-screen mode.

Solution

Listen for the Event.RESIZE, Event.MOUSE_LEAVE, and Event.FULLSCREEN events, respectively.

Discussion

Using stage events can add a real professional touch to your work, and possibly even solve a problem or two. The first event discussed in this recipe is for determining when the user resizes the stage. This can occur when resizing a player, or projector window, or resizing a browser window with a SWF file set to *percent* size mode (instead of *pixels* or *match movie* size).

Before demonstrating the feature, you must set the stage scaleMode and align properties to not scale, and to align to the upper-left corner of the window, when resized, as seen in the first two lines of the following script. Without setting the scaleMode this way, the SWF file *and all its contents* scale to match the window size, instead of just resizing the canvas on which non-scaled content resides. The blue circle in the following script enlarges or reduces based on window size adjustments, rather than just repositioning itself to re-center in a changing stage size.

Similarly, if you don't set the align property to align to the top left of the window, then the content in the SWF file appears to move around unpredictably as the alignment is affected by varying window size. You can witness this behavior, and that of scaling content, by commenting out one or both of the first lines in this script, and setting the SWF file size in the publishing template to percent.

The remainder of the script does nothing more than position a sprite, with a blue circle therein, in the center of the stage—both initially, and every time the stage is resized.

```
stage.scaleMode = StageScaleMode.NO_SCALE;
stage.align = StageAlign.TOP_LEFT;
stage.addEventListener(Event.RESIZE, onStageResize);

function onStageResize (evt:Event):void {
    positionSprite();
}

var sp:Sprite = drawSprite();
addChild(sp);
positionSprite();

function positionSprite():void {
    sp.x = stage.stageWidth/2;
    sp.y = stage.stageHeight/2;
}

function drawSprite():Sprite {
    var mySprite = new Sprite();
    var g:Graphics = mySprite.graphics;
    g.beginFill(0x0000FF, 1);
    g.drawCircle(0, 0, 20);
    g.endFill();
    return mySprite;
}
```

The Stage class also has two other very handy events: Event.MOUSE_LEAVE and Event.FULLSCREEN. The former can tell you when the user's mouse has left the bounds of the Flash Player stage. This feature lets you drop performance demands when the SWF file no longer has user focus (by dropping the frame rate, for example) or merely alerting the user that his mouse is still needed.

The latter event can trigger programmed behavior if the user switches to full-screen mode. This could be used to reposition UI elements or, as in this recipe, display text that reminds the user to return to normal mode using the Escape key (a fact that is only automatically displayed by Flash Player for a brief moment).

These features don't work in the Flash interface's embedded player, so test the following scripts in a browser. To enable both features, change your HTML publishing template (File→Publish Settings→HTML→Template) to "Flash Only - Allow Full Screen." Thereafter, you can test using the Flash shortcut, File→Publish Preview→HTML.

To easily demonstrate the use of Event.MOUSE_LEAVE, the first part of the following script draws a gray background the same size of the stage, and a red box that is 100 × 100 pixels. When the mouse leaves the stage (as shown by the gray rectangle), the red box will fade to 50 percent opaque. After the script, you'll learn how to respond to the mouse returning to the stage.

```
var backSprite:Sprite = drawSquare(0xDDDDDD, stage.stageWidth, ¬
    stage.stageHeight);
addChildAt(backSprite, 0);

var foreSprite:Sprite = drawSquare(0xFF0000, 100, 100);
addChild(foreSprite);

stage.addEventListener(Event.MOUSE_LEAVE, onLeave);
function onLeave(evt:Event):void {
    foreSprite.alpha = .5;

    stage.addEventListener(MouseEvent.MOUSE_MOVE, onEnter);
    function onEnter(evt:MouseEvent):void {
        foreSprite.alpha = 1;
        stage.removeEventListener(MouseEvent.MOUSE_MOVE, onEnter);
    }
}

function drawSquare(col:uint, w:Number, h:Number):Sprite {
    var tempSprite:Sprite = new Sprite();
    var g:Graphics = tempSprite.graphics;
    g.beginFill(col, 1);
    g.drawRect(0, 0, w, h);
    g.endFill();
    return tempSprite;
}
```

 Flash Player doesn't detect the mouse leaving the stage if the mouse is down.

There is no direct opposite of the Event.MOUSE_LEAVE event. That is, using ActionScript, you can't automatically detect when the mouse returns to the Flash stage. However, while the mouse is moving on the stage, MouseEvent.MOUSE_MOVE events are triggered. Therefore, one way to determine if the mouse has re-entered the stage is to set up an event listener that listens for mouse movement.

For greatest efficiency, this recipe adds the event listener only when the mouse leaves the stage, and then removes the listener when the mouse is again detected on the stage. (Removing event listeners was discussed in "14.8 Improving Performance by Removing Event Listeners" on page 314.)

Finally, the Event.FULLSCREEN event is demonstrated in the following continuation of the previous script. This passage picks up from the previous code block by using the foreground sprite as a button. Each time the button's clicked, the screen mode is changed, and a text message is displayed or removed, accordingly.

The first listener just reacts to a mouse event, but it does include the displayState property of the stage. This property can tell you if the screen is in full-screen or normal mode. The second listener dispatches the Event.FULL SCREEN event each time the stage enters or leaves full-screen mode. (Separate events for entering and exiting full-screen mode don't exist.)

Just before creating the second listener, a text field is initialized and positioned, using the stage's fullScreenWidth and fullScreenHeight properties. After the listener detects each display state change, the resulting screen mode value is queried. In full-screen mode, the text field is added to the display list, and the field is later removed from the display list upon return to normal mode.

 Object initializations are typically consolidated at the top of a script, but the text field creation in this example has been placed immediately before the listener for tutorial context. This process simplifies the later option of combining the scripts in this recipe into one cumulative file.

```
stage.scaleMode = StageScaleMode.NO_SCALE;
stage.align = StageAlign.TOP_LEFT;

foreSprite.addEventListener(MouseEvent.CLICK, onClick);
function onClick(evt:Event):void {
    if (stage.displayState == StageDisplayState.NORMAL) {
        stage.displayState = StageDisplayState.FULL_SCREEN;
    } else {
        stage.displayState = StageDisplayState.NORMAL;
    }
}

var noticeFld:TextField = addNotice("Press ESC to return to normal view");
stage.addEventListener(Event.FULLSCREEN, onFull);
function onFull(evt:Event):void {
    if (stage.displayState == StageDisplayState.FULL_SCREEN) {
        addChild(noticeFld);
    } else {
        removeChild(noticeFld);
    }
}

function addNotice(msg:String):TextField {
    var txtFrmt:TextFormat = new TextFormat();
    txtFrmt.size = 14;
    txtFrmt.bold = true;
```

```
        var txtFld:TextField = new TextField();
        txtFld.autoSize = TextFieldAutoSize.LEFT;
        txtFld.text = msg;
        txtFld.setTextFormat(txtFrmt);

        txtFld.x = stage.fullScreenWidth/2 - txtFld.width/2;
        txtFld.y = stage.fullScreenHeight - txtFld.height;
        return txtFld;
}
```

 The resize and full-screen events can be used together. If you copy and paste all of the scripts in this recipe into one file, then not only can you enter full-screen mode but the blue circle re-centers itself into the middle of the screen each time you change screen modes. During full-screen mode, the mouse leave event isn't dispatched.

See Also

"14.8 Improving Performance by Removing Event Listeners" on page 314 for removing listeners.

14.11 Using a Timer to Dispatch Events

Problem

You want to use a recurring event that's not linked to the frame rate, or a one-time event that's delayed.

Solution

Use a timer and specify the duration between event dispatches, and how many events are dispatched.

Discussion

The first step in using timer events is to create and start a timer. ActionScript 3.0's new Timer class essentially provides a consistent mechanism to replace the setInterval() and setTimeout() methods, so you can use them a bit more easily.

The Timer class accepts two arguments. The first is the duration between events, in milliseconds. If you want an event to occur every 5 seconds, this value would be 5000. This duration begins counting when the timer is started, before the first event is fired, so you can also use it to delay the dispatching of a single event. The second is an optional finite number of times you want the timer event to fire.

The following sample uses the syntax for delaying an event (by dispatching it only once), firing an event a finite number of times, and looping an event infinitely by specifying no limit of occurrences, respectively. All samples use a duration of 1000 milliseconds (one second).

```
new Timer(1000, 1);
new Timer(1000, 10);
new Timer(1000);
```

Here's a demonstration of a timer in action. This example, expanded over the remainder of this recipe, and the next recipe, is based on the metaphor of a quiz timer. You may wish to monitor time throughout a quiz or test with regular reminders. If, for example, you wanted to time an hour-long quiz, you might want reminders every 10 minutes to gauge your progress. (To make this code easy to test, it uses an interval of 2 seconds, rather than 10 minutes.)

The first two lines of this block create and start a timer that fires every 2 seconds for a total of six times. The next four lines add an event listener to the timer, to trigger the onRemind() function every time a timer event is received. The function traces "reminder" to the Output panel. (In a real-world example, this might sound a chime, or move a progress bar.)

```
var timr:Timer = new Timer(2000, 6);
timr.start();

timr.addEventListener(TimerEvent.TIMER, onRemind, false, 0, true);
function onRemind(evt:TimerEvent):void {
    trace("reminder");
}
```

The Timer class has another handy event called TimeEvent.TIMER_COMPLETE that notifies you when the timer has dispatched an event the designated number of times. (When an infinite timer is desired, this event never fires.) This ability's very useful for cleaning up after your timer, as the following section of code demonstrates.

The first line of the listener function stops the timer, the second two lines remove both listeners from this recipe, and the last line traces that the result as a simple visual cue of the function's success.

```
timr.addEventListener(TimerEvent.TIMER_COMPLETE, onRemindFinal);
function onRemindFinal(evt:TimerEvent):void {
    evt.target.stop();
    evt.target.removeEventListener(TimerEvent.TIMER, onRemind);
    evt.target.removeEventListener(TimerEvent.TIMER_COMPLETE, onRemindFinal);
```

```
        trace("timer complete, listeners removed");
}
```

 Removing event listeners for timers is a very important concept to understand because, like event listeners, timers can prevent a SWF file from being unloaded. As an extra rub, timers can't be unloaded unless they're stopped first.

See Also

"14.8 Improving Performance by Removing Event Listeners" on page 314 for removing event listeners and "14.12 Dispatching Your Own Events" on page 323 for using custom events.

14.12 Dispatching Your Own Events

Problem

You want to create and dispatch a custom event, rather than rely on pre-existing ActionScript 3.0 events.

Solution

Use the `dispatchEvent()` method to send a custom event and use that same event as the first argument of an event listener.

Discussion

You'll probably find yourself, at one point or another, wishing that an ActionScript class had one or two additional events to fill a void in your project. Moreover, you'll probably want to add events to custom classes that you write yourself.

Any class (including your own) that extends the ActionScript 3.0 `EventDispatcher` class can send an event. This includes many display objects (such as the main timeline), meaning that you can also dispatch events from frame scripts.

This example builds on the previous recipe to dispatch an event when a timer's halfway through its cycle. If you imagine the code required to check for the halfway point of a timer cycle, you might assume an additional mechanism, such as an enter frame event would be required. A listener with a conditional might continuously compare the timer's progress with your desired value, to determine if the halfway point has been reached. This way works, of course, but the ability to dispatch events makes this process a bit easier.

One of the ideas behind event dispatching is to take advantage of something that has already occurred, and use that as an occasion to inform another part of your application that an event has occurred. For example, an event might be dispatched after a load process completes or a sound finishes playing.

In this case, you can take advantage of the fact that the timer is firing at regular intervals and, when a condition has been met, dispatch your own event. This process removes the unneeded overhead of an enter frame event, for example, that might otherwise be required to check to see if the condition has been satisfied. All that remains is to set up a listener to react to your custom event.

If you want to go all the way and make your event follow the same practices as ActionScript 3.0 classes, you can create your own event class. This class could define a public constant for each event, and let you specify your event the same way you would any other—MyLoadEvent.DONE, as a hypothetical example. However, in many cases this is overkill. Since these constants are just consistent, reliable stand-ins for strings, primarily used for more structured data type checking, you can use a string directly, if preferred.

In the following example, (the bold lines of which can be added to the previous recipe) a conditional uses the Timer properties repeatCount and currentCount to see if at least half the timer events have been dispatched. Upon that occurrence, the custom event halfway is dispatched and trapped by its own listener.

```
function onRemind(evt:TimerEvent):void {
    trace("reminder");
    if (evt.target.currentCount >= evt.target.repeatCount/2) {
        dispatchEvent(new Event("halfway"));
    }
}
addEventListener("halfway", onHalfway, false, 0, true);
function onHalfway(evt:Event):void {
    trace("halfway point reached");
}
```

As seen in the added conditional, creating the event is as straightforward as instantiating any object, using the new keyword. The process uses the Event class to form the custom event, and the dispatchEvent() method to send it on its way.

If you want your event to bubble up through the display list, to be available to other display objects, set the optional bubbles property to true when creating the new event:

```
dispatchEvent(new Event("halfway", true));
```

See Also

"14.11 Using a Timer to Dispatch Events" on page 321 for context with using timer events.

14.13 Manually Calling Event Listener Functions

Problem

You want to explicitly call a function used by an event listener without generating argument errors.

Solution

Pass a custom event or null reference to the function when called.

Discussion

The ActionScript 3.0 event model requires that each listener function contain a parameter for receiving event data. This system's very useful for parsing information about the event but can also generate errors when calling the function manually (because no event is being passed to the listener function).

Consider the following example. A listener that triggers the function onClick() is attached to the stage. When trying to call the function manually, an error is thrown.

```
stage.addEventListener(MouseEvent.CLICK, onClick);
function onClick(evt:MouseEvent):void {
    //function contents
}

onClick();
//results in error
```

To prevent the error, you can create a custom event of the type needed by the listener.

```
onClick(new MouseEvent(MouseEvent.CLICK));
```

Alternately, you can pass null with the function call.

```
onClick(null);
```

However, this may create other errors depending on how your function is structured. For example, if your listener function parses event-related information from its parameter, you may receive a null-object error.

The following example demonstrates that generating a stand-in event is handled properly both when the function's purpose is unrelated to the event (as seen in the first line of the function, tracing a string) and when event data is used (as seen in the second line, tracing the target of the event). The result of the latter trace is null because the event is artificial and, therefore, there's no event target, but it doesn't generate an error.

```
stage.addEventListener(MouseEvent.CLICK, onClick);
function onClick(evt:MouseEvent):void {
    trace("onClick executed");
    trace(evt.target);
}

onClick(new MouseEvent(MouseEvent.CLICK));
```

14.14 Capturing an Event Before It Reaches Its Target

Problem

You want to process an event before it gets to its target using the capture phase.

Solution

Use the optional useCapture parameter of the addEventListener() method.

Discussion

The addEventListener() method has three optional parameters. The first is useCapture, a Boolean, that determines the phase of the event. The first line of the following syntax is an example event listener with the two mandatory arguments, while the second shows the useCapture parameter with its default value of false.

```
sp.addEventListener(MouseEvent.CLICK, onClick);
sp.addEventListener(MouseEvent.CLICK, onClick, false);
```

This default value processes the event during the target/bubbling phases, and has been used throughout this chapter and discussed in "14.5 Using the target and currentTarget Event Properties" on page 310. Setting this value to true switches the event processing stage to the capture phase, meaning the event will move through the display list on its first leg of the journey but *not* reach the target.

Most programmers rarely use this phase. The capture phase may sometimes be used to stop an event from continuing to propagate through the display list.

Another use, however, is to prevent a display object container from reacting to an event, but let the container's children respond to that same event.

In "14.2 Capturing Mouse Events" on page 305, you learned how to act only on a target of an event. However, this process required a separate listener for each target. In "14.4 Using Event Bubbling" on page 308, you learned how to apply a listener to a display object container so that all of the container's children could automatically react to the event. In this recipe, you also attach a listener to a container, but use the capture phase so only the children can react.

A scenario that discusses all of these approaches might be dragging two children of a display object container. Applying listeners directly to the children means only the children are draggable, but you need two listeners. Applying a listener to the container requires only one listener but, by default, the container's also draggable. Using the capture phase in the latter instance, however, means that the children are draggable, but the container remains fixed.

The mouse down listener in this example has been changed to use the capture phase (note the third argument, true).

```
var contnr:Sprite = new Sprite();
drawRoundedRectangle(contnr, 0x000099, 130, 130);
contnr.x = contnr.y = 100;
addChild(contnr);

var child0:Sprite = new Sprite();
drawRoundedRectangle(child0, 0x000033, 40, 40);
child0.x = child0.y = 20;
contnr.addChild(child0);

var child1:Sprite = new Sprite();
drawRoundedRectangle(child1, 0x330000, 40, 40);
child1.x = child1.y = 70;
contnr.addChild(child1);

contnr.addEventListener(MouseEvent.MOUSE_DOWN, onDown, true);
contnr.addEventListener(MouseEvent.MOUSE_UP, onUp);

function onDown(evt:MouseEvent):void {
    evt.target.startDrag();
}
function onUp(evt:MouseEvent):void {
    stopDrag();
}

function drawRoundedRectangle(obj:Object, col:uint, w:Number, h:Number):void {
    var g:Graphics = obj.graphics;
    g.lineStyle(1, col);
    g.beginFill(col, .5);
    g.drawRoundRect(0, 0, w, h, 20);
```

```
        g.endFill();
    }
```

See Also

"14.8 Improving Performance by Removing Event Listeners" on page 314 for information about removing event listeners, and "14.14 Capturing an Event Before It Reaches Its Target" on page 326 regarding the capture phase.

14.15 Setting the Execution Order of Events

Problem

You need to use the same event to trigger multiple listener functions, but want to set or change the order in which those functions are executed.

Solution

Use the optional `priority` parameter of the `addEventListener()` method.

Discussion

The second of three optional parameters of the `addEventListener()` method sets the execution order of multiple occurrences *of the same event*. For example, three listeners that use mouse up, down, and click events, respectively, aren't affected by this setting. However, three listeners that all use mouse up events are ordered according to the use of the `priority` parameter.

The following shows this parameter with its default value of 0. Because the order of parameters is fixed, using the second optional parameter requires the use of the first. However, you can simply pass in the default values of any parameters you don't wish to change.

```
sp.addEventListener(MouseEvent.CLICK, onClick, false, 0);
```

This recipe's example traces a message to the Output panel when the mouse button is clicked over the stage. The first unique event dispatched clears the variable used to contain the message, and the last unique event dispatched traces the assembled message. In between, however, are three occurrences of the same event. They consecutively assemble a verb, noun, and adjective based on order of execution because no priority is specified. The result is the question, "is Claire beautiful" (punctuation omitted intentionally).

However, if you comment out the original trio of mouse up listeners, and comment in their twins, then you see that the optional priority parameter has been used. This parameter accepts a non-negative integer, and executes the same events based on the highest priority number first. (Any listener without a priority specified uses the default priority value of 0.) This changes the traced output, executing the functions in the order of noun, verb, adjective. The result is the tracing of the true statement, "Claire is beautiful," to the Output panel.

```
var msg:String = "";

stage.addEventListener(MouseEvent.MOUSE_DOWN, onClear);

stage.addEventListener(MouseEvent.MOUSE_UP, onVerb);
stage.addEventListener(MouseEvent.MOUSE_UP, onNoun);
stage.addEventListener(MouseEvent.MOUSE_UP, onAdjective);

/*
stage.addEventListener(MouseEvent.MOUSE_UP, onVerb, false, 1);
stage.addEventListener(MouseEvent.MOUSE_UP, onNoun, false, 2);
stage.addEventListener(MouseEvent.MOUSE_UP, onAdjective, false, 0);
*/

stage.addEventListener(MouseEvent.CLICK, onShowMsg);

function onClear(evt:Event):void {
    msg = "";
}

function onNoun(evt:Event):void {
    msg += "Claire ";
}

function onVerb(evt:Event):void {
    msg += "is ";
}

function onAdjective(evt:Event):void {
    msg += "beautiful ";
}

function onShowMsg(evt:Event):void {
    trace(msg);
}
```

 You can use variables can be used for priority values, so that you can change the execution order of listener functions on the fly.

14.16 Using Weak Listeners

Problem

In addition to good memory management practices, you want to increase the likelihood that an unwanted object will be removed from memory.

Solution

Use the optional `useWeakReference` parameter of the `addEventListener()` method.

Discussion

The third and last optional parameter of the `addEventListener()` method substitutes a *weak reference* to the listener for the strong, persistent connection used by default. Weak references are support tools to help with memory management. Flash Player uses a common memory management method called *garbage collection* to clear unused elements from memory. It marks any unused elements for collection, and then, during more efficient periods in your application, sweeps through and clears everything up.

If you're not careful about removing unwanted objects from memory, you can run into performance and/or memory problems. A very important part of this process is removing unused event listeners, as discussed in "14.8 Improving Performance by Removing Event Listeners" on page 314. However, using weak references for listeners lets Flash help a bit when determining which objects are set for removal from memory. The basic idea of weak listeners is: if the object to which a reference was being maintained no longer exists, don't let the reference prevent garbage collection.

Think of the relationship between milk and its surrounding carton. If there's milk in the carton, the carton shouldn't be thrown away. However, when the milk's gone, you don't want to keep the carton in your refrigerator. That outcome is the effect with a normal (default) event listener. A reference remains, and the empty carton isn't available for collection.

Metaphorically, the milk's a button, the carton's an event listener, and the refrigerator's the total available memory. Proper memory management requires that you throw the milk carton in the trash when the milk's gone, and wait for the garbage collectors to pick it up and take it away on their next visit. However, if you forget to throw the carton away, a weak reference may help. There's no longer any milk in the carton (the button has been deleted). Therefore, since there's no longer a link between carton and milk (button and listener), the carton can be discarded.

To enable weak listeners, all you need to do is set the last optional parameter of the addEventListener() method to true. You can do this without being forced to use either of the first two parameters simply by reiterating their default values. The following line of script enables a weak reference for a display object called sp, and a listener function called onClick(). Neither the capture phase nor priority features are being used.

```
sp.addEventListener(MouseEvent.CLICK, onClick, false, 0, true);
```

 Using weak listeners is not a substitute for explicitly removing listeners!

See Also

"14.8 Improving Performance by Removing Event Listeners" on page 314 for information about removing event listeners.

CHAPTER 15

How Do I Work with Text?

15.0 Introduction

This chapter will cover the basics of creating, formatting, and interacting with text fields and the text therein. Focusing on the mechanics of using text fields, rather than on string manipulations, this chapter will bring you up to speed with the essentials you need to add text to any project.

Flash uses three different kinds of text fields: *static*, *dynamic*, and *input*. The latter two types can be created and affected by ActionScript; they're the focus of this chapter. Whenever you wish to exert ActionScript control over text, you turn to a dynamic text field. However, if you require user input, including anything from entering a user name and password to completing an essay, then you need to graduate to an input text field—essentially, dynamic fields with added user input features.

You'll see in the first recipe of this chapter that you can very easily create a text field, and setting it to behave as a dynamic or input field is simply a matter of using a single property. This capability also means that you can switch between these two types, if the need arises.

The third text type, static, is accessible via ActionScript to a very limited degree, but only the Flash interface can create static text fields. You can retrieve text from a static text field, using the `StaticText` or `TextSnapshot` classes, but you must walk through the display list to find the desired field. Additionally, the Flash interface may break your text into multiple fields after compilation, as in the case with vertical text, so the ActionScript queries to static text elements are of marginal use.

15.1 Creating a Text Field

Problem

You want to create a text field using ActionScript, rather than the Text tool in the Flash interface.

Solution

You can create text fields in the same manner as other display objects, using the new keyword and appropriate class, TextField.

Discussion

Creating a text field is consistent with creating any other display object, but setting the type property of the field determines its functionality. Regardless of whether you want a dynamic or input text field, new TextField() is still used to create the object, and the field must be added to the display list to be visible. The following example simply creates two different text fields to demonstrate the use of the type property.

```
var score:TextField = new TextField();
score.type = TextFieldType.DYNAMIC;
addChild(score);

var userName:TextField = new TextField();
userName.type = TextFieldType.INPUT;
addChild(userName);
```

New fields will be added to the display list using all their default properties, including a somewhat awkward 100 × 100-pixel size, so it's necessary to style the field after creation. In this case, style is a loosely used term for defining basic appearance and functionality.

15.2 Styling a Text Field

Problem

You want to establish a look and basic feature set for a text field.

Solution

Use a variety of properties of the TextField class that apply to the field, rather than the text therein. Formatting of the text itself is discussed in a later recipe.

Discussion

The following script creates and styles a basic dynamic text field. The first block of code creates the text field.

```
var txtFld:TextField = new TextField();
txtFld.type = TextFieldType.DYNAMIC;
addChild(txtFld);

txtFld.width = 300;
txtFld.height = 20;

txtFld.border = true;
txtFld.borderColor = 0x666666;
txtFld.background = true;
txtFld.backgroundColor = 0xCCCCCC;

txtFld.multiline = true;
txtFld.wordWrap = true;
txtFld.selectable = false;
```

The second block sets the width and height of the text field. This is important because, without this, adding a text field to other display objects conforms those objects to a minimum of 100 × 100 pixels, if the dimensions or size characteristics aren't changed. This process can be confusing at first, especially in situations where the text must be small, such as in the case of a label for a button.

The third block sets the graphical appearance of the field, manipulating the border and background. Both characteristics are optional and, if turned on, can be colored. This example uses a charcoal border and light gray background.

The last block defines three basic behavioral features of the field, letting any text the field may contain wrap to multiple lines and not be selectable. The latter option's useful when you want to prevent text selection highlighting from marring a design. If the ability to select text (to copy to the clipboard, for example) isn't part of your product feature set, setting the selectable property to false is a good way to override this default behavior.

Finally, one more feature can be helpful in a big-picture way. You can, at the field level, set the color of all text in the field. Setting text color would ordinarily be a formatting task but, if you don't need character- or word-specific color formatting, you can set text color this way:

```
txtFld.textColor = 0x660000;
```

See Also

"15.1 Creating a Text Field" on page 334 for creating a text field.

15.3 Creating a Password Field

Problem

You want to hide user input to avoid password entry from being viewable to the casual onlooker.

Solution

Use the `displayAsPassword` property to replace input characters with asterisks.

Discussion

To display asterisks instead of user input characters, you just need to use an input field and set the `displayAsPassword` property to `true`.

```
var pssWrd:TextField = new TextField();
pssWrd.type = TextFieldType.INPUT;
addChild(pssWrd);

pssWrd.displayAsPassword = true;
```

Additional text field properties, however, might also prove helpful for password input. The `maxChars` property limits the number of characters the user can type in the field, and the `restrict` property limits which characters can be entered. The latter can use limited regular expression patterns to specify characters, including simple ranges like lowercase *a* through *z* (which converts all uppercase letters to lowercase) and numbers *0* through *9*, as seen in the next code block.

It also helps to clearly define the size and visibility of the field so the user can easily find it. Here, `width` and `height` are specified, as are the use of a `border` and `background`.

```
pssWrd.maxChars = 15;
pssWrd.restrict = "a-z0-9";

pssWrd.width = 100;
pssWrd.height = 14;
pssWrd.border = true;
pssWrd.background = true;
```

Next, let's create a minimal setup for checking a password. The first two blocks of the following script segment create a button to submit the password. When the button's clicked, the listener at the end of the script checks the text of the field to see if the text entered by the user matches "actionscript3". If so, then it traces "success" to the Output panel. If not, then the script empties the field for a subsequent user entry.

```
var sp:Sprite = new Sprite();
drawSquare(sp, 0x000099);
sp.x = 110;
sp.buttonMode = true;
addChild(sp);

function drawSquare(obj:Object, col:uint):void {
    var g:Graphics = obj.graphics;
    g.beginFill(col, 1);
    g.drawRect(0, 0, 14, 14);
    g.endFill();
}

sp.addEventListener(MouseEvent.CLICK, onClick, false, 0, true);
function onClick(evt:MouseEvent):void {
    if (pssWrd.text == "actionscript3") {
        trace("success");
    } else {
        pssWrd.text = "";
    }
}
```

15.4 Focusing a Text Field

Problem

You want to programmatically place the text insert cursor inside a text field.

Solution

Use the focus property of the stage to give focus to a specified field.

Discussion

When clicking on an editable text field, the text insert cursor is typically placed into the field, letting the user begin typing. This process is referred to as giving *focus* to the field. In some instances, however, you may need to accomplish this goal programmatically.

Consider, for example, the previous recipe, in which a user types a password into an input field. If the password is incorrect, then the field is cleared, but the user must still click in the field to type. The following code block adds one new line (shown in bold) to the last function of the previous recipe, automatically preparing the field for text entry. It does this step by setting the focus property of the stage to the text field reference—in this case, pssWrd.

```
function onClick(evt:MouseEvent):void {
    if (pssWrd.text == "actionscript3") {
        trace("success");
    } else {
        pssWrd.text = "";
        pssWrd.stage.focus = pssWrd;
    }
}
```

The syntax in this new line demonstrates access to the stage through a display object. This line could have been written in a slightly simpler form:

```
stage.focus = pssWrd;
```

However, this would work only because the optional this reference to the main timeline, though omitted, is implied. The stage is, in reality, being accessed through the main timeline, a movie clip display object. Using the syntax featured in the script segment helps remind you that ActionScript 3.0 has no global reference to the stage. You can also remember this principle by always using the this reference.

```
this.stage.focus = pssWrd;
```

See Also

"15.3 Creating a Password Field" on page 336 for creating a password field and "13.11 Referencing the Stage Through a Display Object" on page 300 for referencing the stage through a display object.

15.5 Populating a Text Field

Problem

You want to add text to a text field.

Solution

Use the `text` property of the `TextField` class to replace text, or add text to an empty field. Use the `appendText()` method to add text to the end of an already populated field.

Discussion

While using the `text` property of a text field isn't new for ActionScript 3.0, and was demonstrated in "15.3 Creating a Password Field" on page 336, the new `appendText()` method of the TextField class warrants attention. Briefly, this method achieves the same goal as `txtFld.text += "string value"`, but much faster. That is, rather than manually appending text to a field using the compound operator `+=`, use the `appendText()` method to accomplish the same task.

To easily demonstrate this process, start with the field setup from "15.2 Styling a Text Field" on page 334, and then add the following two lines to your script:

```
txtFld.text = "I Am";
txtFld.appendText(" the Fly");
```

The result is the string "I Am the Fly" because " the Fly" was appended to the starting text without overwriting it.

See Also

"15.2 Styling a Text Field" on page 334 for creating and styling a text field.

15.6 Automatically Sizing a Text Field

Problem

You want a text field to expand to accommodate dynamic input.

Solution

Use the `autoSize` property of the `TextField` class to resize a text field based on input and alignment choice.

Discussion

This recipe continues the previous code example, which has been collected here again for convenience. The first portion of the following script initializes a field and populates it with a single line of text, "I Am the Fly".

```
var txtFld:TextField = new TextField();
txtFld.type = TextFieldType.DYNAMIC;
addChild(txtFld);

txtFld.width = 300;
txtFld.height = 20;

txtFld.border = true;
txtFld.borderColor = 0x666666;
txtFld.background = true;
txtFld.backgroundColor = 0xCCCCCC;

txtFld.multiline = true;
txtFld.wordWrap = true;
txtFld.selectable = false;

txtFld.text = "I Am";
txtFld.appendText(" the Fly");

txtFld.autoSize = TextFieldAutoSize.LEFT;
txtFld.appendText("\nin the ointment");
```

The two new bold lines are responsible for adding a second line to the field, and automatically resizing the field to accommodate. The text field's `auto Size` property is set to automatically resize the field, using its left edge as an anchor for left-justified text. The new line is added using the `appendText()` method, but preceding the string with a new line character, \n.

To see the property in action, test the script with and without commenting the `autoSize` instruction. You find that, despite enabling the `multiline` and `word Wrap` properties, the field shows only one line of text without the effect of the `autoSize` property.

This outcome occurs because the height of the field is fixed at 20 pixels, so, even with the text spanning two lines, the second line isn't visible. The `auto Size` property automatically resizes the field in one or more directions, based on the setting you use.

The constants of the `TextFieldAutoSize` class are LEFT, RIGHT, and CEN-TER. If you choose `LEFT` as the `autoSize` anchor, then the field expands or contracts on the right side, as well as the bottom side, in the case of any new lines or carriage returns. `RIGHT` has the opposite effect, resizing to the left and down, and `CENTER` equally distributes field resizing to the left and right, as well as along the bottom edge if new lines are added.

In all cases, if the `wordWrap` property is turned on, the specified width (or default width, if nothing is specified) of the field is preserved, and only the bottom edge of the field is resized. You can see this in action by commenting in and out the `wordWrap` instruction during testing.

15.7 Scrolling a Text Field

Problem

You want to programmatically scroll text within a fixed field height.

Solution

Use the `scrollV` and `scrollH` properties of the `TextField` class.

Discussion

The first part of the following script is similar to several of the previous recipes in this chapter. It creates a dynamic text field, configures basic appearance and functionality attributes, and populates the field.

In this case, two subtle changes warrant comment. First, the height is fixed at 150 pixels, instead of 20, to show multiple lines. Second, text is added to the field with a loop, using a newline character, which ensures that multiple lines exist for scrolling. However, the bolded code, explained following the script, controls the scrolling.

```
var txtFld:TextField = new TextField();
txtFld.type = TextFieldType.DYNAMIC;
addChild(txtFld);

txtFld.width = 150;
txtFld.height = 150;

txtFld.border = true;
txtFld.background = true;

txtFld.multiline = true;
txtFld.wordWrap = true;
txtFld.selectable = false;

txtFld.text = "I Am the Fly";
for (var i:int = 1; i <= 20; i++) {
    txtFld.appendText("\n" + i + " I am the fly in the ointment");
}

this.addEventListener(Event.ENTER_FRAME, onScroll, false, 0, true);
function onScroll(evt:Event):void {
    if (mouseY < txtFld.height/2) {
        txtFld.scrollV--;
    } else {
        txtFld.scrollV++;
    }
}
```

In this simple example, an enter frame event listener monitors the mouse, and scrolls the text based on the position of the mouse relative to the field. If the mouse is above the horizontal center of the field, the text scrolls up until the top of the field is reached. If the mouse is below the field center, the text scrolls down until the bottom of the field is reached.

If you would rather use a scrollbar to manage text scrolling, you can easily create a dynamic instance of the UIScrollBar component. Making sure you have a copy of the component in your library, you can replace the manual scrolling code (in bold) from the previous example with the following:

```
import fl.controls.UIScrollBar;

var uiScroll:UIScrollBar = new UIScrollBar();
addChild(uiScroll);
uiScroll.scrollTarget = txtFld;
uiScroll.x = txtFld.x + txtFld.width;
uiScroll.y = txtFld.y;
uiScroll.height = txtFld.height;
```

This first line of this new code block imports the necessary class because component classes are not automatically accessible during compilation. The next two lines create a scroll bar instance and add it to the display list. The next line associates the scroll bar with the desired field. Finally, the remaining lines position the scroll bar at the upper-right corner of the text field, and set the scroll bar's height to match that of the field.

You can also scroll a text field horizontally. This ability's useful when you want to enable long lines without line wrapping—for a navigation system, perhaps. In the case of manual scrolling, the principles behind the process are similar, but the scrollH property is measured in pixels, rather than lines (as is the case with scrollV). Proportional typefaces prevent you from relying on character width for consistent scrolling.

When using the component, you need to set the direction property of the UIScrollBar instance to a horizontal equivalent, as when using the ScrollBar Direction.HORIZONTAL constant in the revised code that follows. (Note that you must also import that class if you plan to use the constant.) You also need to reposition the scroll bar (to the bottom of the field in this example.

```
import fl.controls.UIScrollBar;
import fl.controls.ScrollBarDirection;

var uiScroll:UIScrollBar = new UIScrollBar();
addChild(uiScroll);
uiScroll.scrollTarget = txtFld;
uiScroll.direction = ScrollBarDirection.HORIZONTAL;
uiScroll.x = txtFld.x;
uiScroll.y = txtFld.y + txtFld.height;
uiScroll.width = txtFld.width;
```

To see this in action, you can modify the previous script by replacing the scroll bar code as indicated; changing the width and height of the field to narrow and tall (100 and 270, respectively, should work nicely); and setting the field's wordWrap property to false.

See Also

"15.2 Styling a Text Field" on page 334 for defining the display attributes and functionality of a text field, and "15.5 Populating a Text Field" on page 338 for populating a text field.

15.8 Using Embedded Fonts

Problem

You want to use a custom font, but you want to make sure the font is viewable even on computers that don't have that font installed.

Solution

Use the embedFonts property to support the use of an embedded font when formatting text.

Discussion

Using system fonts keeps your files small and efficient, but typically restricts you to using only fonts commonly found in most operating systems. To use a custom typeface reliably, you must use an embedded font so the required font outlines are included in your SWF file.

Furthermore, embedded fonts are required for certain graphical effects, such as rotation and alpha transparency, when used on text fields. Without embedded fonts, text can disappear from fields when these and similar transformations are applied.

To use embedded fonts, you need only one parameter, embedFonts. The following example code uses embedded fonts in a hypothetical field called txtFld. The next few recipes cover specifying the use of a particular font.

```
txtFld.embedFonts = true;
```

In the Flash interface, you can't embed fonts using only ActionScript. See Chapter 7, for an overview of embedding fonts using the Library panel.

 If you enable support for this feature, but fail to specify an embedded font with the correct linkage class, then the text doesn't appear. If this situation occurs, you may be able to quickly test to see if the embedded font is the problem by commenting out the `embedFonts` line of your script and switching to using a local system font. If the text appears, you can then investigate the embedding process and correct the problem.

See Also

"15.9 Formatting Text Using TextFormat" on page 344 through "15.11 Formatting Text Using CSS" on page 348 for specifying font use.

15.9 Formatting Text Using TextFormat

Problem

You want to create a text-formatting object that can be applied to text fields.

Solution

Create an instance of the `TextFormat` class.

Discussion

Arguably the simplest way to use ActionScript to format text is to use `TextFormat` instances. Like Cascading Style Sheets (CSS), you can apply them to many fields, and edits to the instance are reflected across all its uses. However, `TextFormat` instances are somewhat easier to create.

The first step in formatting text this way is to create a `TextFormat` instance. It must exist before attempting to apply it to a text field. The first block of this recipe's code creates the instance, and sets the font and color of the text. It then turns on bold, italic, and underline, but as separate Boolean properties to make it easier to mix and match these effects.

The second block controls common type attributes for size, leading, and letter spacing. All values are in pixels, but the leading value only applies to the space between lines of text.

The last block sets the left and right margins as well as the indent of the first line in every paragraph, both in pixels.

```
var txtFrmt:TextFormat = new TextFormat();
txtFrmt.font = "Arial";
txtFrmt.color = 0x990000;
txtFrmt.bold = true;
txtFrmt.italic = true;
txtFrmt.underline = true;

txtFrmt.size = 14;
txtFrmt.leading = 4;
txtFrmt.letterSpacing = 1;

txtFrmt.leftMargin = txtFrmt.rightMargin = 3;
txtFrmt.indent = 9;
```

The next step is to apply the TextFormat instance to your text field. The following code block instantiates and populates a text field, and shows the first way to use the formatter you just created.

```
var txtFld:TextField = new TextField();
txtFld.type = TextFieldType.DYNAMIC;
addChild(txtFld);

txtFld.width = 200;
txtFld.height = 200;

txtFld.border = true;
txtFld.background = true;

txtFld.multiline = true;
txtFld.wordWrap = true
txtFld.selectable = false;

txtFld.defaultTextFormat = txtFrmt;
for (var i:int = 1; i <= 20; i++) {
    txtFld.appendText("All work and no play makes Jack a dull boy.");
}
```

The for loop in the last three lines populates the field with a single paragraph. Immediately before any text is added to the field, however, the defaultText Format property of the field is set to the TextFormat instance you created. By using this approach, new text added to the field inherits the formatting. This characteristic is most helpful for formatting an empty field for user input.

The next approach is to make a one-time change to text that already exists. Instead of using the defaultTextFormat property before the text's added to the field, you can use the `setTextFormat()` method after the field is populated. To see this change in action, comment out the `defaultTextFormat` line in your script to prevent any initial formatting, and then add the following line after the loop.

```
txtFld.setTextFormat(txtFrmt);
```

The visual appearance doesn't change because you're using the same formatting code, but you can use this approach any time, instead of only before adding content to the field.

When formatting existing text, you can also specify a range of characters rather than changing all text in the field. To do this, you must add two indices to the `setTextFormat()` method, as seen here:

```
txtFld.setTextFormat(txtFrmt, 43, 85);
```

The first is the index of the first character to be formatted, and the last is the index of the character *after* the text you wish to format. That is, the text formatted is *firstIndex* to *lastIndex-1*. (This method is a fairly standard way to identify character ranges, and offers the benefit of being able to specify the length of the string as the last index.)

 Using `TextFormat` instances doesn't work on fields that use a style sheet. For more information, see "15.11 Formatting Text Using CSS" on page 348.

15.10 Formatting Text Using HTML

Problem

You want to use HTML to format a text field.

Solution

Use the limited HTML rendering capabilities of text fields.

Discussion

Flash supports a limited number of HTML tags that you can use to add formatting and functionality to text fields. Table 15-1 lists the tags available in ActionScript, as well as relevant notes, if applicable.

Table 15-1. HTML tags supported by Flash Player

HTML tag	Notes
<font>	Supported attributes include: color, face, size.
<b>	Bold version of font must exist to work.
<i>	Italic version of font must exist to work.
<u>	
<span>	Supported attributes include: class.
<p>	multiline must be enabled to work. Supported attributes include: align, class.
 	multiline must be enabled to work.
<li>	All lists are bulleted. Ordered and unordered qualifiers are ignored.
<img>	Supported attributes include: src, width, height, align, hspace, vspace, id. Can embed external images (JPG, GIF, PNG) and SWF files with automatic text flow around source.
<a>	Supported attributes include: href, event, target.
<textformat>	Used to apply limited subset of TextFormat properties to enclosed text. Supported attributes include: blockindent, indent, leading, leftmargin, rightmargin, tabstops.

To demonstrate that HTML can also be combined with other features for added effect, a simple example will be constructed over the next few recipes. To begin, this script shows the use of paragraph, bold, italic, and font tags to style a line of text. Related upcoming recipes will also make use of span, list, anchor, and break tags.

```
var txtFld:TextField = new TextField();
txtFld.autoSize = TextFieldAutoSize.LEFT;
txtFld.multiline = true;
txtFld.selectable = false;
addChild(txtFld);

txtFld.htmlText = "<p><b>Interactive</b>
  <i>Text</i> <font color='#FF0000'>Demonstration</font></p>";
```

Beyond the somewhat restrictive subset of supported tags, working with HTML is quite straightforward. In the ActionScript 3.0 implementation of HTML, the only point worthy of note is that you no longer need to first enable HTML support. Simply adding text with the htmlText property (instead of the text property) automatically makes HTML features available.

See Also

"15.11 Formatting Text Using CSS" on page 348 through "15.13 Triggering ActionScript from HTML Links" on page 351 for additional use of HTML.

15.11 Formatting Text Using CSS

Problem

You want to use Cascading Style Sheets to format text.

Solution

Use the `StyleSheet` class and corresponding `styleSheet` property of the `Text Field` class.

Discussion

As with HTML, ActionScript supports a limited set of CSS properties. You can see these properties in Table 15-2. Note that, for consistency, the corresponding ActionScript property names don't have hyphens.

Table 15-2. CSS tags supported by Flash Player

CSS property	Notes
`<color>`	Font color in 0xRRGGBB format.
`<display>`	Controls display of item. Values include: `none`, `block`, `inline`.
`font-family`	Font name. Corresponding ActionScript property changed to `fontFamily`.
`font-size`	Font size in pixels. Corresponding ActionScript property changed to `fontSize`.
`font-style`	Font style. Values include: `italic`, `normal`. Corresponding ActionScript property changed to `fontStyle`.
`font-weight`	Font style. Values include: `bold`, `normal`. Corresponding ActionScript property changed to `fontWeight`.
`kerning`	Turns kerning on or off. Values include: `true`, `false`. Works only when using embedded fonts and in SWF files created on the Windows platform.
`leading`	Font leading in pixels. Not officially supported. Similar to: `text-height`. Works well in internal style object, but may not be reliable in loaded CSS.
`letter-spacing`	Tracking in pixels. Corresponding ActionScript property changed to `letterStyle`.
`margin-left`	Positions left margin in pixels. Corresponding ActionScript property changed to `marginLeft`.
`margin-right`	Positions right margin in pixels. Corresponding ActionScript property changed to `marginRight`.
`text-align`	Specifies text alignment behavior. Values include: `left`, `right`, `center` or `justify`. Corresponding ActionScript property changed to `textAlign`.
`text-decoration`	Underlines text. Values include: `underline`, `none`. Corresponding ActionScript property changed to `textDecoration`.

CSS property	Notes
text-indent	Indents first-line paragraph indent in pixels. Corresponding ActionScript property changed to textIndent.

You have two ways to work with CSS in ActionScript. The first is to create style objects inline, which is covered in this recipe. The second is to load an external CSS document, which will be covered in Chapter 17.

The style sheet's application is the same in both cases. So, the basics of the inline method involve creating an object for each style, and then registering that object with its corresponding HTML tag or CSS class. The following script creates a simple example style sheet that contains two arbitrarily named styles for use over the next few recipes. Together, they demonstrate the use of class-based and tag-based styles. The first is called *task,* and is a custom class for adding emphasis to items or subheads. The second style is called *link,* and is associated with the anchor HTML tag for use in the next two recipes.

Building on the HTML of the prior recipe, the bold code is new. The first two segments create custom objects and assign the desired CSS properties and values. The third segment creates an instance of the StyleSheet class, and uses the setStyle() method to associate the objects with the class and tag identifier. Upon completion of this process, the StyleSheet instance css can be applied to a text field (discussed following the script).

```
var task:Object = new Object();
task.fontFamily = "Verdana";
task.fontSize = 14;
task.leading = 4;
task.letterSpacing = 1;
task.textIndent = 14;

var link:Object = new Object();
link.color = "#0000FF";
link.textDecoration = "underline"
link.fontStyle = "italic";

var css:StyleSheet = new StyleSheet();
css.setStyle(".task", task);
css.setStyle("a", link);

var txtFld:TextField = new TextField();
txtFld.autoSize = TextFieldAutoSize.LEFT;
txtFld.multiline = true;
txtFld.selectable = false;
addChild(txtFld);

txtFld.styleSheet = css;
txtFld.htmlText = "<p><b>Interactive</b>
<i>Text</i> <font color='#FF0000'>Demonstration</font></p>";
```

```
txtFld.htmlText += "<br /><span
class='task'>The following tasks are possible:</span>";
```

The last line of this script is standard HTML fare for using CSS. A custom class is applied in a `<span>` tag that surrounds the desired text. (The next two recipes use the anchor tag.)

However, the application of the style sheet is noteworthy because you must apply it *before* text is added to the field. This action happens in the first line of the last code block, before the field is populated with the `htmlText` property.

See Also

"15.10 Formatting Text Using HTML" on page 346 for use of HTML as well as "15.12 Adding Hyperlinks to Text" on page 350 and "15.13 Triggering ActionScript from HTML Links" on page 351 for additional use of CSS.

15.12 Adding Hyperlinks to Text

Problem

You want to place a hyperlink in a text field

Solution

Use HTML, and an anchor tag, to add the link, similar to the corresponding approach of adding a hyperlink to an HTML page.

Discussion

Adding standard hypertext links in ActionScript uses the same process as adding links in HTML. The optional target attribute is also supported for opening links in another window.

```
txtFld.htmlText += "<li><span class='task'>Search:
<a href='http://www.google.com'>Google</a></span></li>";
```

 Although this code works on its own if a field called `txtFld` already exists, it's designed to be added to the previous recipes as an ongoing example. The list tag is added simply to demonstrate additional use of HTML formatting.

See Also

"15.10 Formatting Text Using HTML" on page 346 and "15.12 Adding Hyperlinks to Text" on page 350 for information on formatting with HTML and CSS, and "15.13 Triggering ActionScript from HTML Links" on page 351 for additional functionality triggered from HTML links.

15.13 Triggering ActionScript from HTML Links

Problem

You want to execute an ActionScript 3.0 function from a link in a text field.

Solution

Use HTML and an anchor tag to add the link, but use the ActionScript 3.0 event: protocol instead of the http: protocol, which is reserved for standard links.

Discussion

Triggering ActionScript from HTML links in ActionScript 3.0 is similar to the same process in ActionScript 2.0, but the system now makes use of the ActionScript 3.0 event model. Previously, the link's http: protocol was replaced with asfunction: and a corresponding function was typically created for each unique use of this feature.

Currently, the process is similar in that the http: protocol is replaced with event: but the corresponding executable code is less tightly coupled with the link. That is, the link now dispatches a TextEvent that can be handled in the usual event listener manner, granting much more power and flexibility to the process.

```
txtFld.htmlText += "<li><span class='task'>Trace: <a href='event:showMsg'>
    Show Message</a></span></li>";

txtFld.addEventListener(TextEvent.LINK, linkHandler);
function linkHandler(evt:TextEvent):void {
    if (evt.text == "showMsg") {
        trace("Specific function code executes here");
    }
}
```

Although this code works on its own if a field called `txtFld` already exists, it's designed to be added to the previous recipes as an ongoing example.

See Also

"15.10 Formatting Text Using HTML" on page 346 through "15.12 Adding Hyperlinks to Text" on page 350 for additional HTML and CSS formatting, and hyperlink use.

15.14 Selecting Text

Problem

You want to programmatically select text in a field, akin to if a user selects the text with the mouse.

Solution

Use the `setSelection()` method of the `TextField` class.

Discussion

The following script passage initializes a field, and populates it with a simple line of text. It then attaches a mouse down event listener to the stage that programmatically selects five characters of that text, characters 6 through 10, thereby selecting the second word, "ipsum."

```
var txtFld:TextField = new TextField();
txtFld.width = 200;
txtFld.selectable = false;
txtFld.type = TextFieldType.DYNAMIC;
txtFld.text = "Lorem ipsum dolor sit amet.";
addChild(txtFld);

stage.addEventListener(MouseEvent.MOUSE_DOWN, onSelectWord, false, 0, true);
function onSelectWord(evt:MouseEvent):void {
    txtFld.setSelection(6,11);
}
```

Remember that text operations like this typically specify a range using the first desired character and the last desired character plus 1. Additionally, the character count is zero-based, with the first character having an index of 0, not 1. See "15.9 Formatting Text Using TextFormat" on page 344 for more information.

The next code block adds another feature that lets you replace selected text with a new string. A similar listener structure is used, this time listening for a mouse up event, and replaces the selection, after first checking to make sure a selection exists. This latter task is accomplished by making sure the beginning and end of the selected text aren't the same (which would indicate no selection).

```
stage.addEventListener(MouseEvent.MOUSE_UP, onReplaceWord, false, 0, true);
function onReplaceWord(evt:MouseEvent):void {
    if (txtFld.selectionBeginIndex != txtFld.selectionEndIndex) {
        txtFld.replaceSelectedText("LOREM");
    }
}
```

Finally, if you've struggled with text selection and object focus in the past, you'll be overjoyed to know that ActionScript 3.0 handles this issue quite well. ActionScript 3.0 even has a feature that prevents the selection highlight from disappearing when the field loses focus, as seen here.

```
txtFld.alwaysShowSelection = true;
```

To see this feature in action, add the previous line to the end of the onSelect Word() function, and comment out the listener that invokes onReplaceWord(). (You need to do this step because, if the word is replaced immediately, you don't see the effect of maintaining the selection.) Clicking alternately on the stage and directly on the text shows the visual difference between when the text field has focus and when it doesn't.

CHAPTER 16

How Do I Work with XML?

16.0 Introduction

XML (Extensible Markup Language) is a flexible way to structure data for storage, transmission, and parsing. Traditional name-value pairs, used by standard GET and POST form actions, are fine for transferring small amounts of simple data. However, this technique isn't well suited for large amounts of data or when you have to carefully organize the data.

For example, name-value pairs are limited to associations that link a single value with a single variable. Complex associations where variables must be grouped in some manner are arguably impossible, or would require multiple variables with similar names.. You could get a basic database-like structure this way with name-value pairs:

```
?user1namefirst=John&user1namelast=Public&
user1joined=2007&user1reg=yes&
```

Using XML, however, you can easily associate related variables. The preceding name-value pair submission could be represented this way in XML:

```
<user>
    <first>John</first>
    <last>Public</last>
    <joined reg="yes">2007</joined>
</user>
```

You can imagine, when this data enlarges to many users, how much more easily you can work with a single variable that contains data that's organized consistently.

Although this book discusses ActionScript 3.0's ability to manipulate XML, it can't delve into the basics of XML. However, you'll find a bountiful supply of information online. One such resource is the World Wide Web Consortium home for XML coverage, *http://www.w3c.org/XML/*.

For the purposes of this chapter, you must know only a few basic things, to understand any errors you may see when experimenting.

All but a few administrative tags are self-defined. You need only decide how to structure your content in a consistent manner so that both the server (if present) and client can understand it.

- Tags and attributes must be of a consistent case (lowercase recommended).
- A root node must enclose all other content.
- All tags must be closed (either with a balancing close tag or as a self-closing tag).
- All tags must be properly nested.
- All attribute values must be quoted.
- Whitespace is ignored by default.
- Flash doesn't validate XML by version or Document Type Definition (DTD).

One or two other simple rules apply, and will be covered in the remainder of this chapter, but XML use in Flash is pretty straightforward. ActionScript 3.0 has also gone a long way to simplifying things.

The previous functionality of the XML class has been moved over to the XMLDocument class and included primarily to improve support for legacy projects. Don't use this outdated technique. The new XML class is used mainly for working with your entire XML data set as a whole, and supporting classes such as XMLList are used to work with specific content. Familiar *dot syntax*, like the kind used for ActionScript itself to traverse objects, properties, methods, and so on, is now used in place of the verbose familial navigation from prior versions of ActionScript.

16.1 Creating an XML Object

Problem

You want to create an object to hold XML data for parsing.

Solution

Create an instance of the XML class.

Discussion

You have a few ways to populate an instance of the XML class. Firstly, you can add data to an empty instance, as needed. "16.11 Writing XML" on page 369, discusses this approach. The second approach is to assign data to the instance immediately. ActionScript 3.0 makes this easy because you can type the XML in human-readable form, complete with white space, and carriage returns don't break the assignment. The following example creates an object, products, which nearly all of the recipes in this chapter use.

```
var products:XML =
    <root>
        <season quarter="3">Fall</season>
        <whatsnew>
            <promotion>Fall Sale</promotion>
        </whatsnew>
        <books>
            <book>
                <title series="learning">Learning ActionScript 3.0</title>
                <authors>Shupe and Rosser</authors>
            </book>
            <book>
                <title series="cookbook">ActionScript 3.0 Cookbook</title>
                <authors>Lott, Schall, and Peters</authors>
            </book>
            <book>
                <title series="animal">Essential ActionScript 3.0</title>
                <authors>Moock</authors>
            </book>
        </books>
    </root>;
```

The third method is to start with a string of valid XML, and then pass that to the constructor of the XML class, as seen in the following very concise example — quite handy for dynamic creation of XML starting with a text source (such as user input).

```
var xmlString:String = "<root><username>J. G. Thirlwell</username></root>"
var xml:XML = new XML(xmlString);
```

16.2 Loading XML

Problem

You want to load XML from an external document or server.

Solution

Create an instance of the URLLoader class to load the XML, and then create an instance of the XML class with the loaded data.

Discussion

Although the next chapter discusses working with external assets, people most often work with XML in ActionScript by loading XML from a server or external document. As such, the following example demonstrates the basics you need.

To load XML, you must start with an instance of the URLLoader class. This class is used to load text, variables, and binary data. Because the XML must be loaded before it can be parsed, an event listener is commonly used to process the incoming data after the Event.COMPLETE event is dispatched (indicating that the load is complete). Finally, you must process all URLs using a URLRequest, which can then be passed to the load() method seen in the third line of code that follows.

```
var xmlLoader:URLLoader = new URLLoader();
xmlLoader.addEventListener(Event.COMPLETE, onComplete, false, 0, true);
xmlLoader.load(new URLRequest("store.xml"));

function onComplete(evt:Event):void {
    var xmlData:XML = new XML(evt.target.data);
    trace(xmlData);
}
```

The onComplete() listener function then converts the loaded data into an XML instance (using the last technique discussed in "16.1 Creating an XML Object" on page 356), and traces the data to show you a visual result for testing.

 Using an instance of the URLRequest class may seem extraneous when simply loading an asset (as opposed to just using a string). However, you see in "16.12 Writing XML with Variables" on page 372 that you can configure the instance for sending data, and the consistent use in all cases is a wonderful hallmark of ActionScript 3.0.

See Also

"16.1 Creating an XML Object" on page 356 for creating an XML object.

16.3 Reading an Element Node

Problem

You want to isolate a portion of a larger XML object to work with a single element node.

Solution

Use the familiar dot-syntax object model introduced in ActionScript 3.0 to work with XML, and target an element node.

Discussion

ActionScript 3.0's implementation of XML lifts a pretty big weight off your shoulders when it comes to parsing data. You no longer need to use a series of sequential methods and/or properties to traverse an XML tree. Instead, you need only walk through nodes using dot syntax similar to the ActionScript document object model with which you're already familiar.

To begin, examine this chapter's primary sample XML:

```
var products:XML =
    <root>
        <season quarter="3">Fall</season>
        <whatsnew>
            <promotion>Fall Sale</promotion>
        </whatsnew>
        <books>
            <book>
                <title series="learning">Learning ActionScript 3.0</title>
                <authors>Shupe and Rosser</authors>
            </book>
            <book>
                <title series="cookbook">ActionScript 3.0 Cookbook</title>
                <authors>Lott, Schall, and Peters</authors>
            </book>
            <book>
                <title series="animal">Essential ActionScript 3.0</title>
                <authors>Moock</authors>
            </book>
        </books>
    </root>;
```

The first node, the *root* node, is a requirement of XML. Although its presence is confirmed, it's basically ignored when it comes to parsing. For this reason, some developers prefer to assign it an obvious name, such as "root" (as in this case) or "wrapper," to reinforce that they should skip it when referencing content.

So, to reference a node, start with the XML object as a whole, and then continue to add nested children until you get what you want. You'll learn what to do when you have more than one node with the same name in the same parent tag but for now, look at a simple example. Only one node's called whatsnew, so that node's address is products.whatsnew. Tracing that content in the following script reveals that all data contained in that node is referenced:

```
trace(products.whatsnew);
/*
<whatsnew>
    <promotion>Fall Sale</promotion>
</whatsnew>
*/
```

Other examples include:

- books: products.books
- book: products.books.book
- title: products.books.book.title

If you wish to store a reference to an element node, its data type is XMLList. This is the class used to work with one or more content nodes of the XML object, and will be discussed in "16.5 Working with Multiple Nodes of the Same Name" on page 362. Once you have a reference, you can then parse the content of that particular node.

```
var bks:XMLList = products.whatsnew;
trace(bks.promotion);
```

16.4 Reading a Text Node

Problem

You want to access text nested within an element node.

Solution

Use the familiar dot-syntax object model introduced in ActionScript 3.0 to work with XML, and use the text() method to target a text node.

Discussion

Reading a text node is essentially the same as reading an element node. However, you should remember one subtlety that. When you read an element node that contains no children (also known as *simple content*), ActionScript nicely returns that node's content. The result of reading that node appears to be a String, and even behaves like a String for your convenience. For example, consider the following manipulations of the **season** element node of this chapter's sample XML:

```
trace(products.season);
//Fall;
trace(products.season.charAt(0));
//F
```

Note that even the **String** method **charAt()** functioned correctly when applied to the **season** node, even though it's an element. You can verify the node's element status using the **nodeKind()** method:

```
trace(products.season.nodeKind());
//element
```

This on-the-fly casting is a nice feature when you're dealing with simple content. You can work with the element or its content, based on your own needs. If, however, you specifically need to work with a text node, you need to take an extra step. One such step is to use the **text()** method.

```
trace(products.season.text());
//Fall
trace(products.season.text().nodeKind());
//text
```

Usually you don't need this extra step because ActionScript automatically returns the content of an element node, if it has no children. Furthermore, you can't logically think of complex content (child element nodes) as text, so this characteristic isn't really a limitation. (This issue may be unintentional, as when HTML tags are interpreted as XML child nodes, but this issue's discussed in "16.9 Reading HTML or Entities in XML Nodes" on page 367.)

However, you may still wish to occasionally take the extra step to use the **text()** method to work with text nodes, because of its main purpose. It was designed to create an **XMLList** of text nodes, as explained in the following recipe.

See Also

"16.3 Reading an Element Node" on page 359 for reading element nodes.

16.5 Working with Multiple Nodes of the Same Name

Problem

You want to easily work through one or more nodes of the same name in one data structure.

Solution

Create an instance of the XMLList class by targeting the desired repeating element.

Discussion

One of the ActionScript 3.0's XML implementation's most spectacular features is that it can automatically traverse an XML structure and create a list of all occurrences of a specific node. For clarity of discussion, take another look at this chapter's sample XML:

```
var products:XML =
    <root>
        <season quarter="3">Fall</season>
        <whatsnew>
            <promotion>Fall Sale</promotion>
        </whatsnew>
        <books>
            <book>
                <title series="learning">Learning ActionScript 3.0</title>
                <authors>Shupe and Rosser</authors>
            </book>
            <book>
                <title series="cookbook">ActionScript 3.0 Cookbook</title>
                <authors>Lott, Schall, and Peters</authors>
            </book>
            <book>
                <title series="animal">Essential ActionScript 3.0</title>
                <authors>Moock</authors>
            </book>
        </books>
    </root>;
```

If you look closely, you see that a book node is repeated three times and, thanks to the design of this XML document, each node's contents are consistent. As you can see, title appears in each of these nodes.

Previously, to get to all title nodes, you had to do a bit of juggling. Most often, you could traverse either up or down the tree storing references each time you reached a title node, or create a copy of the most relevant portion of the XML, and then delete unwanted elements. What a pain. Now, with the magic of ActionScript 3.0, you can automatically create a list of all like nodes:

```
var bookTitles:XMLList = products.books.book.title;
trace(bookTitles);
/*
<title series="learning">Learning ActionScript 3.0</title>
<title series="cookbook">ActionScript 3.0 Cookbook</title>
<title series="animal">Essential ActionScript 3.0</title>
*/
```

Since an XMLList instance behaves like an array, you can work with individual nodes in the list.

```
trace(bookTitles[0]);
//Learning ActionScript 3.0
```

One of the things you should watch out for, however, is that length, an array property that returns the number of items in the array, is actually a *method* when you use it on an instance of the XMLList class.

```
trace(bookTitles.length());
//3
```

For data typing purposes, note that even a single node is typed as an XMLList instance, because it's *possible* for more than one node of the same name to exist.

```
trace(products.season is XMLList);
//true
```

Finally, as mentioned in the previous recipe, the text() method creates an XMLList of text nodes (ActionScript's trace() method doesn't insert commas into list output):

```
var titleTxt:XMLList = products.books.book.title.text();
trace(titleTxt);
//Learning ActionScript 3.0ActionScript 3.0 CookbookEssential ActionScript 3.0
trace(titleTxt[0]);
//Learning ActionScript 3.0;
```

16.6 Reading an Attribute

Problem

You want to read an attribute from an element node.

Solution

Use the attribute (@) operator.

Discussion

Attributes are properties found within a node, just like similar properties found within HTML tags. An example in this chapter's sample XML is the `quarter` attribute of the `season` node.

```
<season quarter="3">Fall</season>
```

You can target attributes with the same dot syntax used for element nodes, simply by preceding the attribute name with an *at* symbol (`@`).

```
trace(products.season.@quarter);
//3
```

As with element and text nodes, you can also create an `XMLList` of attributes. (ActionScript's `trace()` method doesn't insert commas into list output):

```
trace(products.books.book.title.@series);
//learningcookbookanimal
```

Finally, if you have an uncooperative attribute name, such as a name containing hyphens, you can use the `attribute()` method to specify the desired attribute. Similarly, if you prefer to remain consistent with the use of the attribute operator, then you can use bracket syntax, as the following hypothetical examples show.

```
simple.example.attribute("hyphenated-name");
simple.example.@["hyphenated-name"];
```

Both these approaches are akin to similar tasks relevant to array manipulation and, as with arrays, are handy for working with dynamically generated names. For example, you could use a `for` loop to loop through a series of numbered attributes:

```
simple.example.attribute("attname" + i);
simple.example.@["attname" + i];
```

See Also

"16.3 Reading an Element Node" on page 359 for reading an element node.

16.7 Finding Content Using Shorthand

Problem

You want to work with content nodes in an XML object without knowing their exact locations.

Solution

Use the descendent (..) or wildcard (*) operators.

Discussion

Sometimes you may want to pull data from separate but similar nodes. For example, you may want to retrieve content from all siblings in a particular node, even if they're unique. In this case, you can use a wildcard (the asterisk, *) to stand in for the element node name.

The following example creates an XMLList of all text nodes within the first book node of this chapter's sample XML. First, revisit the XML, reproduced here:

```
var products:XML =
    <root>
        <season quarter="3">Fall</season>
        <whatsnew>
            <promotion>Fall Sale</promotion>
        </whatsnew>
        <books>
            <book>
                <title series="learning">Learning ActionScript 3.0</title>
                <authors>Shupe and Rosser</authors>
            </book>
            <book>
                <title series="cookbook">ActionScript 3.0 Cookbook</title>
                <authors>Lott, Schall, and Peters</authors>
            </book>
            <book>
                <title series="animal">Essential ActionScript 3.0</title>
                <authors>Moock</authors>
            </book>
        </books>
    </root>;
```

Note that the child nodes are `title` and `authors`. Due to the wildcard, the text from both of these nodes is retrieved.

```
trace(products.books.book[0].*.text());
//Learning ActionScript 3.0Shupe and Rosser
```

In fact, the `book` node itself is an XMLList containing three books. Omitting the bracket and zero index in the preceding script segment returns the title and authors for all three books, easily storable in one XMLList instance, if you want.

The descendent operator, two dots (..), functions in a somewhat similar manner, but stands in for nested levels of nodes. The operator traverses the XML object looking for any specified node, wherever it may be. The following snippet, for example, returns an XMLList of all three titles, even though title isn't at the root of the XML object. Instead, the first level (books) and second level (book) are both traversed to find title in the third level of the XML structure.

```
trace(products..title);
```

See Also

"16.3 Reading an Element Node" on page 359 and "16.4 Reading a Text Node" on page 360 for reading element and text nodes.

16.8 Finding Content Using Conditionals

Problem

You want to retrieve one or more nodes based on a specific value.

Solution

Filter content by element or attribute value using logical comparisons.

Discussion

Another ActionScript 3.0 XML gem is the ability to filter content when retrieving it. A simple test, like those in a basic if statement, can be added to the dot syntax address, and only nodes satisfying that test are returned. You just have to wrap the test in parentheses, and then place the entire expression where the original object would have been.

The following examples retrieve single element nodes based first on the value of another element node, and second based on the value of an attribute. For comparison, however, start with the same path to these items, without the conditionals:

```
//products.books.book.authors
//products.books.book.title.@series
```

The first path references an XMLList of all authors nodes in all book nodes, and the second creates an XMLList of all series attributes in all title nodes of all book nodes. If you know which specific node you want, then you can use bracket syntax and specify an index. If you don't know that information, however, or you want to find every occurrence that satisfies a test, you can rely on conditionals. Using the conditionals filters the content, resulting in the return of only one node in each example.

```
trace(products.books.book.(authors=="Shupe and Rosser"));
/*
<book>
    <title series="learning">Learning ActionScript 3.0</title>
    <authors>Shupe and Rosser</authors>
</book>
*/

trace(products.books.book.title.(@series=="learning"));
//Learning ActionScript 3.0
```

See Also

"16.3 Reading an Element Node" on page 359 for reading an element node and "16.6 Reading an Attribute" on page 363 for reading an attribute.

16.9 Reading HTML or Entities in XML Nodes

Problem

You want to parse an XML object so enclosed XML-valid entities appear correctly, and enclosed HTML isn't interpreted as XML child nodes.

Solution

Use XML-valid entity encoding or enclose content that could be interpreted as XML within a CDATA tag.

Discussion

If you use characters in your data that are also part of the XML specification, they'll probably cause errors or unpredictable behavior because they'll be misinterpreted as part of the XML structure rather than as part of the content. XML has five entities, shown in Table 16-1 in both original and encoded forms.

Table 16-1. The five entities included in the XML specification

Entity	Encoded Form	Notes
<	<	less than
>	>	greater than
&	&	ampersand
'	'	apostrophe
"	"	quotation mark

The following shows how to represent the apostrophe using entity encoding.

```
//incorrect: <publisher>O'Reilly</publisher>
//correct: <publisher>O&apos;Reilly</publisher>
```

You can also successfully include XML-invalid text in a text node by using the
`<![CDATA[ ]]>` tag. This structure basically tells the XML parser to ignore everything within its inner brackets, and treat that content like regular text. You
can use this structure well when you allow HTML tags in an XML text node.
XML nodes are bounded by the < and > signs just like HTML tags are, so the
HTML is thought to be one or more nested XML nodes. The following example
includes both the normal apostrophe and the HTML underline tags without
entity encoding, because it's wrapped within a CDATA tag.

```
//incorrect: <publisher><u>O'Reilly</u></publisher>
//correct: <publisher><![CDATA[<u>O'Reilly</u>]]></publisher>
```

You can encode the < and > signs too, of course, but it can be quite tedious.
The following example adds a publisher node to all book nodes of this chapter's sample XML, and demonstrates the three examples of including XML-
invalid content in text nodes. The last part of the script dynamically creates a
text field, and then populates it with HTML to show that the nested underline
tags aren't misinterpreted.

```
var products:XML =
    <root>
        <season quarter="3">Fall</season>
        <whatsnew>
            <promotion>Fall Sale</promotion>
        </whatsnew>
        <books>
            <book>
                <title series="learning">Learning ActionScript 3.0</title>
                <authors>Shupe and Rosser</authors>
                <publisher>O&apos;Reilly</publisher>
            </book>
            <book>
                <title series="cookbook">ActionScript 3.0 Cookbook</title>
                <authors>Lott, Schall, and Peters</authors>
                <publisher><![CDATA[<u>O'Reilly</u>]]></publisher>
            </book>
            <book>
                <title series="animal">Essential ActionScript 3.0</title>
                <authors>Moock</authors>
                <publisher>&lt;u&gt;O&apos;Reilly&lt;/u&gt;</publisher>
            </book>
        </books>
    </root>;

var txtFld:TextField = new TextField();
addChild(txtFld);
```

```
txtFld.type = TextFieldType.DYNAMIC;
txtFld.htmlText = products.books.book[1].publisher;
```

16.10 Deleting XML

Problem

You want to remove nodes from an XML object.

Solution

Use the delete operator.

Discussion

Sometimes it's easier to delete unwanted XML content than to reference extensive amounts of desired content in an XML instance. In those cases, you can use the delete operator to delete an element, text node, or attribute. The syntax for identifying the XML object in question is the same as referencing it, and the delete operator then precedes this path.

```
delete products.whatsnew;
```

This process is also useful when writing XML, which is discussed in the next recipe.

See Also

"16.11 Writing XML" on page 369 for writing content.

16.11 Writing XML

Problem

You want to dynamically build an XML object at runtime.

Solution

Adapt XML reading techniques to writing content, and consider adding the use of methods such as appendChild(), prependChild(), and insertChild After().

Discussion

You'll often find it convenient to write XML, either for use within the same SWF file, transmission to a database, or even to save to an external file. Most of the tasks you need to write XML are identical to reading the same XML object, except that you find the path to the object on the left side of an equal sign.

To demonstrate each of the major writing techniques, this recipe adds new content to the ongoing sample used throughout this chapter. Excerpts from the XML, enclosed in comments to separate the resulting XML from the ActionScript, demonstrate these techniques. At the end of the recipe, the new content is shown fully assembled. This recipe begins by using writing techniques similar to those used in reading XML.

Writing an element node without any additional qualifying information places the node at the end of the XML object. Here, you can see that a `shirts` node is added to the end of the object, just before the close of the `root` node. (The ellipsis at the start of the comment indicates that output has been removed for the sake of brevity.)

```
products.shirts = <shirts />;
/*
    ...
    </books>
    <shirts/>
</root>
*/
```

Writing a text node simply requires that you add text as a child to an existing element node. (You can also add both element and text nodes simultaneously, as demonstrated in a moment.)

```
products.shirts.tshirt = "Lemur";
/*
<shirts>
    <tshirt>Lemur</tshirt>
</shirts>
*/
```

Adding an attribute requires only the target node and content.

```
products.shirts.tshirt.@size = "XL";
/*
<tshirt size="XL">Lemur</tshirt>
*/
```

You can also write content using methods. The `appendChild()` method is like the first example in this recipe, in that it adds the child to the end of the node to which the method's attached.

```
products.shirts.appendChild(<tank />);
/*
<shirts>
    <tshirt size="XL">Lemur</tshirt>
    <tank/>
</shirts>
*/
```

The prependChild() method offers new functionality by adding the new node to the beginning of the node to which the method is attached.

```
products.shirts.prependChild(<longsleeve />);
/*
<shirts>
    <longsleeve/>
    <tshirt size="XL">Lemur</tshirt>
    <tank/>
</shirts>
*/
```

Finally, the insertChildAfter() method lets you add a node after any specific node. That is, rather than automatically adding to the end of the node to which the method is attached, it's added immediately after the sibling node specified in the method's first parameter.

```
products.shirts.insertChildAfter(products.shirts.tshirt, <onesie/>);
/*
<shirts>
    <longsleeve/>
    <tshirt size="XL">Lemur</tshirt>
    <onesie/>
    <tank/>
</shirts>
*/
```

Including the delete process from "16.10 Deleting XML" on page 369, the altered products XML object should now look like this:

```
<root>
    <season quarter="3">Fall</season>
    <books>
        <book>
            <title series="learning">Learning ActionScript 3.0</title>
            <authors>Shupe and Rosser</authors>
        </book>
        <book>
            <title series="cookbook">ActionScript 3.0 Cookbook</title>
            <authors>Lott, Schall, and Peters</authors>
        </book>
        <book>
            <title series="animal">Essential ActionScript 3.0</title>
            <authors>Moock</authors>
        </book>
    </books>
```

```
<shirts>
    <longsleeve/>
    <tshirt size="XL">Lemur</tshirt>
    <onesie/>
    <tank/>
</shirts>
</root>
```

See Also

"16.3 Reading an Element Node" on page 359, "16.4 Reading a Text Node" on page 360, and "16.6 Reading an Attribute" on page 363 for relevant XML reading techniques, as well as "16.10 Deleting XML" on page 369 for deleting XML content.

16.12 Writing XML with Variables

Problem

You want to use variables, or other dynamic data, when writing XML.

Solution

Wrap dynamic content in braces ({}).

Discussion

If you review "16.1 Creating an XML Object" on page 356, which discussed creating an XML object, it's probably not much of a stretch to imagine using a variable to write dynamic content in the second method, because you could perform any String operation on the content before sending it to the constructor of the XML class. Here's an example adapted from "16.1 Creating an XML Object" on page 356:

```
var uName:String = "Clint Ruin"

var xmlString:String = "<root><username>" + uName + "</username></root>"
var xml:XML = new XML(xmlString);
```

However, another technique is not as obvious. You can also use variables to populate XML content node by node, including element nodes, text nodes, and attributes. To do so, you need only enclose the variable in braces to prevent the XML class parser from seeing the variable name as an XML object name.

Adapting the preceding code snippet, you would use the uName variable this way to write a text node:

```
var uName:String = "Clint Ruin";
var userxml:XML =
    <root>
        <username>{uName}</username>
    </root>;
```

Here's an expanded example demonstrating the addition of an element node, an attribute, and an attribute value. It is certainly unlikely that you would need to do all this dynamically. With this approach, you typically add text nodes or attribute values. However, this example shows that you can dynamically create any of these XML objects.

```
var uName:String = "Clint Ruin";
var reg:XML = <registered/>;
var psswrd:String = "DJ_OTESFU";
var versionAttr:String = "current";

var user:XML =
    <root>
        <username>{uName}</username>
        {reg}
        <password {versionAttr}={psswrd}/>
    </root>;

trace(user);
/*
<root>
  <username>J. G. Thirlwell</username>
  <registered/>
  <password current="DJ_OTESFU"/>
</root>
*/
```

See Also

"16.1 Creating an XML Object" on page 356 for creating an XML object.

16.13 Sending and Loading XML

Problem

You want to send XML to a server, and process XML received from a response.

Solution

Configure a URLRequest instance, and use the load() method of the URL Loader class.

Discussion

XML is ideal for transferring data to and from a server. This very basic example sends XML to a PHP script that saves a file to the server, and then returns an XML object in response. This example is taken from *Learning ActionScript 3.0* by Rich Shupe and Zevan Rosser (O'Reilly), and used by permission.

The first block of the script creates an XML object from a string, as shown in "16.1 Creating an XML Object" on page 356. The second block creates another XML object to contain the XML returned from the server after submission.

The third block creates a `URLRequest` instance, as in "16.2 Loading XML" on page 357 but, this time, configures the instance for sending as well as loading. It specifies the server script location, attaches the XML to the `data` property, sets the `contentType` of the submission to "text/xml," and then specifies the `POST` method for transmission.

The fourth block creates an instance of the `URLLoader`, which you also saw in "16.2 Loading XML" on page 357, as well as adds event listeners for the completion of the response loading, and for the unfortunate possibility of an IO error—both of whose functions are explained after the script.

ActionScript

```
var respTxt:TextField = new TextField();
respTxt.type = TextFieldType.DYNAMIC;
addChild(respTxt);

var xmlString:String = "<?xml version='1.0' encoding= ¬
    'ISO-8859-1'?><root><value>Sally</value><value>Claire</value></root>"
var kids:XML = new XML(xmlString);

var xmlResponse:XML;

var xmlURLReq:URLRequest = new URLRequest(¬
    "http://<your domain>/savexml.php");
xmlURLReq.data = kids;
xmlURLReq.contentType = "text/xml";
xmlURLReq.method = URLRequestMethod.POST;

var xmlSendLoad:URLLoader = new URLLoader();
xmlSendLoad.addEventListener(Event.COMPLETE, onComplete, false, ¬
    0, true);
xmlSendLoad.addEventListener(IOErrorEvent.IO_ERROR, onIOError, false, ¬
    0, true);
xmlSendLoad.load(xmlURLReq);

function onComplete(evt:Event):void {
    try {
        xmlResponse = new XML(evt.target.data);
        respTxt.text = xmlResponse.status;
```

```
            removeEventListener(Event.COMPLETE, onComplete);
            removeEventListener(IOErrorEvent.IO_ERROR, onIOError);
        } catch (err:TypeError) {
            respTxt.text = "An error occured when communicating ¬
                with server:\n" + err.message;
        }
    }

    function onIOError(evt:IOErrorEvent):void {
        respTxt.text = "An error occurred when attempting to load ¬
            the XML.\n" + evt.text;
    }
```

The last two blocks of the ActionScript are the listener functions. When the response is completely loaded, onComplete() is triggered. This function attempts to create an XML object from the response received, put the status node into a text field, and remove both listeners as an example of good memory management. (This example assumes the data will be sent to the server only once, so you won't need the listeners later.) If XML isn't returned successfully from the server, then an alternate message is placed in the text field. A similar error message is placed in the field in the event of an IO error.

Although explaining PHP in depth is beyond the scope of this book, the following simple script is the server component of the example. It receives the incoming data, writes it to a file called *data.txt* in the same directory as the PHP script, and then sends back one of two messages, both formatted as an XML compliant string with the message wrapped in a status node. If successful, the script sends back "File saved." If not successful, the script sends back one possible explanation for the error, "PHP write error. Check permissions."

PHP

```php
<?php

if (isset($GLOBALS["HTTP_RAW_POST_DATA"])){
    $data = $GLOBALS["HTTP_RAW_POST_DATA"];

    $file = fopen("data.txt","w");
    fwrite($file, $data);
    fclose($file);

    if (!$file) {
        echo("<root><status>PHP write error. Check ¬
            permissions.</status></root>");
    } else {
        echo("<root><status>File saved.</status></root>");
    }
}

?>
```

You certainly don't have to save XML files to a server to use the send and load feature. In fact, you're much more likely to send XML to a database or other server script such as a login mechanism. However, this tidy example demonstrates the requisite features, and you can take it from here.

CHAPTER 17

How Do I Work with External Assets?

17.0 Introduction

Flash is capable of many tasks by only using assets that have been created or imported into the authoring environment. However, one of its greatest strengths is its ability to work with external assets at runtime. Flash Player can load several kinds of assets including plain text, XML, HTML, CSS, URL-encoded variables, images, sound, video, and other SWF files, to name some examples. It can even load raw binary data.

This chapter provides a brief overview of loading and unloading a few of these external asset types. You can do very different things with each asset type, depending on the asset, security restrictions, and the version of Flash Player you're targeting. However, the recipes here should give you some idea of what's possible, as well as warn you about some possible pitfalls, to help you along the way.

To improve your memory management efforts, and to save some possible debugging time, you should know a little about how Flash Player 9 and later flushes objects from RAM. In short, you can't immediately remove something from memory. Instead, Flash Player uses a process called garbage collection. When an object is no longer in use, Flash Player marks it for collection. Subsequently, during an optimal low in processor demand, the garbage collector sweeps through and collects all objects previously marked for removal.

Unlike your neighborhood trash removal service, however, you can't predict when garbage collection will occur, and you can't reliably force the process. As long as you're aware of how this system works, you should be able to maintain your code that improves your chances of efficient memory management and more effective garbage collection.

17.1 Loading and Applying a Cascading Style Sheet

Problem

You want to apply the same text styling to one or more text fields, particularly those containing HTML-based content from internal or external sources.

Solution

Use the URLLoader class to load an external Cascading Style Sheet (CSS) into an instance of the StyleSheet class, and apply the latter instance to text fields.

Discussion

The URLLoader class can load plain text, name/value pair variables (such as those in a URL), or binary data. As seen in the first block of the following script, this example uses two such loaders—one for an external HTML file and one for an external CSS document—and a StyleSheet instance to contain the data from the CSS file.

The following two functions are very similar, loading first the CSS document, then the HTML document. In both cases, event listeners for load complete and input/output (IO) errors are added, and the content's loaded. If either process generates an IO error, the onIOErr() function at the end of the script is called.

When the CSS document is loaded, the onCSSLoaded() listener function creates a StyleSheet instance, parses the loaded CSS document to create the requisite styles, and then repeats the loading process for the HTML file.

When the HTML file is loaded, the onLoadHTML() listener function stores the incoming HTML in a local variable, creates a text field, and then sets several basic text field properties (discussed in Chapter 14). It also applies the style sheet, populates the htmlText property with the loaded HTML data, and adds the field to the display list. Finally, the function removes all listeners you don't need any more.

```
var htmlFile:URLLoader;
var cssStyles:StyleSheet;
var cssFile:URLLoader;

function loadCSS() {
    cssFile = new URLLoader();
    cssFile.addEventListener(Event.COMPLETE, onCSSLoaded, false, 0, true);
    cssFile.addEventListener(IOErrorEvent.IO_ERROR, onIOErr, false, 0, true);
    cssFile.load(new URLRequest("demo.css"));
```

```
    }
    loadCSS();

    function onCSSLoaded (evt:Event):void {
        cssStyles = new StyleSheet();
        cssStyles.parseCSS(evt.target.data);
        htmlFile = new URLLoader();
        htmlFile.addEventListener(Event.COMPLETE, onHTMLLoaded, false, 0, true);
        htmlFile.addEventListener(IOErrorEvent.IO_ERROR, onIOErr, false, 0, true);
        htmlFile.load(new URLRequest("demo.html"));
    }

    function onHTMLLoaded(evt:Event):void {
        var htmlData:String = evt.target.data;
        var txtFld = new TextField();
        txtFld.width = 550;
        txtFld.multiline = true;
        txtFld.wordWrap = true;
        txtFld.autoSize = TextFieldAutoSize.LEFT;
        txtFld.selectable = false;
        txtFld.styleSheet = cssStyles;
        txtFld.htmlText = htmlData;
        addChild(txtFld);

        cssFile.removeEventListener(Event.COMPLETE, onCSSLoaded);
        cssFile.removeEventListener(IOErrorEvent.IO_ERROR, onIOErr);
        htmlFile.removeEventListener(Event.COMPLETE, onHTMLLoaded);
        htmlFile.removeEventListener(IOErrorEvent.IO_ERROR, onIOErr);
    }

    function onIOErr(evt:IOErrorEvent):void {
        trace("A loading error occurred:", evt.text);
    }
```

 You must apply a StyleSheet instance to a text field before populating it with text.

Samples of HTML and CSS files required for this exercise to work, follow:

HTML: *demo.html*

```
<body>
<span class='heading'>Use CSS to Style Text</span><br/>
<span class='subheading'>A Simple Example</span><br/>
<p>Lorem ipsum dolor sit amet,sed do eiusmod tempor incididunt ut
 labore et dolore magna aliqua. Ut enim ad minim veniam, quis nostrud exercitation
 ullamco laboris nisi ut aliquip ex ea commodo consequat.</p>
</body>
```

CSS: *demo.css*

```
body {
    font-family: Verdana;
    margin-left: 6px;
    margin-right: 6px;
}

p {
    text-indent: 20px;
}

.heading {
    font-size: 18px;
    font-weight: bold;
    letter-spacing: 1px;
    color: #FF6633;
}

.subheading {
    font-size: 14px;
    font-style: italic;
    text-align: right;
}
```

See Also

"15.1 Creating a Text Field" on page 334 for creating a text field, "15.5 Populating a Text Field" on page 338 for populating a text field, "15.6 Automatically Sizing a Text Field" on page 339 for auto-sizing a text field, "15.10 Formatting Text Using HTML" on page 346 for supported HTML, "15.11 Formatting Text Using CSS" on page 348 for supported CSS.

17.2 Loading and Displaying an Image or SWF File

Problem

You want to display an image or SWF from an external source.

Solution

Use the Loader class to load an external JPG, GIF, PNG, or SWF file, and then add it to the display list.

Discussion

You can fairly simply load a display object, such as an image or SWF file. You need to start with an instance of the Loader class, and then use its load() method to load the content. Consistency is a hallmark of ActionScript 3.0. You must use a URLRequest instance for every URL.

Then you add the image or SWF file to the display list after the load is complete. You add it by using the addChild() method inside an event listener function that triggers when the Event.COMPLETE event is received. This event's not available to the Loader instance, but rather to the related LoaderInfo class. You can immediately access an instance of this class by using the contentLoaderInfo property of the Loader you created, so you don't have to instantiate another class.

After the load complete event is received, the image is added to the display list. Since the event listener was added to the contentLoaderInfo property, rather than the Loader itself, you must add the evt.target.content to the display list, rather than the more typical evt.target. For more information, see Chapter 14.

```
var ldr:Loader = new Loader();
ldr.load(new URLRequest("loadMe.jpg"));

ldr.contentLoaderInfo.addEventListener(Event.COMPLETE, ¬
    onLoaded, false, 0, true);
function onLoaded(evt:Event):void {
    addChild(evt.target.content);
    evt.target.removeEventListener(Event.COMPLETE, onLoaded);
}
```

Although this example loads an image, loading a SWF file uses the same syntax. You need only change the path inside the URLRequest to resolve to a SWF file. However, you may wish to consider other additional features. For example, when loading a SWF file, you may want to delay display or further action until the SWF file has fully initialized. The next recipe demonstrates this approach.

See Also

"17.3 Communicating with an ActionScript 3.0 Loaded SWF" on page 382 for information about working with loaded content after it is loaded or initialized.

17.3 Communicating with an ActionScript 3.0 Loaded SWF

Problem

Having loaded a SWF file that was coded using ActionScript 3.0, you want to communicate between the parent and the loaded SWF file.

Solution

Cast the content of a Loader instance as a movie clip and get or set properties, or invoke methods, of that movie clip.

Discussion

When you load a SWF file into a Loader instance, the content of that instance contains the SWF file and all data therein. Essentially, the main timeline of the loaded SWF file is a movie clip, so you can access the methods or properties of the loaded SWF file the same way you access similar attributes of a movie clip. Hereafter, the host, or parent, SWF file is called "Loader" and the loaded SWF is called "Loadee."

Loadee: *loadee.swf*

Starting with the loaded content, you need a SWF file named *loadee.swf*. To demonstrate a variety of communication tasks, the file should include a pre-created animated movie clip called *anim* on the stage and the following script.

The first line stops the movie clip from playing so that another SWF file may start it later. The first function traces a hard-coded string to the Output panel. The second function accepts a string argument from a function call, and traces a new string that includes that argument value. The last function also accepts an argument value, but this time it's a number, and the function returns a new value (adding 1 to the incoming value) to the script from which it was called. None of the functions are called within the loadee.

```
anim.stop();

function sayHello():void {
    trace("Hello, from your loadee!");
}

function showMsg(msg:String=""):void {
    trace("Loadee here again. You said, '" + msg + "'");
}
```

```
function returnSum(num:Number=0):Number {
    return (num + 1);
}
```

Loader: *loader.swf*

The loadee is then loaded into a host, or parent, SWF file. To do so, you must create an instance of the Loader class, add it to the display list, and then load the desired content, as the first block of the following script shows.

In order to communicate with the new SWF file, it must be fully loaded. Listen for an Event.COMPLETE event before proceeding, to make sure the content is loaded.

```
var loader:Loader = new Loader();
addChild(loader);
loader.load(new URLRequest("loadee.swf"));

loader.contentLoaderInfo.addEventListener(Event.COMPLETE, callLoadee, ¬
    false, 0, true);
function callLoadee(evt:Event):void {
    var loadee:MovieClip = MovieClip(loader.content);
    loadee.anim.play();
    loadee.sayHello();
    loadee.showMsg("Hi, from Loader!");
    trace("Loader sent 1 to Loadee and got back:", loadee.returnSum(1));
    evt.target.removeEventListener(Event.INIT, callLoadee);
}
```

The first line of the callLoadee() function stores a reference to the loaded content, rather than the existing Loader instance. The casting to MovieClip is required because a Loader instance can also load images, for which such communication attempts don't apply. As such, the compiler must know your property and method access is legal.

The second line targets the animated movie clip, and tells it to play. Because the clip was initially stopped, if it plays when loaded, then you know this method did its job.

The third line calls a function in the loaded SWF file. The result is the tracing of the string, "Hello, from your loadee!" The fourth line accomplishes a similar task but passes a value into the loadee to vary the outcome of the function. The result is the tracing of the modified string, "Loadee here again. You said, 'Hi, from Loader!'"

Finally, the last line of callLoadee() also calls a function and passes in a value to affect its outcome. However, in this case, a value is returned to the parent SWF file. Passing in 1 returns a value of 2, at which point the parent traces,

"Loader sent 1 to Loadee and got back: 2" to the Output panel. This demonstrates round-trip communication and getting data from a loaded SWF file.

 You can add a Loader instance without content to the display list without generating an error. However, if you prefer, you can add the instance to the display list with an event listener after the loader issues an Event.COMPLETE event (indicating the content has been loaded).

See Also

"17.2 Loading and Displaying an Image or SWF File" on page 380 for loading a SWF.

17.4 Communicating with an ActionScript 2.0 Loaded SWF

Problem

Having loaded a SWF file that was coded using ActionScript 2.0, you want to communicate between the parent and the loaded SWF file.

Solution

Use a LocalConnection object to communicate between host and loaded SWF file.

Discussion

Although ActionScript 3.0 can easily load SWF files created using ActionScript 2.0, the two versions of the language can't coexist in the same file. ActionScript 3.0 was written from the ground up and exists in its own virtual machine—a player within a player, if you will—in Flash Player.

As such, an ActionScript 3.0 SWF file can't communicate directly with an ActionScript 2.0 SWF file. One way you can get around this limitation is to use a LocalConnection object. Just as you can use local connections to communicate between multiple SWF files in a browser window, or between SWF file and projector, you can use the technique to communicate between ActionScript Virtual Machine 2 (AVM2, used for ActionScript 3.0) and AVM1

(ActionScript 1.0/2.0). Note that an ActionScript 3.0 SWF file can load an ActionScript 2.0 SWF file, but the reverse isn't possible.

This example shows how to control an animation and trigger a function, while passing data into the AVM1 SWF file. To test all functionality, you need an animated movie clip in the loaded SWF file.

Starting with the host, or parent SWF file, the first step in this process is to load the SWF file. In this case, the loaded SWF file is named *as2.swf*, and the parent SWF file, although not referenced by filename in the script, is *as3.swf*.

In this example, the communication is triggered by a button click, but it's still a good idea to enable this functionality only after the loaded content is ready. Otherwise, you may initiate communication prematurely and encounter an unresponsive button or even errors. Here, the local connection, button, and event listener are all created only after the receipt of the init event, as you see in the previous recipe. The listener's contents are explained after the script.

Hereafter, the host, or parent, SWF file is called "Loader" and the loaded SWF file is called "Loadee."

Loader: *as3.swf*

```
var loader:Loader = new Loader();
loader.load(new URLRequest("as2.swf"));
addChild(loader);

loader.contentLoaderInfo.addEventListener(Event.INIT, onInit, false, 0, true);
function onInit(evt:Event):void {
    var as3as2LC:LocalConnection = new LocalConnection();

    var sendBtn:Sprite = new Sprite();
    sendBtn.buttonMode = true;
    sendBtn.graphics.beginFill(0x000099);
    sendBtn.graphics.drawCircle(0, 0, 15);
    sendBtn.graphics.endFill();
    sendBtn.x = sendBtn.y = 30;
    addChild(sendBtn);

    sendBtn.addEventListener(MouseEvent.CLICK, onSendBtn);
    function onSendBtn(evt:MouseEvent):void {
        as3as2LC.send("crossVM","playClip");
        as3as2LC.send("crossVM","showMsg", "Hello, from AS3!");
    }
}
```

The first line of the event listener function initializes the local connection. The second block of the event listener function creates the button used to trigger the communication, and adds it to the display list.

The final block of the event listener function creates the button event listener. When you click the button, two messages go through the local connection. This step uses the send() method of the LocalConnection instance, as3as2LC. The first argument value is the name of the local connection. This connection is like the telephone number or radio channel over which the connected objects communicate, increasing security. Any participating parties must send or receive along this "channel" to successfully communicate. In this case, the host sends over the "crossVM" connection, and the loaded SWF file must connect to this same channel to receive instructions and respond.

The first message sent triggers a function called playClip(), and the second message triggers a function called showMsg() but also passes along the string argument "Hello, from AS3!"

Loadee: *as2.swf*

In the loaded SWF file, the first block of code stops the animated movie clip. The clip is played by instruction issued across the local connection. The variable name used to store the connection in the loadee doesn't have to be the same as the variable used in the parent SWF file. Instead, the correct connection is established because the loadee connects to the same channel created by the loader, "crossVM".

The last two blocks of code are simple functions, but one thing is atypical. Each block is a method of the LocalConnection instance. You can confine access from the connection to only those functions you wish to be executed from a connecting remote SWF file.

```
anim.stop();

var as3as2LC:LocalConnection = new LocalConnection();
as3as2LC.connect("crossVM");

as3as2LC.playClip = function():Void {
    anim.play();
};

as3as2LC.showMsg = function(msg:String):Void {
    if (msg == undefined) { msg = ""; }
    trace("Loadee here. You said, '" + msg + "'");
};
```

See Also

"17.2 Loading and Displaying an Image or SWF File" on page 380 for loading a SWF file.

17.5 Unloading an Image or SWF File

Problem

You want to reduce RAM and performance overhead by unloading an image or SWF file.

Solution

Use the unload() method of the Loader class, but be sure to clean up first by stopping timers, closing streams, removing listeners, and more!

Discussion

The first part of this recipe is simple. A single method unloads a loaded image or SWF file, and the optional additional steps of removing the Loader instance from the display list and nullifying the variable reference are also demonstrated. Hereafter, the host, or parent, SWF file is called "Loader" and the loaded SWF file is called "Loadee."

Loadee: *loadee.swf*

Beginning with the loadee, the first line of the SWF files frame script sets its frame rate to 1 frame per second. This step is only helpful from a tutorial standpoint because it reduces the number of times text will be traced to the Output panel later on during testing.

The next three lines simply draw a maroon circle into the main timeline at point (500, 40) to provide visual feedback to see when the file's loaded and unloaded.

```
stage.frameRate = 1;

this.graphics.beginFill(0x990000);
this.graphics.drawCircle(500, 40, 20);
this.graphics.endFill();
```

Loader: *loader.swf*

Now look at this recipe's host, or parent, SWF file. The first block of the following script loads and displays a SWF file as discussed in "17.2 Loading and Displaying an Image or SWF File" on page 380. The second block creates and displays a sprite that serves as a button. The last block adds an event listener that calls its function when the button sprite is clicked.

The first line of the listener function unloads the Loader instance. The second line removes the instance from the display list, and the last line nullifies the instance so the garbage collector can collect it from memory.

```
var loader:Loader = new Loader();
addChild(loader);
loader.load(new URLRequest("loadee.swf"));

var unloadBtn:Sprite = new Sprite();
unloadBtn.buttonMode = true;
unloadBtn.graphics.beginFill(0x000099);
unloadBtn.graphics.drawCircle(0, 0, 15);
unloadBtn.graphics.endFill();
unloadBtn.x = unloadBtn.y = 30;
addChild(unloadBtn);

unloadBtn.addEventListener(MouseEvent.CLICK, onClick, false, 0, true);
function onClick(evt:MouseEvent):void {
  if (loader != null) {
    loader.unload();
    removeChild(loader);
    loader = null;
  }
}
```

But wait...there's more!

This process appears to be straightforward and, as described, works with simple content such as loaded images in almost every case. However, when it comes to the average loaded SWF file, many problems arise. Put simply, many features, when used, prevent a SWF file from unloading. This recipe covers some of the most common examples of this problem.

This issue's widely discussed, however, so if you run into a situation in which your content isn't unloading, you may be able to find additional information on the web. Grant Skinner, for example, has written several posts about memory management and related topics in his blog. One in particular, covers many of the concerns discussed here, and links to other related topics in his archive: *http://www.gskinner.com/blog/archives/2008/04/failure_to_unlo.html*.

Enter frame events

One of the easiest problems to run into is also one of the easiest problems to miss. If a loaded SWF file contains an enter frame event listener that hasn't been removed, the SWF file can't be unloaded. You can see this in action by adding the following to the loadee script, republishing, and testing the loader/loadee relationship again. This code adds an event listener where none existed before, and then traces a simple string to the Output panel every time an enter frame event occurs.

```
addEventListener(Event.ENTER_FRAME, onLoop, false, 0, true);
function onLoop(evt:Event):void {
    trace("loaded enter frame");
}
```

When you try to unload the SWF file, although the visual feedback appears to show that the content has unloaded, you notice the trace continues forever. You can't unload the SWF file.

The workaround is to be certain you remove all enter frame event listeners before trying to unload the applicable SWF file. One approach to this problem is to add a "clean-up" function to your SWF files. Inside this routine, place any maintenance instructions, such as the removal of event listeners, and call the function before unloading. Here's an example of the function that should be inserted into the loadee.

```
function cleanUp():void {
    removeEventListener(Event.ENTER_FRAME, onLoop);
}
```

The following snippet is an example of code you can add to the parent SWF file, in the existing event listener responsible for triggering the unloading process. The entire attempt is wrapped in a try..catch statement so that any resulting errors can be suppressed from end-user view. The clean-up process is invoked in the first two lines of the try segment.

First a local variable is created to reference the content of loader, as described in "17.3 Communicating with an ActionScript 3.0 Loaded SWF" on page 382. Then the cleanUp() function you added to the loaded SWF file is called prior to unloading.

```
function onClick(evt:MouseEvent):void {
    try {
        var loadee:MovieClip = MovieClip(loader.content);
        loadee.cleanUp();
        loader.unload();
        removeChild(loader);
        loader = null;
    } catch (err:Error) {
        trace("Error unloading:", err.message);
    }
}
```

If you test this improved setup, you find that removing the enter frame event listener before unloading lets the SWF file fully unload. Not only do the visual elements disappear from view, but the tracing caused by the loaded SWF file ceases.

Timers

You can see the same scenario in action with a running timer. If you substitute the enter frame addition to the original loaded SWF file, *loadee.swf*, with this timer addition, then you witness the same behavior. This new code triggers a trace every second.

```
var tmr:Timer = new Timer(1000);
tmr.addEventListener(TimerEvent.TIMER, onTimer, false, 0, true);
tmr.start();
function onTimer(evt:TimerEvent):void {
    trace("loaded timer");
}
```

The solution is similar, but the timer *must* be stopped prior to removing the listener. The garbage collector can't ever collect a running timer. The timer reference should also be nullified after the listener's removed.

```
function cleanUp():void {
    tmr.stop();
    tmr.removeEventListener(TimerEvent.TIMER, onTimer);
    tmr = null;
}
```

Since the host SWF file was set to call the `cleanUp()` function after its button was clicked, no further change to the host is required. Upon adding the preceding code to the loaded SWF file, you find that the tracing ceases and this version can also be collected from memory.

Streams and connections

Unfortunately, the list of steps to remove a SWF file from memory doesn't stop at enter frame and timer listeners. Several other causes may prevent a SWF file from being unloaded, and here are a few of the most common solutions.

Loaded SWFs with Video
Pause and close all `NetStream` instances, remove all related event listeners, and then nullify the `NetStream` instances. Then close all `NetConnection` instances, remove all related event listeners, and nullify the `NetConnection` instances.

Loaded SWFs with Sound
Stop all sounds from playing, close all streams, remove all related listeners, and nullify any `Sound`, and `SoundChannel` instances.

Loaded SWFs with Local Connections
Close all `LocalConnection` instances, remove all related listeners, and nullify the `LocalConnection` instances.

A step in the right direction

Although stated at the outset of this chapter, this section bears repeating. This list of memory management issues and workarounds is by no means complete. However, this peek into the complex world of unloading content in Action-Script 3.0 may give you a head start when it comes to debugging your own projects.

See Also

"17.2 Loading and Displaying an Image or SWF File" on page 380 for loading a SWF file.

17.6 Loading and Playing a Sound

Problem

You want to load and play an external MP3 file.

Solution

Create an instance of the Sound class to load and play the sound, and store the sound in an instance of the SoundChannel class for discrete control.

Discussion

ActionScript 3.0 introduces a much more granular level of control over sound playback. Previously, the Sound class did most of the heavy lifting, but Action-Script 3.0 introduces a few new classes to both add and distribute functionality.

You still begin working with an external MP3 file by creating an instance of the Sound class, loading a file, and playing the sound. People also often wait for the sound to load before playing the file. You do this step in ActionScript 3.0 with an event listener added to the Sound instance, as you see in the following script.

However, a new class is introduced into the equation before the sound is played. The SoundChannel class creates a discrete sound channel that you can control separately from other sound channels (up to 32). When the sound is played, it's played into the new sound channel the way a single musical instrument is assigned to a specific channel in an audio mixing console.

```
var snd:Sound = new Sound();
snd.addEventListener(Event.COMPLETE, onComplete, false, 0, true);
snd.load(new URLRequest("music.mp3"));
```

```
var channel:SoundChannel = new SoundChannel();
function onComplete(evt:Event):void {
    channel = snd.play();
    snd.removeEventListener(Event.COMPLETE, onComplete);
}
```

Finally, after the sound is played into a discrete channel, you no longer need its load complete listener, so it's removed. You can also manipulate ("17.7 Setting the Volume and Pan of a Sound" on page 392) and visualize the sound ("17.8 Visualizing the Amplitude of a Sound" on page 393) without affecting, or being affected by, other sounds in the SWF file.

 "17.6 Loading and Playing a Sound" on page 391 through "17.9 Unloading a Sound" on page 395 can be combined into a single script to demonstrate in one file all the sound features discussed in these recipes.

17.7 Setting the Volume and Pan of a Sound

Problem

You want to change the volume and/or pan (degree of the sound in each of the left and right stereo channels) of a sound.

Solution

Start with the SoundTransform property of the SoundChannel class, and set the values of the volume and pan properties.

Discussion

Building on "17.6 Loading and Playing a Sound" on page 391, this recipe adds volume and pan control. The bolded lines in this recipe's code can be added to the onComplete() function from "17.6 Loading and Playing a Sound" on page 391 to randomly assign a volume and pan level to the sound when it's initially played.

The first bold line creates trans, an instance of another new sound class, SoundTransform, by querying the soundTransform property of the sound channel. Continuing the real-world metaphor started in "17.6 Loading and Playing a Sound" on page 391, using the SoundTransform class (either directly or through a sound channel's soundTransform property) is similar to adjusting the volume slider and/or pan knob on a single channel of an audio mixing console.

These values were formerly in the ActionScript 2.0 Sound class and have been moved to make transforming sounds more consistent with other such alterations, like color transformations, in ActionScript 3.0. As with color transformations, when altering a sound's volume or pan setting you must first edit a transformation instance (either newly created or retrieved from an existing channel, as in this example), and then apply (or reapply) the edited transformation to the sound channel.

```
function onComplete(evt:Event):void {
    channel = snd.play();
    snd.removeEventListener(Event.COMPLETE, onComplete);
    var trans:SoundTransform = channel.soundTransform;
    trans.volume = Math.random();
    trans.pan = Math.random() * 2 - 1;
    channel.soundTransform = trans;
}
```

The second bold line automatically sets the volume of trans to a random number between 0 and 1. The third bold line sets the pan of trans to a random number between –1 and 1.

New to ActionScript 3.0, ranges similar to percentage values (0–100) are now 0 to 1. Values of the volume property range from 0 to 1, and values of the pan property range from –1 to 1. (–1 is far-left, 1 is far-right, and 0 is dead center).

Finally, trans is reapplied to the soundTransform property of channel, resulting in a random volume between mute and full, and a random pan between far-left and far-right each time the SWF file runs.

See Also

"17.6 Loading and Playing a Sound" on page 391 for loading and playing a sound.

17.8 Visualizing the Amplitude of a Sound

Problem

You want to display the amplitude of a sound during playback.

Solution

Use the `leftPeak` and `rightPeak` properties of a sound's channel to control the visual appearance of one or more display objects.

Discussion

This recipe builds on "17.6 Loading and Playing a Sound" on page 391 and "17.7 Setting the Volume and Pan of a Sound" on page 392, and visualizes sound during playback. You can easily do this if you create traditional peak meters that increase in size with a sound's amplitude. The first two blocks of this recipe's script create these peak meters by drawing blue and green sprites (for the left and right stereo channels, respectively), 20 × 100 pixels in size, with a bottom-center registration point.

The last code block contains an event listener that sets the height of these sprites to the value of an ActionScript sound channel's `leftPeak` and `right Peak` properties. These properties contain the left and right stereo amplitudes, respectively, of any sound channel at query time. These values are always between 0 and 1, so multiplying them by 100 yields a maximum height of 100 pixels at full amplitude, and a minimum height of zero during silence.

```
var leftPeakSP:Sprite = createBar(0x0000FF);
leftPeakSP.x = 20;
leftPeakSP.y = 120;
addChild(leftPeakSP);
var rightPeakSP:Sprite = createBar(0x00FF00);
rightPeakSP.x = 50;
rightPeakSP.y = 120;
addChild(rightPeakSP);

function createBar(col:uint):Sprite {
    var sp:Sprite = new Sprite();
    var g:Graphics = sp.graphics;
    g.beginFill(col);
    g.drawRect(0, 0, 20, -100);
    g.endFill();
    return sp;
}

addEventListener(Event.ENTER_FRAME, onLoop, false, 0, true);
function onLoop(evt:Event):void {
    leftPeakSP.height = channel.leftPeak * 100;
    rightPeakSP.height = channel.rightPeak * 100;
}
```

See Also

"17.6 Loading and Playing a Sound" on page 391 for loading and playing a sound and "17.7 Setting the Volume and Pan of a Sound" on page 392 for setting the volume and pan of a sound.

17.9 Unloading a Sound

Problem

To minimize impact on performance and available memory, you want to unload a sound after it has served its purpose.

Solution

Stop the sound, close the sound stream, and nullify the Sound and SoundChannel instances.

Discussion

Building on "17.6 Loading and Playing a Sound" on page 391 through "17.8 Visualizing the Amplitude of a Sound" on page 393, this recipe adds the ability to unload a sound. The first block of code creates a clickable sprite used to unload a sound, and the second block adds an event listener to the sprite that responds when the user clicks on the sprite.

The first step in the listener function is to stop sound playback using the stop() method of the SoundChannel instance. Next, the sound stream is closed. All sound files, whether they're streaming from a server or from a local file, have a stream. This stream essentially refers to the background downloading of file content while the sound is playing.

Closing the stream means you can halt the download process even if data remains to be downloaded. This process is attempted in a try..catch statement because the stream may be fully loaded by the time this instruction is issued. A try..catch statement tries the requested commands, and catches any errors thrown so they can be suppressed from end-user view. For debugging purposes, the statement will trace the error to the Output panel in authoring mode only.

After the channel playback is stopped and the sound stream is closed, you can choose to nullify either or both variables, and remove the enter frame listener (created in the previous recipe) to allow everything to be collected. The remaining four lines are explained after the script passage.

```
var unloadBtn:Sprite = new Sprite();
unloadBtn.buttonMode = true;
unloadBtn.graphics.beginFill(0x990000);
unloadBtn.graphics.drawRect(0, 0, 20, 20);
unloadBtn.graphics.endFill();
unloadBtn.x = 520;
unloadBtn.y = 10;
addChild(unloadBtn);

unloadBtn.addEventListener(MouseEvent.CLICK, onUnloadBtn, false, 0, true);
function onUnloadBtn(evt:MouseEvent):void {
    channel.stop();
    try {
        snd.close();
    } catch (err:IOError) {
        trace("Close stream error:", err.message);
    }

    var trans:SoundTransform = channel.soundTransform;
    trans.volume = 0;
    channel.soundTransform = trans;
    SoundMixer.stopAll();

    channel = null;
    snd = null;

    removeEventListener(Event.ENTER_FRAME, onLoop);
}
```

Depending on how you write your code, you may sometimes find that a sound continues to play even after its stream has been closed, because the portion of the external file that's already been streamed, up to the point of closing the stream, is still eligible for playback.

Stopping playback in the channel may be enough to prevent the sound from continuing to play. If not, you may want to try one or two additional steps. You may also want to mute the sound channel immediately after stopping it, so that if content continues to play it won't be heard, and/or stop all sounds playing through the global SoundMixer class—the last of the new sound classes discussed in this chapter. The SoundMixer class is analogous to the master mixer on an audio mixing console. All discrete sound channels flow through the SoundMixer and, therefore, can be stopped all at once.

See Also

"17.6 Loading and Playing a Sound" on page 391 for loading and playing a sound and "17.7 Setting the Volume and Pan of a Sound" on page 392 for setting the volume and pan of a sound, and "17.8 Visualizing the Amplitude of a Sound" on page 393 for visualizing the amplitude of a sound.

17.10 Loading and Playing a Video

Problem

You want to load and play an external FLV or H.264 video source.

Solution

Create NetConnection and NetStream instances, as well as a Video object for display, and then play the NetStream instance.

Discussion

You have a few ways to play videos in Flash, the simplest of which is to use one of the provided components designed for this purpose. However, in some situations you don't want to commit to the memory/file size to use the components, or you may even be dissatisfied with a component's functionality and want to create your own player.

In these cases, the functionality of a player you create can range from simple to robust, depending on how much time you want to put into coding its features. This recipe covers the bare essentials, adding a few features in descriptive segments. When you've completed this recipe, be sure to look at "17.11 Unloading a Video" on page 399 for information about unloading the video content.

The first step in creating your own ActionScript video player is to create an instance of the Video class, and add it to the display list, to provide you with a display object on which to watch your video. You see this in the first two lines of the following script segment. Describing a real-world parallel, this is like getting a television.

The second step is to instantiate a NetConnection object, as seen in the second two lines of the script. This part lets you connect to a streaming video server, but passing a value of null to the connect() method also lets you work with progressive download video sources. Using a NetConnection is loosely analogous to selecting which video on demand (VOD) service you wish to watch.

The next step is to create a NetStream instance, specifying the NetConnection instance as its argument, and attaching the stream to the Video instance, as seen in lines 5 and 6 of the following script. This step is somewhat akin to selecting which video category offered by the previously selected VOD service to watch (comedy, drama, and so on).

Finally, playing the video of your choice is like choosing and playing the video from the previously selected genre that you want to view.

```
var vid:Video = new Video();
addChild(vid);

var vidConnection:NetConnection = new NetConnection();
vidConnection.connect(null);

var vidStream:NetStream = new NetStream(vidConnection);
vid.attachNetStream(vidStream);

vidStream.play("<your_video_here>.flv");
```

Although the previous bare-bones example works, you may also want to handle automatically triggered events associated with the video. For instance, you may receive notifications or errors associated with metadata embedded or injected into the video, or even data from cue points added when encoding the video.

The following script segment creates an object designed to trap this information to prevent errors from appearing at runtime. This segment creates an object with functions attributed to each of the onMetaData and onCuePoint event handlers. This object is then passed to the client property of the NetStream instance.

As a result, the cited functions respond to incoming metadata and/or cue points. In this example, the duration metadata entry is traced to the Output panel, as well as any cue point text data that may be encoded into the video.

```
var infoClient:Object = new Object();
infoClient.onMetaData = onMetaData;
infoClient.onCuePoint = onCuePoint;
vidStream.client = infoClient;

function onMetaData(info:Object):void {
    trace("duration:", info.duration);
}
function onCuePoint(info:Object):void {
    trace("cuepoint:", info.parameters.text);
}
```

In addition to listening for metadata and cue point information, you may also want to react to any asynchronous errors that may occur when attempting to play a video. This error usually occurs when a server calls a method that the client hasn't defined, so it's handy to have active when scripting a no-frills video player.

The following segment adds event listeners for asynchronous event errors to both the `NetConnection` and `NetStream` objects.

```
vidConnection.addEventListener(AsyncErrorEvent.ASYNC_ERROR, ¬
    onAsyncError, false, 0, true);
vidStream.addEventListener(AsyncErrorEvent.ASYNC_ERROR, ¬
    onAsyncError, false, 0, true);
function onAsyncError(evt:AsyncErrorEvent):void {
    trace(evt.text);
}
```

Finally, if you want your video to do more than just play, then you want to script an accompanying controller. This recipe provides one example of controller functionality by creating a button to toggle the pause state of the video.

```
var pauseBtn:Sprite = new Sprite();
pauseBtn.buttonMode = true;
pauseBtn.graphics.beginFill(0x000099);
pauseBtn.graphics.drawRect(0, 0, 20, 20);
pauseBtn.graphics.endFill();
pauseBtn.y = vid.y + vid.height + 5;
addChild(pauseBtn);

pauseBtn.addEventListener(MouseEvent.CLICK, onPauseToggle, false, ¬
    0, true);
function onPauseToggle(evt:MouseEvent):void {
    vidStream.togglePause();
}
```

See Also

"17.11 Unloading a Video" on page 399 for information about unloading a video.

17.11 Unloading a Video

Problem

You want to unload a video after it has served its purpose.

Solution

Pause and close `NetStream` instances. Close `NetConnection` instances. Remove all listeners and nullify all stream and connection references.

Discussion

Building on "17.10 Loading and Playing a Video" on page 397, this recipe provides a mechanism for unloading the video. The first block of code creates a button to click for unloading, and adds it to the display list. The second block of code creates the button's event listener.

To unload a video, you must first pause and then close the `NetStream` instance (`vidStream`). You must then remove any event listeners added to this instance (such as the asynchronous error listener used in this example) and nullify the instance to let it be collected. You must then close the `NetConnection` instance (`vidConnection`), remove any listeners attached thereto, and nullify that instance to allow it, too, to be collected.

```
var unloadBtn:Sprite = new Sprite();
unloadBtn.buttonMode = true;
unloadBtn.graphics.beginFill(0x990000);
unloadBtn.graphics.drawRect(0, 0, 20, 20);
unloadBtn.graphics.endFill();
unloadBtn.x = vid.width - 20;
unloadBtn.y = vid.y + vid.height + 5;
addChild(unloadBtn);

unloadBtn.addEventListener(MouseEvent.CLICK, onUnloadBtn, false, 0, true);
function onUnloadBtn(evt:MouseEvent):void {
    vidStream.pause();
    vidStream.close();
    vidStream.removeEventListener(AsyncErrorEvent.ASYNC_ERROR, onAsyncError);
    vidStream = null;
    vidConnection.close();
    vidConnection.removeEventListener(AsyncErrorEvent.ASYNC_ERROR, ¬
     onAsyncError);
    vidConnection = null;
    //
    removeChild(vid);
    vid = null;
}
```

Only after all of these steps can the garbage collector remove the video. Finally, if you're also finished with the video object used to display the video, then you can remove it from the display list, remove any relevant event listeners, and nullify that instance, as well.

See Also

"17.10 Loading and Playing a Video" on page 397 for information regarding loading and playing a video.

PART IV

Migration

Part IV distills everything covered in Part I through Part III and applies those skills to the issue of migration—updating legacy projects written in Action-Script 2.0 to shiny new ActionScript 3.0 code.

You'll start by walking through a sample migration of a particle system. The chapter highlights as many migration issues as possible in a simple example, and you'll acquire some practical experience with the various steps required to modernize your code. You'll start to address the important question: should I migrate or rewrite? The answer's not always simple.

The final chapter concludes the book with a dual-purpose cross-reference and code-comparison chapter. Specific migration issues are demonstrated in quick syntax examples, comparing ActionScript 2.0 and 3.0 uses. Where applicable, references to more complete discussions elsewhere in the book are included. Select new material in the same comparative format rounds out the book.

Chapter 18, *A Sample Migration*

Chapter 19, *Where Did It Go?*

A Sample Migration

You'll typically find it fairly straightforward to choose which version of ActionScript to use when you start a new project. You usually decide based on which version of the Flash Player you're trying to target, the need for enhanced performance, or a specific feature you wish to use. Deciding what to do with existing projects, however, is another matter. Often you need to determine whether or not it's worth the time and effort to migrate to ActionScript 3.0 from a prior version of the language, or just to start over.

You can't easily determine what to do; each project's characteristics probably significantly affect your decision. The clarity of your existing code, the extent to which you use particular features, project size, and your comfort level, among other factors, help you decide.

This chapter walks you through a small-scale, manufactured example of a migration from ActionScript 2.0 to ActionScript 3.0. Read the text linearly, as code isn't always explained in detail twice. It is *very important* to understand that this example isn't a demonstration of real-world best practices at work. This example is significantly constrained, and attempts to insert as many migration issues as possible into its tiny footprint. Throughout the example, what may appear to be odd choices, poorly optimized code, or even mistakes, have been intentionally injected into the code to either set up a migration task or bring the two versions into a parallel structure.

For example, objects are added out of order intentionally to demonstrate depth management, different methods of providing or checking default values have been used, objects are created in a variety of ways, both component and custom buttons are used, function/method placement isn't consolidated, and so on. The project demonstrates both timeline- and class-based coding, but is by no means an example of good object oriented programming practices. The class and timeline are coupled too tightly, to mention one example.

If you remember that this scenario is artificial, designed to illustrate migration issues, it may help you form a plan or checklist of sorts to help when it comes time to update your next legacy project.

A Simple Particle System

This representative example creates a particle system that performs a few basic tasks. At startup, it plays an ambient audio loop. It then attempts to draw a blue square particle upon each enter frame event, based on a simple conditional. If successful, the particle moves away from the center of the stage, rotating and fading to transparency. Each time a particle is created, its name is added to a text field.

Finally, two buttons add functionality to the system. The first opens a web page. The second selects the previously created particle, replaces its content with a larger red square, and plays a new random sound. The altered particle affects its associated sound, panning based on the particle's position, and fading based on the particle's alpha.

Both examples require a custom button with a linkage of "BtnLink" and a Button component. The ActionScript 2.0 FLA file also requires an empty movie clip called "Particles." These assets are provided in the downloadable source files (see Preface).

ActionScript 2.0

To start, the complete ActionScript 2.0 code will be presented, with numbered lines. The project features a single class used by a brief frame script in the main timeline. This structure helps demonstrate migration issues related to the use of classes, as well as general syntax. Discussion of each script follows, with a general explanation following the ActionScript 2.0 code, and migration comments following the ActionScript 3.0 code.

Main Timeline

The main timeline builds the user interface, and creates an instance of the Particles class by adding a movie clip to which the class is linked. The class does all the work with the particles, and will be explained in a moment.

```
1  import mx.controls.Button;
2
3  if (!imgURL) {
4      var imgURL:String = "bg.jpg";
5  }
6
```

```
7  var txtFrmt:TextFormat = new TextFormat();
8  txtFrmt.align = "right";
9  var txtFld:TextField = this.createTextField("particleInfo", 1, 380, ¬
      10, 100, 380);
10 txtFld.setNewTextFormat(txtFrmt);
11
12 bg = this.createEmptyMovieClip("bckgrnd", 2);
13 bg.loadMovie(imgURL);
14 bg.swapDepths(txtFld);
15
16 var snd:Sound = new Sound();
17 snd.loadSound("../audio/bass_back.mp3");
18 snd.onLoad = function(success:Boolean):Void  {
19     if (success) {
20         snd.setVolume(10);
21         snd.start(0, 100);
22     }
23 };
24
25 var particles:MovieClip = attachMovie("Particles", "particles", 3);
26
27 var controls:MovieClip = this.createEmptyMovieClip("btns", 4);
28 controls._y = 360;
29
30
31 var linkBtn:MovieClip = controls.attachMovie("BtnLink","link", 5);
32 linkBtn._x = 20;
33 linkBtn.siteLink = "http://www.learningactionscript3.com/";
34 linkBtn.onRelease = function():Void  {
35     getURL(this.siteLink, "_blank");
36 };
37
38 var changePBtn:Button = controls.createClassObject(mx.controls.Button, ¬
      "chng", 6, {label:"Change"});
39 changePBtn.move(changePBtn.x + 120, 0);
40 function changeParticle():Void {
41     var p:MovieClip = particles["particle" + (particles.count - 1)];
42     p.clear();
43     p.beginFill(0xFF0000);
44     makeRect(p, -20, -20, 40, 40);
45     p.endFill();
46     particles.particleSound(p);
47 }
48 changePBtn.addEventListener("click", changeParticle);
49
50 function makeRect(mc:MovieClip, xp:Number, yp:Number, w:Number, ¬
      h:Number):Void {
51     mc.moveTo(xp, yp);
52     mc.lineTo(xp + w, yp);
53     mc.lineTo(xp + w, yp + h);
54     mc.lineTo(xp, yp + h);
55     mc.lineTo(xp, yp);
56 }
```

The following includes discussions of ActionScript 2.0 syntax, but also a basic explanation of the project—much of which applies to both ActionScript 2.0 and 3.0 versions.

Import
> Line 1 imports the `Button` component class to make it accessible to the compiler.

FlashVars
> Lines 3 through 5 check for the presence of a variable called `imgURL,` and then initialize it to the URL of a background image in case no value for the variable is found. This step lets you pass a path to a background image into the project through the HTML host file. If this feature isn't used, the hard-coded background image isn't displayed.

TextFormat
> Lines 7 and 8 create a simple `TextFormat` instance to right-justify text in a field.

TextField
> Lines 9 and 10 dynamically initialize a `TextField`. Line 9 creates the field and gives it an instance name of **particleInfo**, places the field at a depth of level 1, places the field at point (380, 10), and sizes the field to a width of 100 pixels and height of 380 pixels. Line 10 applies the previously *created* `TextFormat` to the field.

Depth Management
> ActionScript 2.0 requires that you set a level for every asset added to your project. Asset levels are hard-coded in lines 9, 12, 25, 27, 31, and 38. This step requires either careful preplanning or arbitrary level assignment (buttons between 100 and 200, movie clips between 300 and 400, and so on) and a good memory.
>
> You can determine the next available level for symbol instances like movie clips, using the `getNextHighestDepth()` method. However, significant problems arise when adding components (which occurs later in the script) because the `getNextHighestDepth()` method can return errant levels beginning with 1048576. Not only does this wreak havoc with your level management, it's outside the valid level range, making it impossible to remove assets dynamically.
>
> To get around this problem, you can adopt the significantly more confusing approach of using the `DepthManager` class, created for managing depths of Version 2 Components, generally making things more difficult.
>
> Line 14 swaps the depths of the text field and background image, making the background image the bottom-most asset. The text field and background were added in reverse order to demonstrate this feature.

Variable Declaration

ActionScript 2.0 allows sloppy variable use such as not declaring or typing the variable bg in line 12.

Image Loading

Lines 12 and 13 display a background image. Line 12 creates an empty movie clip, and sets its depth to level 2. Line 13 loads the image.

Sound

Lines 16 through 23 play a background sound. Line 16 creates an instance of the Sound class. Line 17 loads the sound.

Handling Events

Lines 18 through 23 create an event handler to process, in this case, a load complete event. Upon load completion, it sets the volume of the sound to 10 percent, so you can clearly hear other sounds atop this one, and plays the sound from the beginning, looping 100 times for longer play time. Another event handler appears in lines 34 through 36.

Void

Line 18 uses Void to tell the compiler that no data's returned from the function. This action occurs again on lines 34 and 40.

Percent Values Scale

Line 20 manipulates a percent scale, and uses values between 0 and 100.

Dynamic Creation of Movie Clip and Instantiation of Custom Class

Line 25 creates an instance of a Library-based movie clip with a linkage name of Particles. It gives the clip an instance name of particles, and sets its depth to level 3. Note here that the Particles class responsible for particle control can only easily be integrated into the project by associating the class with a movie clip. This quality means that you have to have at least an empty movie clip in your Library, already set up with the appropriate class name.

Alternatives to this approach include manipulating the movie clip prototype, which is a bit messy and very difficult to bring forward into Action-Script 3.0, or switching to object-oriented techniques and using composition. Both approaches are significantly more involved than relying on a Library symbol.

Lines 27 and 31 also dynamically create movie clip instances. Line 27 creates an empty container (positioned in line 28) to hold buttons, and line 31 creates the first of two buttons, the functionally of which is discussed next. Both lines hard code depths, to 4 and 5, respectively.

Finally, line 38 also dynamically creates a movie clip equivalent, in this case a component. This step is relevant because, in the space of a dozen or so lines of code, you see three separate ways, each with unique characteristics, to place visible content on the stage.

Property Underscores

Line 28 demonstrates that the movie clip's _y property, like most properties in ActionScript 2.0, is preceded by an underscore.

Custom Button Instantiation

Lines 31 through 36 add a Library-based custom button with a linkage name of BtnLink to the project. Line 31 places it into the *controls* movie clip, gives it an instance name of link, and sets its depth to level 5.

Line 32 positions the x location of the button. The y location remains 0, and appears to be 360 because the button is in the *controls* movie clip—which, itself, appears at a y location of 360.

Lines 34 through 36 add a mouse release event handler to the button.

Dynamic versus Sealed Classes

Line 33 dynamically creates a property called siteLink, and then populates it with a string. This step's really nothing more than a variable, but here it's an example of dynamic versus sealed classes. In ActionScript 2.0, you could add properties to instances of most classes, even though this practice wasn't recommended. In ActionScript 3.0, however, most classes are sealed, meaning you can't dynamically alter them in this way. You can use this approach only with select dynamic classes in ActionScript 3.0.

The siteLink property is being added to the button, which you can't do in ActionScript 3.0. The "ActionScript 3.0" on page 413 discusses why this example was included, and also discusses another more directly analogous example.

Opening a URL

Line 35 opens a URL in a new window, getting the URL from the site Link property of the button to which the event handler is attached.

Dynamically Instantiating a Component

Lines 38 through 48 add and empower a Button component. (As with a custom asset, a Button component must be in your Library.) Two different kinds of user-clickable objects demonstrate both the use of movie clips and the use of components.

Line 38 adds the button to the controls container movie clip, gives it an instance name of chng, sets it depth to level 6, and gives it a label of "Change." Line 39 uses the button's move() method to set it to an x position of 120, leaving the y position at 0, to be affected by the position of the parent container. The extraneous use of the x property (rather than setting the value to 120 directly) is to show that ActionScript 2.0 v2 components use properties without underscores, contrary to other properties.

Lines 40 through 48 apply an event listener to the button. Lines 40 through 47 define the function triggered by the button's click event, set in line 48.

Lines 41 through 45 are discussed in the following paragraphs, and line 46 triggers the particleSound() method of the selected particle in the Particles class.

Accessing Objects by Instance Name

Line 41 creates a reference to the previously created particle by accessing the movie clips within the particles movie clip and finding the particle by instance name. The instance name is built with the string "particle" and the number of the current particle minus 1.

Using the Drawing API

Lines 42 through 45 clear the contents of the particle, create a red fill, call a function that draws a centered, 40 × 40 pixel rectangle in the selected particle, and close the fill.

Lines 50 through 56 use the lineTo() and moveTo() methods to draw a rectangle, as the drawRect() method doesn't exist in ActionScript 2.0.

Particles Class

The Particles class creates each particle, establishes its behavior, and ultimately removes it from the project.

```
1 import mx.utils.Delegate;
2
3 class Particles extends MovieClip {
4
5        private var _count:Number;
6        private var _soundNum:Number = 0;
7        private var _tempSound:Sound;
8
9        public function Particles() {
10              _x = Stage.width / 2;
11              _y = Stage.height / 2;
12
13              _tempSound = new Sound();
14              _tempSound.loadSound("../audio/note0.mp3");
15              _tempSound.onLoad = Delegate.create(this, ¬
    onSoundPreloaded);
16           }
17
18        private function onSoundPreloaded(success:Boolean):Void {
19              if (success) {
20                    if (_soundNum < 7) {
21                          _soundNum++;
22                          _tempSound.loadSound("../audio/note" + _¬
    soundNum + ".mp3");
23                    }
```

```
24              }
25          }
26
27          private function onEnterFrame():Void {
28              makeParticle(0x0066CC, Math.random() * 10 + 10);
29          }
30
31          private function makeParticle(col:Number, ¬
    size:Number):Void {
32              if (!col){ col = 0x003366; }
33              if (!size){ size = 20; }
34
35              if (Math.random() * 10 <= 2) {
36                  if (_count == undefined) { _count = 0; }
37
38                  var p:MovieClip = this.createEmptyMovieClip("particle" + _¬
                    count, this.getNextHighestDepth());
39                  _count++;
40                  p.beginFill(col);
41                  _parent.makeRect(p, -size/2, -size/2, size, size);
42                  p.endFill();
43
44                  p.xVel = Math.random() * 10 - 5;
45                  p.yVel = Math.random() * 2 - 1;
46                  p.onEnterFrame = onRunParticle;
47
48                  _parent.txtFld.text += p._name + "\n"
49                  _parent.txtFld.scroll = _parent.txtFld.maxscroll;
50              }
51          }
52
53          public function particleSound(p:MovieClip):Void {
54              if (!p.snd && _soundNum > 0){
55                  var num:Number = int(Math.random() * _soundNum);
56                  p.snd = new Sound();
57                  p.snd.loadSound("../audio/note" + num + ".mp3");
58                  p.snd.onLoad = function(success:Boolean):Void {
59                      p.snd.start();
60                  }
61              }
62          }
63
64          private function onRunParticle():Void {
65              var p:MovieClip = this;
66              p._x += p.xVel;
67              p._y += p.yVel;
68              p._rotation += 5;
69              p._alpha -= 2;
70
71              if (p.snd) {
72                  p.snd.setVolume(p._alpha / 10);
73                  p.snd.setPan(p._x / this._parent._x * 200)
74              }
75
```

```
76              if (p._alpha <= 0) {
77                  p.removeMovieClip();
78              }
79          }
80
81          public function get count():Number {
82              return _count;
83          }
84  }
```

The following features a brief explanation of particle behavior. Where appropriate, comments have been added to address ActionScript 2.0-specific concepts and, occasionally, to explain decisions made to demonstrate migration
issues. Basic syntax issues discussed in the main timeline aren't mentioned
again.

Import
Line 1 imports the `Delegate` class to make it accessible to the compiler.

Class Structure
Lines 3 and 9 make up the key elements of the ActionScript 2.0 class
structure. You'll see later that ActionScript 3.0 begins a class with the
`package` identifier. Line 3 shows that this class extends `MovieClip`. (It's
linked to a Library movie clip.) The class constructor beginning on line 9
centers the particle system on the stage, and creates and preloads the first
particle-specific sound.

Class Properties
Lines 5 through 7 create class properties but only initialize one. This step
factors later into the use of default values.

Number Data Types
Lines 5 and 6 use the `Number` data type for integer counters because no
other number data types are available. You can also see this property in
lines 31 and 55. The value assigned in line 55, as a good example, is always
an integer, but must still be typed as `Number`.

Access to the Stage
Lines 10 and 11 show that Stage is a global object.

Method Closure
Line 15 assigns the `onLoad()` event handler for the sound created and loaded in lines 13 and 14, respectively. `Delegate` is used here, however, to
demonstrate that ActionScript 2.0 does not have method closures. Due to
this setup, the `Delegate` class must pass the relevant scope to the event
handler for it to access the needed properties.

Preloading Sounds
To prevent delays when triggering sounds later, lines 18 through 25 load
seven additional sounds, but don't play them. The name of the audio file

contains indices 0 through 7. The first sound, *note0.mp3*, was loaded in the class constructor, so the soundNum property is incremented before the load.

Class Enter Frame Method

Lines 27 through 29 demonstrate that, because this class extends Movie Clip, ActionScript 2.0 lets you create a method for a movie clip event handler, without any further assignment. That is, because the method has the same name as a MovieClip event handler, it's executed upon every movie clip enter frame event. This method attempts to create a blue particle that's between 10 and 20 pixels square.

Particle Creation

Lines 31 through 51 create each particle. Individual aspects of this function will be discussed in separate headers, but the basic creation process is as follows. Line 35 checks to see if a newly created random number between 0 and 10 is less than or equal to 2. If so, it creates the particle. This action both prevents a particle from being created on every enter frame, and adds a nice feeling of randomness to the process.

Each particle is drawn into an empty movie clip, with its depth set to the next highest available level. It's given an instance name of particle*N*, where *N* is an integer from the _count variable, incremented each time a particle's created. A fill of the color passed into the method is created, a rectangle is drawn using the makeRect() function discussed in the main timeline (using the size passed into the function), and the fill's closed.

Next, random x and y velocities are chosen for each particle, providing movement between 5 and –5 for x and between 1 and –1 for y. The onRun Particle() method is then assigned as the enter frame event handler for each particle. (This step's in contrast to the enter frame event handler assigned at the class level that creates the particles.)

Finally, the name of the particle, and a subsequent new line, are added to the text field in the main timeline (the particle's parent). This step is discussed in detail in the upcoming note, "Manipulating Text Fields."

Default Values

Lines 32 and 33 validate the argument values of col and size, assigning values if none are found. ActionScript 2.0 has no built-in mechanism for assigning default values in functions. As such, you must assign them manually.

Further, line 36 checks for a value of undefined in _count and, if found, initializes the property to 0. This demonstrates a change in the way ActionScript 3.0 handles default values, and this is also why _count wasn't initialized in line 5.

Accessing Objects in the Parent

Lines 41, 48, and 49 all access objects in the parent, in this case the main timeline.

Manipulating Text Fields

The name of the particle, and a subsequent new line, are added to the text field in the main timeline (the particle's parent). The text field is then scrolled to the bottom line so you can always see the newly added name.

Particle Sound

Lines 53 through 62 create and play particle-specific sound. A validation first tests to be sure a sound for this particle doesn't already exist, and that at least one sound has preloaded (via the incremented counter in line 21). If so, a random number is chosen from the current number of preloaded sounds (line 57) and a new sound is created and stored in the snd property within the current particle. The random sound is then loaded and played upon load completion.

(Many people consider it a best practice to group private and public methods (and properties). However, this method's optional, and has been neglected in order to arrange this example in a slightly more linear fashion for easier explanation.)

Particle Behavior

Lines 64 through 79 establish the independent behavior for each particle. For each enter frame event, lines 66 and 67 add the x and y velocity values to the particle's location, line 68 rotates the particle 5 degrees, and line 69 reduces the alpha by 2 percent.

Lines 71 through 74 controls particle-specific audio. The volume and pan of the sound are set according to the particle's alpha and x coordinate, respectively.

Finally, lines 76 through 78 remove the particle when its alpha is less than or equal to 0.

Getter

The last three lines of the class create a getter that returns the value of the _count property when requested, as seen in line 41 of the main timeline frame script.

ActionScript 3.0

The following are the ActionScript 3.0 versions of the two previous scripts. Only language version-specific comments are included here so, if you're unclear on overall functionality, see the equivalent ActionScript 2.0 section.

Main Timeline

The following is the main timeline frame script.

```
1  import fl.controls.Button;
2
3  var imgURL:String = "bg.jpg";
4  if (root.loaderInfo.parameters.imgURL) {
5      imgURL = root.loaderInfo.parameters.imgURL;
6  }
7  var txtFrmt:TextFormat = new TextFormat();
8  txtFrmt.align = TextFormatAlign.RIGHT;
9  var txtFld:TextField = new TextField();
10 txtFld.x = 380;
11 txtFld.y = 10;
12 txtFld.width = 100;
13 txtFld.height = 380;
14 txtFld.defaultTextFormat = txtFrmt;
15 addChild(txtFld);
16
17 var bg:Loader = new Loader();
18 addChildAt(bg, 0);
19 bg.load(new URLRequest(imgURL));
20
21 var snd:Sound = new Sound();
22 snd.load(new URLRequest("../audio/bass_back.mp3"));
23 snd.addEventListener(Event.COMPLETE, onSoundLoaded, false, 0, ¬
     true);
24 function onSoundLoaded(evt:Event):void {
25     var sndChannel:SoundChannel = new SoundChannel();
26     sndChannel = evt.target.play(0, 100);
27     var sndTransform:SoundTransform = sndChannel.soundTransform;
28     sndTransform.volume = .1;
29     sndChannel.soundTransform = sndTransform;
30     evt.target.removeEventListener(Event.COMPLETE, onSoundLoaded);
31 }
32
33 var particles:Particles = new Particles();
34 addChild(particles);
35
36 var controls:MovieClip = new MovieClip();
37 controls.y = 360;
38 addChild(controls);
39
40 var siteLink:String = "http://www.learningactionscript3.com/";
41 var linkBtn:SimpleButton = new BtnLink();
42 linkBtn.x = 20;
43 controls.addChild(linkBtn);
44
45 linkBtn.addEventListener(MouseEvent.CLICK, onShowLink, false, 0, ¬
     true);
46 function onShowLink(evt:MouseEvent):void {
47     navigateToURL(new URLRequest(siteLink), "_blank");
48 }
```

```
49
50 var changePBtn:Button = new Button();
51 changePBtn.x = 120;
52 changePBtn.label = "Change";
53 controls.addChild(changePBtn);
54
55 changePBtn.addEventListener(MouseEvent.CLICK, onChangeParticle,¬
      false, 0, true);
56 function onChangeParticle(evt:MouseEvent):void {
57    var p:MovieClip = MovieClip(particles.getChildByName(¬
    "particle" + (particles.count - 1)));
58    if (p != null) {
59        p.graphics.clear();
60        p.graphics.beginFill(0xFF0000);
61        p.graphics.drawRect(-20, -20, 40, 40);
62        p.graphics.endFill();
63        particles.particleSound(p);
64    }
65 }
```

The following is an explanation of ActionScript 3.0-specific issues that appear in the main timeline frame script.

Import

Notice in Line 1 that the class path has changed from mx to fl.

FlashVars

FlashVars are no longer stored as global variables in the root timeline. Instead, they're stored in the parameters object of the LoaderInfo instance of the root, as seen in line 4.

TextFormat

Although you can use appropriate string values, it is a best practice to use relevant constants for many property values in ActionScript 3.0. In this case, the format's align property is populated with the RIGHT constant of the TextFormatAlign class, used in line 8.

The application of the TextFormat instance in line 14 has been changed from setNewTextFormat() to defaultTextFormat().

TextField

All display objects are created with a simple consistent new *<class name>*() structure. The ActionScript 2.0 TextField creation method is replaced with the ActionScript 3.0 instantiation (line 9) and followed by the assignment of property values (lines 10 through 14).

Depth Management

The ActionScript 3.0 display list automatically handles depth management so you don't have to manually assign levels or worry about methods like getNextHighestDepth() or the DepthManager. As such, you don't see any level assignments in any of the object instantiation routines.

However, you can still control depths. For example, you still have a `swap Depths()` method for moving the background image below the text field, as seen in line 14 of the ActionScript 2.0 main timeline frame script code. However, you have an easier way to handle this when objects are added to the display list. In ActionScript 2.0, existing objects are replaced when a new object is added to the same level. ActionScript 3.0, however, moves all objects above the target level one level higher, and then inserts the addition where specified.

Therefore, you can easily place the background image behind the text field when the image is added, as seen in line 18. The `addChildAt()` method is used, specifying level 0. The background image appears in level 0, and the text field is moved to level 1.

Variable Declaration

While you can in some cases omit typing a variable, all variables must be declared with the `var` identifier.

Image Loading

Rather than creating an empty movie clip, a `Loader` display object is used lines (17 through 19). Instead of using the image path as a string for the `load()` method, ActionScript 3.0 requires a consistent use of the `URLRequest` class for processing the URL prior to use.

Sound

Although the creation of the `Sound` instance is the same (line 21), sound management diverges significantly from that point on. Loading is similar, with a change of method name to the more consistent `load()` and the ever-needed `URLRequest` instance instead of a string. The event handling is significantly different in ActionScript 3.0 (and is explained in a moment), but the idea behind it, as it pertains to sound, is the same: wait until the sound is loaded, and then proceed.

However, three new classes play a big part of sound management. First, each sound is typically played into its own discrete sound channel, an instance of the `SoundChannel` class (lines 25 and 26). This step is a requirement if you wish to perform sound transformations. Where the `volume` and pan properties existed in the `Sound` class in ActionScript 2.0, they're now accessible through the `soundTransform` property of the `SoundChannel` class.

To effect such a change, an instance of the second new class, `SoundTrans form` is derived from the `SoundChannel soundTransform` property (line 27), the desired property is changed (`volume`, line 28) and the new instance is reapplied to the `SoundChannel soundTransform` property once again (line 29).

The third new class, not used in this example, is the `SoundMixer` class. This class lets you manipulate all the sounds at once. The isolation of sounds into their own discrete channels lets you control each sound separately and with greater precision.

Handling Events

Event handling is very different in ActionScript 3.0. For detailed information, see Chapter 14. From a migration standpoint, event handlers are no longer attached to the target of the event. Instead, event listeners are created, specifying an event to listen for, and a function to trigger upon an occurrence of that event (lines 23 through 31).

A mandatory parameter is used to receive information from the event that can be used inside the function. For example, the target of the event in the mentioned listener is the `snd` object. That is referenced by `evt.target` in lines 26 and 30.

The events are specified as constants, as discussed previously with the `TextFormat` align property, and optional parameters allow more granular control over when the event is processed (capture or target/bubbling phases and priority) as well as whether weak references are used for a little backup help in the memory management department.

Finally, you should remove the listener when you no longer need it, for optimal memory management (line 30). You also find event listeners in lines 45 through 48, and 55 through 65.

Void

Void is now lower case (lines 24, 46, 56).

Percent Values Scale

Percent value scales are now from 0 to 1 (instead of 0 to 100).

Dynamic Creation of Movie Clip and Instantiation of Custom Class

ActionScript 3.0 lets you much more easily use custom classes as display objects. You don't need to rely on a Library-based symbol, or more convoluted methods, to instantiate the class. Instead, provided the class extends `MovieClip`, `Sprite`, Shape, or another applicable display object, you just need to instantiate it the way you would any other display object: `new <classname>();` (line 33). You must then add the instance to the display list for the user to see it.

Another movie clip is dynamically generated in line 36. Note the simplicity of creating an empty movie clip container (to hold buttons). Rather than using one of many methods, such as `createEmptyMovieClip()`, the consistent `new MovieClip()` approach is all you need, coupled with the `add Child()` method on line 38.

Property Underscores

Line 37 is one example of the fact that ActionScript 3.0 properties are not preceded by an underscore.

Custom Button Instantiation

The same custom button used in the ActionScript 2.0 version can be instantiated here as a proper button (`SimpleButton`, line 41) rather than using a `MovieClip` method and typing the instance as a `MovieClip` or `Object`. It's then positioned, and added to the display list (lines 42 and 43, respectively).

Dynamic versus Sealed Classes

In this case, however, the `SimpleButton` class is a sealed class, so you can't add the site URL used by the button as a property. In this case, it's stored in a standard variable.

You could have brought these two examples into a more parallel structure by using movie clips for buttons in both cases, because `MovieClip` is a dynamic class and would allow the addition of a property. However, the purpose of this chapter is not to change the way you want to work, but to understand how best to migrate a legacy project to the new syntax of ActionScript 3.0. Taking advantage of the new `SimpleButton` class is desirable, and even lets you create a button entirely from code (no Library assets) if preferred.

To see an exact parallel, you can add an example property to the text field instance in both versions of the project. In the ActionScript 2.0 version, adding

```
txtFld.inUse = true;
```

after line 10 works. However, adding the same line in the ActionScript 3.0 version after line 15 generates an error because the `TextField` class is sealed in ActionScript 3.0.

Opening a URL

Line 47 shows the new syntax for accessing a URL, using the `navigate ToURL()` method and `URLRequest` instance.

Dynamically Instantiating a Component

Adding a component to your project on the fly is really no different from adding a movie clip or other display object. Just use the `Button` class as you would another display object class, as seen in line 50. (As with a custom asset, a Button component must be in your Library.)

Accessing Objects by Instance Name

You can't access a dynamically created object directly by instance name. That is, setting the name property in ActionScript 3.0 doesn't make it possible to reference the object using the dot syntax object model. Instead, you must use the getChildByName() method, as seen in line 57.

Using the Graphics Class (formerly the Drawing API)

Although the clear(), beginFill(), and endFill() methods are the same in ActionScript 3.0, they're methods of the Graphics class, accessed through the graphics property instance of each relevant display object. Further, you don't need a custom function to draw a rectangle, as the new drawRect() method does that for you.

Particles Class

The Particles class functionality is the same in ActionScript 3.0. It creates each particle, establishes its behavior, and ultimately removes it from the project.

```
1 package {
2
3      import flash.display.*;
4      import flash.events.*;
5      import flash.media.*;
6      import flash.net.*;
7
8      public class Particles extends Sprite {
9
10         private var _count:int;
11         private var _soundNum:int = 0;
12         private var _tempSound:Sound;
13
14         public function Particles() {
15             addEventListener(Event.ADDED_TO_STAGE, onAdded, ¬
                   false, 0, true);
16             addEventListener(Event.ENTER_FRAME, onLoop, false, ¬
                   0, true);
17             _tempSound = new Sound(new URLRequest( ¬
                   "../audio/note0.mp3"));
18             _tempSound.addEventListener(Event.COMPLETE, ¬
                   onSoundPreloaded, false, 0, true);
19         }
20
21         private function onAdded(evt:Event):void {
22             x = this.stage.stageWidth / 2;
23             y = this.stage.stageHeight / 2;
24             removeEventListener(Event.ADDED_TO_STAGE, onAdded);
25         }
26
27         private function onSoundPreloaded(evt:Event=null):void {
28             _tempSound.removeEventListener(Event.COMPLETE, ¬
                   onSoundPreloaded);
29             if (_soundNum < 7) {
30                 _soundNum++;
```

```
31                          _tempSound = new Sound(new URLRequest(¬
                                "../audio/note" + _soundNum + ".mp3"));
32                          _tempSound.addEventListener(Event.COMPLETE, ¬
                                onSoundPreloaded, false, 0, true);
33                      }
34              }
35
36              private function onLoop(evt:Event):void {
37                  makeParticle(0x0066CC, Math.random() * 10 + 10);
38              }
39
40              private function makeParticle(col:uint=0x003366, ¬
                    size:Number=20):void {
41                  if (Math.random() * 10 <= 2) {
42                      var p:MovieClip = new MovieClip();
43
44                      if (isNaN(_count)) { _count = 0; }
45                      p.name = "particle" + _count;
46                      _count++;
47
48                      p.graphics.beginFill(col);
49                      p.graphics.drawRect(-size/2, -size/2, size, size);
50                      p.graphics.endFill();
51
52                      p.xVel =  Math.random() * 10 - 5;
53                      p.yVel = Math.random() * 2 - 1;
54
55                      p.addEventListener(Event.ENTER_FRAME, ¬
                            onRunParticle, false, 0, true);
56                      addChild(p);
57
58                      MovieClip(parent).txtFld.appendText(p.name + "\n");
59                      MovieClip(parent).txtFld.scrollV = ¬
                            MovieClip(parent).txtFld.maxScrollV;
60                  }
61              }
62
63              public function particleSound(p:MovieClip):void {
64                  if (!p.snd && _soundNum > 0) {
65                      var num:int = int(Math.random()*_soundNum);
66                      p.snd = new Sound(new URLRequest(¬
                            "../audio/note" + num + ".mp3"));
67                      p.channel = new SoundChannel();
68                      p.channel = p.snd.play();
69                  }
70              }
71
72              private function onRunParticle(evt:Event):void {
73                  evt.target.x += evt.target.xVel;
74                  evt.target.y += evt.target.yVel;
75                  evt.target.rotation += 5;
76                  evt.target.alpha -= .02;
77
78                  if (evt.target.snd) {
```

```
79                    var trans = evt.target.channel.soundTransform;
80                    trans.volume = evt.target.alpha / 10;
81                    trans.pan = (evt.target.x / this.x)  * 2;
82                    evt.target.channel.soundTransform = trans;
83                }
84
85            if (evt.target.alpha <= 0) {
86                if (evt.target.snd) {
87                    evt.target.channel.stop();
88                }
89                evt.target.removeEventListener(Event.ENTER_FRAME, ¬
                    onRunParticle);
90                removeChild(MovieClip(evt.target));
91            }
92        }
93
94        public function get count():int {
95            return _count;
96        }
97    }
98 }
```

As with the ActionScript 2.0 section, basic syntax issues discussed in the main timeline won't be mentioned again.

Class Structure

Line 1 shows that all ActionScript 3.0 classes must be enclosed in a package statement. This line would also be where you would include a path to the class, if desired. Lines 8 and 14 remain consistent with ActionScript 2.0.

Import

Lines 3 through 6 import all the classes to make them accessible to the compiler. Unlike ActionScript 2.0, even classes in Flash Player must be imported.

Class Properties

Lines 10 through 12 are consistent with ActionScript 2.0.

Number Data Types

Lines 10 and 11 use the int data type because you don't need float values. You can also see this characteristic in lines 40 and 65. 40 is a good example, as the uint data type is used, because a color value can't be negative.

Much has been made of the performance of the uint data type and, to a lesser degree, the int data type, so you can decide whether or not to use them. This is just an example.

Access to Stage

Unlike ActionScript 2.0, the stage isn't a global object. Instead, you must access the stage through a display object. The Particles class both extends MovieClip, and is added to the display list in the main timeline frame script, so you can access the stage without passing a reference to it through the constructor.

However, you can access the stage only after the display object has been added to the display list. Therefore, this class can't access the stage within its constructor, as the class hasn't yet been fully initialized. Instead, a new event listener is added to listen for the Event.ADDED_TO_STAGE event (line 15). Once this event fires, the display object is part of the display list, and the stage reference doesn't return null.

Lines 21 through 25 contain the function used for this purpose and, because the listener is no longer necessary, it's removed upon execution of this function. (The this keyword is not strictly needed because the relevant scope is the class itself, but it's been added to emphasize that you're accessing the stage through a display object.)

Class Enter Frame Event

The use of the enter frame event for the class is the same; however, note that, because event handlers no longer exist, you can't just name a function onEnterFrame() and expect it to work. You must convert that structure to an event listener design, seen in lines 16 and 36 through 38.

Method Closures

You no longer need the Delegate class, as ActionScript 3.0 supports method closures.

Preloading Sounds

The sound preloading routine hasn't changed, and doesn't include any ActionScript 3.0 syntax issues that haven't already been discussed, with one small exception. If you pass a valid URLRequest instance to the Sound class constructor, as in line 31, the load() method is automatically called.

It's also a good idea to look this method over with regard to removing listeners. It's important to remove the load complete listener from _temp Sound after each sound has been loaded (or, if you prefer, after the last sound has loaded) to prevent the listener from remaining on the last sound.

Particle Creation

ActionScript 3.0 has nothing unique in the makeParticle() method that hasn't been, or won't be, discussed elsewhere. However, be sure to read about changes to default values, accessing objects in the parent, and using the Drawing API (now commonly referred to as the Graphics class).

Default Values

ActionScript 3.0 allows the assignment of default values to method arguments, as seen in line 40. This action makes the associated arguments optional, but all optional arguments must appear at the end of the method signature.

Further, default values for data types have changed in ActionScript 3.0. For example, line 44 can no longer test for undefined, as the default value for number data types is NaN (not a number). As such, you must use the isNan() method to validate its value.

As is true with many intentionally injected migration issues in this exercise, this could have been handled a different way. This property could have been initialized in line 10, for example, but was not so this issue could be discussed.

Accessing Objects in the Parent

In Lines 58 and 59, the particle must cast the type of its parent before it can access the parent's methods or properties. Without this step, the compiler knows only that the parent's a display object container, but not what kind. The compiler, therefore, doesn't recognize the txtFld property of the parent.

When cast to a MovieClip, however, the compiler knows that MovieClip is a dynamic class and can, therefore, have custom properties. It then looks for txtFld in the parent. and finds the text field you created.

Manipulating Text Fields

When adding text to the text field (line 58), the appendText() method was used, as it's much faster than the compound operator +=. Furthermore, the property scrollV must be updated to the value of maxScrollV (line 59).

Particle Sound

Nothing about the particleSound() method that is unique to ActionScript 3.0 hasn't already been discussed. Line 64 checks to make sure the particle's Sound instance hasn't already been created, and that _soundNum has been incremented to be sure the sounds have preloaded. Line 65 creates a random number within the count of available sounds, line 66 creates an instance of the Sound class and loads the sound, and lines 67 and 68 create a SoundChannel instance and play the sound.

Particle Behavior

The behavior of the ActionScript 3.0 particles isn't unique, but a few very important concepts should be discussed. To begin, the first number of the product used for the sound transformation pan value is calculated using the particle's x divided by the Particles class' x (line 81). This step's in contrast to the ActionScript 2.0 calculation, which divides the first number by the class's *parent's* x value (line 73 of the ActionScript 2.0 class code). ActionScript 2.0 requires the Library movie clip to instantiate the class this way, so the movie clip must be referenced in the calculation. ActionScript

3.0 lets you add this class to the display list directly, so only the class needs to be referenced.

Next, you must stop the sound, and remove the event listener, before removing the particle. Otherwise, the particle and its attendant objects, (such as listeners) won't be collected by the garbage collector and purged from memory.

The compiler must be told that the object is a `MovieClip` to prevent an error from occurring, because the compiler sees only the target of the method as an `Object` that may or may not be removable. However, this issue has already been addressed in the "Accessing Objects in the Parent (Type Casting)" section of this discussion.

Getter

Nothing unique about the `count()` getter method is unique to ActionScript 3.0 hasn't already been discussed

Migration Sample Summary

This is a small example of one possible migration path used to update a legacy project to ActionScript 3.0. Although awkward coding choices were made to show the largest number of migration issues practical in this size example, the exercise is still relatively close to a real-world scenario.

Having read this chapter, you may want to see if you can migrate this example on your own. Once you try the process a few times, you'll have a pretty good idea of what you need, and you can evaluate the effectiveness of migration on a case-by-case basis. Depending on the extent of the changes, you may wish to use the old project as a kind of template, and then code the new version from scratch.

CHAPTER 19

Where Did It Go?

Introduction

Migrating from ActionScript 2.0 to ActionScript 3.0 is as much a matter of following subtle changes in the development of the language as learning new features. In many cases, all you'll need to do to upgrade a script, you just have to change a class name or, perhaps, change from a method to a property. These kinds of changes are typically easy to identify because you need minor adjustments. In other cases, however, you may find yourself searching for missing functionality. Like looking up an unfamiliar word in the dictionary, you need a place to start.

What's Included

This chapter is essentially a cross-reference to material covered elsewhere in this book, but also includes additional material not otherwise discussed. The primary goal is to help you find something you used in ActionScript 2.0 but appears to be missing or significantly changed in ActionScript 3.0.

Itemizing every change introduced by ActionScript 3.0 is beyond the scope of this book. However, you can find a concise, table-based guide called "Action-Script 2.0 Migration" in the Help system by searching for "migration" or by looking online at *http://livedocs.adobe.com/flex/2/langref/migration.html*. While this table doesn't include examples, it does point you to the correct new Help entry in ActionScript 3.0 syntax, if one exists.

When you know specifically what to look for, and in which package or class to look, the Help table is probably the best place to start. However, you can use this chapter as a supplemental tool to *preplan* migration efforts by identifying known issues that affect a broader category such as asset display or sound, for example. Loosely organizing topics into larger categories this way is particularly helpful when changes affect more than one property, method, or event, and even span multiple classes.

In all cases, the code snippets are not fully realized scripts but rather syntax examples to point you in the right direction.

What's Not Included

A few things won't be addressed here, so that the chapter can cover as much as possible of what you're most likely to run into during a migration session. So, this chapter doesn't cover:

Syntax deprecated in ActionScript 2.0
   Some ActionScript syntax introduced with version 1.0 of the language was replaced with better, or more standards-compliant, syntax in ActionScript 2.0. Examples include operators like gt (string greater than), <> (mathematical not equal to), and or (logical or), global functions like tellTarget() (for object addressing prior to the use of dot-syntax), and object properties like __proto__ (an early OOP technique).

Features entirely new in ActionScript 3.0
   This chapter is primarily designed to help you find ActionScript 3.0 solutions to problems you're used to solving with ActionScript 2.0. New material's included here, but the focus is on migration rather than taking advantage of features introduced for the first time with ActionScript 3.0. Much of the entirely new material is discussed in earlier chapters of this book.

Repetition of consistent changes across multiple categories or topics
   One of the concepts stressed throughout this book is the consistency that version 3.0 of ActionScript brings to the language. Some changes, such as the new event architecture, apply to many classes and aren't repeated herein.

Code Comparisons

Half the battle when upgrading existing projects is knowing how to change older code. The remainder of this chapter identifies select migration issues and compares ActionScript 2.0 and 3.0 syntax.

Language Fundamentals

Several very basic changes introduced in ActionScript 3.0 affect the way a script is structured. Ranging from default values to scope issues, these language fundamentals are not category-specific.

Examining and using default values

ActionScript 2.0: Checking variables for initial values often involves a comparison against null or undefined.

```
var userNum:Number;
if (userNum == undefined) {
userNum = 1;
}
```

ActionScript 3.0: A value of undefined can be used only for untyped variables. Every data type now has a default value, as seen in Table 19-1.

Table 19-1. Data type default values

Data type	Default value
int	0
uint	0
Number	NaN
Object	null
String	null
Boolean	false
untyped (*)	undefined
all other (including user-defined classes)	null

Equality can be used for most default value validations, but the isNaN() method should be used for the Number data type.

```
var userNum:Number;
if (isNaN(userNum)) {
    userNum = 1;
}
```

Additionally, ActionScript 3.0 allows the assignment of default values for function parameters. See Chapter 18, for more information about default values.

Referencing objects by evaluated expression

ActionScript 2.0: You can dynamically build a reference to an object using the eval() to evaluate an expression. For example, you can refer to

```
trace(eval("this.myClip" + i));
```

ActionScript 3.0: The eval() method is gone. Although using scope bracket syntax, such as this["myClip" + i], is still possible, using getChildByName() is the recommended practice.

```
trace(this.getChildByName("myClip" + i));
```

See "13.5 Finding a Display Object" on page 291 for more information about finding a display object by name.

Creating global variables and functions

ActionScript 2.0: The declaration _global lets you create global variables and functions.

```
_global.userName = "David Thomas";
_global.pereUbu = function ():Void {
    getURL("http://ubuprojex.net/");
}
trace(userName);
pereUbu();
```

ActionScript 3.0: Global variables and functions have been removed. Use a static class member, a Singleton (a class that allows only one instance), or, for variables accessible to an entire display list (which isn't really global), you can rely on the **root** reference. See the next entry. The following snippet is an example of the static class member approach. The Global class allows the storage of variables in a dynamically populated object.

Global.as

```
package {
    public class Global {
        public static var vars:Object = {};
    }
}
```

Elsewhere, in another class or frame script, you can store variables as object properties, including functions. To demonstrate, the last three lines of this snippet trigger the global function after a one-second delay.

```
import Global;
Global.vars.userName = "David Thomas";
Global.vars.pereUbu = function():void {
    navigateToURL(new URLRequest("http://ubuprojex.net/"));
}

trace(Global.vars.userName);
var tmr:Timer = new Timer(1000, 1);
tmr.addEventListener(TimerEvent.TIMER, Global.vars.pereUbu, false, 0, true);
tmr.start();
```

Be aware that, like ActionScript 2.0 global variables, this simple approach doesn't use type checking for variable values.

Accessing the root of a SWF file

ActionScript 2.0: The _root is the host SWF file played by Flash Player regardless of whether it is standalone (which makes it the _root) or loaded into

---

another SWF file (which makes the *parent* SWF file the _root). This makes addressing a movie clip, or storing a variable, unpredictable. The _lockroot property helps work around this problem by allowing _root references to remain SWF-file-specific. If _lockroot is set to true, when a SWF file is loaded into a parent SWF file, _root in the loadee SWF file is still the main timeline of the loadee, and _root in the loader SWF file is still the main timeline of the loader.

```
_root.mc._x = 100;
_root.userName = "Kramer";
```

ActionScript 3.0: The new root is the senior most display object in the current scope, and functions somewhat as if _lockroot is true in ActionScript 2.0. If you choose to use root as a variable repository, then you must first cast it as MovieClip so you can dynamically assign properties (variables).

```
MovieClip(root).mc.x = 100;
MovieClip(root).userName = "Kramer";
```

See "13.8 Working with Parents of a Display Object" on page 296 and "13.9 Casting a Display Object from One Type to Another" on page 297, as well as Chapter 18, for more information about dynamic versus sealed classes.

Using delegates

ActionScript 2.0: The Delegate class is used to link scope with the execution of a function or method.

```
_tempSound.onLoad = Delegate.create(this, onSoundPreloaded);
```

ActionScript 3.0: This is now unnecessary due ActionScript 3.0's method closure. See the "Method Closures" on page 8 of Chapter 18 for more information.

Display

Controlling visual elements in Flash is entirely different in ActionScript 3.0, so you see many changes from previous versions, large and small. For an in-depth look at display objects and the display list, see Chapter 13.

Accessing the Stage

ActionScript 2.0: The Stage is a top-level class and you can get to it from anywhere.

```
trace(Stage.width);
```

ActionScript 3.0: You can access the Stage only through a display object that's part of the display list. This example also demonstrates a subtle difference in the name of the property to specify width, changing from width in ActionScript 2.0 to stageWidth.

```
var sp:Sprite = new Sprite();
addChild(sp);
trace(sp.stage.stageWidth);
```

See "13.11 Referencing the Stage Through a Display Object" on page 300 for more information about accessing the stage through a display object.

Accessing a parent

ActionScript 2.0: The _parent property identifies the parent of a symbol instance or loaded SWF file.

```
this._parent.gotoAndStop(2);
```

ActionScript 3.0: The parent property works the same way, but ActionScript 3.0 has many more display object types, so the compiler sometimes needs to be told that the requested property or method of a parent is legal. For example, a parent could be a sprite, rather than a movie clip, in which case frame navigation actions wouldn't apply. Telling the compiler that the parent's a movie clip by casting it as such eliminates any possible confusion.

```
MovieClip(this.parent).gotoAndStop(2);
```

See "13.9 Casting a Display Object from One Type to Another" on page 297 for more information about accessing a parent of a display object and casting from one data type to another.

Creating an empty movie clip

ActionScript 2.0: Creating an empty movie clip requires the createEmptyMovieClip() method, a new instance name, and a level. The clip is automatically displayed.

```
var mc:MovieClip = this.createEmptyMovieClip("clip", 1);
```

ActionScript 3.0: You create all display objects using the new keyword and appropriate class, and you must add them to the display list to be visible.

```
var mc:MovieClip = new MovieClip();
addChild(mc);
```

See "13.2 Creating a New Display Object" on page 286 for more information about creating a new movie clip.

Adding a library movie clip to the stage

ActionScript 2.0: Adding an existing movie clip to the stage requires the attachMovie() method, the symbol's linkage name, a new instance name, and a level. The clip is automatically displayed.

```
var mc:MovieClip = this.attachMovie("Help","helpHeadline",2);
```

ActionScript 3.0: You create all display objects using the new keyword and appropriate class. Instead of using a linkage name, you use a symbol's class name, and instantiate the clip just like an empty movie clip. You can type the reference variable to the class type if it helps clarify your intent, but you need not write a custom class for this feature to work. You can also type to Movie-Clip, for example, if you prefer (as seen here). See "Creating a bitmap" on page 431" for more information. You must add the instance to the display list to make it visible.

```
var mc:MovieClip = new Help();
addChild(mc);
```

See "13.2 Creating a New Display Object" on page 286 for more information about adding a library element to the display list.

Duplicating a movie clip

ActionScript 2.0: You can duplicate a movie clip instance using the duplicateMovieClip() method, a reference to the original clip, a new instance name, and a new level.

```
duplicateMovieClip(mc, "mc2", 2);
```

ActionScript 3.0: This functionality has been removed. The recommended approach is to use new to create another instance of the relevant movie clip, but this will not inherit any of the original movie clip's attributes. To accomplish something similar in ActionScript 3.0, you must create a custom clone method that analyzes the original and attempts to apply all of its attributes to the copy.

Creating a bitmap

ActionScript 2.0: Create a BitmapData object, and attach it to a movie clip using the attachBitmap() method, specifying a level.

```
import flash.display.BitmapData;
var bmpMC:MovieClip = this.createEmptyMovieClip("bmpContainer", 1);
var bmpData:BitmapData = new BitmapData(200, 200);
bmpMC.attachBitmap(bmpData, 2);
```

ActionScript 3.0: Create a Bitmap instance and add it to the display list.

```
var bmp:Bitmap = new Bitmap();
addChild(bmp);
```

Adding a library bitmap to the stage

ActionScript 2.0: This process is similar to the ActionScript 2.0 method for creating a bitmap but, rather than creating a new `BitmapData` instance, you use `loadBitmap()` method and the library bitmap's linkage name to create an instance from the bitmap.

```
var bmpD:BitmapData = BitmapData.loadBitmap("Logo");
var mc:MovieClip = this.createEmptyMovieClip("mc", 2);
mc.attachBitmap(bmpD, 2);
```

ActionScript 3.0: Specify a linkage class for the bitmap in the library, and create a new instance of the class. You must add it to the display list for it to be visible. Here again, you can type to the custom class, or to the base class. In this example, the custom class is used. See "Adding a library movie clip to the stage" on page 431 for more information.

```
var logoBmp:Logo = new Logo(100,100);
var bmp:Bitmap = new Bitmap(logoBmp);
addChild(bmp);
```

Checking the level of a display object

ActionScript 2.0: You can get the level of a symbol instance by using the `_level` property.

```
var mc:MovieClip = this.createEmptyMovieClip("clip", this.getNextHighestDepth());
trace(mc._level);
//_level0
```

ActionScript 3.0: The `_level` property has been removed. Use the `getChildIndex()` method of a display object container instead.

```
var mc:MovieClip = new MovieClip();
addChild(mc);
trace(getChildIndex(mc));
```

Getting the highest unused depth

ActionScript 2.0: Use the `getNextHighestDepth()` method (or the `DepthManager` class when using version 2.0 components).

```
var mc:MovieClip = this.createEmptyMovieClip("mc", this.getNextHighestDepth());
```

ActionScript 3.0: Depth management is automatic and the highest level is automatically used when adding to the display list.

```
var mc:MovieClip = new MovieClip();
addChild(mc);
```

See "13.3 Adding a Display Object to the Display List" on page 287 for more information about adding a display object to the display list using the highest available depth.

Swapping display object depths

ActionScript 2.0: Use the `swapDepths()` method.

```
mc1.swapDepths(mc2);
```

ActionScript 3.0: For corresponding functionality, use the `swapChildren()` method to swap known display objects, or the `swapChildrenAt()` method to swap the children in two depths. However, you can also use the `addChild()` method to place a child at the top of the display list, or `addChildAt()` method to place it at a specific level. All children above move up a level, accordingly.

```
swapChildren(mc1, mc2);
swapChildrenAt(0, 1);
```

See "13.4 Specifying the Depth of a Display Object" on page 289 for more information about specifying the depth of a display object.

Accessing a display object by name

ActionScript 2.0: You can access a symbol instance using a programmatically created instance name instead of a variable reference.

```
this.createEmptyMovieClip("clip", 1);
trace(clip._x);
//0
```

ActionScript 3.0: This option's no longer a part of the display object creation process, so you can't use a programmatically created instance name to access display objects.

```
var mc:MovieClip = new MovieClip();
addChild(mc);
mc.name = "clip";
trace(clip.x)
//error
```

Instead, use the `getChildByName()` method.

```
trace(getChildByName("clip"));
//[object MovieClip]
```

Actually, this method's consistent with ActionScript 2.0. The only difference is that you can assign an instance name during creation. Even in ActionScript 2.0, you can't access a movie clip through the value of its `name` property.

```
var mc:MovieClip = this.createEmptyMovieClip("clip", 1);
mc.name = "clip2";
trace(clip2._x);
```

```
//undefined
trace(clip._x);
//0
```

See "13.5 Finding a Display Object" on page 291 for more information about finding a display object by name.

Removing a display object

ActionScript 2.0: Use the `removeMovieClip()` method to remove a movie clip or button instance.

```
removeMovieClip(mc);
```

ActionScript 3.0: Use the `removeChild()` method to remove any display object.

```
removeChild(mc);
```

See "13.6 Removing a Display Object from the Display List" on page 292 for more information about removing a display object from the display list.

Using the drawing API

ActionScript 2.0: Drawing API methods are part of the `MovieClip` class, letting you draw into movie clips without reference to any other classes.

```
mc.lineStyle(1, 0x000000);
mc.lineTo(10, 10);
```

ActionScript 3.0: Drawing API methods have been moved to the `Graphics` class, and you can access them through the graphics property in shapes, sprites, and movie clips.

```
mc.graphics.lineStyle(1, 0x000000);
mc.graphics.lineTo(10, 10);
```

See all of Chapter 12, for more information about using the `Graphics` class.

Checking for display object collisions

ActionScript 2.0: Use the `hitTest()` method to check for a collision with another symbol instance (the first line) or point (the second line).

```
trace(mc.hitTest(mc2));
trace(mc.hitTest(100, 100));
```

ActionScript 3.0: Use the `hitTestObject()` method or `hitTestPoint()` method to check for a collision with a display object or point, respectively.

```
trace(mc.hitTestObject(mc2));
trace(mc.hitTestPoint(100, 100));
```

Assigning a mask to movie clip

ActionScript 2.0: Use the setMask() method to assign one movie clip as a mask for another movie clip.

```
mc.setMask(mc2);
```

ActionScript 3.0: The process is the same as in ActionScript 2.0 but mask is a property.

```
mc.mask = mc2;
```

See "12.11 Using a Drawn Shape as a Dynamic Mask" on page 278 for more information about assigning a mask to a display object.

Events

Like the display architecture, the ActionScript 3.0 event model differs greatly from previous versions. From handling built-in events to dispatching custom events, significant changes present new migration challenges.

Using event handlers

ActionScript 2.0: Event handlers commonly take the form of onEventName() and are methods of the object meant to react to the event. The following is an example of a button frame event:

```
helpBtn.onRelease = buttonRelease;
function buttonRelease():Void {
    trace("button action here");
}
```

ActionScript 3.0: Event listeners now handle all events exclusively.

```
helpBtn.addEventListener(MouseEvent.CLICK, onClick, false, 0, true);
function onClick(evt:MouseEvent):void {
    trace("button action here");
}
```

See all of Chapter 14, for extensive discussions about events, as well as Chapter 18, for information about components and a comparison of event listener use in ActionScript 2.0 and 3.0.

Adding and removing listeners

ActionScript 2.0: Some classes, including Key, Mouse, MovieClipLoader, Stage, TextField, and Selection use the addListener() method to register event listeners, and the removeListener() method to remove listeners.

```
var txtListener:Object = new Object();
txtListener.onChanged = function(tf:TextField):Void {
    trace(tf.text);
```

```
    tf.removeListener(txtListener);
};
txtFld.addListener(txtListener);
```

ActionScript 3.0: All listeners are registered using the addEventListener()
method, and removed using the removeEventListener() method.

```
txtFld.addEventListener(Event.CHANGE, onChange);
function onChange(evt:Event):void {
    trace(evt.target.text);
    evt.target.removeEventListener(Event.CHANGE, onChange);
};
```

See all of Chapter 14 for extensive discussions about events, as well as information about components and a comparison of event listener use in Action-
Script 2.0 and 3.0.

Enabling event dispatching

ActionScript 2.0: You must prepare an object for event broadcasting.

```
AsBroadcaster.initialize(obj);
```

ActionScript 3.0: You no longer need to prepare an object for event dispatching. All classes that extend EventDispatcher, including all display objects,
can automatically dispatch events.

Dispatching events

ActionScript 2.0: Use the broadcastMessage() method of AsBroadcaster to
broadcast events.

```
obj.broadcastMessage("edited");
```

ActionScript 3.0: Use the dispatchEvent() method of the EventDispatcher
class to dispatch events.

```
dispatchEvent(new Event("edited"));
```

See "14.12 Dispatching Your Own Events" on page 323 for more information
about dispatching custom events.

Trapping a mouse up event outside a display object's boundaries

ActionScript 2.0: Use the onReleaseOutside event.

```
mc.onReleaseOutside = function ():Void {
    trace("onReleaseOutside called");
};
```

ActionScript 3.0: This event has been removed from ActionScript 3.0. Attach
an additional mouse up event listener to the stage to simulate a mouse up

outside the display object. See "14.6 Simulating a Mouse Up Outside Event" on page 311 for more information about simulating a mouse up outside event.

```
mc.addEventListener(MouseEvent.MOUSE_UP, onUp, false, 0, true);
function onUp(evt:MouseEvent):void {
    trace("mouse up behavior");
}
stage.addEventListener(MouseEvent.MOUSE_UP, onUp, false, 0, true);
```

Text

Several changes have been made to the TextField, TextFormat, and related classes, affecting everything from creating text fields to triggering functions from hyperlinks.

Creating a new text field

ActionScript 2.0: Use the createTextField() method, supplying an instance name, level, x and y coordinates, and width and height. The instance is automatically added to the stage.

```
var txtFld:TextField = this.createTextField("txt", 1, 0, 0, 100, 100);
```

ActionScript 3.0: Use the new keyword and TextField constructor, and add it the display list. The level is determined automatically, and the default values of x:0, y:0, width:100, and height:100 are used. Alternatively, each property can be set individually.

```
var txtFld:TextField = new TextField();
addChild(txtFld);
```

See "15.1 Creating a Text Field" on page 334 for more information about creating a text field.

Populating a text field with plain text

ActionScript 2.0: Populate the first string using the equal (=) operator and add to that text using the plus-equal (+=) compound operator.

```
txtFld.text = "start";
txtFld.text += "continue";
```

ActionScript 3.0: Populate the first string using the equal (=) operator and add to that text using the appendText() method for better performance. See "15.5 Populating a Text Field" on page 338 for more information.

```
txtFld.text = "start";
txtFld.appendText("continue");
```

Populating a text field with HTML

ActionScript 2.0: Use the same techniques for populating a field with plain text, but set the html property to true and use the htmlText property instead of the text property to assign the text.

```
txtFld.html = true;
txtFld.htmlText = "<b>start</b>";
txtFld.htmlText += "continue";
```

ActionScript 3.0: The same process is used for ActionScript 3.0, but the html property is unnecessary, and it's been removed. Note that, unlike when working with plain text, there's no append method, and you use the plus-equal (+=) compound operator.

```
txtFld.htmlText = "<b>start</b>";
txtFld.htmlText += "continue";
```

See "15.10 Formatting Text Using HTML" on page 346 for more information about using HTML in a text field.

Setting a default text format

ActionScript 2.0: Use the setNewTextFormat() method to assign a text format before adding text to the field.

```
txtFld.setNewTextFormat(txtFrmt);
txtFld.text = "Rex Stout";
```

ActionScript 3.0: The same process is used for ActionScript 3.0, but default TextFormat is a property.

```
txtFld.defaultTextFormat = txtFrmt;
txtFld.text = "Rex Stout";
```

See "15.9 Formatting Text Using TextFormat" on page 344 for more information about formatting text with a TextFormat instance.

Using a text field as a variable

ActionScript 2.0: You can assign dynamic and input text fields variable names in the Property inspector. The field then displays the value of the variable throughout its use.

ActionScript 3.0: This feature has been removed.

Scrolling a text field

ActionScript 2.0: Assign to the scroll property a number of the line to which you wish to scroll. Using the maxScroll property for this value scrolls the field to the end of the text.

```
txtFld.scroll = txtFld.maxscroll;
```

Horizontal scrolling is also possible, using `hscroll` and `maxhscroll`, respectively.

ActionScript 3.0: You use the same process for ActionScript 3.0 but the properties are `scrollV` and `maxScrollV`.

```
txtFld.scrollV = txtFld.maxScrollV;
```

Horizontal scrolling is also possible, using `scrollH` and `maxScrollH`, respectively. See "15.7 Scrolling a Text Field" on page 341 for more information about scrolling a text field, as well as Chapter 18 for a comparison of text scrolling in ActionScript 2.0 and 3.0.

Triggering an ActionScript function with a hyperlink

ActionScript 2.0: Use the `asfunction` protocol to trigger a function. You can pass an argument to the function by following the function name with the argument value.

```
function doIt(msg:String):Void {
    trace(msg);
}

txtFld.htmlText = "<a href='asfunction:doIt,Hello'>link</a>";
```

ActionScript 3.0: Use the event protocol to trigger an event listener. You can pass a value to the function by querying the text properties.

```
txtFld.htmlText = "<a href='event:doIt'>link</a>";

txtFld.addEventListener(TextEvent.LINK, linkHandler);
function linkHandler(evt:TextEvent):void {
    if (evt.text == "doIt") {
        trace("doIt");
    }
}
```

See "15.13 Triggering ActionScript from HTML Links" on page 351 for more information about triggering ActionScript functions from text hyperlinks.

Sound

For all code snippets in this category, the following variables are used.

```
var snd:Sound = new Sound();
var sndChannel:SoundChannel = new SoundChannel();
var sndTransform:SoundTransform = new SoundTransform();
```

The `Sound` class is available to both ActionScript 2.0 and 3.0, while `SoundChan nel` and `SoundTransform` are available to ActionScript 3.0 only. The `SoundChan` nel class lets you play sounds in discrete channels for more granular control. The SoundTransform class contains transformation controls like pan and volume. You use a fourth class, SoundMixer, in ActionScript 3.0 to control all sounds in all channels, but it's a static class and doesn't need instantiating.

Loading and playing an external sound

ActionScript 2.0: Use the loadSound() method of the Sound class, and pass the sound path name to the method as a string. Play the sound using the start() method of the Sound class.

```
var snd:Sound = new Sound();
snd.loadSound("sound.mp3");
snd.onLoad = function():Void {
    snd.start();
};
```

ActionScript 3.0: Use the load() method of the Sound class and use the sound path name in a URLRequest instance. Play the sound using the play() method of the Sound class, assigning the sound to a channel.

```
snd.load(new URLRequest("sound.mp3"));
snd.addEventListener(Event.COMPLETE, onComplete, false, 0, true);
function onComplete(evt:Event):void {
    channel = snd.play();
    snd.removeEventListener(Event.COMPLETE, onComplete);
}
```

See "17.6 Loading and Playing a Sound" on page 391 for more information about loading and playing sounds.

Playing an internal sound from the library

ActionScript 2.0: Use the attachSound() method of the Sound class, passing the library linkage name to the method. Play the sound using the start() method of the Sound class.

```
snd.attachSound("beep");
snd.start();
```

ActionScript 3.0: Use the sound's class name to create an instance of the sound, and play it into a channel using the play() method.

```
var beepSound:Sound = new Beep();
sndChannel = beepSound.play();
```

Stopping a sound

ActionScript 2.0: Use the stop() method of the Sound class.

```
snd.stop();
```

ActionScript 3.0: Use the `stop()` method of the `SoundChannel` class.

```
sndChannel.stop();
```

Getting or setting a sound's volume or pan

ActionScript 2.0: Use the `getVolume()` and `setVolume()` methods of the Sound class.

```
snd.setVolume(snd.getVolume()*.5);
snd.setPan(snd.getPan()*-1);
```

ActionScript 3.0: Modify the SoundTransform instance of the sound using the volume and pan properties, and reapply the transformation. See the next entry for more information.

```
sndTransform = sndChannel.soundTransform;
sndTransform.volume *= .5;
sndTransform.pan *= -1;
sndChannel.soundTransform = sndTransform;
```

Further, the complexity of ActionScript 2.0's simultaneous volume and pan transformation approach is no longer needed.

ActionScript 2.0: Use the `getTransform()` method to store the current sound transformation of a sound in an object. Set the sound transformation properties. (The `ll` and `lr` values dictate what percentage of the left channel sound plays in the left and right channels, respectively. The `rl` and `rr` values dictate what percentage of the right channel sound plays in the left and right channels, respectively.) Reapply the transformation to the sound.

```
var sndTrans:Object = snd.getTransform();
sndTrans.ll = 0;
sndTrans.lr = 0;
sndTrans.rl = 100;
sndTrans.rr = 100;
snd.setTransform(sndTrans);
```

ActionScript 3.0: The general idea behind the sound transformation process is the same as with ActionScript 2.0 but less cryptic. You need only adjust the volume and pan properties of the `SoundTransform` instance rather than building the confusing object required in ActionScript 2.0. Note that percentage values are between 0 and 1, not 0 and 100. To transform a single sound, use the `SoundChannel` instance.

See the "Getting or setting a sound's volume and pan" entry to modify a single sound or, to transform all sounds, use the `SoundMixer` class.

```
sndTransform = SoundMixer.soundTransform;
sndTransform.volume = 1;
sndTransform.pan = 1;
SoundMixer.soundTransform = sndTransform;
```

See "17.7 Setting the Volume and Pan of a Sound" on page 392, as well as Chapter 18 for more information about setting the volume and pan of a sound.

Getting a sound's duration

ActionScript 2.0: Use the duration property of the Sound class.

```
trace(snd.duration);
```

ActionScript 3.0: Use the length property of the Sound class.

```
trace(snd.length);
```

Getting a sound's current time

ActionScript 2.0: Use the position property of the Sound class.

```
trace(snd.position);
```

ActionScript 3.0: Use the position property of the SoundChannel class.

```
trace(sndChannel.position);
```

Getting a loaded sound's bytes loaded or total bytes

ActionScript 2.0: After using the loadSound() method, use the getBytesLoaded() and/or getBytesTotal() methods of the Sound class.

```
trace(snd.getBytesLoaded() + " of " + snd.getBytesTotal() + " bytes loaded");
```

ActionScript 3.0: Use the bytesLoaded and/or bytesTotal properties of the Sound class.

```
trace(snd.bytesLoaded + " of " + snd.bytesTotal + " bytes loaded");
```

Stopping all sounds

ActionScript 2.0: Use the global stopAllSounds() method.

```
stopAllSounds();
```

ActionScript 3.0: Use the stopAll() method of the SoundMixer class.

```
SoundMixer.stopAll();
```

Setting the buffer time of loaded sounds

ActionScript 2.0: Set the global _soundbuftime property to the number of seconds you wish to buffer.

```
_soundbuftime = 3;
```

ActionScript 3.0: Set the bufferTime property of the SoundMixer class to the number of seconds you wish to buffer.

```
SoundMixer.bufferTime = 3;
```

Network

Much of the IO (input/output) processes in ActionScript have changed with version 3.0. URLs are handled consistently, loading content classes are more specialized, and unloading assets requires quite a bit more attention. For additional information not covered here, see Chapter 17.

Using FlashVars

ActionScript 2.0: FlashVars are stored in the main timeline of a SWF file and, if you don't find them, then you can use default values instead.

```
if (!imgURL) {
    var imgURL:String = "bg.jpg";
}
```

ActionScript 3.0: FlashVars are stored in the parameters object of the Loader Info class, and can be accessed through the loaderInfo property of the root.

```
var imgURL:String = "bg.jpg";
if (root.loaderInfo.parameters.imgURL) {
    imgURL = root.loaderInfo.parameters.imgURL;
}
```

See Chapter 18 for another example of using FlashVars.

Getting the URL of a SWF file

ActionScript 2.0: Use the global _url property from the _root.

```
trace(_root._url);
```

ActionScript 3.0: Use the url property of the root loaderInfo instance.

```
trace(root.loaderInfo.url);
```

You can see another example of accessing a URL, this time of loaded content, in the next section.

Loading and unloading an image or SWF file using loadMovie

ActionScript 2.0: Use the loadMovie() method of the MovieClip class.

```
var bg:MovieClip = this.createEmptyMovieClip("bgImg", 1);
bg.loadMovie("image.jpg");
```

To unload the image or SWF file, use the unloadMovie() method of the Movie Clip class.

```
bg.unloadMovie();
```

ActionScript 3.0: Use the load() method of the Loader() class, a display object that can load images or SWF files. To unload the image or SWF file, use the unload() method of the instance.

```
var bg:Loader = new Loader();
addChild(bg);
bg.load(new URLRequest("image.jpg"));

bg.contentLoaderInfo.addEventListener(Event.INIT, onImageLoaded, false, 0, true);
function onImageLoaded(evt:Event):void {
    trace("bg URL:", bg.contentLoaderInfo.url);
    bg.unload();
}
```

See "17.2 Loading and Displaying an Image or SWF File" on page 380 and "17.5 Unloading an Image or SWF File" on page 387 for more information about loading and unloading external SWF files or images.

Loading and unloading an image or SWF file using MovieClipLoader

ActionScript 2.0: You can also use the MovieClipLoader class to load images or SWF files, in conjunction with a listener.

```
var bg:MovieClip = this.createEmptyMovieClip("img", 1);

var mclListener:Object = new Object();
mclListener.onLoadInit = function(mc:MovieClip) {
    trace(mc._url);
}

var bg_mcl:MovieClipLoader = new MovieClipLoader();
bg_mcl.addListener(mclListener);
bg_mcl.loadClip("image.jpg", bg);
```

ActionScript 3.0: MovieClipLoader has been removed. Use the Loader class instead. See the "Loading and unloading an image or SWF file using loadMovie" entry for a sample use of the Loader class.

Loading variables using LoadVars

For both ActionScript 2.0 and 3.0 versions of this example, a text file called *userdata.txt* contains the following URL-encoded variables.

```
user1=Sally&age1=2&user2=Claire&age2=0
```

ActionScript 2.0: Use the load() method of the LoadVars class to load the variables. After loading, use the decode() method to convert the loaded string to object properties.

```
var ldVar:LoadVars = new LoadVars();
ldVar.onLoad = function(success:Boolean) {
    if (success) {
```

```
        trace(this);
        ldVar.decode();
        trace(ldVar.user1);
    } else {
        trace("Error loading variables.");
    }
};
ldVar.load("userdata.txt");
```

ActionScript 3.0: Use the `load()` method of the `URLLoader` class to load the variables. Due to the `dataFormat` property of `URLLoaderDataFormat.VARIABLES`, the loaded data can already be queried by variable name.

```
var req:URLRequest = new URLRequest("userdata.txt");
var vars:URLLoader = new URLLoader();
vars.dataFormat = URLLoaderDataFormat.VARIABLES;
vars.addEventListener(Event.COMPLETE, onVarsLoaded);
try {
    vars.load(req);
} catch (err:Error) {
    trace("Variable load error:", err.message);
}

function onVarsLoaded(evt:Event):void {
    var ldr:URLLoader = URLLoader(evt.target);
    trace(ldr.data);
    trace(ldr.data.user1);
}
```

Sending variables using LoadVars

ActionScript 2.0: To send data to a server, define both send and receive instances of `LoadVars`, create variable properties and values in the send instance, and use the `sendAndLoad()` method of the class. The following example assumes that a server-based script returns a name-value pair with a variable called `confirm`.

```
var result_lv:LoadVars = new LoadVars();
result_lv.onLoad = function(success:Boolean) {
    if (success) {
        trace(result_lv.confirm);
    } else {
        trace("LoadVars error.");
    }
};
var login_lv:LoadVars = new LoadVars();
login_lv.user = "pfj";
login_lv.pass = "isn";
login_lv.sendAndLoad("http://<yourdomain>/login.php", result_lv, "POST");
```

ActionScript 3.0: To send variables to a server in ActionScript 3.0, first create the variables as properties of a `URLVariables` instance. Then assign the instance to the data property of a `URLRequest` instance that links to your server script.

To receive data returned by the server, use the `load()` method, as seen in the previous ActionScript 3.0 example in this entry. If you don't need a response, use the `sendToURL()` method, as seen here.

```
var vars:URLVariables = new URLVariables();
vars.name = "Graham Lewis";

var req:URLRequest = new URLRequest("http://<yourdomain>/login.php");
req.data = vars;

try {
    sendToURL(req);
} catch (err:Error) {
    trace("Error sending vars:", err.message);
}
```

Connecting to a URL in a web browser

ActionScript 2.0: Use the global `getURL()` method.

```
getURL("http://www.google.com", "_blank");
```

ActionScript 3.0: Use the global `navigateToURL()` method with a `URLRequest` instance.

```
navigateToURL(new URLRequest("http://www.google.com"), "_blank");
```

See Chapter 18 for additional examples of opening a URL.

Miscellaneous

Entirely written from scratch, changes permeate every nook and cranny of ActionScript 3.0, and some don't necessarily warrant their own category.

Examining property underscores and name changes

ActionScript 2.0: Many, but not all, properties are preceded by an underscore:

```
toolTip._x = this._xmouse;
```

ActionScript 3.0: Property names don't begin with an underscore and, on occasion, have been renamed to be more consistent with ActionScript 3.0 naming conventions, including the use of camel case.

```
toolTip.x = this.mouseX;
```

See Chapter 18 for additional examples of property underscores.

Using event and constant names

ActionScript 2.0: Event and constant names (as well as properties serving the role of a constant), don't share any particular naming or usage conventions. Seen here, the value for the `autoSize` property is a string.

```
var txtFld:TextField = this.createNewTextField("txt", 1, 0, 0, 100, 100);
txtFld.autoSize = "left";
```

ActionScript 3.0: Corresponding structures are stored in classes for consistent use and reliable recall. The value for the `autoSize` property in this syntax is a constant.

```
var txtFld:TextField = new TextField();
txtFld.autoSize = TextFieldAutoSize.LEFT;
```

See "15.6 Automatically Sizing a Text Field" on page 339 for information about automatically sizing a text field, including the use of the corresponding constant.

Using Intervals and Timeouts

ActionScript 2.0: Repeating timed executions of functions are achieved with the `setInterval()` method and halted with the `clearInterval()` method, as seen in the following code. Note that you must manually halt the process if you want a finite number of executions.

```
//setInterval
var i:Number = 0;
var intID:Number = setInterval(showMsg, 1000);
function showMsg():Void {
    trace("interval");
    i++;
    if (i == 5) { clearInterval(intID); }
}
```

A single, delayed execution of a function is achieved with the `setTimeout()` method, and halted by the `clearTimeout()` method, as you see in the following new example.

```
//setTimeout
var timeoutID:Number = setTimeout(showMsg, 1000);
function showMsg():Void {
    trace("timeout");
    clearTimeout(timeoutID);
}
```

ActionScript 3.0: The `Timer` class makes intervals and timeouts easy. An ongoing timer functions much the same way as an interval, but with the consistency of event listeners. (Note that the timer must be started.) All timers must be stopped, and their event listeners removed when no longer needed, or the file containing the timer cannot be unloaded.

```
//ongoing interval
var i:int = 0;
var timr:Timer = new Timer(1000);
timr.addEventListener(TimerEvent.TIMER, onTimer, false, 0, true);
function onTimer(evt:TimerEvent):void {
    trace("interval behavior");
    i++
    if (i == 5) {
        timr.stop();
        timr.removeEventListener(TimerEvent.TIMER, onTimer);
    }
}
timr.start();
```

A single execution (as in when setTimeout() is desired), or even a finite number of executions not limited to 1, is even easier to use. An optional second parameter of the Timer class lets you specify how many times the timer fires and automatically stops the timer after the last execution.

```
//single execution
var i:int = 0;
var timr2:Timer = new Timer(1000, 1);
timr2.addEventListener(TimerEvent.TIMER, onTimer, false, 0, true);
function onTimer(evt:TimerEvent):void {
    trace("timeout behavior");
    timr2.removeEventListener(TimerEvent.TIMER, onTimer);
}
timr2.start();
```

See "14.11 Using a Timer to Dispatch Events" on page 321 for more information about using Timers.

Getting and setting the year of a date instance

ActionScript 2.0: The getYear() method of the Date class returns a year integer since 1900. (The year 2008 yields 108, for example.) Similarly, the set Year() method lets you set the year of a date object.

```
var today:Date = new Date();
today.setYear(today.getYear() + 1);
```

ActionScript 3.0: This method was removed because it was not ECMA-compliant. Use the getFullYear() and setFullYear() methods instead, which use full years, such as 2008. (Consider switching to these methods exclusively in any ongoing ActionScript 2.0 projects, as well, to make future migration to ActionScript 3.0 easier.)

```
var today:Date = new Date();
today.setFullYear(today.getFullYear() + 1);
```

Accessing private namespaces

ActionScript 2.0: Subclasses can access private properties or methods of a super class.

ActionScript 3.0: The private namespace now restricts access to a class.

Index

Symbols

" (quotation marks), XML entity, 367

& (ampersand)

&& (logical AND) operator, 249

XML entity, 367

' (apostrophe), encoding as entity in XML, 368

* (asterisk), wildcard operator, 365

+= (plus-equal) operator, 438

. (dot), 16

(see also dot syntax)

. . (descendent accessor) operator, 11, 365

: (colon)

: : (name qualifier) operator, 14, 82

< and > (angle brackets), XML entities, 367

= (equal) operator, 437

@ (at sign), attribute operator, 363

[ ] (square brackets)

array access operator, 76

scope bracket syntax, 427

_ (underscores) in property names, 246

{ } (curly braces)

enclosing dynamic XML content, 372

{ (open curly brace) on new lines written with Flex Builder 3, 40

A

access control specifiers, 80

Accordion Panel V3 component, 227

Accordion.selectedIndex property, 222

Actions panel, 105

new features, 112

tree view of keyframe code, 111

ActionScript 2.0, 4

(see also migration to ActionScript 3.0)

explanations of syntax in particle system code, 406

ActionScript 2.0 Migration table, 72

ActionScript 3.0

additional resources, 84

API restructuring, 15

binary data and sockets, 18

changes from ActionScript 2.0, 59–84

major changes in API, classes, and language, 60–72

major syntax and structure changes, 77–83

obsolete code, 72–77

ECMAScript for XML (E4X), 10

event handling, 15

learning after version 2.0, 21

method closures, 8

migration to versus writing code from scratch, 22

namespaces, 14

new primitive types, 14

new sound APIs, 18

regular expressions, 12

runtime types, 6

sealed classes, 7

writing using external code editors with Flash, 32

writing with FlashDevelop, 50

writing with Flex Builder 3, 37–46

caching vector as bitmap, 280
creating display object dynamically,
    268
creating gradient fill, 277
defining fill style, 273
defining line style, 270
drawing a curve, 272
drawing a line, 271
drawing a rectangle, 274
drawing circles, 276
drawing rectangle with rounded
    corners, 274
referencing display object's graphics
    property, 269
using shape as dynamic mask, 278
duplicateMovieClip( ) function (obsolete),
    75
duration of sounds, 442
dynamic attribute, 7
dynamic classes, 7
dynamic text fields, 333
dynamic tone generator, 18

E

E4X (ECMAScript for XML), 10
easing classes, 107
Ebert, Michelle and Joa, 18
Eclipse IDE, 24
ECMAScript, 3
    characteristic of languages
        implementing, 5
ECMAScript for XML (E4X), 10
editors (see code editors external to Flash)
efficiency of ActionScript 3.0, 93
element node, reading in XML object,
    359
embedFonts property (TextField), 343
endFill( ) method, 273
entity encoding (XML), 367
equal (=) operator, 437
errors, 244
    (see also Compiler Errors panel)
    compiler errors, 232
    documentation, 242
    helpfulness of error messages, 236
    identifying and understanding
        common errors, 244
    runtime, 235

runtime error handling in ActionScript
    3.0, 5
runtime errors
    display in Flash Player 9, 239
eval( ) function, 76
event handlers, 72
    (see also events)
    obsolete practice of direct attachment
        to objects, 72
    referencing by instance name in
        ActionScript 3.0, 73
Event.ENTER_FRAME, 107
Event.ENTER_FRAME event, 312
Event.FULLSCREEN event, 317
Event.MOUSE_LEAVE event, 317
Event.RESIZE event, 317
Event.target property, 10
event: protocol, 351
EventDispatcher class, 323, 436
    addEventListener( ) method, 16, 98,
        132
    components' inheritance from, 188
events, 303–331, 435
    adding and removing listeners, 435
    animation responding to mouse clicks,
        175
    associating with functions, 131
    calling event listener functions
        manually, 325
    capturing before reaching target, 326
    capturing frame events, 312
    capturing keyboard events, 315
    capturing mouse events, 305
    capturing when leaving or resizing
        stage, or switching to full
        screen, 317
    dispatching, 436
    dispatching using a timer, 321
    dispatching your own, 323
    DOM3 event model, 15
    enabling event dispatching, 436
    event flow in ActionScript 3.0, 307
    event handling in ActionScript 2.0,
        407
    event handling in ActionScript 3.0, 98,
        417
    event listeners, 303

data property, 446
loading sounds, 440
navigateToURL( ) method, 446
URLs
connecting to a URL in a web browser, 446
getting for SWF files, 443
URLVariables class, 445
Uro, Tinic, 18
useCapture parameter, addEventListener( ) method, 326
user input, content requiring, 179
useWeakReference parameter (addEventListener( ) method), 330

V

var keyword, 61
changes in ActionScript 3.0, 61
variables
changes in ActionScript 3.0, 61
data types, 83
declaration in ActionScript 2.0, 407
declaration in ActionScript 3.0 code, 416
declaration once per timeline or class, 248
defined in keyframe scripts, 7
differences between ActionScript 2.0 and 3.0, 428
loading, 444
private variable names, 35
sending to a server, 445
specifying intended type, 6
text field used as (ActionScript 2.0), 438
undeclared timeline variables, inability to reference, 248
untyped, 83
writing XML containing variables, 372
Variables panel, 255
vectors
caching vector as bitmap, 280
manipulation with Graphics class, 267
version detection, 29
version property, Capabilities class, 19
vertical scrolling in text fields, 341

video
displayed in full-screen mode, 196
loading and playing external video, 397
removal of loaded SWFs with video from memory, 390
unloading video files, 399
Video class, 285
creating instance and adding to display list, 397
video components, 179
available with Flash CS4 Professional, 188
virtual machines
ActionScript Virtual Machine 2 (AVM2), 85
AVM1 and AVM2, 4
visual assets, display of, 283
visual containers, DisplayObjectContainer base class, 17
void type, 14
volume control
getting or setting a sound's volume, 441
for loaded sound file, 393
volume slider (example), 192

W

Warnings mode, 125
warnings, compiler, 233
weak listeners, 330
web browsers
embedding Flash applications, 29
Flash Player Debug and Release versions, 25
standards and portability of content, 100
web page for this book, xix
WebService component extension, 217
WebServiceConnector scenario, 215–219
creating in ActionScript 2.0, 215
recreating in ActionScript 3.0, 217
wildcard (*) operator, 365
windows
draggable (example), 310
resizing, 317
wordWrap property (TextField), 340

About the Authors

David Stiller is a resident author at *www.communitymx.com* (over 50 articles), co-author of Foundation Flash CS3 for Designers (friends of ED) and contributor to *How to Cheat in Adobe Flash CS3* (Focal Press). He blogs regularly at quip.net/blog/ and is a longtime regular on the Adobe Flash and ActionScript support forums.

Rich Shupe is the co-author of *Learning ActionScript 3.0* (O'Reilly) and has been teaching ActionScript programming to students of all levels since the language became available. He founded his own training and development company, FMA, in 1995 and is a faculty member of New York's School of Visual Arts' MFA Computer Art Dept. He writes about ActionScript at *www.LearningActionScript3.com*.

Jen DeHaan is a software quality engineer on the Flash authoring team at Adobe Systems, Inc. She is an author and co-author of 17 books (and tech editor for several others) over the past five versions of Flash. Jen's latest blog is at *www.flashthusiast.com*.

Darren Richardson is a technical editor for O'Reilly Media. He gained high visibility among Flash and ActionScript developers by writing over 50 articles for Web Designer Magazine and community-related sites. He can be found on a nearly daily basis blogging at *www.playfool.com/blog/*.

Colophon

The reptiles on the cover are ophiops.

The cover image is from the Dover Pictorial Archive. The cover font is Adobe ITC Garamond. The text font is Linotype Burka; the heading font is Adobe Myriad Condensed; and the code font is LucasFont's TheSans Mono Condensed.

The Premier Community Site for all that is RIA!

InsideRIA.com brings some of the sharpest minds—and opinions—in the Rich Internet Application community together, creating the leading resource of its kind. Check in daily for all the news on topics including Flex and ActionScript 3, User Experience, Standards, Adobe® AIR™, Microsoft Silverlight, JavaFX, Google Gears, and other open source topics. InsideRIA also features monthly articles, screencasts, tutorial series and more. If you're a part of the RIA development and design community, you belong here.

InsideRIA.com